10 0679525 5

D1760211

UNIVE...
WITHDRA...
ROM THE LIBRAR

PLANNING MAJOR INFRASTRUCTURE

PLANNING AND PROVIDING INFRASTRUCTURE is politically controversial, right across the world. European countries are engaged in major programmes to adapt and modernise their infrastructure systems, especially in energy and transport. This is in part to meet the need to restructure to low carbon living, and is also driven by the concern to compete economically. Infrastructure is seen as critical to economic success.

This book analyses this planning and policy world as it is currently developing in Europe and the UK. How can decisions about large infrastructure projects be taken better? Have some countries managed to generate genuine consensus on how the large changes are progressed? What can we learn from the different ways in which countries manage these challenges, to inform better spatial planning and more intelligent political steering?

Case studies of the key features of policy and planning approaches in France, Germany, the Netherlands, Spain and the UK form the core of the book. High-speed rail, renewable energy deployment, water management, waste treatment – all raise critical planning issues. The case studies are articulated alongside the big issues of principle which haunt this field of public policy: how can democratic legitimacy be secured? How can ecological and economic transitions be managed? What is the appropriate role of the national government in each of these areas, as against those of regional and local government? These are some of the central themes raised in this innovative exploration of this high profile field.

TIM MARSHALL is a Reader in Planning at the Department of Planning in Oxford Brookes University. He is a planner with a mixed practice and academic career. Major interests include high level strategic planning at urban, regional and national levels. His past books include *Transforming Barcelona* and *Regional Planning* (with John Glasson).

PLANNING MAJOR INFRASTRUCTURE
A CRITICAL ANALYSIS

TIM MARSHALL

University of Nottingham
Hallward Library

Routledge
Taylor & Francis Group

NEW YORK AND LONDON

First published 2013
by Routledge
2 Park Square, Milton Park, Abingdon, Oxon OX14 4RN

Simultaneously published in the USA and Canada
by Routledge
711 Third Avenue, New York, NY 10017

Routledge is an imprint of the Taylor & Francis Group, an informa business

© 2013 Tim Marshall

The right of Tim Marshall to be identified as author of this work has been asserted
by him in accordance with sections 77 and 78 of the Copyright, Designs and Patents
Act 1988.

All rights reserved. No part of this book may be reprinted or reproduced or utilised in
any form or by any electronic, mechanical, or other means, now known or hereafter
invented, including photocopying and recording, or in any information storage or
retrieval system, without permission in writing from the publishers.

Trademark notice: Product or corporate names may be trademarks or registered
trademarks, and are used only for identification and explanation without intent to
infringe.

1006795255

British Library Cataloguing in Publication Data
A catalogue record for this book is available from the British Library

Library of Congress Cataloging-in-Publication Data
Marshall, Tim, 1950–
Planning major infrastructure : a critical analysis / Tim Marshall.
    p. cm.
1. Infrastructure (Economics)—Planning. 2. Infrastructure (Economics)—Europe—
Case studies. 3. Public works—Planning. 4. Public works—Europe—Case studies.
5. City planning. 6. City planning—Europe—Case studies. I. Title.
    HC79.C3M367 2012
363.6068'4—dc23
2011052713

ISBN: 978-0-415-66954-2 (hbk)
ISBN: 978-0-415-66955-9 (pbk)
ISBN: 978-0-203-11212-0 (ebk)

Designed and typeset in Univers by Alex Lazarou

MIX
Paper from
responsible sources
FSC® C004839

Printed and bound by CPI Group (UK) Ltd, Croydon, CR0 4YY

CONTENTS

LIST OF FIGURES

ACKNOWLEDGEMENTS

A cliché but true: innumerable debts have been run up in working towards this book, over many years. The numerable ones include the following. Firstly I am grateful to the UK Economic and Social Research Council, which provided funds for a Fellowship when I could devote time to research on "Infrastructure and Spatial Planning", between 2008 and 2010. During that time I was able to discuss the issues in this field with numerous people around Europe, and these are listed after the References section by country, stressing that they bear no responsibility at all for what I have done with their contributions. I am extremely grateful for all their help, which often went well beyond the immediate answering of what no doubt sometimes seemed to be irrelevant questions. Though it is risky to do so, I pick out for their special help, from this very long list, the following: Arjen van der Burg and Andre Rodenburg in the Netherlands, Patrick Le Gales in France, Manfred Sinz in Germany and Graeme Purves in Scotland.

No less important has been the support of colleagues, at the Department of Planning in Oxford Brookes University and in more occasional modes elsewhere. Elizabeth Wilson, Steve Ward, Peter Headicar and John Glasson have given consistent help in my varying endeavours over many years, and my gratitude to them especially is very great. Richard Nunes covered my teaching with exemplary efficiency, and Sue Brownill and Dave Valler also carried some of that burden, as well as giving support over much more than just the fellowship period. Help beyond Brookes must include mentions of Graham Haughton, Greg Lloyd and Erik Swyngedouw, all of whom supported the original fellowship application. Other members of my very valuable Sounding Board were Tony Baden, Roger Levett, Simon Marvin, Tim Stansfeld and Corinne Swain, all of whom made probing contributions at different times.

Considerable personal support has come from friends, over this period and longer, and a very short list must include Riki Therivel, Jon Shapley and Angeles Garcia, Nando Sigona and Nancy Lindisfarne, as well as my brother, sister and mother, at various distances.

PREFACE

This book is about big challenges. Many interests regard the provision of major infrastructure as a critical issue, whether in developed or developing countries. But equally large forces and sentiments are often ranged against the physical implantation that would be necessary to achieve infrastructural transformations. The large political and economic changes of recent decades (liberalisation, globalisation) may have made such achievement harder. Planning processes are caught up in this wider force-field of tensions.

The planning orientation, or the planning project as Patsy Healey (2010) has called it, is at the forefront of this study. Decisions about the location of large infrastructure are planning decisions, as well as often decisions of major principle in the direction of a policy field: not just meeting a generic demand to fly, but where to place an airport. The "where" of such decisions, with all the ramifications back to the nature of the provision of the service, can often be critical to whether development goes ahead at all.

A contemporary UK example is a high-speed rail project to link London with the north of England and perhaps Scotland. This is called High Speed Two (HS2), to distinguish it from the only other British high speed line, linking London with the Channel Tunnel. From 2007 all political parties apparently supported this scheme, although before that almost no one favoured spending the large sum needed to make it happen. The reasons for the shift are not clear: whether it is economic (helping non-southern parts of the UK), social and economic (creating extra capacity on a now congested network) or environmental (to take some of the aviation market, the proclaimed reason for the support of the Conservative Party, who pledged not to expand London's airports). But what is clear is that one part of the outcome over the next decade, as to whether this line is built, and if so where, is naturally a planning issue. The where of infrastructure is not always the most vital in any complex of factors which determine its nature. But here this looms very large, because of the geographical nature of the proposal.

Already, only a few weeks after the government announced the revised line for the route from London to Birmingham, eight local authorities had expressed their opposition to the scheme (Townsend 2011). By 2011 the Stop HS2 campaign was a highly organised national force, covering the whole route from the edges of Birmingham to the fringe of London. The most critical parts are where a new line is needed, cutting through the scenic Chiltern Hills. This area is the home of many very rich residents, and has been solidly Conservative Party territory for generations. Planning approval must eventually be given, if the scheme is to go ahead, most likely through a parliamentary process (Hybrid Bill), or possibly by government executive decision after an almost certainly long drawn-out public inquiry. Even if financial obstacles can be overcome, planning issues may finish the chances of this only plausible high speed line in Britain.

HS2 is just one example of where planning will matter a great deal. In Britain many other schemes are also affected by this dimension. These are, not surprisingly, above all the most controversial schemes – airports, motorways, waste incinerators, ports and power stations. For any sort of "unwanted land use", of which most infrastructure is a major type, the locational decisions in developed western European countries are nearly always contested, often passionately. It is not that planning (spatial planning, land use planning) is necessarily the determinant factor in all or even most cases. It is important that finance and regulation matter a great deal too. This is a continuing thread throughout this book, working against the impression that might often be obtained in recent years, that the main "barrier" to the achievement of infrastructure production is this sort of planning.

This book is the result, in part, of the rising importance given to infrastructure in many countries in recent years. I had long been considering doing some research on infrastructure and planning, since at least the late 1990s. I finally wound up the energy to apply to the Economic and Social Research Council in 2007. It is clear the timing was good, as the bid was successful. I do not put this down to the proposal being better than others I had done or those of colleagues. It was rather that infrastructure's time had come in the outside world. So this book, and the research behind it, are as much a product of the recent "infrastructure turn", as the realities analysed.

RESEARCH PHILOSOPHY AND APPROACH

Research philosophy

One principle in thinking about any area is, for me, to connect widely to other areas. It may be that everyone would say they do this. My preference is for an understanding which sees concepts as internally related, in the sense described by Bertell Ollman (1993). There are limits to how far one can stick to the strong form of this philosophy, which finds everything implicated, to varying degrees, in everything else. But the basic idea has always seemed correct. There is in this perspective little or no safe ground for an "objective" view of reality, firmly splitting facts and values. There are then long social philosophical debates, from social constructionism through critical realism to dialectical materialism to sociological positivism, as to quite where this takes research.

In my view this is helpful to understand the very different, and in a sense equally valid, perspectives of economists, engineers, planners, ecologists and so on, on infrastructure, as well of those of the "general public" in so far as such a construct exists. There is, as argued above, no "innocent" position from which to view and judge these issues, hence the need to state value positions openly and remain sceptical of arguments – perhaps of international bodies like the OECD, for example – which claim some sort of objective truth. This does not have to be the weaker sort of relativism, but simply an open framing of argument and debate. Probably my own approach is partly affected by a planner's mindset, which is obliged to see issues from many angles, often aiming to synthesise rather than get into great detail. The experience of planners may encourage them to see internal relations to some degree, more than many other more "focused down" actors.

This is not necessarily the same as taking a relational position, one that has become commonly supported in urban and planning fields in recent years (Healey 2007). While there may be good philosophical reasons for relational theorising, my own perspective is rather Euclidean – the power of conventional maps, distances and proximities. This may be taken as intellectual conservatism, or simply an inability to understand the full implications of relationalism for planning. Despite cheap oil for a century or more now, distance and the material implications of space remain critical everywhere, and although sensitisation by relational thinking is valuable, everyday planning will remain obliged, as far as I can see, to use traditional approaches to steering land change, transport and energy applications.

This book puts considerable stress on inter-country variation. I see generalisation in this field as possible only up to a limited point. Much social theory has perhaps higher aspirations in this sense, imagining that what applies in one country can fit elsewhere – prominent social theorists often read strangely, as if they are taking the problematic evolving in their home country in recent years as common to a much wider area (Beck 1992, Giddens 1998). None of this is to deny powerful wide-reaching forces. But in this field, where political, social and geographical specificities are so important, such forces are mediated strongly by those specificities, and it is the job of theory to uncover this mediation, its mode of operation (Marsh et al 2008).

Research approach

This book is based largely on work carried out under a fellowship funded by the UK government Economic and Social Research Council (ESRC) in 2008–2010, on "Infrastructure and Spatial Planning". This allowed research on all the European countries treated in Chapters 5 to 10 and, if briefly, on the European Union (discussion of which had to be excluded for want of space). It also allowed time to read behind and round the issues, to access part of the wide field of literature which can be said to impinge on the field of infrastructure and its planning. Details of the research processes in each country are to be found on the project's webpages, which are to be maintained for some time, and whose main outputs were lodged with the ESRC in 2011. The working papers are also listed at the end of this book. Research consisted of interviews with experts in the fields of infrastructure and planning in each country, backed by as much reading as could reasonably be done in the time given to each case study. Except in the case of the Netherlands, this was in the language of the country. In the Netherlands, much was available in English.

The choice of countries was based on finding cases within the European Union with similar challenges (hence the richer western states), alongside some differences, in constitutional form (federal, semi-federal, unitary), and in planning approach. This was backed by practical considerations of the number of countries one researcher could reasonably study in the time available, and the familiarity with languages, or relatively full availability of English-language publications. This resulted in a choice of four large west European states (UK, France, Germany, Spain), and one smaller state, the Netherlands, marked by its history of national spatial planning.

The research process was therefore deliberately framed around national studies, not around projects or around individual infrastructure sectors. This was quite different from other work in this field, for example that of Flyvbjerg et al (2003) or Altshuler and Luberoff (2003) or the Omega project.[1] All of these took a project-based approach, although with varying features, which will be described in a little more detail in Chapter 4. Examining just a sector or subsector would have had other advantages and disadvantages – an example would be the literature on wind energy (such as Szarka 2007), or on airports (Forsyth et al 2010).

The reason for taking a national and overview approach was related to the interest in understanding the significance of planning systems and approaches, and seeing across infrastructure sectors that have some common features. The research strategy was thus to view systems, whole pictures, not look at the details of projects or sectors. The project approach has undoubtedly reaped very valuable knowledge, and may be of more value to some more "practical" actors or interests. The approach taken here may be of more value to those more interested in synthesising perspectives, and to those concerned with institutional design and with how political framing and democratic factors influence what happens in this field. No doubt the results here will be best read alongside the full future publication of the vastly more extensive OMEGA research project, for example, as well as other work already existing across sector- and project-based approaches.

---

1   Details of this large and global project on 30 major urban
    transport projects in 10 countries can be found on the webpages:
    www.omegacentre.bartlett.ucl.ac.uk/about_us/index.php

LAYOUT OF THE BOOK

The book has two main parts, before a concluding chapter. Chapters 1 to 4 tackle some important themes of infrastructure and planning common to all the European case studies, and are intended to set the scene for those studies. Chapter 1 looks at the overall theme of infrastructure and how it is dealt with in the contemporary world. There is a simple storyline here. We live in an "infrastructuralist" era, driven by the forces of the political economy of our times and the massive tensions caused by the search for progress on contradictory paths: more growth, lower carbon societies, more well-being globally. Infrastructure making is caught up in all this, and the planning component of that is best understood not within some separated off compartment, but within that envelope of understanding, catching the real relations.

Chapter 2 is about the way infrastructure is provided, which means studying both industrial structures and actors, and governmental systems which structure or regulate the producers. This is the economics and politics of making infrastructure. Chapter 3 tackles the "softer" themes regarding the way in which "need" for infrastructure is generated, and how this relates to the geographical and historical framing of making infrastructure, a feature of significant importance for how we think about the "where" of infrastructure, and hence for its planning. Much of this is a study of the mental or imaginary aspects of these framings, as much as the "real" geographies or histories. Chapter 4 moves to the terrain of spatial planning, and examines the way in which we can analyse planning in relation to major infrastructure. This involves looking at strategy work, how big schemas or plans may frame our forward planning of infrastructure, as well as project planning. The way in which strategy and project relate to each other is of importance, and varies a lot between countries. It also affects the legitimacy of decision making, and "success" in achieving public consent to schemes.

Then follow six chapters on individual European countries. Four of these are simply country studies covering all the aspects of infrastructure planning seen as important to my concerns. The first chapter on the UK looks at the "traditional" ways in which infrastructure was planned before the present, looking across all the main sectors. Chapter 10 then explores the paths to the forming of new systems, and their natures, looking at England, Wales, Scotland and Northern Ireland, and considering how much difference they may make.

The final chapter aims to synthesise important conclusions arising from the combined understandings of the analytical and country chapters. Particular focuses include sectoral differences, country differences, and the implications of work on this field for broader planning, political and social theory.

PART I
Framing infrastructure and planning

CHAPTER 1
INTRODUCING INFRASTRUCTURE AND "INFRASTRUCTURALISM"

BIG INFRASTRUCTURE

For a very long time, societies have been building large physical structures or objects, which support the way they interact with their surroundings. Enabling travel (ports, roads) and managing water (reservoirs, aqueducts) go back several thousands of years, and are especially associated with powerful states and empires. With the industrial revolution, this process became much more dynamic, creating ever larger systems, moving faster, using enormous quantities of energy. The globalisation of industrialism since the mid-twentieth century means that ever fewer parts of the planet are free of these systems – roads, bridges, power stations, pipelines, airports. They are the objects analysed here. Just type in any of these words to a search engine and you will find dozens of pictures of these objects, worldwide. Many of them will be very recent, and will have gone through lengthy planning processes. Missing will be many elements of infrastructure, proposed but halted by planning processes (amongst other forces).

No attempt is made to match this global reach in this book, with research limited largely to western Europe. This is the result of a personal capacity, as well as prior experience, easy with the planning systems and governing schemas of this part of the world. Many of the basic analytical approaches and principles are doubtless transferable to other world regions, given the nature of globalisation, especially in the force of global finance and globalising companies, but also given the power of neoliberal ideology, insistent in its effects almost everywhere. But there would also be big differences in any attempt to extend analysis elsewhere. In particular, much of what is said about planning approaches will not travel too well to other regions. But politics, economics, geographies and much more also differ radically. So the balancing of commonalities and differences would be quite a complex one.

WHAT DO WE MEAN BY INFRASTRUCTURE?

Infrastructure is one of those words for which, if you ask people for a definition, you will get different answers. Each person will start by saying that they know roughly what they mean by it. But there will be subtle (or not so subtle) differences between each definition. This will apply just as much in everyday talk as in academic disciplines. So we need to start with some idea of these varying understandings. There may be no "correct" answer in the end, but there will be a useful and practical one for the purposes of this book on the planning of major infrastructure.

Sometimes quite wide definitions are adopted, such as that which appears in one of the most entertaining books on infrastructure (perhaps a small field), by Brian Hayes that focuses on the US (Hayes 2005). He includes mining, farming and food industries, although not by and large manufacturing industries more generally, as well as the networked industries.

Planners may see infrastructure as all the physical things needed to support a new development – roads, sewers, water supplies and energy sources, for example. They may then add on social sorts of infrastructure, such as schools or clinics or hospitals. And in recent years, "green infrastructure", open spaces of various biotic forms, may be put on to the list. The definition used by the UK government for its Community Infrastructure Levy in 2010 had all of this, including "transport schemes, flood defences, schools, hospitals, and other health and social care facilities, parks, green spaces and leisure centres" (DCLG 2010a). Engineers may be more comfortable with

Figure 1.1 Classification of infrastructure assets by a leading fund operator, RREEF (Source: RREEF 2005 *Understanding Infrastructure,* from RREEF internet pages 2008).

	Economic Infrastructure		Social infrastructure
Transport	**Energy and Utility**	**Communications**	
Toll roads	Gas	Cable networks	Healthcare facilities
Bridges	– Distribution	Satellite systems	Education facilities
Tunnels	– Storage		Housing
Sea ports	Electricity		Judicial and correctional
Airports	– Generation		facilities
Rail	– Distribution		
Ferries	Water		
	– Treatment		
	– Distribution		

just the basic products of their trade – roads, sewers etc. Economists may regard it as everything which supports the economy, which can be as wide as all the built environment and all the training of the labour force, so houses or universities become infrastructure. One understanding of this is shown in Figure 1.1, from RREEF, the infrastructure investment arm of Deutsche Bank. So already we see big divergences, escaping out of the bounds of common sense usage.

An older dictionary definition is this: "inner structure, structure of component parts; a system of communications and services as backing for military or other operations" (Chambers Twentieth Century Dictionary, 1972/1977 edition, Edinburgh: Chambers). To an extent this carries us back to the Latin derivation, with "infra" meaning below. Early usages were indeed particularly military. It was only in the later twentieth century that, in English at any rate, the word began to be used more widely to cover the sorts of matters referred to above. The intention was to separate out a part of social equipment from the use of that equipment, just as armies distinguished the physical preparation from the actions of war or potential war. But this has been a creeping growth of usage, one reason for the fuzziness which infuses the concept.

One might have thought that the meaning would be illuminated by contrast with the apparent opposite, superstructure (or suprastructure to be exact). But this has never come to be in common use in the same way. For Marxists it was often one half of the "base–superstructure" duality, with crude versions of this having the economy as the base which in turn "determined" the rest – values, ideologies and so on reflecting economic fundamentals. But this was always uncomfortable for most of the more complicated Marxisms, and never brought in the discussion of infrastructure. English speakers use the word superstructure just to mean the outer part of a building or structure, or metaphorically as some sort of addition or accretion, not really as any sort of opposite to infrastructure.

If derivation or linguistic research does not help us much, we may turn to recent historical impressions. It would appear that the word began to become more common from about the 1960s, in fields like engineering, economics and planning. Until then, and to an extent much more recently, and often still today, it was more normal to be direct and concrete, to refer to transport systems, or just roads and railways, or to sewer systems, or to power stations. There was not much need to have an overarching or more abstract category, even though there was some awareness that such a thing existed. Frey (2005) argues that the rapid economic growth of the post-war years showed up bottlenecks in communication. He says the term was used first of all in the French railway system to refer to the lines, bridges and tunnels (but not trains themselves), and that NATO then adopted it when talking of provisioning depots, radar stations and barracks (but not weapons systems). Already by the 1960s a literature had grown up in West German academic circles (Jochimsen 1966, Jochimsen and Simonis 1970, Frey 1972). However, my impression is that this remained largely within these circles, not spreading much until later, and then hardly using the insights of this literature. We will come back to this, particularly in discussing the approach of economists – probably the discipline which gave the field most attention theoretically, as against the practical concerns of the engineers.

It appears that the word was rising hand-in-hand with another term, "logistics". In his fascinating history of the container, Levinson (2006 p.266) says that "before the 1980s, logistics was a military term", but had by 1985 become a routine business function. This he ascribes to the advance of global supply chains and just-in-time practices made possible by containerisation, which he sees as a key material carrier of globalisation. The whole new profession of logistics management, spreading across the manufacturing, transport, wholesaling and retailing sectors, places infrastructure issues in the spotlight, in a way in which they were not before.

The struggle with definition has continued, with Edwards (2003) trying "essentially any important, widely shared, human-constructed resources" (p.187), though falling back by the bottom of the same page to the idea that it may be "best defined negatively, as those systems without which contemporary societies cannot function".

More on the reasons for infrastructure's rise will follow in this and the next chapter. From the 1980s, in particular, the now elastic usage developed. Some theorists drew the lines very widely, some very narrowly, depending on their substantive or value concerns. Development economists were aware from an early stage of the varying usage, and it is not surprising that some of the first discussions of the usefulness of infrastructure creation came from World Bank economists, who were therefore obliged to draw lines round the object they were studying. Urban planners were less concerned with the category, working rather with their headings of transport or water supply and so on, but by the 1990s it was beginning to be a target of discussion in English speaking countries.

By the early 2000s, the term was increasingly prevalent, at least in the developed world. It had by no means elbowed aside the more specific terms, either in common discussion or in academic fields. But it was, again especially in English speaking countries, seen as a significant policy zone of states alongside others of older standing – welfare, environment and security, for example. We will see frequent evidence of this as the details of the themes and country studies unfold. For example, in 2010 the Dutch government changed the organisation of its ministries – not, as in many countries, a common event, but something that tends to happen every 20 or 30 years. Two rather venerable ministries ceased to be: that of VROM, including environment, housing and urban affairs and planning, and that of transport and water management. Most of what had comprised the two ministries was combined as a single ministry titled Infrastructure and Environment. Infra-structuralism had become institutionalised in the Netherlands.

All this is important, as it should alert readers to the historical specificity of the whole field. It is useful for us to remember the inherent slipperiness of the concept. This should put up warning signs. Though by necessity it will be essential for me to define what I mean by infrastructure, so that you can understand what I am saying, it is worthwhile remembering that, just like any other concept, this carries with it histories and drives. Infra-structure is not innocent. As long as we know what we are talking about, it is not dangerous or necessarily liable to mislead. But the framing is still criti-cal. This is in line with the movement within the social sciences, in recent decades, which stresses such framing – interpretive social science (Fischer 2003, Hajer and Wagenaar 2003, Jensen and Richardson 2004). This is not to say that this book will be primarily written in those terms. My approach is in fact much "flatter", once the basic terms are defined. This is as much a matter of personal comfort and basic thought patterns, as thought-out theory. But the interpretive approach is most valuable in reminding us of the constructedness of the field we are looking at here.

THE INFRASTRUCTURE STUDIED HERE

The focus of this book is on "hard" or "networked" infrastructure, and on the major elements of this. Thus hard/networked infrastructure means water, energy, transport and waste treatment systems. This means that "social" infrastructure such as health and education systems is not treated here. It is noteworthy that Infrastructure UK (HM Treasury 2010) adopted this division of "economic" and "social" infrastructure in its National Infrastructure Plan, signalling the critical importance of the first, as against the second, which was being very heavily cut back by the new Conservative–Liberal Democrat government. Such social infrastructure raises different issues, because of the nature of the functions and the way they have been classically dealt with by governments (mainly in the public sector), as well as the public reactions in planning (people rarely campaign against the building of a local school). It is true that the advance of neoliberalism, tending to commodify all social pro-visioning, may in due course make social infrastructure more similar to the areas examined here. But differences will remain – hospitals and the health sector are largely private in the US, but they are still quite different from the networked infrastructure industries.

Not included are information-technology systems and telecommu-nications. These are widely regarded as just as critical to economic progress and social existence as the other forms. They are excluded here for two rea-sons. The primary one is that they raise far less significant planning issues. It is true that mobile-phone masts have been an issue in some places at certain times, in the UK at least. But this has been occasional, and it is clear that the enormous project of rolling out broadband around the advanced world has not been held back, or raised big confrontations, in the way that has happened in other sectors. Equally, the companies involved and the regulatory machinery invented by governments have not been so newsworthy or subject to such big societal debates. In addition, any way of cutting down the range of areas about which I needed to learn was seized, so this sphere, though doubtless of much greater interest from several economic or sociological perspectives, was left aside. Graham and Marvin's original groundbreaking book, *Splintering Urbanism* (2001) valuably brought in this sector, making the links to the other networked industries, and related work can be traced by those who are interested in this area.

The other exclusions are the "minor" elements of these infrastructure sectors. Normally the consumer end of these systems is not so problematic, as pipes or wires or small roads enter neighbourhoods. This may not mean that the issues involved are insignificant, especially in financing and maintenance. In the UK there has been a long-running discussion about how some of this local infrastructure should be financed (Ennis 2003, Morphet 2011). Since the 1980s the cuts in public financing have pushed local authorities to extract "planning gain" or "planning obligations" from private developers of housing or other schemes, paying for roads, open space or often larger facilities like schools or health centres. In the 2000s the Barker reports on housing and planning (2004, 2006) suggested reforming this system, either by means of a development tax, a weak version of the sort of systematic approach used in Spain, or by a weaker Community Infrastructure Levy (CIL), a more systematic approach to the existing planning gain system, which was legislated for in the 2008 Planning Act. The post-2010 UK government retained the CIL, but it remains to be seen how well this will work alongside, or instead of, the planning obligations system (DCLG 2010a). Whilst of critical importance in themselves, these issues are not dealt with here. They relate very much more to how development as a whole is regulated and paid for, and to the compensation and betterment issues which have implicitly dogged most planning systems since their foundation, than to the kinds of issues which frame major infrastructure development (or non-development). Naturally the two fields are not wholly separate, affected as they are by some common trends, particularly the retreat of public funding and public ownership. But they can be relatively easily separated out, and that is done here.

WHY HAS MAJOR INFRASTRUCTURE BECOME A BIG ISSUE RECENTLY?

As explained above, infrastructure has been around for a very long time, whatever it has been called. No answer that claimed that there is something dramatically new about the infrastructure now proposed would have much validity. So we have to search for an explanation in other aspects of the contemporary world, as to its current prominence in debate and politics.

Neoliberalism

The word "neoliberalism" is for some a key concept, for others a lazy resort to ideological explanation when more specific factors should be called on. Here it is treated as an essential element of understanding the current world. There is no doubt that it is a fuzzy concept. Recent academic discussion has noted its "variegated" form (Brenner et al 2010). But we need some shorthand for the changes that the world, and above all capitalism, has undergone in recent decades. The generally accepted account is that the post-1945 form of capitalism started to come under pressure in the 1970s, and that the political transformation was led in earnest by leaders like Reagan, Thatcher and Pinochet in the 1980s (Harvey 2005). In due course this has led to a much more market driven world, with almost all countries affected, since the collapse or internal transformation of virtually all Communist regimes since 1990. Bob Jessop (2002, 2008) analyses this as the shift from the Keynesian Welfare National State (KWNS) to the Schumpeterian Workfare Post-national Regime (SWPR). Neil Brenner (2004) uses the phrase Rescaled Competition State Regime (RCSR). Each therefore draws on different features. Jessop contrasts the roles of the two famous economists John Maynard Keynes and Joseph Schumpeter, the way that labour and welfare are treated, and the partial supersession of national state powers. Brenner stresses competitiveness as being at the core of the change, but also emphasises power shifts at the sub-national level (cities and regions) and at the level of bodies such as the European Union and global organisations like the World Trade Organisation.

These acronyms can be used as shorthands to the changes that have occurred. It must be remembered, and the country chapters will make this very clear, that these changes were very variable in space and time and that they remain in process, and not necessarily unilinear. In other words, neoliberalisation is by no means "complete", whatever that could mean, and it could still be reversed – as it has been in some countries, mainly in secondary ways (such as taking water systems back into public ownership). The global economic crisis which began in 2008 is playing a part in this, above all in the global North, and the outcome remains uncertain as to how this will unfold over the years.

A simple bedrock idea of this book, hardly a novel one, is that this neoliberalising epochal change is at the base of the new ways in which infrastructure has come to be treated, in western Europe and worldwide. It is not the only element, but without this, large parts of what is analysed here would be different. A more detailed account of this shift is reserved for Chapter 2. The essential features in this field are that infrastructure is now regulated, financed, owned and managed in new ways, and this affects its planning: the search is on for new regimes of planning to fit these new realities.

The precise way in which neoliberalisation impinges on infrastructure fields will emerge throughout the book, so the details will not be explored here. The essence lies in the creation of new forces, both economic and political, which create a new urgency and salience to many infrastructure fields. State policies respond to these pressures, though in different ways in each country, and to an extent within countries.

Sustainability and nature

The same period in which neoliberal ideas and practices have developed their sway over the planet has seen the rise of ideas about nature and sustainability that are very different from those before the 1960s or 1970s. There are some links between the two shifts, but only indirect ones – they are largely autonomous, though how environmental or ecological ideas actually get expressed or acted on is greatly affected by the political economy, more or less neoliberalised. Again in shorthand, green thought has moved through changing understandings of nature and development, marked by gradual learning about how ecological and natural systems are impacted on by human society, as well as underpinning society. Over 40 or 50 years, terms like environment, ecology and sustainable development have marked this change. In the 2000s climate change debates have come to dominate the field, bringing the energy sector into the core of state policy. Time has been a critical component here, with longer timescales due to climate change issues (Wilson and Piper 2010) intersecting with infrastructure's slow changes and its normally long lives. This generates some odd and difficult dynamics, alongside the variable speeds of natural systems.

How this impacts on infrastructure policy can be easily understood. It has made it increasingly high-profile politically, working from several directions. Some of the detail here will be explored in Chapter 3. One direction is from the global downwards, discussing energy issues and travel. How should energy sources be developed, should there be a concerted drive to shift to low carbon energy generating systems and does this imply localised rather than centrally organised energy systems? Should the saving of energy, and travelling less, be at the core of state policies? The implications for all infrastructure fields are direct, from energy to waste to travel. This book will accept the realities of these challenges, though on occasion trying to problematise the ways they work. I happen to accept the case for lower-carbon and lower-impact living. But it is clear that most people even in rich countries do not, so the reality of the continuing development of infrastructure, even of a high carbon kind, will remain a target of policy making, and hence a valid target of the kind of academic consideration that wishes to be relevant to policy making. In less developed countries, the case for certain kinds of major infrastructure development is very widely accepted, and so although this book is not about those places, what is said here can have relevance to those contexts too. Much of this development will be high carbon, and it should be planned as well as it can be.

Another way in which the changed relationships to nature matter is in the changes in local consciousness of places and landscapes. Already in the early twentieth century many developed countries possessed countryside protection movements, but these have become much more generalised and powerful in recent decades. The relative ease with which the electricity transmission lines were built across the UK in the 1950s, for example, shows this. Building similar lines now would be, if not impossible, fraught with conflict and would necessitate the building of a new public consensus, against likely universal rejection across the country. Planners, politicians and businesses are all fully aware now that any development, of almost every kind, including the apparently "greenest", will be fought tooth and nail by campaigning organisations.

How far can this changed consciousness be rolled in with the wider greening of politics? It is important to understand that they are linked together, fixed to new views of nature, landscape, agriculture and so on. But they are also in part separate, and link in this way to the third element in the rise of infrastructure up the political pecking order.

Changes in governing and politics

It is widely understood that politics in developed countries is less predictable and less driven by ideological divisions than a generation ago, although these are only trends and not absolute changes. This is often seen to go with a decline in trust of governments, and a certain weakening of democratic processes. However, this is a highly contested field and no academic or wider consensus exists here, or at least even less than for the two other zones analysed above. My view is that democracy has indeed weakened across western Europe over recent decades, so that a sense that what people vote for is what they get in government is now far from as common as it might have been, in very broad terms, 30 or 40 years ago (Crouch 2004 refers to "post-democracy"). The title of Hay's 2007 book *Why We Hate Politics* points to the issue. A term like "de-democratisation", though ugly, may help to name this trend. From a UK perspective (and especially in England, after devolution to the rest of the UK since 1998), one can pick out the loss of powers of local government since the 1980s, the drift of powers to the

European Union (especially after the single market drive of the 1980s–1990s), and the weakening of political parties as a functioning transmission-belt of public opinion formation in the same period.

Many readers may disagree with this position, which argues that neoliberal politics has driven through measures over these decades which did not have wide support, and that this has meant that governments can indeed rely on less trust and public acceptance across most policy fields. This applies especially, it seems to me, to the infrastructure field. Here the building of a motorway or power station always rests on an implicit national or at least wider social contract, that this infrastructure is needed in the public interest. If the conception of the public interest is fading, then arguing for such developments, whether apparently beneficial or not, becomes much harder. Independently of the rise of green consciousness, this trend would have made infrastructure development harder and so raised its profile as a planning issue and challenge.

Another way in which this has been conceptualised recently has been in the decline of "the public" (Newman and Clarke 2009) or the "public sphere" (Habermas 1989). If more and more zones of life are commodified or made private, subject to mainly commercial or personal transactions, it is understandable that such individualisation may make wider democratic functioning harder. Giddens (2009) reflects on this issue in discussing the politics of climate change. Debates on science and science policy have pointed in the same direction (Hajer 2009), as had (in other ways) the conceptualisation of the risk society (Beck 1992). We are here in a wide landscape of social scientific work, by no means all of one mind or pointing to the same understandings, let alone solutions. But this political and governing dimension surely matters to the planning of infrastructure. And it is important to note its link to neoliberalism. Controversial though this is, my position is that the decline of democracy is indeed related to the shift in power from a more widely beneficial welfare-state era to a harder, more selfishly governed and violent world. Infrastructure is then caught up in this set of pressures from two directions, making such development more desirable for certain powerful economic interests, while making it more difficult to organise a consensus. When we add in the largely autonomous push coming from our evolving understanding of the complex ecology of the planet, it is clear that we are dealing with a challenging zone of public policy.

INFRASTRUCTURE CHALLENGES – INFRASTRUCTURE GAPS?

As will have become clear, this is not an area where it is likely that everyone will agree on what is to be done. Here, rather than making a list which might be treated as more solidly "true" than it can be, I will discuss the main logics which lie behind normal discussions of infrastructure development. It will become obvious after this that the search for consensus in academic terms, let alone politically, will be hard.

One common way to phrase the current challenges is to say that there are "gaps" in infrastructure provision. Often so called "research" is comprised of no more than surveys of businesses or public officials asking for their impressions – useful to show common concerns or mantras, but little more (KPMG 2009a, 2009b, 2010). Business lobbies such as the European Round Table from the 1980s argued that there were "missing links" in European transport systems (European Round Table 1984). In Canada the Ontario "Minister for Public Infrastructure Renewal" was only one of a swathe of politicians round the world making this sort of argument: "Investment in infrastructure in Ontario has not kept pace with economic and population growth for at least two decades, and the accumulated 'infrastructure deficit' has become burdensome" (Caplan 2005). Academics have made the same point in discussing UK provision (Clark and Root 1999). Sometimes this is phrased as a contrast between pre- and post-privatisation regimes, as with Helm who, though a supporter of privatisation, chronicles how this led to the "asset sweating" by energy companies not keen to invest, from the 1990s onwards (Helm 2004a). He subsequently sought to calculate the investment needed in the main infrastructure sectors in the UK up to 2020, coming up with a figure of over £400 billion (Helm 2009).

The gaps identified were primarily guided by criteria related to developing low carbon systems. It will become clear in the following sections that it is, in my view, not so easy to set out such a "gap and shopping list" approach. This may seem like academic fence-sitting. At any rate, it will be clear that this book is not written with an adherence to the basic argument of the UK government in the last few years, that there is a clear and self-evident problem of infrastructure gaps. This is not to say that there may not be serious non-investment, in either new development or maintenance, in some sectors. But an all-society and long-term perspective will be needed to arrive at what these are, dealing with questions of basic value.

INFRASTRUCTURE CHALLENGES AND THE ECONOMY

Business lobbies and governments

There is a very widespread understanding that infrastructure is necessary for economic success. The organisation Business Europe brings together the most successful business groups from across the European Union. Amongst its top priorities in 2009 was infrastructure. Interestingly, by 2011, this phrasing had retreated, with a much less openly-strong pressure for infrastructure development, although the references to the need for the completion of single markets in energy and transport remain – the long-term code for new infrastructure development.

In the UK the Confederation of British Industry (CBI) has shown no such lightening of its long-term campaigning for more infrastructure, above all in transport. John Cridland, CBI Director General, commented on a recent KPMG survey:

> This survey paints a disturbing picture. Firms across the country say that the infrastructure they depend on every working day is just not good enough and is stifling growth. High quality infrastructure swings boardroom decisions when companies are looking where to invest, and pays dividends in terms of future jobs and growth.
>
> The UK is still a long way down the international infrastructure league table and languishes behind key competitors. So, if we are serious about boosting exports – especially in emerging markets – and achieving sustainable growth, the Government must put infrastructure investment firmly at the top of its agenda.
>
> (CBI press release 9 September 2011)

Thus, the argument of business is that infrastructure spending is vital to competitiveness. The argument can work at any level – local, regional, national or continental, depending on the circumstances – and is normally, as above, conducted comparatively in the sense that others are doing more than "we" are doing.

Many individual OECD governments certainly subscribe to this view, and have set up overall bodies to oversee this policy area in recent years, such as Infrastructure Canada (2002), Infrastructure Australia (2008) and Infrastructure UK (2009). These are the countries, it might be noted, that have been at the forefront of the privatisation and liberalisation of infrastructure sectors, as well as of pressing for private-public partnerships in this field, and developing new private equity funds for infrastructure. Those countries a little further behind in this trend have been less oriented towards setting up this kind of overview body, though most countries have been equally or more energetic in particular sectors.

The economics discipline

More broadly, the position of the economics discipline is not clear cut on what infrastructure does to achieve economic growth, or economic development where the two are distinguished. There is a long tradition of seeing land and natural resources as critical for a country's development, with the mercantilist and physiocratic schools in several European countries stressing these aspects from at least the seventeenth-century onwards, aspects which easily embrace most infrastructure sectors too (Meek 1962). By the twentieth century, economists argued that transport and energy systems were generally "natural monopolies" that could not be subject to competition but rather should be managed or regulated by the state (O'Neill 2010). This became very widely accepted, in all capitalist countries, including the United States.

The natural monopoly argument was based on certain features of infrastructure which were held to distinguish it from other industrial sectors. These were its indivisibility, its largeness, its network character, its long life, its expensiveness and its very extensive externality effects. More generally, it was normally an input into a whole range of societal activities, as it underlay all production and consumption (a point emphasised in recent years by Helm, for example, 2009). In this sense it was often seen as being like other general actions of government, such as the provision of defence or police forces, or institutional supports in legal systems like company forms or support for contracts. For much of the twentieth century such arguments in economics textbooks were broadly supported. Only with the advance of neoliberal economics arguments from the Chicago school, particularly in the 1960s, were the foundations of natural monopoly challenged. The features identified were not generally dismissed, as it was widely accepted that building two roads or two electricity transmission lines next to each other would be wasteful. But the ways in which the various features could be resolved by "unbundling" the services involved, and introducing markets to each step of the process, were developed and then implemented, initially in the US and the UK from the 1970s on. The economics argument was perhaps never really finished, whilst political practice sped ahead. We will see the effects this had. The facts of very large investments, long pay-back periods, systemic externalities and geographical difficulties did not change, and so infrastructure remained different. That meant that exceptionally intricate and complex regulation was needed to make the new non-public systems work, after a fashion. The search for effectively functioning liberalised systems is still continuing, and arguably the problems are far from resolved.

The other aspect that has never been very convincingly pinned down from an economics perspective is *how* infrastructure provision may matter for economic growth. Its importance may seem obvious from a common sense viewpoint. Economists looking at development referred to "social overhead capital" as against "directly productive activities", in an attempt to theorise its distinctive importance (Hirschman 1958). But economists who have tried to quantify the impact have had difficulties. Starting with World Bank researchers in the 1980s (Aschauer 1989, Gramlich 1994), they seemed to find some effect, but critiques of the econometrics followed. Calderon and Serven (2004) seem to have carried out more robust work, covering transport, power and telecommunications. They argue that if Latin American countries caught up with the infrastructure provision of median

Asian countries, like South Korea, they could increase their annual growth rates by between 1 and 5 per cent – most for the worst provided states, and least for those like Chile, already relatively well stocked. These results are impressive, and in fact surprising.

The collective representative of developed countries, the OECD, makes broadly the same argument, though often with rather less insistence and intellectual conviction. It carried out a large research project on infra-structure needs to 2030, and concluded that these were indeed high (OECD 2006, 2007). Around the same time, OECD economists worked hard to pin down the importance of infrastructure in contributing to GDP growth, and it is worth quoting the conclusions:

> investment in physical infrastructure can boost long-term economic output more than other kinds of physical investment ... the gains have been larger for countries with comparatively poorly developed energy and telecommunications networks ... additional investment raising provision in such countries by 10% has been associated with around a 0.25% percentage point increase in long-term growth rate (almost four times larger than for countries with more developed networks) ... at present almost all countries have reached levels of provision where additional expansion would have relatively small effects on economy-wide activity.
>
> (OECD 2009 p.167)

Although there was also an effort to identify which sectors helped most – energy, roads, rail, telecommunications – this was seen to vary a lot between countries, and the final view came to rely on wider OECD policy posi-tions: that private sector provision was more efficient, backed by independent regulators (a staple of neoliberal ideology unrelated to the research).

Doubters can point to countries like India with clearly very deficient transport, energy and water systems, and quite low new investment, but with respectable economic growth rates. Relatively speaking, countries like the US and those of western Europe have gold-plated infrastructure sys-tems, and from an economic efficiency point of view it is hard to be sure whether infrastructure defects are the primary causes of failures in one country or region compared with other factors. Spanish regional economists have spent an enormous amount of energy in recent years trying to assess the impact of the massive, largely EU financed, infrastructure investment across all the sectors examined here, and have, as far as I am aware, found it hard to prove that this has been critical to the success of the country as a whole, or to particular regions with the largest investments. So, some recent work does point to significant impacts of infrastructure investment on growth, but there remain, it would appear, doubts and gaps regarding what can be inferred from this.

Whilst the precise link between infrastructure and growth may be uncertain, there is probably more evidence for the link between public spending as a whole and economic growth. This relation, originally called "Wagner's Law" after an economist of the 1880s, has been shown to hold in survey after survey (Hall 2010c). The difficulty is then to find out which part of the public spending has the most causal power: whether in network-infrastructural, educational, health or social-security spending.

Marxist analysis

Marxist positions on infrastructure naturally begin from a very different place. Harvey (1982, 1985) starts from the position that the reproduction of both capital and labour power requires a wide range of physical and social infrastructures. This whole built environment "hangs together as a spatially specific resource complex of humanly created assets to support both production (fixed capital) and consumption (the consumption fund)" (Harvey 1985 p.144). This requires large amounts of geographically immobile and long-term capital investment. This will age unevenly, depending on maintenance and technical progress, and will be renewed piecemeal, with the established spatial configuration constraining this renewal.

Harvey therefore analyses physical infrastructures from a different perspective, both as a call on overall capital needed to support accumulation, and as a way that surplus capital can be absorbed during general crises to avoid system-threatening capital devaluation. If he were analysing the post-2008 economic and financial crisis, he would certainly be looking at the intricate tying together of financialised capitalism and circuits of infrastructure investment. The same logics can apply to social infrastructures, which he defines as welfare, legal and political systems, but these are less firmly immobile and less linked to built-environment processes. His analysis simply assumes that the provision of infrastructure is integral to the circuits of capital accumulation, from observing how this has progressed during the history of capitalism. It is clear in such a long historical view that, in fact, capitalism has always dedicated significant efforts to providing physical infrastructures. This is not the same as saying that all such provision was perfectly or rationally judged, that the amount was "correct", but it does argue that the provision reflected dynamics integral to capitalism's moving forward.

One further feature emphasised in Marxist accounts is competition: the tendency to competition between modes of infrastructure and between cities, regions and countries is endemic in capitalism. This may well be counteracted by state policies, as has been very often the case historically. But there is an internal drive to competition, which pushes for more and more value creation. Ideologies or academic arguments may be mobilised to support this drive and remove the "chains" of state involvement. But this already finds a ready dynamic existing in capitalist systems – not something "natural" but something already naturalised by the existence of capitalism. When, in Chapter 2, the economic development of infrastructure industries is examined, we will refer again to this underlying tendency. In the present period, competition and competitiveness are the twin motors held by the hegemonic powers to be ideal for the infrastructure world, and much of what we will observe in this book picks up on the problems and tensions this creates, generating insistent pressures for state action, including action within spatial planning.

These observations may well be more useful to us than the large-scale empirical efforts made to try to establish the contribution of infrastructure to economic growth. A Marxist will say that capitalism, by definition, is concerned with capital accumulation, not with economic growth, which is an "accidental" side product of accumulation. Given that now, and in the foreseeable future, we are living in a largely capitalist world, we may reasonably expect the dynamics that have been observed over the long term and in the recent past, to continue, in the broadest sense in the same manner. We need to see infrastructure creation (and for that matter destruction and decay) as being within capitalism, as well as within the history of industrialism.

Understanding the economy–infrastructure nexus

So, on the competitiveness, or economic success, side, we have an unclear situation. Business organisations, governments and "common sense" promote infrastructure investment for these goals, whilst main-line economists express some reservations, even though the more applied ones would doubtless add their support. More critically, and taking on Marxist understandings of the effects of existing within a capitalist system and of the pervasiveness of competitive forces, a wider perspective could argue that gains in overall welfare might not necessarily be obtained by every country competing to raise its infrastructure investment. Would that not just leave them on the same level again, but at great cost? Organising the reduction of energy and transport growth, largely related to these investments, might make more economic sense. This points to the need to discuss the overall nature of infrastructure, within the global development schema as a whole, which follows in the section on infrastructure in historical perspective.

INFRASTRUCTURE CHALLENGES AND THE ENVIRONMENT

A large amount of investment in infrastructure has partly environmental goals. This has long been the case, back to public-health aims through the last two centuries and more. But it has become more important with the rise of ecological consciousness. That consciousness has worked as a double-edged sword. In part it has driven against development, arguing for energy efficiency or moderated consumption. But in some sectors, such as public transport, waste-water treatment or, more recently, renewable energy, it presses for investment. This has become more insistently so as climate change has risen up the agenda since the early 1990s. There is now, therefore, a new and powerful lobby for infrastructure development for low-carbon reasons. In most countries there are now strategies laying out how such investment could contribute to such goals by 2050 or whatever date is chosen. This sits rather oddly alongside the economic challenges discussed above, which are normally about economic growth, or more simply business profitability. The two logics can be used rhetorically by lobbying groups, with one side or another stressed depending on the audience. But it is clear that they have different relationships to fundamental political or moral positions. One is about business success, however conceived, with an instrumental, local and short-term utilitarian logic. The other is about very long-term, global ecologies, a whole-planet and rather ethical logic. Coming together in a pro-infrastructure development discourse is clearly strange, if not actually dishonest and philosophically incoherent.

At the same time it is possible to have doubts about the widespread adoption of low carbon arguments in the last few years. Erik Swyngedouw has suggested that this, following the fate of "sustainability", is as much about the depoliticisation of a potentially very system-challenging issue, as about making real differences to what is done day-to-day in economies (2010). He points out that the environmental challenges have been present for decades, untackled in most respects in many parts of the world. The headlining of low carbon by almost every international body and state may not be in good faith. This, therefore, cautions against fully buying into the environmental arguments for infrastructure investment, or at least for maintaining some scepticism about claims regarding what new power stations or railway lines may do, given the failure to advance programmes of demand management or energy efficiency, despite these being pushed by many environmentalists for 30 or 40 years. The work of Flyvbjerg and colleagues (Flyvbjerg et al 2003, Priemus et al 2008) is supportive of such a sceptical position, though their interest is especially in the political dynamics of particular projects. Flyvbjerg documents effectively how projects always cost far more than originally thought, and that the nature of the decision-making process is in some senses normally corrupted.

This book inclines towards this scepticism, on the topic as a whole. There may well be good economic, social and environmental reasons for major infrastructure development in some places. But it is always important to look at alternatives, which may be cheaper (societally speaking – that is, looking with some overall rationality). The existing systems always need to be examined, to understand how they are managed and maintained. For example, if one is looking at a proposal for a high-speed rail line, it would be wise to look at the whole transport picture. This would include accessibility: Who would benefit from the system, how would fares be structured, what would be the cost to the government budget and what else might be done with that funding? In other words, how one sees the infrastructure challenges brings in one's overall goals. These are as much social as economic and environmental, taking an overall welfare perspective. There is a tendency in the infrastructuralism of the present period to roll up the argument into a competitiveness and low-carbon imperative, in each country, implying that the investment is "obviously" needed. The publications of bodies like the Institution of Civil Engineers in the UK, though extremely well put together, tend to have this character (Institution of Civil Engineers 2010, for example). Looking at the overall picture, the challenges may not be so simple. A critical and questioning approach to the challenges will be the best one in many circumstances.

INFRASTRUCTURE IN OVERALL HISTORICAL PERSPECTIVE

It is worthwhile standing back and thinking about what most infrastructure investment is enmeshed in. More detail of specific histories (and geographies) will be given in Chapter 3. For now, just a reminder of the very big framing will be useful, alongside the understanding of capitalism given above. The core of this is about living in a high-energy world. Simms and Boyle (2010), in a chapter on the history of British Petroleum (now BP), bring out the profound implications for all the developments of the last century and more, of the shift to oil-based living. This infuses all daily existence and all politics – the entire world of material objects. Quite directly it is the lifeblood of almost all infrastructure, which has become essential to high-energy societies. Altvater (2005) has analysed this in relation to "fossil capitalism", its absolute requirement for petroleum as well as other fossil fuels (or, in desperation, high-cost alternatives like nuclear power). In a different analytical register, Martinez Alier (1987) tracked the relation of economy and ecology, through the development of the prehistory of ecological economics. Humans have learnt to substitute external energy sources for "natural" ones deriving from the planet's surface (solar power, wind, photosynthesis). This has transformed agriculture, manufacturing and movement.

One influential zone of work on these issues is on Large Technical Systems (LTS). This emphasises the blending of technical and social factors in the spread of infrastructure systems, concentrating on the period since the Industrial Revolution (van der Vleuten 2006). This draws attention to the profound importance of these transformations of nature, the creation of new "human-made deep structures" in society (van der Vleuten 2004. p399). Each LTS can generate second order LTSs, say a food system, which is made up of transport, energy and other systems. In a sense spatial planning is making second order links of this kind through its influence over location of development, though only as one of many factors.

Everything under discussion in this book is part of the externally powered, LTS-rich, world, even if these have a green form such as wind energy or biocrops. Such sources are after all desired to meet such external energy demand, however much that might be sensibly reduced. Even the most ascetic prophets of change do not imagine a full return to pre-industrial forms of life, without electricity, the internet, or some form of public transport. In other words, we are immersed in speed, high energy, globalised consciousness and practices. Some of this could easily be imagined as different, but much of it we would only lose with intense resistance. The point that follows from this developed form of historical addiction, is that we are bound into a major-infrastructure-filled world, at least for the moment – a moment we may think of as lasting several human generations. So at the least, the issue of such big infrastructure is likely to be with us for some time yet: not an argument for stasis or doing nothing new, but a caution about where we have got to in human history, as well as a call to understand this and, in the long run, question it. After all, the history of oil, the largest component of this addiction, is not a pretty one, as a reading of BP's (or any other oil company's) history will soon inform us.

CONCLUSIONS

We have seen that infrastructure has risen to be a prominent theme, on the back of economic and environmental concerns. But this relatively recent phenomenon has been placed here within a wide and deep framing, which includes the emergence of industrialism and the dynamic developments of capitalism, in some cases over centuries. Given infrastructure's often very long life, and its deep implication in resource flows and lifestyles, such framing is appropriate. In the next chapter we move to look at the ways in which infrastructure industries have been changing and have been governed. These together constitute the overall provision systems for each sector, which form the context or frame for the ways in which planning and geography relate to major infrastructure.

CHAPTER 2
INFRASTRUCTURE INDUSTRIES AND INFRASTRUCTURE GOVERNMENT

Planners and planning academics have rarely focused on infrastructure fields as a separated area of interest, and the same applies to the social sciences as a whole. As made clear in the first chapter, economists, amongst others, did theorise some of the issues. Once one goes down to the level of individual industries, there are also empirical surveys. But there are rarely overviews that try to keep the whole picture of reality together. One theme in this chapter is the need to provide an overview to make any sense of what has been, and is, going on, which is of central importance to understanding the context in which planning is operating. The tendency to separate off thinking about planning is, in my view, always problematic: a disciplinary and professional curse which needs to be continually resisted. For the purposes of presentation and analysis, it is essential to separate out more economically oriented dimensions and more governmentally oriented dimensions in this chapter, and then geographical–historical aspects in Chapter 3, and planning ones more precisely in Chapter 4. But the issues are to be understood in relation to each other, and they are presented that way in the national case studies.

This holistic view has always been understood by radical thinkers and reformers. The drives to take public control, across numerous sectors and countries, were always rooted in such a wide view, as was the movement of privatisation and liberalisation, now equally widespread and taking equally varied forms. It is important to start by taking this long view, before examining the current state of infrastructure industries and governance. The "economic" and "political" are utterly intertwined, as they always have been, and so the links between the two will be continuous in this presentation.

INFRASTRUCTURE PROVISION OVER TIME

In the industrialised world of the last two centuries or so, there has been a continuous oscillation in the systems of provision (Dupuy 1991, Hughes 1983). In some states, provision was taken into state hands early on (railways in Germany, for example), but elsewhere private companies were normally in the lead, either in quite independent modes (water and gas systems in British cities) or being strongly regulated (water concession systems in France, management of private rail construction in Britain). Where early systems were private, there was a very generalised tendency for public takeover of responsibility, from the late nineteenth century onwards. This often had a strong ideological component – "municipal socialism" in Europe, "progressivism" in the United States – but it was backed by wider pragmatic arguments arising from all the features recited in Chapter 1: externalities, high investment costs and long returns. So by the early twentieth century the typical infrastructure provision systems, in energy, transport, water and waste, were in locally and publicly controlled organisational forms, in Europe as much as in North America. Then, from the First World War onwards, there was a common tendency, at least in Europe, for centralisation to occur, handing these local bodies to state-run or coordinated corporations. In Britain this often took place in two steps, as in electricity and railways, with first private ownership largely being retained, but then with decisive nationalisation after 1945. The other common trajectory was from municipal to regional or national public control (water, waste, gas, roads). Different forms and trajectories marked each country. France maintained its water concession systems, but nationalised energy and transport after 1945, whilst Germany kept transport systems in public central control by and large, while continuing with decentralised public systems in water, waste and to some extent energy.

Thus, the well known publicly owned or managed pattern of the Keynesian or Welfare State era was formed, running most infrastructure systems from the 1940s to the 1980s or later (Graham and Marvin 2001 give much more detail). This affected planning deeply, in several ways. Firstly, it reduced the geographical variations in provision, because of the public commitment to universal service. If an area or region was developed, it could expect that the relevant state body would provide services – often the two processes would have been planned together. Secondly, and related to this, the need for infrastructure was often taken to be almost self-evident. The publicly owned bodies normally did not have to get planning permission, or at least were assumed to already embody public legitimacy because of their public corporation status, when an inquiry came up. Hills (1984) describes how, in the 1970s, the National Coal Board tended to assume that what it was doing was in the public interest when discussing the development of new coal fields with local authorities or other interests. The same applied to the Central Electricity Generating Board in its transmission system construction from the 1950s, although in both cases public opposition began to challenge this basic assumption.

Thirdly, and perhaps obviously, public control did give at least potential scope for integrated spatial planning, whether at national, regional or local levels. Instances of this did exist, as in French national planning from the 1960s to the 2000s, in UK regional planning in its strongest era in the 1960s to 1970s, or in the capacity of German municipalities to plan with their Stadtwerke (municipal water, waste and energy bodies), in places up until the present day. There was by no means a neat mesh of public infrastructure control and integrated planning, for a host of reasons, but with the Keynesian period structures the possibility was there to be worked towards, and certainly in Scandinavian countries and the Netherlands the potential became often the norm. And this is by no means purely historical. Ontario's government spelled out its aim to link its infrastructure spending capacity, especially in public transport, with its spatial planning under its Greenbelt Act 2005 and Places to Grow Act 2005 (Caplan 2005). Some of the post-2008 crisis infrastructure investment plans also saw the scope for such linking up (for example, the stimulus packages in France and the Netherlands).

The neoliberal revolution, started in the late 1970s, has not swept away the whole of this publicly owned infrastructure model. Certainly the landscape is completely transformed in many countries, with private and sometimes competing companies now the key actors. But there are some areas in many countries which have resisted this trend, as will become clear in the sectoral survey below. Roads are one very obvious case, but several other fields – ports, airports, water and energy – retain significant portions of public ownership.

The first cases of privatisation came through governments of the most radical right-wing character in the 1970s and 1980s, based on the thinking of the Chicago school of economists (Milton Friedman and others), first in Chile after the 1973 coup, and then under the Reagan and Thatcher regimes in the 1980s (Funnell et al 2009, Parker 2008). Practice was developed, by trial and error as well as in tandem with academic advisors, as to how the privatisation of public bodies would be best managed, and what regulatory systems were needed to make infrastructure systems achieve some generally acknowledged wider goals. This dynamic of "re-regulation" came to be recognised as an integral part of the transformation of infrastructure industries, creating a new zone of academic study – some further analysis is given below. The nature of regulation depended on how far the stress was on privatisation alone, or on liberalisation and competition (the more normal goal, driven by conventional economics doctrines). That division rested, in turn, on the nature of the sector: in some it was much easier to create liberalised competition (telephones, some energy systems) than in others (water, rail, roads).

THE NEW INFRASTRUCTURE INDUSTRIES

The new world of privatised infrastructure industries was coming into being and into focus by the 1990s. It was driven at several levels, predominantly nationally, but also from the 1990s by the European Union's core policies, as well as in international bodies such as the World Trade Organisation and the International Monetary Fund, though these had most impact on weaker and poorer countries. Gradually, and very variably between countries, this impacted on planning, counteracting all three effects mentioned above. Universal provision could no longer be assumed, but had to be fought out and negotiated at each step. Public legitimacy of infrastructure providers declined. This is not easily proven by reference to data, but most observers have tracked a decreasing respect for the new infrastructure companies, at least in the UK, which has had a negative effect on the acceptance of new schemes. Clearly this is a complex issue, to which we will return in the concluding chapter. There was already plenty of evidence for lesser public acceptance before the structural reforms (for example, in France in the 1990s, with providers still largely public). The third clear effect was to reduce the potential for integrated planning, matching new development and infrastructure provision, at whatever scale. As noted above, this had never been easy in the publicly managed systems, but would become a very different sort of challenge under the post 1990s regimes.

Figure 2.1 Largest transnationals in infrastructure industries, ranked by foreign assets, 2006. (Source: Whitfield 2010 p. 138)

Rank	Electricity	Telecoms	Transport	Water/sewage	Natural gas	More than one infrastructure industry
1	Electricite de France (France)	Vodafone Group (UK)	Grupo Ferrovial	Veolia (France)	Gaz de France (France)	Suez (France)
2	E.ON (Germany)	Telefonica (Spain)	Albertis (Spain)	Grupo Agbar (Spain)	Spectra Energy Corp. (US)	Hutchison Whampoa (Hong Kong, China)
3	Endessa (Spain)	Deutsche Telekom (Germany)	AP Moller-Maersk	Waste Management Inc (US)	Centrica (UK)	RWE Group (Germany)
4	Vattenfall (Sweden)	France Telecom (France)	DP World (UAR)	Shanks Group (UK)	Gas Natural (Spain)	Bouygues (France)
5	National Grid (UK)	Vivendi (France)	China Ocean Shipping (China)	Waste Services Inc (US)	Transcanada Corp (Canada)	YTL Power (Malaysia)

Source: United Nations Conference on Trade and Development 2008

From the 1980s a new set of infrastructure corporations emerged and gathered power: economic and political. At first, in Britain, there was some US influence, with corporations such as Enron moving into the electricity business. Then European companies became dominant, with private or part-private national companies like Suez, Veolia, RWE, E.ON, EDF and DB (previously Deutsche Bahn) becoming continent-wide giants in the water, waste, energy and transport fields. This had resulted, by 2011, in a variable landscape of industries, as we will see in detail later, with French, German and Spanish based companies tending to dominate the European peripheral-country systems. Figure 2.1 shows the rankings in six main infrastructure sectors of such companies, estimated by UNCTAD in 2008.

But alongside this mega-corporation world of companies, with their main interest in providing infrastructure services, there emerged from the early 2000s a private equity model of control. This is often known as the "Macquarie model", after the Australian bank which began to specialise in infrastructure funds in the 1990s (O'Neill 2010, Whitfield 2010). This is related to the wider phenomenon of Public Private Partnerships (PPPs), which have sought to increase the attractiveness of private investment in infrastructure by giving state guarantees of long-term returns. In this way states manage to combine the peculiar "natural" features of natural monopolies (lack of competition) with the equally "natural" features of the state (long-term existence and hence generally credible commitment). This can then give solid bases for higher debt-ratios, a situation that private equity companies took full advantage of from about 2002 onwards. As Whitfield makes clear (2010 pp.98–99), the approach used by Macquarie was only one among several ways in which infrastructure funds developed during these years. He also describes how closely the growth of this sort of investment in infrastructure was tied to the other well-known elements of financialising capitalism, such as securitisation, derivatives, hedge funds and almost universal use of tax havens (Macquarie often using Bermuda). The related rise of sovereign-wealth funds also comes into the picture, as these funds (from the Middle East and Far East) have started to make large investments in infrastructure.

So in the years before the 2008 financial crisis, more and more interest was being shown in infrastructure by finance companies world-wide, including some representing pension funds. These were searching for reliable returns over long periods, which some infrastructure sectors were thought to be able to provide. Figure 2.2 shows the leading funds in this area before the crisis. Analysts in bodies like RREEF, run by Deutsche Bank, were examining the growth and attractiveness of the sector since the early 2000s, and the financial press saw infrastructure investment as a valuable path for the diversification of rich funds, including sovereign-wealth funds. RREEF tried to calculate the global values of infrastructure, if with the crudest methodology, evidently imagining this as all a fair target for financial investors. The number came to 18.9 trillion dollars, 83 per cent of this in developed countries

Figure 2.2 Value of assets under global fund management 2009. (Source: Whitfield 2010 p. 119)

Rank	Type of Fund	Assets US$ billion	%
1	Pension Funds	25,000	32
2	Investment/Mutual & Managed Funds	22,000	28
3	Insurance Companies	17,000	22
4	Foreign Exchange Reserves	7,400	9
5	Sovereign Wealth Funds	3,900	5
6	Hedge Funds	1,700	2
7	Private Equity Funds	700	1
8	Real Estate Investment Trusts	700	1
	Total	**78,400**	**100.0**

Source: International Financial Services London 2009, Sovereign Wealth Fund Institute, 2009.

(RREEF 2008). Given capital's restless search for ways to create value, such calculations may not be so far fetched. But only a month after this report, in October 2008, the press was reporting a big slowdown; it was expected the asset class might be saved by government infrastructure-based rescue packages, smoothing the coming years financing picture (Davis 2008). Hall's view (2009 p.10), admittedly from a long term critic of PPPs, was that infrastructure funds were much less stable than they appeared, working profitably only at particular moments in an economic cycle and under very particular conditions.

Some argue that these funds could be a big part of the future for infrastructure provision, with everything from roads to schools to hospitals to airports following the investment patterns of Macquarie and being cut up into fundable parcels. We will consider this further in the concluding chapter. It may represent one plausible end to the processes of privatisation begun 30 years ago. However, the post-2008 crisis conditions have slowed the progress of infrastructure funds, with some companies like the Australian firm Babcock and Babcock going bankrupt. Infrastructure company indices showed them growing rapidly in value from around 100 billion dollars in 2001 to 350 billion in 2007, falling back to 200 billion in 2008 (Whitfield 2010 p.95). So the "Macquarie model", in the broadest sense, appears to be tied up with the fate of hyper-financialising capitalism and especially with how that is regulated. At present, the survival and growth of the "traditional" infrastructure corporations like RWE, EDF or Veolia seems just as likely an outcome, if infrastructure industries remain largely in their current "private but strongly regulated" forms in Europe.

REGULATION OF INFRASTRUCTURE INDUSTRIES

"Regulation" can mean many things, depending on context and theoretical lens. Some regard planning (land use or spatial) as a form of regulation. It certainly has some similarities to the forms of regulation set up after the privatisation of utilities or network industries, in the sense of being institutionally formalised systems governing the use of assets to obtain publicly validated goals. In the case of land-use planning, the assets are the services provided by land and buildings, and the goals are variously social, economic and environmental. In the infrastructure industries the objects are the provision of various services (transport, heat, water, waste disposal, electricity), and the goals a mix of low prices, wide-scale availability and minimised environmental impacts. The similarities are clear in the services and the wider goals, but the systems of regulation are extremely different. Planning systems are essentially geographical; about adjoining spaces, in particular, territories governed broadly with the involvement of inhabitants and users of those territories, and so normally with a strong local component, if more widely framed. The regulation of infrastructure industries is highly varied, but often exceptionally complex, with separate economic and environmental arms. Rules often impinge from associated state-policy fields like competition authorities and health and safety agencies. Regulatory institutions are not normally especially geographically focused, and tend to be nationally organised. We will come back to the contrasts and interrelationships of these two forms of regulation later. For the moment, when I refer to regulation I take the normal usage in this field, meaning the post-privatisation bodies created to manage the new industry structures and behaviours.

Just as privatisation and liberalisation progressed at widely different speeds and in varied forms, so regulation took on nationally distinct characteristics. It is true that, in a very general sense, the outcomes had some similarities given EU rules and the broad tasks of regulation. Some kinds of state sponsored bodies were needed, with the infrastructure provider having some sort of independence (including from the government if that still provided infrastructure services). So a survey in the mid 2000s of France, Germany and the UK found that the regulated competitive model – privatised suppliers, liberalisation of supply, independent regulatory agencies – could be applied to all three countries (Thatcher 2007).

However, at a finer grain the differences are considerable. Earlier Thatcher (2002) suggested five types of regulatory regime, which he stressed were not designed to fit a whole country but should be applied to individual sectors. At one extreme was the public ownership regime, where the government and public monopolies simply set all rules. At the other end of the spectrum was the private competition regime, where all suppliers were private and the regulation system was set up to secure real competition. Between these were the semi-liberalised public-service regimes, mixed economy competition regimes (when several companies were still public) and protected competition regimes, where re-regulation effectively damp-ened or prevented competition. The point here is not to list or detail which of these were or are present in which countries, but to emphasise that they have been very common in Europe in recent decades, and so in many of the country cases described later some versions of these were present at vari-ous times in certain sectors.

It is true that since 2002, EU and national government policies have pushed the range of cases towards the private competition regime desired by the EU and many other policy makers. But this has not removed the "in-between" cases, at least in some sectors – perhaps only telephone and related services are very solidly in the "final" stage, and even there this by no means implies the absence of state regulation. Furthermore, the "end state" regime has numerous possible variations, depending on how strong the regulatory agency or agencies are, and what the policy priorities are seen to be (generating strong competition, helping "national champions", achieving environmental goals of one kind or another, and so on). Regulatory institutions might take different forms (Finger 2005): at different levels (EU, national, subnational), of varying independence, of varying powers (budgets for research or enforcement etc), and either sector/goal specific or cross sectoral (say for competition or for environmental aims whatever the infra-structure industry).

All this matters when considering planning, because planning natu-rally exists only to create certain effects. If some of those effects are achieved by other public instruments or institutions, then planning's role is reduced or different. If an ecologically sound house is achieved by a national law or some other general means, there is clearly no point in seeking to negotiate this on each housing development by means of planning regulation. In the case studies, reference will at times be made to the role of regulatory sys-tems other than planning, and how the two relate to each other.

THE NATURE OF INFRASTRUCTURE SECTORS IN CONTEMPORARY EUROPE

As the above discussion reveals, there are some common tendencies across infrastructure industries. This means that some firms are active in more than one sector. However, there remain real differences, so here the approach is to look at the main industries separately and note links where these are occurring. The main emphasis is on the ownership and control of industries, not on regulation. The dividing up is the one adopted throughout this book. The four transport sectors (ports, airports, road, rail), water, energy and waste, are thus examined in turn. More detailed information is given on the UK industries.

I have not, at present, found good pan-European statistical data on each transport sector, and so these sections will not have the generalised figures on the industries that are given for water, energy and waste. There are several cross-European transport companies emerging, primarily to run buses and train *services*. These established themselves in the privatised British system, and companies like Stagecoach, First Group, Go-Ahead and National Express have a European reach (and wider), as have Veolia, Transdev (both French) and DB (owning Arriva), with bus and, to a lesser extent, rail operations in many countries. But this has extended less to the infrastructure *systems* discussed below. At present these tend to either be more nationally arranged, or more globally infiltrated by private equity or global transportation corporations. Whilst one cannot fully separate out the infrastructure components from those using the infrastructure, the division does have some significance.

PORTS

Ports were often in public ownership, and subject to significant public planning processes during the twentieth century, and this continues to varying degrees in many European countries. The public forms have varied, with central government being the usual owner in France and Spain, but variations with municipal or regional ownership more common in Germany and the Netherlands, and, until the 1980s or 1990s, in the UK. Shipping lines had long been in mainly private hands, and the transformation of world shipping brought by containerisation from the 1960s onwards (Levinson 2006) changed both the leading maritime companies and countries, and started to impact on the functioning of ports. This then intersected with the political drive for privatisation, centred on the UK in its early stages. But this has been very uneven around Europe and the world as a whole, with governments in one shape or another keeping ownership of many important ports. Details will appear in the country chapters, but here a broad idea of the variety is given.

In the UK the conglomerate of major ports put together by governments in the 1960s and 1970s, Associated British Ports, was sold off in the early 1980s, followed by a number of smaller ports in the early 1990s. The Labour government of 1997 to 2010 did not continue this process, but immediately on the arrival of the Conservative–Liberal Democrat government, the privatisation of the remaining trust ports was initiated. Up to 2008 there was a significant rise in private equity ownership in the 2000s (ABP, PD Ports), but still major holdings by "traditional" port or maritime companies, based in Hong Kong/China, Dubai and in the case of Peel Holdings, in the UK. This privatisation and globalisation of UK port industries was very much reflected in planning policy towards port expansion in the 2000s, as we will see in Chapter 9.

Other countries were not affected so fundamentally by the forces of privatisation, though globalisation's pressures were naturally very visible. The massive increase in world trade from the 1960s, picking up speed with the rise of China in the 1990s, called for the expansion of European ports. This was largely carried out under publicly owned and managed bodies, although these were increasingly run under principles and management structures of a private sector or commercial character. Thus Rotterdam's port is held by a consortium of local and central government, and that of Amsterdam by Amsterdam City Council. Bremen and Hamburg are run by the respective city states, though with arms-length bodies entrusted with day-to-day management. Bremen is developing the large new deep water JadeWeserPort with the state of Lower Saxony – a publicly led and partly publicly financed response to the competition on the "north range" from Hamburg via Rotterdam and Antwerp to Le Havre.

Spanish and French ports remain, in most cases, still formally owned by central governments, but many have been passed, in effect, to regional and local governments to manage. In France the seven largest ports are retained in central government control, because they are seen as strategic national priorities. We will see how this gives a rather different character to public decision-making on ports and their expansion during this dynamic period of trade growth, in all these countries as opposed to the UK. Nevertheless, there are common features of intense inter-port competition that have developed since the 1990s (Notteboom et al 2009, Wang et al 2007). The difference is that the non-British governments are content to give certain amounts of public support to their port agencies, in contrast to Britain since the 1990s. Whilst the EU frowns on such support, it was unable to bring in a ports directive in the early 2000s to directly regulate this, and has to use softer measures and quiet threats to discourage "unfair competition" in this sector (Pallis and Tsiotsis 2008).

AIRPORTS

The twentieth-century pattern for airports was similar to that for ports, with public ownership and development the almost universal norm in European airports. The UK had had a major state-holding company, the British Airports Authority (BAA), set up in the 1960s and 1970s primarily to manage London's airports, and then privatised in 1986. In addition there was a mix of municipal and private airports, which filled in regional gaps but until the 1990s had nothing like the significance of BAA's set of larger airports. The picture in 2011 is more complex, with the rise of low-cost airlines since the 1990s boosting some regional airports and government action leading to the partial breaking up of BAA in 2009–2011. A few airports remain municipally run (Manchester, Luton) but these also have a strong commercial orientation.

Other European countries have a much less privatised landscape, although whatever the ownership structure, a strongly commercialised orientation is the norm. German airports have seen significant sales of public shares since the 1990s, with two or three smaller airports growing on the back of low-cost carriers. But a recent survey found only 11 out of 35 larger airports with private investors as part owners, very often with majority public control even in these cases (Malina 2010). Frankfurt airport is, for example, 52 per cent owned by Hesse state and Frankfurt Stadtwerke, whilst Munich remains publicly owned by a mix of federal and state shares, as do the Berlin airports. Schiphol and the smaller Dutch airports remain in public ownership, though with full commercial freedom in normal operation. French and Spanish airports are being gradually transferred to mainly regional public ownership, though with central control retained in the most important cases. The Paris airports are still in a state owned holding, and transfers in Spain are occurring more due to political pressures than in the more systematic transfer taking place in France. In all cases, the rise of inter-airport competition has been noticeable since the emergence of the low cost airlines, although in only a few cases has this led to new or almost new airports appearing. In most cases the already important regional centres have consolidated their positions, with a few airports becoming intercontinental hubs (Frankfurt, Munich, Paris, Schiphol, Madrid, with Barcelona and Lyon less definitely established).

It is clear in all countries that the role of the large airlines, the national or ex national carriers, remains critical, especially for intercontinental travel. As in the ports industry, the competition between the carriers impinges on the competition between the end points. In almost no cases are airlines the owners of airports, so the complex tensions in these relationships continue and develop. The 2000s have seen the beginnings of the arrival of private equity firms buying airports, as in the UK case of Gatwick in 2010. Some, like Macquarie, may aspire to build up portfolios of European airports, which would change the balance of competition. Where airlines have merged, as in the case of Air France and KLM, they have begun to cooperate in their strategies towards their key airports, and this appears to be generating pressures for the Paris airports and Schiphol to also work together. The EU has pressed "open skies" dimensions of aviation strongly since the 1980s, and has also been active in fighting state aid. But it has had to tread gently in the face of implicit national defence of powerful airports. As is often the case, the drive for liberalisation can rarely be finally "sealed" by tightly framed and equally applied regulatory regimes.

The complexities of competition in the airports business are widely discussed by academics (Forsyth et al 2010), with the normal issues of partial spatial monopolies: there are rarely two airports serving exactly the same markets. How this works out will emerge during the next few years, if privatisation and liberalisation progress. This will then affect the dynamic of inter-airport competition and the pressures on planning regimes in each country or region. How powerful these pressures are will depend partly on whether growth remains as vigorous as it has been in the last two decades or more. A slackening off of this growth, a possibility for either economic or public policy reasons, would naturally remove the urgency of expansion plans and also reduce the attractiveness of airports for private equity or similar buyers.

ROADS

It is clear that roads are an odd case in the infrastructure world. They have often had certain forms of private concession management, as toll roads (turnpikes in eighteenth-century England), but by far the most common form has been as essentially publicly developed and owned. The motorway systems built since the 1950s have had toll systems in some countries, but this has been subject to continuous review, and sometimes the removal of tolls or their replacement by other financing mechanisms. Where motorway tolling has been common, and where this has been privatised (as in France and Spain), significant economic sectors have developed by exploiting these assets. Another direction of change has been from private equity firms buying toll roads, as in the case of the West Midlands M6 toll road. This was built by a consortium of the Macquarie Infrastructure Group and Autostrade, the Italian motorway operator, who soon sold their share to Macquarie (Whitfield 2010). Other recent cases in the United States and Canada suggest that this mode may be on the increase internationally, and that the exceptionalism of roads may be under strong pressure in the coming years (for analyses of the Toronto 407 Express Toll Route, see Torrance 2007a and Torrance 2007b).

The implications for planning and spatial development are considerable. Roads have always, like other elements of transport systems, been used as instruments of regional development and to a certain extent of spatial planning. The assumption that this is one of their functions lies alongside the more obvious one of providing immediate traffic capacity for vehicles (normally private ones, not subject to direct public control). If toll roads (and related bridges or tunnels) become partly or largely machines for generating revenue streams, this clearly puts any planning goals in a different light. A company such as Macquarie managing a long concession (50 years) may aspire to use any technique to increase traffic flows, including the encouragement of development that might have such an effect. The armoury of instruments for public steering, and particularly spatial planning, changes accordingly. Equally, the decisions on network expansion, or for that matter contraction should such reduction of motorway systems be seen as sensible (as occurred with canals and railways), take on a different character, with an altered balancing of public and private interests.

For the moment such fundamental issues are largely in the future. In recent decades roads and motorways have continued to be built in many countries, but with increasing resistance in most regions. The number of new projects coming forward is now, in most of western Europe, quite small, and so immediate challenges in this sector are not great. In most countries, change consists of adding lanes to existing roads, or lesser management changes, not raising large spatial planning issues. However, given the consistent failure to hold back the rise of motorised traffic, certainly up until 2008, we cannot be sure that this will continue to be the case in the future.

RAIL

Despite often having begun as private and local or regional ventures, most European railways were state owned until the 1990s. As usual the UK took the first radical steps to privatisation, in 1994, with other countries only setting up semi-private structures or track/train separation arrangements in the late 1990s or 2000s. In the Dutch and German cases this has generated a series of switchbacks, maintaining public ownership of track and rail companies, but with strong commercial pressures to change services and cut costs. Deutsche Bahn (DB AG in recent years) has, since its formal privatisation in 1994, become only secondarily a manager of the German rail system, having diversified into road, air and other sectors worldwide. UK privatisation was highly problematic, with the government obliged to take back responsibility for tracks in 2002 in order to improve the system's safety and functioning. However, rolling stock companies (ROSCOs) have got fully caught up in private equity deals in recent years, forcing train-operating companies to make decisions in peculiar situations. In a highly politicised context, they are squeezed between the government-run rail-track body, a government regulating agency, and the companies providing trains and carriages.

This strange mixed model sits alongside the more comprehensible Dutch and German ones (hardly any more loved by their citizens, it would appear) and the remaining state-run systems in France, Spain and elsewhere. These systems are under considerable pressure to change, having already been forced to separate track and train operating systems by EU directives. EU rules do not strictly impose the privatisation of railway operators, but do require full opening of rail systems to competition. This has been coming into force variably for freight and passengers and is supposed to be completed by 2012. Already several European countries have open competition in freight rail. Competition is not currently developing as quickly in passenger systems, for various reasons, and it is not yet clear how far and fast this will go. Governing and regulating systems vary enormously in different states, with local and regional services often now financed at local and regional levels, and national systems being governed by nationally set concession arrangements as in the UK. High-speed systems might become subject to take overs, if the large Spanish and French operators are threatened financially. Again, as in the roads sector, this is largely in the future, and the case studies mainly examine practices under the more stable systems functioning until the present. Should some of the potential of a new, fully liberalised, European rail system come to be realised, this will dramatically change the prospects for investment, system integration, financing and cross subsidy, and much more.

The zone of controversy and development in recent years has been in high-speed rail development. But this has been very diverse, with varying tensions felt in different countries regarding the development of new routes. Several countries have been busy shrinking their rail systems since the 1990s, especially Germany, France and Spain (again the UK led the way in the 1960s in such network cutting). This, although of great importance to planning as a whole, does not of course raise issues relating to the building of new rail infrastructure. Equally the work underway in, for example, France and Spain to improve regional systems, can normally use existing track, and in doing so does not raise planning and development issues. The main focus in the case studies will therefore be looking at the macro scale, largely of high-speed rail system construction, and seeing how this relates to macro planning questions.

WATER

Water supply and waste-water treatment have traditionally been sectors with heavy public involvement. Hall and Lobina (2010b) show this to be the case over the long historical run, and emphasise that new investment remains overwhelmingly public-led in most countries, whether directly via taxation or by loans raised on the security of the flows of taxation.

The ownership of private water companies in Europe has become increasingly concentrated since the 1990s (Hall and Lobina 2010a). The French companies Suez and Veolia are dominant in the private sector, with subsidiaries stretching, between them, across most EU countries. Both are heavily involved in water and waste sectors, with Veolia also having a big role in transport. But the majority of water operators remain in public ownership. Suez, Veolia and SAUR are, in any case, part state-owned. The big shift to private control has slowed, with no major privatisations in the EU in the 2007–2010 period. In fact one return to public control occurred, when the city of Paris remunicipalised water services for eight million

Figure 2.3 Water company ownership 2010. (Source: Hall and Lobina 2010a pp. 8–9)

Company	Owner	Country	Type of owner	Comments
Anglian Water	Osprey/AWG	UK	PE	Consortium of 3 PE funds, inc. 3i
Northumbrian Water	Northumbrian Water Group	UK	SEC	27% owned by Ontario Teachers Pensions, 15% by fund managers Amvescap,
Severn Trent Water	Severn Trent	UK	SEC	
Southern Water	Greensands	UK	PE	IIF 28%, Challenger 23%, UBS 16%
South West Water	Pennon Group	UK	SEC	Pennon is 30% owned by 5 financial investors
Thames Water	Macquarie	Australia	PE	Owned via Kemble Water
United Utilities Water	United Utilities	UK	SEC	
Welsh Water/Dwr Cymru	Glas Cymru	UK	NPC	Not for profit private company
Wessex Water	YTL	Malaysia	M	Malaysian power company
Yorkshire Water	Saltaire Water	UK	PE	Private equity consortium: Citi, GIC, Infracapital
Bournemouth and West Hampshire Water	Sembcorp	Singapore	M	Singapore based company http://www.sembcorp.com/
Bristol Water	Agbar/Suez	ES/FR	M	
Cambridge Water	Cheung Kong Infrastructure	Hong Kong	M	Hong Kong based multinational
Cholderton Water	Cholderton Estate	UK	P	Private family owned
Dee Valley	–	UK	SEC	35% of shares owned by Axa SA.
Folkestone and Dover	Veolia	FR	M	
Portsmouth Water	South Downs Capital	UK	PE	15% owned by directors, 36% owned by SMIF/Land Securities
South East Water	UTA and HDF	Australia	PE	Utilities Trust of Australia, Hastings Diversified Utilities Fund
South Staffordshire Water	Alinda	USA	PE	Alinda Capital partners, a US PE firm
Sutton & East Surrey Water	Aqueduct Capital	DE	PE	Canadian funds CDPQ 25%, AIM 17.5%, PSP 22%; plus Aqueduct Capital 25%, GBP 10%
Tendring Hundred	Veolia	FR	M	
Three Valleys	Veolia	FR	M	

(Type of owner: SEC = stock exchange quoted (UK); M = multinational; PE = private equity;

NPC = not-for-profit company; P = privately owned company)

people in January 2010, after the two 25-year concessions to Suez and Veolia expired. Various systems exist in Europe, with French style long-term concessions given by public authorities to private firms more common in Latin countries, and local or regional water companies, often in public ownership, more the norm in Germanic states.

The pattern in the UK is, as so often, different from that elsewhere. Full privatisation occurred in England, whilst Scotland retained public ownership. Welsh Water became a not-for-profit company in 2000, leaving the normal fully private pattern of England behind. Figure 2.3 shows the mix of ownership as of September 2010. It reveals an extensive takeover, since the early 2000s, by private financial companies of one kind or another, including Thames Water (owned by Macquarie), with other important UK stock exchange listed firms (Severn Trent, United Utilities), and some smaller water companies owned by Veolia or Suez. So the English industry is both heavily involved in the financialisation of infrastructure, and heavily internationalised, in stark contrast to Wales (though there the management is subcontracted to United Utilities) and to Scotland.

EU policy has been critically important for water industries since the 1980s. The Urban Wastewater Directive of 1991 led to an enormous infrastructure investment programme rolling out across the continent, especially as new countries joined the EU. Most of this investment is not very controversial in spatial planning terms, mainly involving the rebuilding of plants in situ to higher standards. However, water supply issues are significant in some parts of Europe, especially in the drier Mediterranean regions.

ENERGY

Energy industries vary significantly, primarily between the main branches of electricity, gas and oil. The oil companies have, for a century or more, been heavily internationalised, with the global "seven sisters" already massive presences by the 1960s (Yergin 1991). Although nationally owned companies have also been significant in several states, including in Norway, they have remained active mainly in their own territories. This pattern contrasts with the gas industry where, until privatisation took hold in the 1980s and 1990s in many European countries, the production and distribution of gas was under municipal or national government control. Subsequently, many gas companies have become private, and some have started to be involved in electricity ventures. The process of internationalisation began in the 2000s, particularly with Dutch and German companies, if not yet as widely extended as in the electricity industry.

Thomas (2009) analyses the electricity industry alongside the gas industry, in view of their increasing links. He shows that the "seven brothers",

Figure 2.4 Largest European electricity and gas companies. (Source: Thomas 2009 p.12)

	Home markets	Other markets	Deb/equity	Asset sales	Transmission networks ownership	Greenhouse gas reduction	New capacity
GDF Suez	France, Belgium	N'lands, Germany	0.50	No	France (G)	Nuclear, coal	Gas, coal, biomass
EDF	France, UK, Germany	Italy	1.06	Yes	France (E)	Nuclear	Gas, nuclear, coal
ENEL	Italy, Spain	Bulgaria, Slovakia	1.90	Yes	No	Nuclear	Gas
EON	Germany, UK, Sweden	France, Italy, Spain, N'lands, Czech, Bulgaria, Romania	1.16	Yes	Germany (E & G)	Nuclear, coal	Gas, coal
RWE	Germany, UK, N'lands	Poland, Czech, Hungary	1.47	Yes	Germany (E & G)	Nuclear, coal	Coal, gas, renewables
Iberdrola	Spain, UK		1.24	No	No	Renewables	Renewables
Vattenfall	Sweden, N'lands, Germany	Denmark, Poland	0.47	No	Germany (E)	Nuclear, coal	Gas, coal, renewables

Notes: E = electricity, G = gas

as he calls the largest companies, are beginning to dominate these sectors across the continent, although there are other significant regional and local firms. Figure 2.4 shows the main features of these largest companies.

Network companies, whether in electricity or gas, are gradually being separated from distribution and generation (supply). But normally these are highly regulated and do not offer very profitable opportunities. Many remain national, and in quite a lot of cases are in public ownership. Rather like roads in the auto sector, or rail tracks for trains, they may remain "more public", whether or not literally in public ownership, as an essential base material for the rest of the energy system. How such "publicness" interacts with planning, whether at strategic levels or in project consents, is an issue that will emerge in the case studies. We may assume that it is a very different publicness from that once contained in the fully publicly-owned models, where whole systems were state owned and managed together. It may be more similar to the publicness of financial infrastructure, such as banking systems, which were seen in the 2008 crisis as essential components of economies. But this hardly attracted consensus or much sympathy for such supposedly essential elements of contemporary life, and the same may apply to network infrastructure's new forms of publicness. This would affect their planning.

Thomas also shows the nature of new-generation investment, bringing out the dominance of gas- and coal-fired power stations, of those actually under construction in 2009. Renewables rhetoric has thus been powerful since the early 2000s, but corporations' decisions give another story.

WASTE MANAGEMENT

Municipal companies or bodies traditionally ran most of the waste operations in Europe until the 1980s or 1990s. They remain important in many countries, especially in Germany. Furthermore, the public sector retains a dominant role in regulating and organising the waste industry, in almost all dimensions, with a powerful lead from EU directives and systems of waste planning at various levels. However, private waste companies have become increasingly important in most countries. Figure 2.5 shows the pattern of ownership in

Figure 2.5 Largest municipal waste companies in Europe 2009. (Source: Hall 2010a p. 3)

Company	Parent	Parent country	Parent type	Sales 2008 (€m.)	Notes
Veolia	Veolia	France	S	7668	a
Suez Environnement	GdF-Suez	France	S	5770	a
Remondis	Rethmann	Germany	P	5600	b
FCC	FCC	Spain	S	2788	c
Alba	Alba	Germany	P	2700	d
Urbaser	ACS	Spain	S	1480	b
AVR/Van Gansewinkel	KKR/CVC	USA/UK	PE	1197	d
Biffa	Montagu PE	UK	PE	788	e
Shanks		UK	S	697	e
Séché-SAUR		France	S	695	f
Cespa	Ferrovial	Spain	S	606	d
Ragn-Sells		Sweden	P	408	d
Delta		Netherlands	Mun	405	a
Lassila & Tikanoja		Finland	S	300	a
CNIM		France	S	271	a

Notes: a. Waste management, Europe, b. Includes water, c. Environmental services, excluding water
d.Total company sales, e. Year to March 2009, total company sales, f. including waste business of SAUR
P=private; PE=private equity; S=stock exchange listed; Mun=municipal

Source: Orbis; company reports; PSIRU calculations (combining sales of merged companies);
Lindauer Managementberatung 2006[1]

the municipal waste sector (industrial and hazardous, and nuclear waste, are somewhat different sectors). The biggest companies are French, with major government holdings, whilst the Spanish firms are parts of construction groups and others are "traditional" private waste firms (Hall 2010a).

GOVERNMENT AND INFRASTRUCTURE

The above makes it clear that the "infrastructure industries" are not separable from the operation of government and politics. Equally, planning systems and decisions are pervaded by governmental and political processes. So both "sides" of this exploration are infused with the varying realities of these processes. This section will outline how these matters can be most usefully framed comparatively, guiding the treatment in the country studies. This will be presented in two steps. First, the broadest large-scale issues will be discussed, normally treated as parts of constitutions. Secondly, the scale related mainly to the internal organisation of governments will be examined. Clearly the two are really intertwined, but the first generally changes only "geologically", over decades of national history, while the second may, in parts, shift much more quickly.

Constitutions

Political scientists classify states by certain conventions, most simply into unitary and federal states. Lijphart's study, though now not up to date (published 1999), covered this dimension of variation in full. He charted the importance of changes in this aspect over a 50-year period across 36 countries. There was considerable movement from "pure" unitary forms to much more mixed varieties from the 1970s in many countries, but at any one time both the constitutional form and the practical degrees of (de)centralisation were critically important in infrastructure matters. Flinders has updated Lijphart for the UK (2009) as we will see in Chapters 9 and 10.

The two aspects (federalism, centralisation) together have of course considerable implications for the working of planning systems, as has been explored by students of comparative planning (Commission of the European Communities 1997, Newman and Thornley 1996). It will be impossible to avoid extensive reference to this dimension in the case studies, and especially the movements in the last 20 years or more, which have affected arrangements for deciding on infrastructure so much.

In Europe the EU is an increasingly important element of the constitutional conundrum. This is often addressed in terms of "multi-level governance" or "multi-level polity" (Wallace et al 2010). This is increasingly significant in the infrastructure field, but it is not possible to address such a large issue in this book. My broad position is that the national level remains critical for most of the vital decisions and for the framing of infrastructure planning. But this is not to deny that the EU matters (sometimes a lot). So a perspective that merely emphasises "intergovernmentalism" would not do justice to the (in some senses) independent force of the EU dimension of politics and policy. This confirms the constitutional shift that the rise of the EU represents, which may well become more pronounced in this field over the coming decade or more. Part of this relates to how influence is mediated by national states, all in quite varying ways: some exploiting it, some resisting it, some bending it, and so on (Marsh et al 2008).

Governmental organisation

The parallel dimension is the internal arrangement of governments, including their connections to external circuits of power. Here the most critical issues are around the integration, coordination and delegation of governmental powers. The reason why these matter for my study is because I am continually focusing on the relationships between the functional organisation of government, say of transport systems, and the link to spatial issues that is implicit or explicit in spatial planning decisions. Spatial planning continually strives for integration, across scales and across sectors, whilst governments naturally settle into what are often pejoratively termed "silos". This is the tendency to departmentalism or the autonomy of even very small parts of departments, ministries or agencies. This is not an oddity, but natural to all organisations, probably of whatever form, and certainly across public and private sectors, and across many historical and societal variations. The striving against these tendencies is equally ingrained, with "joined up government", for example, becoming a theme of the New Labour governments of 1997 to 2010 in the UK (Bogdanor 2005).

We can give a few examples of the reflections of those who have studied coordination issues in government in recent years. Hayward and Wright (2002), in studying the central government machinery of France, use a scale of policy coordination. All sorts of coordinating tools are used, though independent decision-making, the first of the nine types, may be as common as any others, as even the effective coordination of the tasks of one ministry is a large challenge. They conclude that French interministerial or cross-governmental coordination was relatively weak during the 1990s, and is possibly getting less effective over time. Further significant attempts have been made since that time to deal with the question, as we will see in the French study.

The history of the search for integration perhaps passed its high point in the UK with the work of the Institute for Operational Research (IOR) school in Coventry, which sought to clarify that planning was always about inter-agency working, or "reticulation" (Friend and Hickling 1987). The aspiration to include everything within the plan or planning process or governing body was, they argued, always doomed, so planning would always be about the skills needed to "keep everyone on board", or similar metaphors so beloved of practising planners. This has been especially tough in the era of public–private partnerships and ever more complex funding and organisational governance challenges, often much sharper than in the heyday of the Institute for Operational Research school in the 1970s. The Bogdanor volume as a whole (2005) takes a highly sceptical position towards the chances of integration, emphasising the more subtle arts of governing (Hood 1998), which can be used by skilful operators to keep numerous governing challenges on roughly common tracks.

Flinders (2008a) puts special emphasis on the phenomenon of delegation to so-called independent agencies, as well as the tendency to public–private partnerships. He finds that the result is often a decline in the strategic capacity of government, with an increasingly fragmented state structure. He refers to governments across the world:

> experimenting with innovative tools of governance in an attempt to maximize efficiency within the public sector. This drive to "get more bang from each buck" is increasingly based upon delegating responsibilities away from the core state and entering into 3Ps (public private partnerships). As a result the relationship between state structures and democratic frameworks is becoming more opaque and this risk of disconnectedness becomes more pressing.
>
> (Flinders 2008b p.246).

This shift is seen by Flinders as being accompanied by a decline in legitimacy, as governments try to depoliticise zones of government. This he sees as a retreat from democratic governing, with delegation being used more as a device to redistribute power to areas less open to public influence. So the creation of so-called arms-length bodies is often not a move to "independent" forms of decision making, but an "arena shifting" device which removes control from elected representatives and often from other mechanisms of democracy such as pressure-group activity.

Here it is clear that we have moved from a largely "internal" consideration of governmental arrangements and linked across to outside bodies, the overall form of the polity and its links to the economy and society. This appears to be a critically important perspective for the study of infrastructure planning. This zone of politics, along with many others, has found itself in the core of this whirlwind of governing change. There are many possible positions in relation to these changes. Flinders sometimes seems to ascribe them to the weight of governing problems hitting states in recent years, or to the complexity of governing in an abstract sense, rather than something governments have brought upon themselves for ideological reasons. Saalfeld

(2006) also speaks of complexity, but inclines towards analysing how this has been constructed by governments, however we may judge the pressures on them.

"Consensualist" versus "majoritarian"

Saalfeld also draws on the broad distinctions at the core of Lijphart's work, in identifying a "consensus model" in many countries. This was seen by Lijphart to operate especially in the Netherlands, Germany and Scandinavia. Saalfeld sees this as imposing high decision-making costs:

> Governing has become a more time-consuming, multi-level bargaining process in which governments are agenda setters and co-ordinators, but often do not have the resources and expertise to impose a policy "from above".
>
> (Saalfeld 2006 p.105)

He sees this as, in fact, affecting all countries, under the impact of globalisation, regionalism within states and increasing demands from citizens. However, he and Lijphart still see another sort of less consensualist governing model, with a more hierarchical and top down approach to governing, often but not always based on a majoritarian voting system and a unitary state. So we have the split between "top down" centralising states like France and the more cooperative models in the Netherlands. We will have plenty of occasion to see some value in these distinctions, especially in the "high Keynesian" era up to around 1990. But such a consensual/hierarchical split can often raise more questions than it answers. If the UK was such a smoothly running centralised model, why was the chorus of complaint about the difficulty of infrastructure decision-making so great there, much more so than in any other country? To deal with such complexities, we have to configure the elements discussed into a slightly more complex model. This is presented briefly here, and will be discussed further in the concluding chapter.

Governing overall

In the very broadest sense the above analysis can be combined to set up two overall contrasting tendencies, if one looks at European governing in recent times. These may be seen to correspond to the degree of neoliberalisation of polities in the last 30 years. One type is the concentrated power model, which has come through in the English part of the UK (and to a certain extent in the UK as a whole, moderated by the 1998 constitutional reforms). This struggles to bring together different sectors, however much it wishes to, as it is not designed, or willing, to spend the political energy to create consensuses.

Silos and top down modes are the norm, but do not always work well, and are subject to varying reforms: "streamlining", "speed up" and so on. Some other countries show signs of this tendency, as does the EU.

However, most other countries, at least the four in my case studies, are in another type. The articulation of this is more complex, with the search for consensus having either continued, as has been the norm for the last 60 years in Germany and the Netherlands, or been invented under the pressures of a declining centralism as in France and Spain. This is far from idealising these cases, where consensus is often seen as horrendously difficult to build, with log-jams of decision making a constant theme of public and academic discussion. It is also not to necessarily paint the English case as especially dire. The system before the 2008 reforms gave a relatively fair balance between citizen responsiveness and the need to get decisions. It will be the implementation of the model invented in 2008 which will be the test of real practice, as against the intentions (which were, as I will explain, well characterised as neoliberal and far from extending democracy).

This dualism is clearly highly simplifying, and is intended only to apply to the period of the last ten or 15 years, where the distinction between the UK and most other EU states (at least in my four cases) has been rather sharp. Before that time, other models would be needed, in particular, that form of top down centralism common to most unitary states, where legitimacy was rather more easily obtained, with the cases of France and Spain taking something like this form until around 1990. However, I do think the distinction is important, as it draws attention to the cluster of features of consensus building, legitimacy and democracy, all of which are important for the quintessentially "public" infrastructure field (public in the fundamental sense discussed above). Like all ideal types it glosses over differences.

CONCLUSIONS – MAKING INFRASTRUCTURE, GOVERNING INFRASTRUCTURE

Major features of the regime which now structures infrastructure provision are as follows.

- A thorough intertwining of the economic processes of producing infrastructure goods and services by companies or public agencies, with regulatory and political management of these processes.
- Extensive commodification across most infrastructure sectors in Europe, backed by EU policy, but advancing very unevenly over two or three decades, and by no means complete. This has been forwarded by the key tenets of neoliberal ideology, in particular, the appropriateness of private ownership and liberalised competition as the best ways to provide utility services, if properly regulated by

the state. New financial models are struggling to emerge within the ups and downs of financialised capitalism.

- New power balances, with private or semi-private corporations exercising power in many countries, influencing governmental policies in ways that are different from those in the Keynesian period of generalised state ownership.
- New balances of risks in several of these industries, most obviously in the energy and transport sectors, where the largest and most complex investments are present or under consideration. This places pressure on state regulatory systems to lessen or manage these risks, including those present from planning regimes.

As a whole, then, we have seen how significantly the substantive and governmental landscape has changed in recent decades in relation to utility or infrastructure sectors. It would be odd if this did not have knock-on effects for the spatial planning part of the jigsaw. But before we start examining how that planning is structured generally, we need to look more closely at the substantive challenges the present period is throwing up, and how different interests and countries think about these challenges, the imaginaries generated by particular geographies and histories. These are the themes of the following chapter.

CHAPTER 3
POSSIBLE NEW INFRASTRUCTURE: GENERATING THE NEED AND IMAGINING THE FORMS

Much of what has been said up to now takes it for granted that infrastructure ought to be forthcoming, whether pushed by a societal need or driven by an economic demand. There are then issues about how it is provided (the last chapter), and the planning of where it goes and what shape it takes (the next chapter). But there is clearly another question, as to how the need is generated, and how that need is imagined. These in a sense lie underneath or behind the other questions: not how or where, but whether. This chapter looks at these issues. The first part is on the relatively straightforward aspect of the generation of need or demand. This is followed by an exploration of the issues of imaginaries and the subjective aspects of infrastructure, something less easy to be definite about, but still of considerable significance for the way in which infrastructure provision is understood, and therefore for its public acceptability and legitimacy.

There are more fundamental considerations in thinking about how anything in society comes to emerge or be "required". Social theory has long struggled with the basic questions of the construction of society or social forms. All major social theory schools have explicit or implicit theories of this, whether the versions of vulgar Marxism where the economics determines the rest, the more plausible schemas of historical–geographical materialism, or the more idealist or postmodernist varieties where ideas or the exercise of interpretation are at the core of the explanations. Critical realism sees generative structures (say patriarchy, or a mode of production) as in some sense creating the "real" or "actual" which in turn is what gets experienced. Here there is no definite adherence to one approach or another. The discussion does rest on a complex understanding of the generation of social processes, where materialities and imaginaries blend together. We cannot expect to pin down chains of causation and power in any simple way, given the tortuous interweavings of history. Scientific and technological developments infuse potential change just as cultural and economic transformations do. So the account here stays more on the surface, to steer clear of these complexities. I refer to them here only in order to indicate the basic approach, which is not to take for granted the need or demand that "more practical" actors may accept as unavoidably present.

OVERALL FORCES BEHIND INFRASTRUCTURE CHANGE

There is no simple calculus that can tell us how much infrastructure, and which kind, is needed for a particular society, at whatever level is being examined. Analysts at the Australian Treasury explored this issue quite inten-sively, and concluded that calculating the adequate or appropriate amounts of infrastructure was a highly perplexing issue (Coombs and Roberts 2007). As economists and quantitatively minded analysts they clearly aspired to a general cross-society ruling which would tell them if Australia had, in inter-national terms, more or less infrastructure provision than it should have. But after much number crunching they concluded that this depended on numer-ous factors, linked to both geographical particularities and to values, which would dictate trade offs. What is adequate was soon seen to vary between sectors, places and systems, so that in the end the possibility of confirming the size, or even existence, of "gaps" tended to fade away. They found, for example, that one measure of relevance was the population distribution of a country. A measure developed by the OECD identified countries with populations more concentrated in a few regions, and this led to the idea that these countries could give equal services of energy or accessibility for less investment than more dispersed population patterns. But this needed qualification, because the scale at which the density measure was worked out matters. Within-urban-region densities, the nature of whole country spa-tial distributions, and overall geographical scale were all relevant. Because Australia and Canada had spread-out populations *within* regions, they could need *more* infrastructure than apparently more dispersed countries like France and the UK.

So the initial indication, that Australia might get by with less infra-structure per unit of GDP than some other countries, was seen to be based on risky analysis, though the study inclined to that conclusion for want of a better one. This sort of thinking can be related to the discussion of green economists (Jacobs 1991), in which they suggested that the aim should be to raise the environmental efficiency of economic activity, or of societal activity as a whole. We might extend the idea of this environmental coefficient to one of an "infrastructure coefficient". Despite the practical difficulties in calculating what this might be, we may accept that such a measure can be conceived of. One very broad aim might then be to make the relationship of "social wellbeing" and "infrastructure equipment" as high as possible. Of course, this is highly abstract. Just as bundling together wellbeing into one index can be problematic (Anderson 1991, Jackson and Marks 2002), so one cannot imagine an overall level of infrastructure in any meaningful quantitative form, adding up the capital elements of roads, pipes, ports, etc, with the resources needed to make these work, in one number. But, conceptually at least, we can imagine a list of elements, related to environmental throughputs, ecological impacts and social arrangements, each estimated in relation to social wellbeing. This may sound like the old dream of comprehensive cost–benefit analysis, suitably updated ecologically. But, the complexities alluded to above (and many more) mean that we already know that such a quantified approach is going to be beyond reasonable analysis. The point is simply that societies can at least be imagined as possessing such infrastructure coefficients, and that in principle these could be subject to societal choice.

Of course in the real world we have known that since at least the start of the industrial revolution, the prime motor of infrastructure creation is economic growth. For whatever historical period we choose to focus on, the growth of industrial production drives the need for infrastructures, mainly in energy and transport terms. The bases of the British industrial revolution (canals, coal, ports) and of the Chinese one now (coal, ports, road and rail) are clear enough. Technological change is the intervening variable, driven forward by economic growth and forming the basis for the next round of change. This was theorised in its simplest form as "stages of development", with development "take off" seen as linked with infrastructure capacity (Rostow 1960). This is equally associated with the growth of world trade, with more and more types and amounts of commodities traded across the whole planet, as the oil era facilitates cheap long-distance movement (Calderon and Serven 2004). Thus the "logistics revolution" (Bowen and Leinbach 2010) is seen as transforming the positions of ports and airports across the world in the last 20 years, with cities rising and falling as large companies (FedEx, DHL) choose them (or discard them) for continental or national centres.

So the tandem of growth and trade generates demand for infrastructure, along long and often not easily visible logistics chains and energy flows. This is visible for the earlier industrial revolutions (Hobsbawm 1962, 1975), and is now very clear, with Chinese growth generating the need for new transport and energy investment across every continent, for example, not just within China itself. The infrastructure stock of a country like Britain is now more outside its borders than within its own territory, probably to an even greater extent than at the height of the British Empire. This naturally makes the practical challenges of any calculus of an infrastructure coefficient within one country even harder than they would be otherwise.

The Infrastructure Planning Commission created after 2008 may have relatively few major projects to decide upon within England or Wales – though some in the transport field are definitely linked to the growth in world trade. But if it had to consider all indirectly generated infrastructure projects, it would have to hold hearings about rail schemes in China, port projects in Brazil and new runways in big European freight airports.

But what if we probe behind the not terribly controversial statements about growth and infrastructure: What about the drivers of growth? Brenner's work (2004) is one major source of theorising on the spatial economic drivers of recent decades. He regards the push in almost all rich countries for "premium infrastructure" as due to the international competition unleashed by neoliberalisation. He analyses how this generates pressures at all levels, from global organisations to small localities fighting to make places attractive to investment. Sometimes this is phrased in Marxist terms (Harvey 1989 as a classic statement), sometimes as simply the "competition state", seen by Cerny (2006) as simply a norm of current international political economy, perfectly expressed in conventional terms. Brenner's focus on infrastructure is rather more localised than mine, with the stress on the urban level. But the overall point is transferable. Like many regulation-influenced theorists, most consistently Jessop (2002, for example), Brenner takes national state projects as one building block of his analysis. This can include spatial dimensions, thus effectively national spatial strategies, articulated at several levels, but led by the state. National state projects can indeed be seen to drive growth, and to contain infrastructure as important parts of this. So neither growth nor infrastructure is to be seen as a *deus ex machina*, floating in from the ether. They come from the drive embedded in competition, whether or not this is conceived as neoliberalised capitalism and so understood in its present history, or as an ever present reality of societal existence by those who prefer to "normalise" competition.

So where does this leave us with the growth–infrastructure relationship? If economic growth were in some miraculous manner turned off in high GDP countries, would we see a collapse of demand for new infrastructure? This question is more complicated than it looks. It depends in part on how the current (or lower) levels of consumption are satisfied, within the country or by world trade. Clearly a shift to more self-sufficient societies would have major implications for infrastructure systems, as industrial production was "repatriated", food production adjusted and energy systems altered. The latter points to the more specific issue of transitions in just one element of social functioning, of which the most prominent now is low carbon. If a low-carbon transition is to be achieved within a few decades, most infrastructure systems need massive transformation, even with lower consumption levels. So many apostles of low-carbon societies, alongside some more conventional analysts of intelligent economic adaptation, press for a switch to renewable energy sources, including for transport systems and building, heating and powering. In most European countries such a transition has only begun in very recent years, with even the most advanced wind-power countries obtaining very small proportions of their total energy needs from renewable production.

But, if we take the position of accepting recent history to be that of neoliberalising capitalism, we need to reflect on how this leaves our understanding of growth and the infrastructure link (O'Connor 1994). Does *this* form of capitalism at least tend to drive on growth in this high-octane infrastructure character, with little evident scope for lower carbon pathways? This political economy question always rears its head if we stand back historically. The previous paragraph was written from the perspective that we can change our direction if we so wish, without worrying ourselves about the basic economic motors, a position shared by most mainstream green and liberal commentators. Marxists, and, to an extent, strong believers in market mechanisms, do not see such an easy disconnection. The most market-committed analysts will say that the system is problematic because not all factors are internalised within market systems, but if all factors could be then the system would solve any questions addressed to it, including those around growth, infrastructure and ecological limits. Marxists see the capitalist system as all encompassing and with enormous power, but do not see that it can be redirected by processes of internalising costs by full commodification. On the contrary, they see systemic forces, working especially powerfully in the present period, which are driving growth ever onwards with very high carbon and infrastructure components, if marked by crises of various sorts.

Clearly we have now reached the outer shores of the discussion on what generates infrastructure creation. Consensus has been left behind, and readers have their positions on these questions. Here I accept the broadly systemic position, that current neoliberalising capitalism is indeed driving the underlying forces requiring more ports or airports or motorways. States compete for their share of the internationally available infrastructure funds (this thinking is clear in the UK National Infrastructure Plan, HM Treasury 2010). This fundamentally undermines the "sensible" position of demand management, which could change the "infrastructure coefficient", at all levels. But for the purposes of discussion in this book, I would maintain that there is some room for manoeuvre within this historical dynamic which we are living through. States do maintain spaces for reform, as do other bodies, which means that infrastructure can still, in principle, be designed in better and worse ways, some of which will be more fitting and less expensive to alter when (or if) more sensible societal arrangements are created. This can be seen to be occurring now, in the different approaches across Europe. Planning can be part of this choice, if pressed in the right directions.

THE MACRO SPACING OF INFRASTRUCTURE GENERATION

Reference was made to density above. The location of the demand for infrastructure provision is not a neutral issue. Normally it responds to a set of
factors reflecting the growth of markets. Depending on the conception of
regional or spatial development (Pike et al 2006), this process may be termed
as a necessary feature of capitalism, in the shape of combined and uneven
development, or as one creating an accidental set of externalities, with which
states will always have to contend, in whatever mode of production.

Congestion on a transport system (whether of goods, people or
energy) normally results from a rise in market demand set up by numerous
smaller or larger decisions. These "private" decisions then generate "public"
needs, for new roads or ports or transmission lines. Some areas are emptied
out by market forces, leaving unused infrastructure capacities. Other areas
(for example, south-east England) get filled up and face ever more jammed
infrastructure networks. One currently fashionable theory does indeed argue
that there is no alternative to such unequal dynamics (partially critiqued in
Martin 2008). This is seen to be because agglomeration economies naturally
generate some winning regions (as in the south of England) and some losing
ones, and that betting against the winning regions in the hope of boosting
the losing ones is doomed to failure (Leunig and Swaffield 2008). The implications for infrastructure are clear, and were already the basis for government
policy in the UK in recent decades, as has been seen in port and airport decisions since about 2000 that prioritise investment in southern England. The
UK is no doubt the extreme version of such regional policy, with most other
European countries maintaining more emphasis on territorial balance.

THE TIMING OF INFRASTRUCTURE GENERATION

Time issues always complicate provisioning questions. This is evidently the
case with infrastructure, which generally has long lifetimes. This can parallel the often long turnover of ecological systems (carbon flows and sinks,
waste systems, forming of fossil fuels over millions of years), and the complex rhythms of social change (cultural attachments, migration movements
etc). It can run against the often short turnover time of capital (Harvey 1982),
which therefore is heavily challenged in funding infrastructure investment.
This turnover time is seen by some as getting ever shorter under the financialising capitalism of the last 20 to 30 years.

This forms a complex picture for infrastructure generation pressures. Private companies will work on various timescales, some only very
short term, but with larger corporations often looking forward several years.
The financialised elements coming into infrastructure industries discussed in

the last chapter are equally divided, with some linked to large pension funds having long time-horizons, and others seeking quick returns. But the needs, as perceived by governments and societies, may be also very uncertain, or at least variably assessed. The long-term transitions now discussed for low carbon (ranging from one or two decades to whole centuries) are much longer-term than was normal in the past. Such a perspective would, we may assume, immediately exclude all new investment which reinforced lock-in to high carbon systems such as new roads or airports. But we know that such investment is far from excluded, revealing the short-term horizons of many governments and individuals.

A typical example of such time politics has been the debate in Germany about nuclear power phase-out. This took a formalised shape under the Social Democrat–Green coalition, with the 2002 agreement to phase out the last nuclear power-station by about 2022. This was then rescinded under the Christian Democrat–Free Democrat coalition, with the proposal in 2010 to extend the life of power stations by ten years. After the Japanese nuclear events of 2011, policy returned to approximately the 2002 agreement position. This shows the complex play of future time-promises. Opponents of the 2010 change had argued that this simply gave the electricity companies ten years more of profits, and took the pressure off the government and companies to promote renewable alternatives by the now nearer date of 2022. Infrastructure generation pressures are seen as totally tied up with state decisions on timing.

THE PARTS OF INFRASTRUCTURE

Infrastructure is never a whole, undivided thing, either there or not there, new or old. It is always being maintained and often extended (usually quite incrementally). The maintenance or extension of existing systems are often alternatives to new construction. Assets are often "sweated", seen as financial objects (Helm 2004a). Harvey (1982) analyses the whole stock of the built environment as something that grows piecemeal. Each generation inherits a certain stock of infrastructure, which it can keep, maintain, extend, but rarely (except at moments of major technological transition) discard wholesale. This has just as many societal as commercial dimensions, though the two may not coincide. What is "profitable" to society may not be to an individual system operator. This suggests the importance of "whole system" reviews of each infrastructure sector, factoring in maintenance and minor investments as much as larger investments. This has come into the more sophisticated recent planning exercises, as in the SNIT in France (see Chapter 6).

GEOGRAPHICAL SHAPES OF INFRASTRUCTURE SYSTEMS

There is more to the geography of infrastructure than the spacing or locational dimensions discussed above. Infrastructure systems also have particular morphologies or shapes. The most evident distinction is between linear and point features, with points sometimes elaborated as nodes (van der Vleuten 2006). Most infrastructure systems are a complicated mix of these things, with points at one place, linked by long linear elements. Ports and airports are essentially points, though with linear implications in the protection of sea lanes and the linking to territorial transport systems in the case of ports, and the effect on air corridors, stacking systems and noise contour areas for airports. Energy and land transport systems are dominated much more by the linear side, though power stations are always significant points within such systems, as can be railway stations or even motorway service stations. Waste-treatment centres are points, though linked in some ways by transport systems for the waste to where it is generated.

There are no simple general rules as to the implications of these distinctions. But the varied combination of linear and point features, given the way they are affected by various technical features – noise, visual appearance, occasionally smell, risk of danger – does have a strong effect on how these elements are perceived, received and planned. Their relationship to geography can be critical. The fact that wind speed may often be greatest in exposed and coastal areas may make the siting of wind power more problematic, given the visual prominence of the technology required. Ports are mostly on coasts and traditionally were seen as creating less problematic impacts because of that, tucked out of the way on a possibly not very valued edge zone. Coastally-sited airports have been seen in the same way, able to cast much of their noise effects over the largely uninhabited seas. Power stations, especially nuclear ones, were often sited on coasts, in remote areas if possible, giving chances to obtain cooling water and dispose of waste heat, alongside easier security arrangements.

More generally, the way in which the nature of the country interacts with the various infrastructure types can be important. It is frequently said that countries with lower population densities can fit in infrastructure with less conflict. Whilst anecdotally this may be supported, it is hard to prove very scientifically, given that most European countries have at least seen struggles over infrastructure, often in areas of low population. No doubt the generalisation needs modifying, by referring both to the nature of the "more empty" countrysides, and to the attitudes towards these spaces in each country. It is at least reasonable to suppose that featureless plains or monotonous deserts may stir up less opposition currents than more varied and inhabited landscapes – and in general Europe has less of these than some other continents.

Another geographical dimension relates to where the functionality of different industries "requires" them to be. This naturally depends on technologies and on economic–ecological factors. During an earlier period water sources needed to be near users in cities or elsewhere, but more recently remote sourcing may be seen as practical. Early airports and ports were always very close to urban centres, but recently, with ideas of hub airports and trans-shipment ports, this link is not seen as so inevitable as in the past. Some analysts speculate about a small number of intercontinental airports for Europe, and although these would (as a result of the path dependency of growth patterns) tend to be near the largest cities, this might not be inevitable. Shipping specialists have wondered about creating enormous ports in places like the Shetlands, where mega tankers from Asia might shed their cargos, to be distributed round Europe by smaller vessels. Nevertheless, broadly speaking, these various forms of transport points are normally near cities, and in some cases, above all with airports, this creates inevitable conflicts.

The same sort of issues affect terrestrial transport, where the ends of systems (road and rails) must normally connect conveniently into the core of major urban areas. In Victorian times this meant cutting train lines ruthlessly through some British cities, and more recently the impact of urban motorways was very powerful in some European and American cities. Such heavy urban surgery for infrastructure purposes is now almost unimaginable in European countries, though it may still be possible in more authoritarian states such as China. So technology interacts with geography to heavily constrain real possibilities.

This can work at a very high geographical scale. The form of the world's seas and their depths constrains the size of ships, with the Malacca–Max debate on what will stop ever larger ships being built: at present the size of the Straits of Malacca between Malaysia and Indonesia is seen as the key constraint. But lower down than this the forms of states and seas and land masses/continents partly determine what role each country or region plays in the unfolding of transport and energy systems. We will see this clearly enough in the country chapters. It was not determined that Rotterdam would become Europe's premier port, but its location near the mouth of the largest river gave it a good start. This sits alongside the geography of European industrialisation: some of the largest industrial and urban areas have been and still are not too far from Rotterdam. Something similar is unlikely ever to work for Barcelona, Marseille, London or even Le Havre.

Many other examples of these partly invisible, but sometimes quite critical, workings could be given. Energy systems have had a complex geographical play, becoming gradually more flexible, with the cheapening of fuel itself feeding this progressive delocalisation and partial globalisation of energy systems. Before, it was useful for a district to have coal to hand to create an iron or steel industry. There are still signs of such localised linkings in the study by Humphrys (1982) of UK energy geographies. Now contracts are being signed for liquefied natural gas to be brought in ships across the whole planet, and ports are adapting to receive this new form, and pipelines built, as in the case of the new LNG plant and pipeline in Milford Haven and across South Wales, built in the early 2000s. This does not mean that all logics of local linkings have disappeared. The complexities of the challenge of low-carbon adaptation may bring back such logics, with on-site genera-tion and heating having great attractiveness for some goals. The question of storage, whether of gas for security purposes, of CO_2, or of electricity (as in pumped storage systems), raises acutely the importance of local and regional geographies, as it may be far too expensive to carry such products over long distances. An empty underground gas field nearby may give a big advantage in some of these processes, as may ways of "storing" electricity in mountainous landscapes.

The same can be seen to apply to water systems, whether of waste water or fresh supply. This may include the advantage of being near seawa-ter, now that the Spanish experience is showing Europe the importance of desalination in some urban regions. The natural heritage of regions interacts with the enormous changes made to them over recent centuries, in making reservoirs and altering river courses, and building water treatment plants. Where rivers and lakes and seas are, and how these relate to centres of demand, affects how "easy a hand" different countries and regions have in confronting new challenges.

Waste is also caught up in these morphological–geographical plays. Until only two or three decades ago, the interaction of urban waste genera-tion with available "holes in the ground" more or less dictated the waste strategies of many urban regions. Now the approaches are more sophisti-cated and in part planned, but the geographical choices, of the boundaries of waste treatment self-sufficiency for different technologies, are no less stark. Waste incinerators may or may not be accepted in urban areas, or in the countryside, and the same may apply up to a point to recycling centres and surviving landfill sites. Scaling up generally means a drastic reduction of the number of waste sites in Europe, with each one being larger, and some internationalisation, especially with hazardous waste, with famous cases of European waste being shipped to Africa or Asia. Probably only policy, including at EU and international levels, is restraining, to a certain extent, this globalisation of waste streams. This means, as in so many sectors, that "our" waste infrastructure may sometimes be as likely to be constructed in China as within our own territories. More than the other environmental infra-structure sectors, waste is often seen as just another part of manufacturing, if differently situated in the chain. But even so, local factors remain critical for many purposes.

HOW INFRASTRUCTURE IS UNDERSTOOD – SEEING INFRASTRUCTURE

The above has been largely based on the "real" and "material" aspects of infrastructure generation. But in some ways equally important, for planning and thinking about future infrastructure provision, is what is *thought* about these sectors. I will look at this first in terms of perception and subjectivity. Then the more fuzzy area of imaginaries is explored.

Hayes's wonderful "field guide" to infrastructure systems, mostly in the US, starts with a reflection on how we see such landscape elements. A dramatic photo of a New Mexico oil refinery against the red sandstone buttes of Red Rock State Park leads into the thought that most viewers would see this as an industrial desecration. He says:

> I might offer the counterargument that the juxtaposition of natural landforms with the geometrically simpler cylinders and spheres adds visual interest to the composition, but I don't expect to win many converts to that view.
>
> (Hayes 2005 p.2)

No doubt the same arguments have reverberated around countries since the beginning of the industrial revolution, the discussions about the aesthetics of pylons in Britain in the mid-twentieth century being a well known example. The work by the Bechers on industrial buildings raises similar debates (Becher and Becher 2002).

This book does not need to get into the deep waters of "nature" and society, or the social psychology of perception. What we know from experience is that some sorts of modern "intrusion" are accepted, and some are not. This varies between countries and cultures and probably between different parts of each society. What is desecration to someone may be just a useful feature (a transmission line, an airport, a rail line) to the next person. Wind farms have been much studied in this respect, and it is clear that perceptions do vary a great deal, with community involvement or ownership sometimes coming into the levels of acceptability, but with many other factors touching this too (Szarka 2007). Crises and wars may overturn the priorities of populations. Less dramatically, the French government famously uses the offer of community facilities for areas ready to accept nuclear power stations or the identified nuclear-waste storage facility – such offers being more readily taken up in poorer regions. A power station may very well mean a job, not a threat. Areas such as Cumbria in northern England are deeply caught in this fight of perceptions, with a struggling economy pressing many towards accepting all investment offered, alongside many retired or higher-wage incomers (or locals, or visitors) who resent any infrastructural intrusions.

The main point to take from this for my purposes is the complexity of these dimensions of infrastructure. Planners and other public (or private) policy makers are in the forefront of difficult societal judgements, as the literature around the risk society and about science policy and the environment has explored over the last 20 years (Beck 1992, Hajer 2009, Irwin 1995). A major lesson has been, for some, the need for humility – for making few assumptions, for working through the real perceptions of all actors involved in as careful and honest a way as possible. All sorts and levels of democracy are challenged in this force field. Some of the new approaches to project decision-making discussed in the next chapter need to be assessed in this light. All concerned are pitched into a whirlpool, into many possible infrastructural futures, and the somewhat easier answers of earlier decades are unlikely to be available.

This does not mean that the use of intelligence in creating more beneficial institutional framing cannot help. Hajer's work (2009) on the UK Foods Standards Agency in the early 2000s suggests ways of doing things better, with a gradual and subtle melding of open and transparent governing, media-aware policy making and competent political leadership actually bringing some good results. Trial and error is important: perceptions and reactions cannot often be guessed in advance. Infrastructure planning, caught up in this contradictory set of subjectivities and evolving perceptions, is similar in some ways to our confusions about food. We want many of the gains that new infrastructure can give (some of us, some of the time), but our perceptions are, in part, old constructions. In Britain this is often wrapped up in anti-urbanism and anti-industrialism, with a (highly variable) distrust of new technology. In other European countries there are generally different cultural assumptions and structures of feeling, towards the new, towards nature, towards development – though some say such gaps are narrowing, with the processes of modernisation gradually generating more inclination to a sort of heritage-oriented ruralism of the English variety. This ruralism is built on the car and on the low price of oil, and so is already fully implicated in infrastructure systems and the provisioning of non-urban areas. So images and perceptions are based on decades of real material and geo-demographic change.

Overall, the difficulty of these subjectivities points to the need for deepened democracy, deliberation, genuine conversations, with the powerful listening. But this may be much easier said than done. The hard materialities are perfectly real, and carry their own powers and power holders. I will come back to these challenges in the concluding chapter.

HOW INFRASTRUCTURE IS UNDERSTOOD – NATIONAL IMAGINARIES

The above discussion is bound up with the ways in which places are imagined, and the ways that countries think about themselves. In a sense this is the macro equivalent of the examination of subjectivities. We will see in the case-study chapters the very different understandings that countries (or the EU) have of themselves. There are, as far as I can discover, no extended considerations of these issues in just the form I am searching for. There are of course discussions of matters close to this area in the study of history or in the social sciences. The explorations of "imagined communities" (Anderson 1991), or of nationalism more generally (Smith 2010) do touch on these concerns tangentially. Marxist thinkers like Castoriadis (1987) discussed social imaginaries as the ideas that individuals and societies had in their minds and actions, about their situation, and their historical possibilities. This is the sort of sense in which I use the term imaginary here.

There are some discussions within the planning field of areas close to this issue. Peel and Lloyd (2007) explore the process of "civic formation" in relation to Scotland and use terms like "collective territorial imagination" (p.403) and "national spatial public interest" (p.407). They see the search as being to widen the national vocabulary to explore possibilities, and part of that is necessarily attached to spatiality. Duhr's work (2007), on the visual language of planning, focuses on the use of maps in planning. One interesting dimension of this is work she cites by Brunet on French "*cartes-modeles*" – the most famous example was probably the presentation of the changed time-geography of Europe, which would be generated by successive rounds of high-speed rail investment. Once such non-Cartesian geographies became very widely diffused, imaginaries would evidently be much changed: we are into the territory of the correspondence with people's mental maps of places, including at the widest scale. Other valuable discussions of visualising spatiality, using images and mobilising spatial conceptions, whether used to good or poor effect, include Neuman (1996) and Zonneveld (2005).

The question of interest here is: How does a social unit (most importantly in the present period, a country ruled by a state) imagine its operation and particularly the shape of its territory? Within this, subsidiary issues emerge: How is such a conception reached, whether by public discussion, by some powerful historical legacies accepted widely as starting points, or by some other means? How does this link to other broad areas of politics and culture, such as shared or collective approaches to society, or purely individualist conceptions? How is the country imagined physically: as a "green and pleasant land", as a collection of cities, as a blend of sea and mountains, as a threatened territory (whether by neighbours or by nature) and so on?

The reason these matters are seen as important for the study of infrastructure, is that the scope for public thinking about new infrastructure (or existing infrastructure, to an extent) is conditioned in part by these national imaginaries. Whether explicitly or implicitly, countries (and sometimes levels above and below these) conceive of their presents and futures around certain templates. Very often this may be highly simplified, just the French "hexagon" or the US "from sea to shining sea", but some more politically involved or influential interests may have more developed conceptions. These may be axes of the country, or features seen as needing most conserving – or, more in the past, developing: reading early industrial period writers in England like Defoe or Young, we find a passion to develop, to improve, much of it wrapped up with infrastructure; China is no different now. In the absence of explicit national spatial thinking or planning (the norm in current times), such imaginaries may have an important effect on decision-making, as ministers, pressure groups and local actors mobilise around certain shared or contested ideas of the whole territory or, more commonly, ideas of localities.

There is nothing to say that there will be only one imaginary, or even that there is a small set of fixed ones. There is much more work to do in this area, linking up with that of geographers and other disciplines. As is often the case in the social sciences, the work may be plausible but needs firmer foundations. Here I put forward my own framing of the issue, in the hope that others will develop this further. This is done under three headings, continental, national and historical.

The continental

First, it is important to note that so far in Europe there is very little idea or imagining of the European continent. Naturally all decision makers, public and private, national and EU, have an idea from maps of the land-masses and seas and states. But I find it hard to imagine that this is rooted in much of a personal feeling linked to real territories. This may gradually emerge (McNeill 2004), as mobility increases and as technology and language smooth out borders. Jensen and Richardson (2004) certainly thought that a "monotopic" European spatial imaginary was being constructed, the drive for a frictionless place, through an accumulation of spatial practices pressing in this direction. The EU's policy development work for trans-European networks may gradually be bringing such thinking into the minds of policy makers and associated actors, at least. But more widely, I would assume that any conceptions remain amorphous. The makers of the European Spatial Development Perspective avoided the inclusion of any meaningful maps in the final document (CEC 1999), largely to avoid political difficulties (Faludi and Waterhout 2002) – but also perhaps in part because the reading of these maps by an outside audience with no formed imaginary would have been inevitably confusing, in only being able to focus on their own territory. The situation in Europe is no doubt different from that in a country of continental size like Australia, China or the US, where a much more coherent polity over long periods gives different grounds for imaginings.

The national

Planners use maps to present policies and ideas with the extra power of images. They use them variably, between different planning traditions in

Europe (Duhr 2007). Occasionally these maps are national, if less so now than some decades ago. I will discuss this in the chapters below on the Netherlands, France and Scotland. For some infrastructure sectors (transport, energy) the national level is often the critical one. How far should we think of policy makers as having a formed idea of the country? I would suggest that such ideas do exist in all states, even though there may be several versions, partially or totally in conflict or competition.

These ideas are doubtless in significant part linked to nationalist conceptions. These relate to general principles that are widely accepted, or thought to be widely accepted, like fair conditions across the country, or good general accessibility – these two being obviously spatialised, as against others with less direct geographical implications. Being nationalist, the dominant conception will tend to be unitary, of the whole country viewed as one (an undivided republic in France, the United Kingdom with a monarchy, Spain in its peninsula, the Netherlands with its history of land reclamation and vulnerability to natural forces, and so on). Some of these conceptions may be quite shaky or fuzzy, especially where the nation has been buffeted, as in Poland's history of losing itself and its territory so drastically. But this may lead to pressures to reinforce the dominant idea even more, given the historical insecurity.

In most countries it would be normal for other conceptions to exist. This would obviously be the case in countries like Spain or the UK, which have other non-central nationalisms that from their very existence have had competing ideas of territory and probably different basic principles. Nationalisms, dominant or sub-central, are full of ideas about landscapes, about cities (their qualities and ills) and about the cutting up of territory below themselves (Marshall 1996, Nogue-Font 1991). Lowenthal (1994) looks at European and English landscapes as national symbols, finding how English conceptions are especially ruralised, and marked by insularity, artifice, stability and order, significantly different from some European cases he considers. Edensor (2002) discusses how the "elements of national space are linked together to constitute practical and symbolic imaginary geographies which confirm the nation as the pre-eminent spatial entity" (p.67). He sees the nation as embedded in notions of space in a multifaceted way – power, meaning, aesthetics, identity and so on (p.65). Allen et al's (1998) study of the south-east of England gave a practical example of how the UK had been embedded in this corner of England by the continued flourishing of economic, political and cultural power. This led to a later call to "decentre" these processes, in effect a call to reformulate the spatiality of UK and English nationalisms, to change fundamentally the spatial imaginaries at work (Amin et al 2003).

Nationalisms intersect with ideas of ecology, of socio-ecological projects (Harvey 1996, Marshall 1994), as the Nazi experience made clear (Blackbourn 2006, Zeller 2007). Green thinkers have different ideas of territories from others, and this has fuelled numerous struggles *against* infrastructure that is viewed as unnecessary, as well as (to a lesser extent, given the weakness of Green political forces), *for* more ecologically stimulated infrastructure. Small nations seem to be particularly keen on different understandings of infrastructure systems – Denmark, Portugal, Scotland and Catalonia, for example. Partly, this may be from a wish to be different, and have a base from which to stand up to larger national states.

Regionalism may add to this, and with Europe being replete with varied regionalisms (Harvie 1983, Keating 2005), this could have widespread impacts, even in the absence of plausible competing nationalisms. As a result there could be all sorts of balances of imaginaries, some solid and perhaps largely shared, some mildly distinct but able to converse, others fractured (as in Northern Ireland), some tortured (as in much of ex-Yugoslavia). I will suggest how I see the situation in each country studied, although as said above, this will inevitably be speculative in the absence of more extensive research.

The historical

All of this is historically infused. In this world of ideas and territories the *longue durée* is the basic currency (Braudel 1973, Cunliffe 2008). Naturally there can be breaks and revolutions, but at least in the west of Europe, a lot is based on old foundations. When Hayes explains why the oil company "destroyed the view" in that part of New Mexico (Hayes 2005 p.2), the reason goes back to the corridor of communication along this pathway from pre-colonial times, copied time after time by later travellers. This is why Harvey (1982) refers to "historical-geographical materialism", in trying to find a name for his approach to understanding the world. Ideas can have extremely long lifespans, especially when tied in some way to a real territorial template, with all its ecological and built environment relations. Cities rarely move, regions are often no more than incrementally rejigged. So the ideas of these places may show lots of continuity. Does this necessarily make thinking about infrastructure geographies inclined to conservatism, given that the imagined template of territories tends to follow past tracks? Possibly that is so, though it does depend on the overall movement in the society. Times of radical change, like that in China at the present, do not necessarily follow in old tracks. The breaking of trends may be imposed in the near future, if predictions of peak oil are correct, with enormous implications for infrastructure in the medium-term. History would no longer serve as a marker, because not making radical changes would impede at least some sorts of survival. So this might drive big and rapid changes in the idea of how a country is and should be, driven by real, visible threats and problems. Much of the "sunk" investment, that which has already been made, might just be ditched as no longer functional, and new systems invented in new geographical configurations.

My overall starting point is that these conceptions are likely to have an important interplay with the "non spatial" dimensions of policy making, which often have a dominant position in political discussions: the commitment to competition in infrastructure industries free of any particular consideration of place or territory, for example. Such commitments may be grounded (brought down to earth) by geographical conceptions or brought out in political struggles. They may get developed openly in countries with national planning traditions. They may intersect with debates on transport systems such as road or rail networks. So far I have not tried to give many examples of the content of the imaginaries. It is best to leave that to the country chapters, and return briefly to the significance of this dimension in the final chapter.

CONCLUSIONS

This chapter has come at the issue of infrastructure from two sides. On the "demand" side has been an examination of what generates the push for new infrastructure. This considered growth, trade and globalisation, but also particularities of territories, timing, shaping and piecemeal accretion, all of which can affect the extent and nature of the forces generating the demand or need for new infrastructure.

The geographical shapes of infrastructure systems were also surveyed, showing important interactions with territories to which planning can usefully be alerted. This is, in part, simply a case of being more aware of how one thing relates to another – a normal part of planners' mental equipment, but seen perhaps from fresh angles.

Finally, the ideas of territories were examined to see how they might affect the "supply" side of the provision of infrastructure, and especially its planning, conscious or otherwise. Seen from the perspective of individual subjectivities and perceptions this was shown to raise large challenges for planning and public policy making. It calls for extended public deliberation and deepened democracy, it was suggested. From the perspective of whole societies or nations a fuzzier world was explored that related to how countries think about themselves and their futures. The implications of this will be explored in the country studies. Before that, one more prior zone is examined in the next chapter: that of the process of planning itself.

CHAPTER 4
PLANNING MAJOR INFRASTRUCTURE – STRATEGIES AND PROJECTS

It may seem that we have been skirting the real core of a book on planning infrastructure, with little so far on planning. Now the moment arrives for presenting the framework for dealing with planning issues in the coming case studies. As a planning insider, I am aware that to those within planning discussions this will look curiously schematic and perhaps oversimplified, and to those outside (quite likely the majority) as a curious walk around issues that may appear straightforward. Planning theory, or reflective discussions on the purpose and process of land use planning, city planning or spatial planning (the activity even has no agreed English-language terminology) has been enormously vigorous over the last half-century, but this is hardly known outside the bounds of planning. In fact, even to those within planning such theorising has often been seen as too arcane to compete with the apparently more central and substantive discussions of how to organise urbanisation or revive existing places. Here I will not go into any depth about the underlying choices for the framework used. The book does not make claims of any originality in planning theory, and the links to these deep and wide debates are not the most critical element of the framing, contrary to what some might expect.

Nevertheless, certain assumptions about how planning is understood are important for the analyses in the coming chapters. These fall broadly into three boxes. One is the initial way in which planning activity is seen to be cut up: the overarching schema. This is followed by the two divisions actually chosen: one section on the roles of strategic planning, and one on the project level of planning. While the way these are related is critical to the whole discussion they have a certain autonomy, analytically and in practice, and so are best discussed separately.

Given that we have got this far without considering planning in any detail, the question may arise as to its significance. Unplanned infrastructure development has certainly been common historically. The early story of the London Underground is a memorial to non-planning, as lines grew in a topsy-turvy fashion with almost no relation to each other and certainly no considered linking to the growth of London (Wolmar 2004). Wolmar makes very clear the enormous costs that later generations had to bear because of this, though the tone of his history is more towards celebrating the entrepreneurial dynamism that kept investment moving during the first 50 years of system building. The contrast with the Paris Metro is striking: the first line opened 40 years later than in London, but within a fully planned system. Ultimately, it is hard to prove the importance of planning, either by historical examples or contemporary analysis. For many, the value of coordinated forethought for such massive investments may seem obvious. For a few, the value of dynamic individual or market-driven action, unconstrained by public integrating efforts, may be equally clear. Readers of this book are more likely to be in the first camp, but doubtless divided about the extent of integration and coordination desirable

THINKING ABOUT PLANNING IN THIS FIELD

Ultimately most planning, at least in relation to infrastructure, is about things being constructed and land being altered, however much demand management is advocated. But that is a long "ultimately", the end of a chain of causes and effects. The natural tendency of many observers and actors is to see the project only or primarily in its isolation. The emphasis in this book, on the stages "before" the project, reflects in part my own interests and research capacities, which tend to be the natural tendencies of a planner with a social science background as against an engineer or architect (or perhaps accountant). But it also reflects my view that the project is, in reality, only a part of the story, with the other part at least as significant and interesting.

That said, there could be several ways to examine the infrastructure planning phenomena. One could have been to identify "governance lines", as suggested and practised in a recent UK research project (Haughton et al 2010). This would have tracked through individual projects and looked back to their "origins", however they might have been conceived. Another, closer to the approach used here, would be to start from the highest level, and "look down" from a national and strategic level. Clearly there are risks in this approach, in overstressing the systemic aspects of the insertion of large infrastructure elements. As will be apparent, in some sectors and some countries such coordinated top down influences are less strong. It is important to have an awareness that this is so, and to realise that "looking down" only catches part of the reality.

It should be noted that the way in which the strategy/projects division is treated below is not quite the same as an apparently similar distinction made by Faludi (2000). What he describes as a "project plan" can be any localised and specific instance of planning. An infrastructure project, especially a large one, may require strategic plans, especially, he argues "by virtue of the persistent uncertainty and conflict surrounding it" (2000 p.304). So his division is, rather, by the nature of the planning challenge, with manageable uncertainty (project plan) or not (strategic plan). The division here is more concrete, between the project in the physical sense and the steps or phases behind it. Faludi's perspective is rooted in the IOR school, centred on the deep impact of uncertainty on all planning. His comments on strategic planning as a whole are relevant, but not the strategic/project plan distinction.

At any rate, the contention here is that there are, in principle, two distinct moments or divisions in the planning of infrastructure: the project, and the preceding phases or dimensions. The empirical question is then whether and how these are related to each other. There are evidently, in principle, several possible relationships:

- At one extreme would be the almost "free floating" project, perhaps promoted by some local or special interest, without any acknowledged link to wider framing. Marketised thinking could be a strong support for this sort of project – the demand is there, in this place, for this development, and this is seen to substitute for any wider conception – planning is an irrelevance or worse.
- At the other extreme would be the tidy "top down" or "integrated" logic beloved of the rational planning paradigm, where an overall view of the society, economy and so on indicated a need for certain infrastructure, which was then factored into an articulated spatial planning process, including all feedback effects.
- In between these two are any number of intermediate possibilities. Simple ones include just having a sectoral strategy that is partially spatialised, a roads strategy, for example, or relating a project proposal to some wider spatial considerations, even without any strategic "written down" guiding framework. More complex variations of this are considered below.

Historically, in the last 30 years, there has been a gradual drive to "less planning", away from the extremely integrated model. The move from a planning doctrine which promotes much top down coordination by national and regional governments, to one more oriented to decision-making by private developers or local public or semi-public agencies, is a critical one in the infrastructure planning field as elsewhere in planning. But there is an understanding in many quarters and countries that there are limits to this change in the major infrastructure field at least, and so there are all sorts of hybrids and innovative responses to the steering in these fields (as in fact is the case across planning's encounter with neoliberalisation). Space, territory and investment remain difficult intersections so public action of one kind or another remains, with spatial planning processes part of this. The question remains: How, who for, and where? This affects both sides of the picture, strategy and projects, if in different ways. It will be clear that, with a typical planner's mentality, I favour the more integrated strategic approach. Examining how that works, or does not work, has been a prime focus of the research, and much more important than understanding how projects work "on their own".

STRATEGIC PLANNING FOR MAJOR INFRASTRUCTURE

Since the 1990s there has been intensive debate in planning theory on the nature of strategising in planning. This has been affected by certain areas of management thinking (Mintzberg 2000), particularly in the drive for strategic planning for cities and regions (Bryson 2004). A swirl of conceptual work has been flowing around the zones of strategic framing, planning doctrines, institutional and governance forms (Faludi and van der Valk 1994, Healey 1997, 2007, Salet et al 2003, Salet and Gualini 2007, to name a few key texts). The most concentrated work has probably been that of Patsy Healey, with her 2007 European comparative study representing the forefront of extended consideration on what strategies do, can do and ought to do. This includes some connection to the thought on strategic projects, more the field of south-European architect-influenced planning theory, where the strategy may be built up more from below by major projects, or even by many minor schemes (Majoor 2008). In particular, really major projects can carry framing strategies with them. Here the theorists were thinking of big urban projects, but to some extent the same could apply to some infrastructure projects, not necessarily in especially beneficial ways. That is to say, if big infrastructure projects frame territory in an overweening way without wider strategic planning, this could easily set off distorted and counterproductive spatial trends.

A simple message from this work is that strategies need to be only loose, orienting policy phenomena, not trying to do too much work on the objects below or downstream. The popularity of "framing" has been enormous in expressing this feeling: a strategy constrains, but not too much, just indicating the concepts and the discourse, not the precise content of "later" planning. It is worth quoting Healey on strategies at some length:

> Strategies are selective constructions, "sense-making" devices, created from a mass of material. Their formation occurs through time,

but not necessarily in defined stages and steps. They are created through processes of filtering and focusing attention, highlighting some issues and pushing other issues to the sidelines ... Persuasive strategies orient and inspire activity ... mobilise intellectual and social resources to create the power to carry a strategic frame forwards, just as they may also mobilise resistances.

(Healey 2007 p.185)

So in this sense an integrated spatial strategy at national or regional level might do work by bringing sectoral infrastructural policy fields into some sort of coherence, but not necessarily in a tidy way, at one time and evenly across infrastructures or policy agendas. In these terms, it might only be a loose, orienting framework, possibly constraining some infrastructure fields very little if not of core interest for some reason.

This strategy conception connects to the Dutch planning debate on the conformance and performance of plans (Mastop and Faludi 1997). That is, "traditional" plans were seen as requiring development to conform to the rules of the plans. This may be seen as outdated and too inflexible. At any rate, for many plans, including most strategic plans in Faludi's sense, "performance" would be enough. In particular, national and regional plans are seen as offering a starting point, setting the shape of discussion. If in the end the plan is not followed, that is not seen as something bad: the plan may have been well worth doing, if it was taken into account or played a part in the planning and public process. Strategies are just "structuring devices" in Faludi's words (2000 p.314), no more and no less.

This poses a considerable challenge to infrastructure planning. How much "looseness" is plausible before it makes little sense even to try and plan infrastructure, whether locations or linear features? However, the relevance of the debate is clear enough in this field, given the way in which the real-world relationships of strategies and particular projects ebb and flow through time. The purpose of strategising for infrastructure is some sort of framing, and the question is: What sort – tighter or looser, longer or shorter term, integrated or disintegrated?

The great majority of the discussions on strategic planning have been at the urban or city–region level. Whilst, as Brenner makes clear, that is an important level for the consideration of some kinds of infrastructure, the focus here is on the larger infrastructure systems, and so the national and regional levels have to come into view. Planning theorists have been much less engaged with these levels, although what has been said above, and in texts such as Healey's, can be used in these contexts too – as long as relevant adjustments are made. At the EU or international scale such adjustments would be needed even more, though this is only emergent in most sectors at most. Here discussion is divided primarily into the national and subnational, with a short section on EU/transnational planning.

NATIONAL STRATEGISING

Whether in federal or unitary states, the central governments of European countries maintain important roles in overall policy-making and steering infrastructure systems. This is what is treated here, with all subnational levels reserved for the next section. It is clear that the differences between the two categories in federal (or semi federal) states and unitary states are considerable. But even in federal states the importance of infrastructure means that, on balance, central governments keep the key roles in their hands, if to a lesser extent than some years ago. There are essentially three fields of action: general, broadly non-spatial policy; sectoral strategising with spatial dimensions; and comprehensive spatial strategising (of some stronger or weaker variety). The first need not concern us here, having been discussed to some extent in earlier chapters. But we must remember how "non-spatial" policy-making often has definite spatial implications. Nationalising infrastructure systems, as occurred widely in the twentieth century, generally led to more universal coverage and quite different spatial allocations of investment. The reverse process had an equivalent spatial impact more recently, fragmenting or shifting investments (Graham and Marvin 2001). Neoliberalisation may well be carrying more "spatial punch" by now than the other two specifically planning fields together.

Sectoral strategising

Sectoral strategising with spatial elements is very important – in fact, it is the dominant policy-making form met in most countries in recent decades. This is often called pejoratively "silo" based decision-making (sectoralism that does not understand the need to integrate one area of state action with another). There is also the risk of capture by interests connected to ministries or agencies, so that they pursue the agenda of these sectional interests. But sectoralism is the norm, reflecting not only the universal organisation of government in ministries, headed by the ministers responsible and their particular agendas, but also other ubiquitous features of policy making including the force of sectoral policy communities and professionalised zones of interest. Very large ministries grouping related policy areas under one roof have often not lasted for a particularly long time (in the UK the Department of Environment only included transport from 1970 to 1976, and the Department of Environment, Transport and the Regions only lasted from 1997 to 2001, for example). The need to focus on particular targets (improve water quality, invest in transport etc) can often override more long-term aspirations for improving governmental coordination and reviving particular cities or regions. So sectoral planning is very important in real government action.

This sort of strategising is affected to some degree by planning ideas, but rarely by those of the spatial planning variety. One feature of the current understanding of strategies described above, is that it is hard to see how it could apply to most sectoral strategising, which by its nature is less encompassing and less likely to allow the mobilisation of societal creativity. Actors will most likely come from within one policy community. In all probability road engineers will plan road systems, water engineers will plan water systems and so on – activities that are set within the relevant ministries or agencies. The influence of spatial planning may only come in through the force of thinking imported by planners in the spatial planning department, or by politicians with some spatial planning conceptions. The latter is most likely in those few countries with strong planning traditions (the Netherlands being the famous example). Sometimes too the force may come from below, as the ministry sectoral planners work with planners in regions or localities, and encounter the need to work in more integrated ways.

There are significant differences as to the form of strategising. One distinction is the breadth of coverage, whether covering a whole sector (say energy, transport, water and waste, as I have defined them here) or subsectors (just roads, or even just major roads, or just gas systems, and so on). The more subsectoralised the planning, the less able it will be to take in spatialised and non-spatialised relations between subsectors. In fact, highly subsectoralised planning is common, though in most countries there have also been efforts to combine fields, for say both gas and electricity (but rarely linked to oil), or both road and rail (but rarely linked to ports or airports).

Another distinction is the nature of planning: how long term and how linked to implementation it is. The norm is to take relatively long horizons overall, perhaps a decade or more, but for this to be followed by more short-term implementation plans – for example, the last German road and rail plan ran from 2001 to 2015, but has a rolling investment programme for the next five years, which only becomes concrete on an annual basis. Clearly this dimension is very important, as it affects how far it impinges on lower-level (city and local) planning, how it intersects with project planning, and how far real-world state and private sector investment is tied into such planning. Powerful sectoral planning, as often exists now in the water and the road and rail sectors, can be very influential, in nearly all cases much more so than any residual or aspirational comprehensive spatial planning (the Netherlands, as usual, is perhaps an exception). This planning may not be predominantly spatial planning. The regulatory agencies require planning in many cases, for example, in the English water industry, where companies have to gain the approval of the Environment Agency and Ofwat (the economic and social regulator) for their investment plans. If a water company wishes to build a new reservoir, for example, the investment plan approval may be tough, and will normally predate the seeking of planning consent by some years.

Comprehensive spatial planning

Comprehensive spatial planning, the old integrated high-level ideal, was a common aspiration in the high-Keynesian era. The Netherlands began its tradition of national spatial planning in the Second World War, institutionalised it in the 1960s, and retained it, in modified form, until at least 2010. Germany moved towards such a form in the 1970s, but this was resisted by federalism and ideological pressures, leaving a transport-planning residue. France had a unique form of comprehensive national planning from the 1960s to 1990s, and in minor form to the present. The devolved administrations of the UK have picked up versions of such planning since the 1998 devolution settlements. Ireland also developed a distinctive if light version since the 1990s. Some other European states have, for periods, had significant amounts of comprehensive spatial planning: the Baltic republics in varying degrees since 1990, Denmark in the shape of non-binding national reports in the 1990s. Overall though, this form is abnormal and resisted by a mix of pressures: ideological, constitutional, organisational and professional. It is not just that the form has decayed to some extent with the erosion of Keynesian social democracy. It is that even in the heyday of such state projects, comprehensive national spatial planning, like comprehensive economic planning, never established itself in most states. Even globally Alterman (2001) struggled to find strong cases in the 1990s to compare with her base-level case of Israel (Japan being one interesting exception).

We will see how, in the Dutch case (and to a lesser extent in France, and most recently in Scotland), the presence of a comprehensive system affects the planning of infrastructure. All the doubts about the looseness of planning, about long-term strategies, will emerge from such study. But the significance of such systems is also relevant, at least to this outsider view, to how the debates and understandings are framed in ways that are different from those states lacking such formalised consideration.

The previous chapter discussed how there may be understandings "behind" all national strategising, whether that is comprehensive or sectoral. At the highest and most abstract level are the national spatial imaginary, and the national state project, perhaps with a spatialised version (as Brenner argues) – a national spatial project. These are not easy concepts to manage. One of the distinctive features of countries with lots of national strategising, especially if it becomes comprehensive, is that these abstractions "come out", getting argued through in the light of day in public discourse. Spatial conflict does the best job in making the imaginaries (often by no means consensual ones) visible. In the Netherlands there can be at least discussion of spatial concepts at this scale, even if academics may be highly critical of the maladroit way in which they have been manipulated in recent national planning (Zonneveld 2005). Reference was made in the last chapter to the importance of spatial imaging in this process (Duhr 2007, Neuman 1996). Healey (2007 p.206) also discusses the search by planners for the "appropriate fit" between experienced reality (we might include mental images) and the spatial conceptions which planners themselves mobilise: the spatial organising ideas (green belt, technology corridor etc). It will be important to try and track this relationship, between mental maps and actual maps in planning efforts, through the case studies. There are big differences in the form of arguments, when discussing high-speed rail routes, for example, between countries like the Netherlands and England that are at opposite ends of the explicit national-strategising spectrum.

Therefore, we now have a schematic approach for discussing national strategising, which will be given substance in the case studies. This ranges from more abstract to more concrete:

- enduring national spatial imaginary;
- national state (spatial) project;
- comprehensive national spatial strategy; and
- sectoral and subsectoral infrastructure strategies.

SUB-NATIONAL STRATEGISING

The key feature that distinguishes sub-national planning from national planning is that the full potential range of authority and tax power is lost. This loss is, however, quite different in the cases of Germany and Spain (where the states and regions have considerable legitimacy, powers and funds), compared to those of England or the Netherlands (where dependence on central government is far greater). Even within countries there are considerable differences. In Germany a state such as Bavaria may have considerable control over its infrastructure futures in several sectors, just as in Catalonia or other powerful Spanish autonomous communities. So in those cases, we will see confident strategy-making at this scale, even though dependence on central government powers will always be visible. The governing challenge in these states is one of continuous cooperation and bargaining, with strong cards held by both sides, and to varying extents also by the largest cities within each state. Smaller states and regions will need to cooperate with neighbours, and will have less power.

In England there are anomalies such as London, which now parades a whole panoply of strategies in most infrastructure areas despite having formal competences only in limited parts (mainly in some transport fields). Recent work in England has brought out this strong difference when comparing the capacity of cities as influential even as Manchester to affect their critical infrastructure equipment with that of London (SURF 2007a, 2007b). In England the aspiration may have been to start to guide change in this area, but the SURF reports shows how limited the local or regional powers were at that time (even during a period of central government support for regionalism). The key issues they raise relate to how far central government action can facilitate innovation lower down, or (in parallel) how far central policies may cascade downwards – whether in transport, climate change or waste management fields. Certainly, significant efforts to guide future infrastructure in English regions has been the exception rather than the rule, though we will see some instances in English regional planning in the early 2000s where efforts were being made in these areas. The same applies in other unitary states, though French regions and major cities can in some fields make a more significant attempt to wield influence than in England and the Netherlands, forming an intermediate case with some negotiating power and therefore some incentive to think independently about at least some aspects of their infrastructure futures.

What is potentially significant at this sub-national level is that spatial planning is, generally speaking, much more alive and well. This means that it could form a significant pole of integrating force, even if for somewhat smaller territories. There was an argument in the 1990s that such regions could be ideal spaces for forging more ecologically advanced infrastructure systems (Marshall 1994, 1996). From 2010 this regional-level potential no longer applies in England, but otherwise all the cases show significant planning presence at this level, between the local and the national. In some cases, as in Spain, Germany and the Netherlands, this consists of legally-backed plans which must be taken account of by lower level governments, even if they are often not exactly binding. In France the regional spatial planning efforts have been much more uneven, with few regions making this a consistent priority since the 1980s. However, this does not mean that infrastructure necessarily enters into these regional or provincial-level planning strategies in a big way: the existence of such a potential or capacity does not mean it is used. The position noted at national level may well be so here, in which sectoralised planning is again the thriving relation, able to "push around" the less well connected spatial cousin.

This brings us back to the classic situation of spatial planning, in which the planner works in a collaborative milieu, as reticulist or connector, sometimes able to knit together spatial and infrastructure drives in mutually supporting ways at state or regional government level, and sometimes not. At certain moments integrative discourses may have political support or public resonance, whether for more economic or ecological policy directions. So the question will be present in each country study: How far can sub-national strategising, primarily at the level of the region, substitute for national gaps? Putting it another way, one aim is to see the ways in which articulations of European polities support effective infrastructure planning, with the intersection of national and regional efforts. Given current circumstances and the nature of the (mostly) quite large countries studied, this is a very important zone of study.

It may be argued that more focus should have been placed on the locality, especially the city region. There is little doubt, from my overall knowledge of European city planning, that there is often some effective integration at this level, through normal planning processes and lively political public spheres. This is indeed extremely important. The reason I have studied this at most in passing is that the infrastructure systems examined do, I would argue, require coordination at higher levels if they are to be steered more than marginally. Policy makers in cities like London may perhaps challenge this with some force, but even they lack effective levers over national rail, airport or water systems. Systems like the German municipal Stadtwerke or the French water concession arrangements do retain some local force, but from an overarching perspective this is hard to use to guide whole systems, especially given the tendency to erode these municipal systems via privatisation over the last 20 years. It is important to remember that cities do have much leverage, especially where strongly decentralising options may be emerging. But for the moment, the limitation to the bigger scale of sub-national planning seems reasonable.

EUROPEAN UNION/INTERNATIONAL STRATEGISING

The forces of globalisation and Europeanisation, political and cultural as much as economic, have pressed the importance of wider infrastructure systems. Increasingly some infrastructure is cross-border, transport and energy most obviously. This has begun to escalate the role of EU and related planning or strategising processes. This can hardly be spoken of in the same tone as the sorts of strategies discussed above by planning theorists. The EU polity is a quite different animal, with even similarities to national-level spatial and sectoral planning (where they exist) being quite limited. The fuzzy, floating world of EU policy making may need another planning-theory mode altogether, which would be full of political framings and complex multi-meaning discourses, but hardly in planning or strategy language (Faludi 2010). Here there is no space to examine this very different world, even though emerging reforms of Trans-European processes in 2010–12 make this of increasing significance.

INFRASTRUCTURE AND PROJECTS

As noted above, this is much less the central focus of the study here. Other academic studies, for example, in the transport field the OMEGA project, or in the work reported in Priemus et al (2008), have taken this as their prime orientation. This has allowed these researchers to connect much more easily to the immediate world of investors, corporations and engineers, as I have observed in the effective network built up around the OMEGA project, both in London and internationally. The struggles around project consenting are without doubt the front line of infrastructure interest, whether for those opposing development or driving it forward. People are much closer to this stage, usually both physically and psychologically, in spite of the growth of virtualised politics, and this is where most passions emerge, with the heaviest contestation. It might be said that most higher-level strategising rests in some sense in the shadow of these specific reactions, trying to second guess their nature.

Nevertheless, detailed work on these dimensions was not carried out within this research process, for reasons already given. This does not mean that the projects were invisible – which would have been somewhat absurd, given their prominence in the public mind – it simply means that their study was not in the foreground. This section therefore only looks at the broad area of project consenting, and briefly at the issues of public deliberation and politics related to this.

STATE CONSENTING FOR PROJECTS

For reasons analysed in earlier chapters, it is generally perceived that getting permission to build major infrastructure has been getting harder. Often this is accepted as something natural, a feature of advanced democratic life. This is almost certainly a common position in liberal democracies meaning that, in general, planning systems have not been massively altered in response to this perception. The pressures for fair and full participation possibilities are very strong in most countries, so any measures seen as reducing these tend to be heavily fought. However, business lobbies have been very persistent in some countries in arguing for the need to speed up consenting processes. Occasionally this call has been joined by more reflective contributions, such as that of an actor advising the Mayor of London on the Crossrail and London river crossing schemes from around 2000 (Rosewell 2010). She finds the decision-making process, still in part based around cost–benefit analysis, quite inadequate, and also criticises the inflexibilities of planning. But her focus is more on the overall decision-making problems, which are largely financial, rather than problems with spatial planning.

It is in fact hard to get comparable data on the typical lengths of time that consent for different kinds of project may take, let alone of the costs this may create (these are not the same thing – good programming may mean a five or ten year decision-making period generates no extra costs). This is partly because of the different institutional regimes, meaning that where one places the starting point of the consent process varies between systems. Equally, projects are all different, not just physically but organisationally. An apparently similar major port project may have certain key features which distinguish it from a counterpart in another country. I did not, therefore, seek to collect "objective" information to be able to answer the question undoubtedly of interest to developers: Which country is fastest, or slowest, in consenting? In part that is because I do not regard the question as necessarily a critical one. Slow decision-making may be both appropriate and beneficial in many cases, so although a good database of dates and time periods, ideally running over several decades, would be of some value, it would certainly mean different things to different interests. Nevertheless, where I have encountered data which does seem reliable, I will note it, if often with caveats.

Broadly speaking, it may be said that there are three "layers" to consenting such projects. One is the "normal" planning consent, typically given in major projects with lots of opportunities for consultation and a public inquiry. Final decisions will normally lie, at least formally, in central government with the relevant minister – in politicised cases, decisions are virtually certain to be made directly by the minister. Secondly, this process is now conjoined with the needs of EU legislation on environmental impact assessment and appropriate assessment (for habitats protection). This has been variously merged into national planning procedures, or tacked on. It is probably one of the most difficult and controversial elements for many businesses, giving ample work to planning lawyers across Europe. As NGOs have found, this a particularly effective set of levers with which to oppose projects. Thirdly, there are other kinds of sectoral consenting, particular to ports, reservoirs or rail lines, including financial and environmental regimes separate from spatial planning. These may be as onerous as planning regulation, though they have not been the target of so much business lobbying, perhaps because, being less visible, simplification and "speed up" can be more easily managed within the government machinery. Together these three layers make up the "barriers" of regulation – or the defences of the citizen.

Where the focus has been on planning process deficiencies, the responses have been, as we will see in each country, quite varied. The tendency to discuss speeding-up processes may be universal, but the resultant measures are not the same, up to the present. In any case consenting systems vary widely, despite the common requirements of EU regulations. So the baseline positions are quite different. We will see in the final chapter whether there is any tendency for convergence along some dimensions.

PROJECTS, AGONISM AND DEMOCRACY

One feature of ongoing debates in planning theory has been discussion of the role of conflict. Some have seen this as something to be avoided, with the search for consensus and collaborative solutions being one natural track of thinking. Others see conflict as a universal and beneficial feature of societal processes, which can increase the quality of decision-making. Public inquiries, for example, have been seen as giving plenty of space for such contestation in British planning (Cowell and Owens 2006). More widely, this area opens up democratic challenges, with a wide range of deliberative or representative devices on which institutional designers might in principle draw (Saward 2003). We will see the various national approaches which have really emerged in recent years. The main focus will be on changes in process, affected (if unconsciously) by new understandings of open, transparent deliberative approaches. It will be important to grasp the link to wider strategy and how far that has closed off debate "lower down". This has been an area of some innovation, for example, with the Commission Nationale du Debat Public in France and the Infrastructure Planning Commission in the UK.

For some theorists "agonism" is seen to be at the core of democracy (Hillier 2002, Mouffe 2000), with mutually opposed interests obliged to come to arrangements after struggle and debate: neither permanent antagonism nor settled consensus but somewhere between the two. The idea is to use rather than to suppress antagonisms, be adversaries rather than enemies. This can be very well applied to the field of infrastructure projects, as some planning commentaries have noted (Barry and Ellis 2011). So, in their object of study, wind farms, they hope that full public and meaningful engagement might be about communities bargaining an appropriate energy-future package, from as wide a choice of options as possible. So, if a community agreed to reduce its overall greenhouse gas emissions, for example, it might do this by hosting a wind farm, by committing to energy conservation or reducing car dependency, and enter into partnerships with many bodies to secure this. This would need to meet some sort of national carbon plan, disaggregated to areas, to secure what has been called "energy descent planning" (Hopkins 2008). So, this combines ideas from different sources, around dealing with conflict, but also higher-level government validated programmes. Recognition of agonism is not likely to be much comfort to "practical" people, but does give some valuable purchase for analysing real world events in this field. I will come back to the value of this perspective in the final chapter, when it will be possible to reflect on the experiences noted in different countries, where conflicts have indeed been important parts of the process.

STRATEGIES AND PROJECTS

A major issue introduced here has been the relationship of different kinds of strategic approaches to infrastructure projects. We need to understand how the linking (or non-linking) works, what force planning strategies have, and also to consider what force they *ought* to have. We can get ideas and sometimes inspiration about this from case studies. These also ground us in the varied realities of the present. The concluding chapter will come back to many of the issues raised in the first four chapters. But for now, we move into the real worlds of European infrastructure planning.

PART II
National case studies

CHAPTER 5
THE NETHERLANDS

Countries are wholes. How infrastructure is planned is best studied within these whole contexts – hence the next six chapters. The implications for the transfer of lessons and approaches between countries are obvious: such transfer is done with considerable risk. All institutional arrangements should have a sign on them: beware, transfer at your peril. One of the most intensive studies on international transfer was undertaken in the Netherlands, by Martin de Jong in 1999, on the scope to transfer transport infrastructure innovations (De Jong 2008). Because the Dutch are very aware of international practice, such transferability debates occur all the time. Equally, planners at least often look in on Dutch practice, and have tried to bring good ideas that they have encountered there back home (Ward 1999). More recently, Dutch planners and planning academics have tended to view such external admiration with scepticism, doubting whether they have any practice worth exporting (Wolsink 2003). There is a fine line to walk, therefore, for an outsider student of recent Dutch planning of any kind, and perhaps most of all in the fields of infrastructure and national planning, the primary targets of this chapter. I am obliged to be sceptical by Dutch expert views, but remain on the search for wisdom and good practice, even if I know this must be tempered with Dutch realism.

GOVERNING AND PRODUCING INFRASTRUCTURE

Politics and governments

Political decision-making in the Netherlands is concentrated in the central government, inside a unitary state. But that state has considerable elements of fragmentation, both vertically (significant powers lying with municipal and provincial authorities) and horizontally (spread around ministries, agencies and different elements of government: parliament, cabinet, judiciary). Political scientists have stressed different features. Lijphart, we have seen, presented consensualism plus some decentralisation as critical. Andeweg and Irwin (2005) put the emphasis on sectorisation and division within government and politics. Some writers present change as having been central during the 2000s, with the arrival of right wing/anti-Islam parties in positions of influence since 2002 seen as ending the liberal consensualised settlement of the previous decades. Here I attempt to blend these insights:

- Policy making does try to take all the key elites along with it. Elections and wider pressures can often extend this to a broader responsiveness. The coalition agreement drawn up after elections is a key part of this machinery, and contains many of the primary substantive policy changes of the coming government term. The model of consensualism does therefore apply to the Netherlands, and deeply affects all policy making on infrastructure and how planning is done.
- There are real divisions in government, but these are probably less than in many countries. The departmental arrangements are detailed below.
- The search to build viable programmes and actions across many influential constituencies does make for a viscosity in the system (noted in Dutch as "stroperigheid" or "syrupiness"), and means that all actors are used to fairly slow governmental action, though not all may be happy with this.

So this is a system that is very much *sui generis*, in some respects nothing like the other case studies examined here. Political culture is an enduring feature of systems, bolstered by constitutional and institutional continuities. The Netherlands cannot be said to have suffered major changes in any of these areas for a half century or more. At the time of writing the country is adjusting to a strong push to the political right, aimed at cutting back the remains of the social democratic post-war system even further than has happened since the 1980s. Several changes within the coalition agreement made in autumn 2010 are of importance for the areas surveyed here, alongside the big budget reductions. In particular, governmental structures are being cut back, with central ministries slimmed and functions passed down in some cases to provincial governments. New boundaries for the provinces are also being considered. It remains to be seen how far this programme shifts the general way of operating of the governmental and political culture. For the purposes here, the generalisations above can stand for understanding the last two or three decades.

Infrastructure industries

The Netherlands sees itself as an early convert to the wave of liberalisation, with accommodation to such a wave a main feature of governments since the 1980s, often with much enthusiasm. The already powerful private sector in many industries has been able to expand, with partial or full privatisations in energy, water and transport industries. However, to a UK observer, this has seemed rather mild in many cases. As shown in Chapter 2, much in the transport sector remains essentially in public ownership, whether ports, airports, roads or railways, even though it is all within thoroughly commercialised structures and mindsets in most cases. Similarly gas and electricity transportation remains in public hands, and water companies have a broadly public orientation, even if with a company structure. So, although the language and practice of private business may appear to be everywhere, the state retains levers that it can use if needed, meaning that policy making on all these infrastructure sectors can start from a stronger public hand than would be the case in the UK or probably in most respects in the US. For now, the system is a hybrid.

This also applies to regulatory policy, which has been set up quite energetically across most sectors (affecting the fields of roads and water least). Reports by the government research agency surveyed the field and expressed concerns about the disintegrated landscape of regulation, and how far it was fit for achieving public goals (Arts et al 2008, WRR 2008). The fact that such a major inquiry was set up is indicative of the continuing concern for public and societal aims in the Netherlands. "Public values" were seen as the key issue (De Bruijn and Dicke 2006, Steenhuisen et al unpublished). The main worry was that as some sectors came increasingly under private control (for example, Rotterdam's three waste incinerators being taken over by a private equity firm), the investment needed in the future would not be forthcoming. However, the government reaction to the report was muted, suggesting that an approach which was more interventionist or coordinated was unlikely to be acceptable to the right and centre parties then running government.

THE NETHERLANDS AS A COUNTRY, AND THE WAY INFRASTRUCTURE NEEDS ARE GENERATED

The geographical uniqueness of the Netherlands is even more well known than its political culture. The "waterland" is held responsible for all sorts of national characteristics (Verbong and Van der Vleuten 2004). The country is essentially a delta, and in large part owes its independence to this position, setting it a little apart from Germany, perhaps the "natural" owner of its territory (viewed from a continental perspective). It is a relatively old state, based on this geography, which has required continuous defence from the sea, the rivers and the neighbouring powers. Belgium, the only other small state in this zone of Europe, arrived much later, and has had a history that is less solid. The Netherlands is small, enabling easy communication in recent times, but not that small, inciting the careful arrangement of spaces within its territory. It fits intricately into the mosaic of the continental land-mass, despite having only Belgium and Germany as immediate neighbours. So, dealing with territory has always been, in part, about international relations, something developing through the twentieth century as continent-wide organising took increasingly solid institutional forms.

Some of the generation of "needed infrastructure" flows out of this geographical base. These "needs" are listed briefly here, and will be returned to in later sections.

- The maintenance of *physical forms*, of land and water as they are (or perhaps marginally altered). This was bound up with territorial planning in much of the twentieth century, with defence from the sea and the reclaiming of land prime goals for most of this period. This has been less insistent since the cancellation of the last proposed polder in the Ijsselmeer in the 1980s, and the winding down of the massive flood defence programme from the 1990s. But the issue has not gone away, making a comeback with river flooding threats in the 1990s and climate change fears of a long-term nature in the 2000s.
- The making of *connections*, on land, by water and in the air. The country has always seen itself as a place of transit, economically and culturally. Its situation on the main seaway of northern Europe and on the largest navigable river of the continent encouraged this, especially as the industrial revolution of Germany picked up speed. This became a renewed theme in the 1980s, with the "mainport" construction, whereby "Netherlands distribution country" was established as a main pillar of state policy, and was wound into planning doctrine (Van Duinen 2004). There has always been a drive behind land connections, whether water, rail or road, with passions being raised by the challenge of fitting these into a densely occupied territory, at least in the western Netherlands.

- The search for reliable *power*. With few indigenous fuel sources beyond peat, water and wind, the country always had to think about how it would get energy, as demand rose through the twentieth century. Exploitation of indigenous gas from the 1960s to (it is estimated) the 2020s, has long made a difference and been built into state policy. Other options, whether nuclear power stations or wind farms, have been more controversial. No ability to promote massive cutting of demand has yet emerged, perhaps in part due to the half-century bonanza of home-produced gas.

These have been, in bald terms, the forces creating infrastructure policy dilemmas, to be fitted into a quite limited territory with a dense occupation of humans, animals and growing crops: the formidable Dutch agro-horticultural machine. Like all the countries surveyed here, the Netherlands is of course a highly industrialised, high consumption, high energy, capitalist society. Whether through electoral democracy, or business pressure politics, the drive is for economic growth, and for the increasing use of infrastructure of many kinds which normally goes with growth. In some areas, higher "infrastructural efficiency" has resulted in "demand diversion". Recycling has cut the demand for waste landfill sites, alongside acceptance of incineration of waste for the remaining proportions. High-quality public transport and much use of rivers and rail for freight have managed to stop road transport completely congesting the roads network – major public policy achievements in the twentieth century.

But the way in which the pressures above translate, if at all, into infrastructure depends on several factors. Verbong and Van der Vleuten (2004) chronicle the "material integration" of the country between 1800 and 2000. They show that this happened around the growth of networks and nodes. This is valuable in bringing out, in one sweeping view, the succession of effort on waterways, railways and then roads, and the growth of non-local power sources after the 1940s. This has led to a country far more tied together (on several levels) than one or two centuries ago, and hence at the same time far more vulnerable to failures in these interlocking infrastructure systems.

The main Dutch infrastructure is shaped around a small area, relatively speaking, on the North Sea coastline, squeezed in with the urbanised core of the country in a way which is geographically very distinctive. As the twentieth century wore on, the two nodes of Rotterdam and Amsterdam became even more than before the essence of this configuration. The ports of Rotterdam and Amsterdam gathered the great majority of marine and inland water traffic, with Rotterdam being by far the bigger growth machine, and with the most hunger for infrastructural servicing. Schiphol airport became the other key node, and the invention of the term "mainport" recognised the centrality of Schiphol and Rotterdam to the country's transport systems. Of course, many linear elements have made these nodes the base of whole networks, radiating from these essential locations. Thus the key transport decisions of the 1990s, on the freight Betuwe line and the high-speed line to Amsterdam, revolved around links to these locations.

Other sectors did not have quite the same shapes, with water having its more intricate development logics related to the national agenda for protection, land recovery and water supply. Both energy and waste treatment needed to orient themselves towards servicing the western Netherlands core above all, and so maps of pipelines and the transmission grid and waste incinerators relate to feeding the big western cities. However, in order to do this the energy grids are national, with major electricity and gas investments creating new systems in the 1950s and 1960s. Up until that time the provision systems had been largely province based, with power stations serving each province relatively separately, and gas being produced in each city, with waste treatment equally localised.

During the recent period of interest to this study, the main demands for investment have been on the above issues of the core nodes and the transport links to them, alongside more dispersed challenges on water management and renewable energy in the shape of wind farms. These have been argued out in the full open process of Dutch democratic planning, generating heavy controversies at every step. As we will see, they have been framed very strongly by the primary spatial doctrines or imaginaries of the country. Planning has been the institutional home of these controversies, within the wider polity.

SPATIAL PLANNING AS A WHOLE

In the planning world, the Netherlands has always been seen as a world champion, a leader in innovation, taking planning more seriously than most other states. This is seen to be so at all levels, and across a range of sectors. It is based on certain "planning doctrines" (Faludi and Van der Valk 1994, Needham 2007), which became established in the mid-twentieth century, and still more-or-less guide the sense of planning at the present. They are in part spatial (such as the idea of the Randstad, the urbanised western core of four larger cities and the Green Heart sitting in the midst of this core) and in part more general (about guiding the areas of investment in housing and economic activity and making the drives for economic competitiveness and for ecological sustainability compatible in the long term). Since the 1990s observers have seen these doctrines coming under pressure (Zonneveld 2005, 2006), with weaker conceptualisation in spatial terms. The 2010 coalition agreement gave less support for such traditional ideas, even explicitly mentioning the need to build on parts of the Green Heart, and wishing to delegate locational decisions for housing and economy to the lower levels of government.

The Dutch call their overall system "ruimtelijke ordening", roughly spatial planning (here I draw on Needham 2007, as well as Faludi and van der Valk 1994). The system grew up through the twentieth century and gained its "mature" form in the 1962 Act. An idea developed in the 1960s that this activity formed part of the overall planning of government and society. This consisted of "sectoral" planning, for each field of activity, and "facet" planning, which was essentially cross-sectoral and included financial and spatial planning. This gave the spatial planners a good niche in the governmental system, making it seem on a par with the budgeting side, and may have helped to maintain the profile of the ministry that contained spatial planning. For many years this ministry was called the Ministry of Housing, Spatial Planning and the Environment (I use the Dutch initials, VROM). Mastop (2001) suggests that this sectoral / facet doctrine has died away. However, some of the mindset may remain and this is relevant to the relationship to infrastructure.

It is not clear at present how far the system is being fundamentally scaled back by the 2010 government decisions, after the more modest steps of the 2005–2008 reforms. In particular, a new national spatial and infrastructure strategy was prepared in draft in 2011, but it is not possible to discuss that here. For this study it is the evolving system between the 1980s and 2010 that is relevant. Following these introductory sections, we will look at the relationship between infrastructure and spatial planning at the strategic level, before moving on to the projects dimension.

NATIONAL PLANNING

The old planning act had been revised many times, but finally in 2006 a fully new act was passed, which came into effect on 1 July 2008. It will be necessary to describe both the old and new systems, as most of what has happened was done under the old system. How the new system will work is only now being developed, and will depend largely on the multiple interactive practices built up during the first years of operation by ministers, through leading incidents and fights and no doubt court judgments.

The pre-2008 system

National government made Planologische Kernbeslissingen, or PKBs, (which translates as national spatial planning key decisions). The most important of these was a sort of national spatial strategy, which until recently was called the Third or Fourth (etc) Report on Physical Planning. But the current strategy is called the Nota Ruimte, and that is translated to English simply as National Spatial Strategy (NSS). There are two other forms of PKB: sectoral schemes (say for transport), and theme schemes (say for rural areas). In addition, government could include specific decisions in any of the PKBs on detailed aspects. For all PKBs there was a prescribed process for production of the documents, with ample time for public and parliamentary debate, as the process went through from Part 1 (the draft) to Part 5, the final version approved by Parliament. Usually this process took several years.

Needham (2007) lists the PKBs in force or under revision. The sectors/themes are:

- Second electricity supply scheme, including detailed revisions on the near-shore wind park, the cable to Britain and on the Randstad 380kV lines (dates from 1992, under full revision now);
- Pipelines scheme (dates from 1985, under revision now);
- Military lands scheme;
- Regional airports scheme;
- Traffic and transport scheme (revised 2006 as Nota Mobiliteit);
- Policy plan on drinking and industrial water supply;
- Green space structure scheme; and
- Space for the rivers.

The specific projects or areas are:

- Wadden Sea;
- Schiphol and surroundings;
- Main port, Rotterdam;
- High speed line south; and
- Betuwe line.

The PKBs have been a way of coordinating the actions of central government (and being "self-binding" on the government itself), but also have to be taken into account by lower levels of government. According to some commentators it was not always clear whether they had the form of firm guidance or just statements of policy. However, given the normal operation of Dutch public policy making, through cooperation and discussion, it is unlikely that this was so critical as it might have been in some countries. Zonneveld considers that:

> spatial planning key decisions have been written through the years in such a way that their content became more binding for provincial and local government. The end stage of this was formed by the use of so called binding decisions (*concrete beleidsbeslissingen*) in the latest spatial planning key decisions, a policy instrument which

seems inconsistent with the basic decentralised philosophy of the 1965 Spatial Planning Act.

(Zonneveld 2006 p.12)

The important feature is that this was a form of forward planning led by VROM, or at least where VROM had always a significant input. In principle it therefore spatially informed many of the key areas of infrastructure planning in the government.

The post-2008 system

The 2008 act ("Wet ruimtelijke ordening", effective since July 2008) brought in structural visions ("Structuurvisies") as the effective replacement for PKBs. These can be prepared by all three levels of government and are only meant to be strategic documents, with no legally binding effect. For central government to achieve such binding effect there are other new instruments, in the form of general orders and specific instructions, as well as the right to make directly "integration plans". Critics such as Wolsink (2003) regard this armoury as evidence of a continuing strong centralisation, whilst others such as Roodbol-Mekkes and van der Valk (2008) are more confident that the balance of centralisation and decentralisation in the new act and the Nota Ruimte will not change too much in practice.

We may assume that the structural visions will work in a way analogous to PKBs. There are no laid-down procedures for the making of structural visions in the legislation itself, and there are worries that not as much importance will be given to public debate. Wolsink (2003) fears that the new instruments will be used to instruct much more than the PKBs. So far, what is of interest for international comparative purposes lies in the old system, rather than in seeing valuable innovations in the new arrangements. It may well be that, in conjunction with the other speeding up/revision procedures now under way (see below), there is some similarity to what is occurring in the UK, with some centralisation and the removal of the right to object. The extent to which this is the case will depend on how all the factors work together, in association with the fundamental aspects of Dutch government and politics and the reforms to the whole system of infrastructure provision. It is at least these four elements together (planning reforms, speed up reforms, political and governmental culture, infrastructure industry restructuring) that will condition the trajectory in the Netherlands.

The research base

One essential ingredient for the effective coordination of infrastructure planning and high-level spatial planning must surely be a sound data and research base. The part of this base in central government in the Netherlands has undergone changes and some slimming down in the last decade, first being made a semi-autonomous agency in 2002, and then being merged with the environmental research body in 2008. However, there were still around 80 planning research staff in the Spatial Planning Bureau at the time of the merger, giving a sound research capacity at the heart of government. As van der Wouden et al (2006) argue, the "vast number of full-time planning professionals" allow the system to be "expert-driven and the principle of 'survey before plan' plays an important role" (p.35). Ministries also work openly and continuously with the universities and consultancies, much more tightly than has been the norm in the UK. Some argued that the transport and water ministry (VenW) lacked good research capacity in the past, but the creation of the KiM in 2007, the "knowledge institute for mobility", should have changed that. In some areas there may be a tendency to shelve difficult decisions by carrying out another research programme, but it can be argued that this can often be a better path than taking a wrong and often expensive decision. Sectoral planning areas like water also dedicate considerable resources to long-term research, as can be seen in the National Water Plan of 2009.

An example of the sort of long-term research common in the Netherlands is the Scenarios to 2040 exercise (CPB 2006), a joint exercise of the research bureaux. This looked at four development paths for the country, and explored the implications for different policy areas, including energy and transport. While like all scenario exercises, this did not have heavyweight messages, it shows the ability to carry out integrated and long-term research to inform ministries in a cross-sectoral way, and in reflective spaces far enough from individual ministries to maintain detachment. The space is literal: the three research bureaux are in different buildings from the ministries with the newly merged planning and environmental one being partly in Bilthoven, far from The Hague.

COORDINATION OF INFRASTRUCTURE AND SPATIAL PLANNING

The integrated approach to planning depends in part on an integrated approach within central government. This has rested on several pillars in the Netherlands. Here I look at departmental roles and mechanisms for securing cooperation across departments.

Two ministries dominated infrastructure and planning issues up to 2010, VROM, the Dutch initials for the environment, housing and planning ministry, and VenW, the transport and water ministry. However, others were significant regarding energy issues, including the ministry for farming and nature (LNV), and the economic affairs ministry (EZ). Departmentalism can always pose a threat to effective infrastructural–spatial planning. Dutch experts consider that some ministries are always in tension, the main example always being VenW and VROM. Some saw this as being down to different world-views, coming from different briefs and backed by different professional backgrounds. It could be argued that the basic outlook in VROM was environmental and social, in VenW, infrastructural and in favour of construction. Professional backgrounds are mixed: there are many engineers in VenW (especially in the Rijkswaterstaat directorate) and evidently a number of planners, with social science and geography backgrounds dominating in VROM.

The cabinet decided in April 2009 to let the policy directorates of VenW move in with the ministry of VROM from 2015. EZ would share the LNV building. But the 2010 coalition agreement immediately merged VROM and VenW, under the title Infrastructure and Environment. This seems unlikely to strengthen the hand of spatial planners. However, there may be opportunities to blend infrastructure and planning together effectively – much will depend on the new structures and the ministerial agendas.

From interviews in 2008–2009, some experts saw the departmentalism threat as overplayed. They noted that on many issues the traditionally non-cooperating ministries, VROM and VenW, did in fact work amicably together, giving the examples of the high-speed train project and the stations rebuilding projects. Priemus saw the Nota Ruimte as having brought together departmental agendas much better than in the Fifth Report (2004, p.581). New techniques have been developed over the last decade to ensure that working together is more effective, although officials are mainly referring to the budgetary arrangements (see MIRT below), but with the argument that this sort of cooperation then brings previously separated mindsets together.

There may be conflict between ministries, but this does not have to be seen as a problem. An example was the proposal to base the Fifth Report on corridors concepts, pushed by VenW, but resisted by VROM and many outside interests. The idea was finally abandoned, but by being fought out within government, the basic alternatives for future urbanisation became clear in the public realm.

Nevertheless, the challenge of budgets being by and large departmental, and that this can generate "tunnel vision" for ministers, is recognised. This appears to be the inevitable limitation of any departmental system in any organisation, and where responsibility for budgets must rest in some reasonably clear place. Spatial planning tends to push for cross-departmental decision-making, as in the MIRT process, but there appear to be strong limits to this.

There are in fact many administrative and political mechanisms for spatial planning coordination, including cross-departmental committees normally meeting on a three weekly cycle to ensure all spatial planning matters are understood across the key departments, with civil servants' groupings linked directly to Cabinet committees. Whilst VROM has always had a considerably smaller budget than VenW, and less clout than some other ministries, it did have significant resources to argue its positions. One relatively recent instrument should be mentioned: the MIRT process.

In 1999 a body was set up to coordinate infrastructural investments, called the MIT (Multi-Annual Plan for Infrastructure and Transportation – an annexe to the annual VenW budget). Some argued that this body assessed projects with little notice being taken of planning goals. So, in 2007, the title was widened to MIRT, with Ruimte (Space) added. This has been refined into a large-scale agreement process, with provinces and municipalities meeting all together twice a year and working according to carefully agreed "rules of the game". This can tie project decisions into a more spatialised understanding of goals across the big-spending ministries. This therefore became a way for VROM to achieve spatial aims, rather analogous to the way it worked with housing and agricultural interests in the 1970s and 1980s, but now attuned to the programmes of transport, water and economy (Faludi and van der Valk 1994 Mastop 2001 and Needham 2007 comment on these "twin harness" developments). The National Water Plan extends MIRT practice to the water projects sector, with the MIRT starting from area agendas, to be drawn up for nine years by the regional partners and central government (Netherlands Government 2009 p.37). The 2010 coalition agreement gave renewed support to the MIRT role.

STRATEGIC PLANNING AND INFRASTRUCTURE

As has been seen, there has been a systematic approach to issues considered of national importance, tied into the national spatial strategy process. This has covered all matters affecting major infrastructure. The 2006 National Spatial Strategy (NSS) starts with an infrastructure map of the Netherlands, primarily of transport but also indicating the role of infrastructure as a prime building-block in country-wide planning (Figure 5.1). So the critical questions are: How has this affected the major infrastructure process? Has the presence of comprehensive spatial planning at the national level made decision-making on major infrastructure different/better than it would have been in its absence? We have no other European country where we can ask this question against some sort of long-term evidence, and although the answer would not provide a recipe necessarily applicable elsewhere, given the problems of international transfer, it will be of considerable interest.

My simple answer, not perhaps surprising given a personal commitment to the value of planning, is that it has made a very great difference. From my perspective that difference is for the better. Some Dutch observers might be much less definite, as will become clear in the discussion on projects. As we saw in Chapter 4, the dominant way to think about the force of strategising is in terms of framing. This seems to me to be epitomised

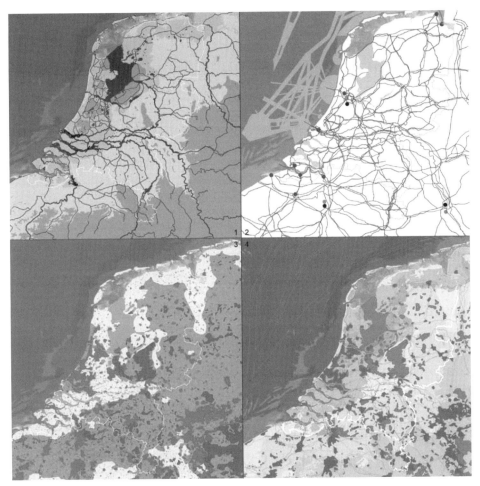

Figure 5.1 Infrastructure maps from the National Spatial Strategy 2006.
(Source: VROM 2005. Audiovisual archive Dutch Ministry of Infrastructure and the Environment)

by the way in which Dutch national-level planning works. The national spatial strategy, under its various incarnations in the last 30 years, gives a very long-term time-frame for thinking and discussion, in a sense on a nearly continuous loop:

- The preparation of the Fourth Report ran from 1985 to 1989, and it was then revised in the following two years as the Fourth Report Extra. The preparation of the Fifth Report began around 1998, was completed in 2002, but was then revised as the Nota Ruimte in 2005. The major regional study Randstad 2040 took up the discussion immediately, to be issued in 2008–2009, covering many of the key issues in the centre of the country, effectively revising parts of the Nota Ruimte.

- Within these frames a series of PKBs were prepared, as shown above. These had very long discussion lives, for example, from the late 1980s to the early 2000s for the Maasvlakte 2 Rotterdam port extension. But some were sectoral planning strategies, not project exercises, like the national transport plans or the national water plans. As part of the spatial planning system, these had to have the participation and assent of VROM, that is of the spatial planning community. So the key state ministry, Verkeer en Waterstaat, was brought into the frame – in fact, some argued that it started to set the framing, given its budget power and support at the highest level for the competitiveness and mobility agenda, in part represented by this ministry.

- The detailed design of projects and of consenting processes then followed, but there was always the possibility of reversion to high-level strategic discussion should pressures or circumstances change sufficiently. However, such re-opening or stalling would always be set within the above two macro-framing stages.

This is not to present the framing as anything tidy or cleverly phased from A to Z. Neither Dutch nor most other planning works that way, at least in democratic or relatively responsive polities and in recent times. Most infrastructure remains continuously controversial, open for debate and conflict. This is surely the norm of contemporary life, given the conflicting pressures that infrastructure industries and decisions encapsulate. We will see below how the realities of some key cases show how messy this can be, to some extent casting doubt on the broad position taken above regarding the value of high-level framing.

The core of the national spatial strategy

So what is at the heart of the NSS, and what lies behind it? There are different views as to how coherent the NSS is. Zonneveld's work explores the strength or weakness of spatial models such as the Randstad, the Green Heart or the mainports. He sees the spatial concepts within national planning as weakly structured in recent years, particularly in the Nota Ruimte of 2005 (Zonneveld 2005). Alongside these weaknesses I would still see the NSS/Nota Ruimte and its supporting and developing work as presenting a clear model of the country, maintaining the pattern of urbanisation in concentrated areas, supporting the economic spatial structure that has emerged over the last 40 years and supporting certain green and blue imaginary elements. This is continued by the National Water Plan of 2009, designed to maintain the Netherlands as it is. This therefore retains the existing country model, with only adjustments, not radical shifts.

There are of course tensions in this, particularly around the priority given to growth, especially of mobility, and what this means for infrastructure development and management. The emphasis is mostly on growth, in all transport modes and in all resource use, except perhaps in the stress on materials efficiency and to some degree on energy efficiency. This tends to press for more infrastructure, even if this is not always spatially specified, as going more in one place than another.

Brenner's argument for the Netherlands is that the model shifted in the 1980s to one of more targeted support for the growth success stories, with mainports and the Amsterdam area as gainers, seen as essential for national competitiveness, and with less stress on the equal development of all areas. Again, this clearly contains much of the truth, but the presence of an explicit NSS, linked to all the sectoral strategies, surely gives considerable weight to the old model, spreading gains around the country, protecting central blue and green assets as far as is compatible with the thriving of the mainports. So although clearly affected by the detected shift from Jessop's Keynesian Welfare National State (KWNS) to Schumpeterian Workfare Postnational Regime (SWPR) or to Brenner's Rescaled Competition State Regime (RCSR), the change appears, to an outsider at least, to be only partial. The maintenance of an explicit NSS "keeps under control" alternative strategies which may be at times in tension with this.

Some of these issues are explicitly fought out, such as with the mainports or the big new rail lines. But even these, it can be argued, essentially confirm the Randstad's national dominance, the story of the country for a century or much more. The Netherlands picture can still be described with the same keywords making up a mental map – concentrated, well knitted together (especially to outside), protecting blue and green and safe from "environmental attack" (sea, pollution, lack of fuel).

The national spatial imaginary of the Netherlands

Chapter 3 discussed the role of ideas and imaginations in the forming of national spatial futures, including those affecting infrastructure. The above section on the core of the NSS already began to touch on the essential thinking "underneath" national spatial strategising: maintaining current physical forms and environments, facilitating growth and business success and balancing development around the country. There is no scientific way to prove what the national spatial imaginary or imaginaries are within the heads of the key actors behind the NSS. Because of the way in which the NSS is prepared, there are many such actors, over extended time-periods. There will be contested versions. However, the very process of making an NSS, integrated with many more substantive policy areas, including the major infrastructure decisions of the country, must, I would argue, drive the defining of a more shared imaginary. The NSS is precisely a corralling of ideas on the existing and future shape of the country. This means that the national spatial imaginary is forced within narrow boundaries, broadly continuing according to existing patterns. It may therefore be reasonably coherent in the Dutch case.

The idea of the country (the national spatial strategy) is affected by the public debate and commitment of the state to steering certain futures. We might liken this to a patient "talking out" internal conflicts and issues in psychotherapy, thus reducing the divergences or at least becoming clearer about what these are. This may be seen as an important dimension of democracy, part of the package of democratic elements (Saward 2003), deliberative as much as representative, which can increase intelligent governing. Here we are seeing some of the value of having real, live plans, as suggested by Neuman, who mentions that plans can mobilise hope, use images, allow conflict and form links to power structures (Neuman 1998). All of this has gone on in the NSS processes of recent decades.

So in the Netherlands the interplay of the explicit national spatial strategy and the national spatial imaginary (or imaginaries – to the outsider some sort of very broad consensus appears to exist) is kept under control by the explicitness of the strategy. Public debate brings out the zones of tensions and conflict, even if politics often requires considerable fuzziness in this relationship, and therefore within the NSS. Debate about the geography of the Netherlands, and of its insertion in Europe, is continuous and reasonably conscious. This facilitates talking about space- and time-futures, even though this cannot wave away the tangles of political economy and power struggles embedded in any state's governance. This is therefore a more public coherence.

SECTORAL PLANNING AT NATIONAL LEVEL

Several contributors to the national level planning survey of Alterman (2001) made the point that in their countries the most likely way in which spatial planning might come into higher-level policy making was through sectoral plans. In many countries these exist in one form or another, for whole sectors (energy, transport) or for subsectors (gas, roads). The Netherlands has certainly been a keen promoter of such sectoral plans in the post-war period. Some have been, as we have noted, designated as PKBs, and therefore obliged to be brought into spatial planning thinking to certain extents. This applies to water (the National Water Plan of 2010), transport (the Nota Mobiliteit of 2006) and to individual energy plans like those for pipelines and transmission plans. Equally, plans for the mainports are so important that they virtually count as plans for their sectors (ports and airports), and have to be, in principle, woven into the national spatial doctrines.

Even in the absence of a comprehensive national spatial strategy, it can be argued that these would have generated some degree of integrated approach in these sectors, given the presence of a spatial planning research and policy making capacity in the relevant ministry (until 2010 VROM), and a minister able to make the political arguments. However, it can equally be argued that, in the absence of the continuing effort to make national spatial strategies, the above capacity would tend to be reduced significantly. This argument will be tested in our other European cases. They have no national spatial strategising – do they therefore lack capacity for spatialised thinking?

So the scope for the spatialisation of sectoral planning evidently is dependent on its existence at all. To a large extent I judge that where it does (still) exist in the Netherlands (transport, water and energy in some respects), spatial tying in does work to a fairly high degree (some test cases are treated below). The situation can be divided in the following way:

1. Sectoral planning exists and is formally tied into spatial planning processes and understandings – the normal case in the Netherlands.
2. Sectoral planning exists and is largely separated from spatial planning – rarely the case in the Netherlands.
3. Sectoral planning is weak and therefore cannot be tied in much to spatial planning, partly reflecting the advances of liberalisation – does not apply to the Netherlands.

To demonstrate or at least exemplify the above propositions, it is necessary to examine some of the most important sectoral plans, but this is very selective. Here I look briefly at the energy sector and at two examples of formal strategies.

Energy

There is no real national energy plan in the Netherlands, although there is strong coordination at national level which includes spatial planning in some respects. But the sector is affected by liberalisation drives, even more than the transport and water fields, and so overall government policy is less ambitious than in the past. The last overview, the Energy Report (EZ 2008), was nothing like a fully rounded strategy. But substantial powers remain with national and other government levels, and whilst the Fourth Report of 1991 appeared to say nothing at all about energy planning, and the NSS relatively little, there are significant intersections of the strategic thinking in each field in a number of ways. One has long existed, in the shape of PKBs for electricity production and transmission, SEV-III, which allocates sites for large power stations and routes for transmission lines and for pipelines. Updated versions of both were issued in 2010. That for pipelines is worked down to the detailed plans for each local authority area. These were prepared jointly by the energy division of the Economic Affairs ministry and VROM, and reflect the careful working together for that purpose, although with the energy policy lead coming from within the Economy ministry. Another example is the joint work on energy in the North Sea Plan, including allocation of space for wind farms. Onshore wind has had a problematic history, with neither top down nor more locally-generated planning giving very good results (Breukers and Wolsink 2007).

The whole energy-policy field has been marked by ambitious rhetoric in the last decade regarding energy transitions. This has ebbed and flowed, and has not caused a very large dent in the more normal ministry priorities of competition and liberalisation (Kern and Smith 2008). However, government agencies have done large amounts of research and analysis on this area (for example, Senternovem 2008), and cooperation with the gas and electricity transport companies that are still state owned means that levers remain in state hands which could be used if the political desire was present. The other drive that has affected this field, like that of transport, has been the push to speed up consent procedures. In 2004 the government centralised procedures in this area for all larger schemes in order to shorten timescales (and, we may assume, to ease the risk of refusals), and this was made permanent in 2008, under the "state coordination programme" (RCR).

National Water Plan

The National Water Plan (NWP) was published in 2009, superseding the Fourth National Policy Document on Water Management of 1998. A long-evolving raft of national water policy making had ensued in the intervening 11 years, including the report of the Delta Committee in 2008, and the completion of river basin plans under the Water Framework Directive in 2009. The NWP is a summary document of sectoral policy making, dealing with every major aspect of water matters: water supply, water quality, flood protection and varied uses of water, all set within the long-term framework given by the Delta Committee on climate change effects for the next century or more. It also includes a full detailing of these matters for nine regions and features of the country: coast, rivers, Randstad, higher parts etc. Figure 5.2 gives some idea of the main proposals.

The Plan is also a document amending parts of the NSS, given that many water matters come into the national spatial structure of the NSS, with four identified framework vision maps (for the coast, rivers, Ijsselmeer lake area and North Sea), and each chapter concludes with a section on "spatial aspects". As a "structure vision" under the 2008 Planning Act, VROM's full involvement was essential, and the plan does appear to be integrated with the NSS, including with the revision work already done by the Randstad 2040 Strategic Agenda. It therefore fits into the normal Dutch strategy and policy

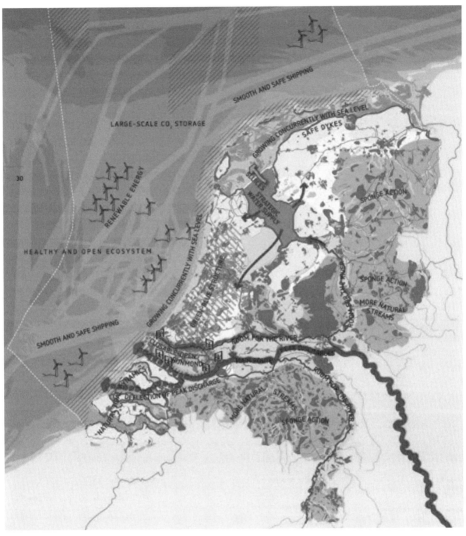

Figure 5.2 Target Situation, National Water Plan 2009. (Source: Netherlands Government 2009. Audiovisual archive Dutch Ministry of Infrastructure and the Environment)

target situation

— safe dykes
●●●●● closable-open Rijnmond ring
🏠 flood defences
growing concurrently with sea level
Waal, main route for peak discharges
⬅●● deflecting rivers' peak discharges via delta to the sea
area around the rivers: Room for the River
green-blue structure
natural tidal dynamics
strategic water supply
drain excess water to Wadden Sea
sponge action
more natural streams

smooth and safe shipping
renewable energy
nature areas at sea

subsoil

urban area (situation around 2015)
nature and forests
sandy soils
area around rivers
peat grassland
marine clay
dunes
lakes
sea

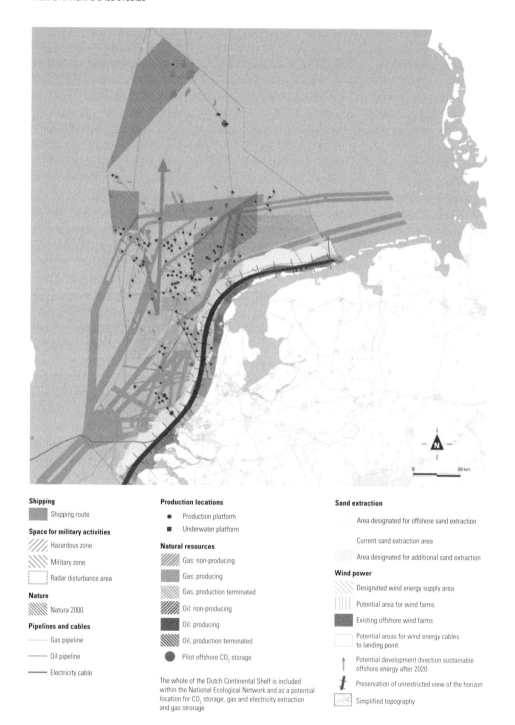

Shipping

Shipping route

Space for military activities

Hazardous zone

Military zone

Radar disturbance area

Nature

Natura 2000

Pipelines and cables

— Gas pipeline

— Oil pipeline

— Electricity cable

Production locations

● Production platform

■ Underwater platform

Natural resources

Gas: non-producing

Gas: producing

Gas, production terminated

Oil: non-producing

Oil: producing

Oil, production terminated

● Pilot offshore CO_2 storage

The whole of the Dutch Continental Shelf is included within the National Ecological Network and as a potential location for CO_2 storage, gas and electricity extraction and gas strorage

Sand extraction

Area designated for offshore sand extraction

Current sand extraction area

Area designated for additional sand extraction

Wind power

Designated wind energy supply area

Potential area for wind farms

Existing offshore wind farms

Potential areas for wind energy cables to landing point

Potential development direction sustainable offshore energy after 2020

Preservation of unrestricted view of the horizon

Simplified topography

Figure 5.3 Structural vision map (proposal) from Draft Policy Report for North Sea.
(Source: VenW 2008. Audiovisual archive Dutch Ministry of Infrastructure and the Environment)

making approach, of continual national and multi-level adjustment of plans with spatial implications.

It also includes a specific chapter on the North Sea. This constitutes the framework vision, as can be seen in Figure 5.3. This allocates competing uses to the Exclusive Economic Zone of the Netherlands, following an exercise led by VenW (2008). The plan prioritises "activities of national importance, being shipping, oil and gas recovery, CO_2 storage, wind energy, sand extraction and replenishment, and defence" (Netherlands Government 2009, p.211). As this is a structural vision under the Planning Act, it was also a joint exercise with VROM. The Cabinet was to decide later whether to make a government zoning plan, or whether the structural vision would suffice.

National transport strategy

The Nota Mobiliteit, the latest incarnation of the national transport strategy, was approved by parliament in 2006. It had become separated from the NSS. This left behind the original intention to combine them, stemming from the wish in the late 1990s to reduce the large number of national strategies, possibly not integrated among themselves. The post-2003, more conservative, government was very concerned to deliver on transport policies. With plans to widen motorways and introduce national road charging, this made the transport strategy a big policy area, too important to be subsumed in the NSS. It remained a document worked out with VROM and approved as a PKB, but the evidence of much of the strategy (not all sections were translated to English) suggests a somewhat sectorally-focused plan. No doubt it was formally consistent with the NSS, prepared at just the same time, using the same database and population, development and traffic modelling. But the main concerns are simply dealing with traffic increase, despite the road charging scheme being part of the package (subsequently scrapped by the 2010 government, to the surprise of few experts).

So, the message from the Nota Mobiliteit may be that some basic coordination remains a continuing virtue of the Dutch system, as achieved here, but that a number of factors can combine to reduce the integrating effect of national spatial planning. These factors can play into any governing system, whatever the intentions of designers. In this case they relate to political and ideological drives of the moment, to address the car-driving constituency, at the same time as trying to appear concerned with green issues. This probably pulled against any more sophisticated attempt to plan the country's future on a more long-term basis – as had been more evident during the 1990s with the Fourth Report. This political moment would have reinforced the ever-present tendency towards silos in all governments and organisations – tendencies which naturally have their advantages as well as advantages. Other mechanisms could be called on to reduce siloisation in other parts and stages of policy making, such as the MIRT process, which could bring spatial aspects together at the area and implementation levels.

So, in the case of these two national sectoral strategies, we see differing degrees of linking with spatial planning at national level, reflecting both the timing and circumstances of their making and the relationship between the two fields. For water, spatial planning and water policy needed each other from the mid 1990s, and so were obliged to work together. This was still generally the case for transport, but not very insistently in the 2000s, allowing some degree of separate development. Such coming together and veering apart must always be a feature of governing, which even the best designed set of arrangements could not obviate.

SPATIAL PLANNING AND MAJOR INFRASTRUCTURE PROJECTS

The "sharp end" of projects will be dealt with here only in limited respects. Dutch academics are extremely interested in this dimension that, as in most countries, attracts the most attention, especially in public fights over individual projects and in poor management such as cost and time overruns. A recent book edited by Priemus et al (2008), though international in coverage, draws much of its energy from discontent with major project management over the previous ten years. Here the main focus is on the degree of linking to the strategic elements discussed above, including the issue of strategic projects, and the question of state attempts to speed up decision making in the last 20 years.

Strategies, strategic projects and projects

Mastop (2001) and the WRR (1999) discussed the issues of the rise of project-led and infrastructure-led planning. This overlaps with the long-running debate in the 1980s and 1990s about whether urban strategies should have an overall global view, whether in more master planning or more strategic planning forms, or whether picking out exemplary or influential projects was the way to go. Mastop suggests that planning since the Fourth Report has tended to have a project-led colour, and that this is one reason for the emphasis since the early 1990s on speeding up and making project management more efficient.

Faludi and van der Valk (1994) argue that "strategic projects" form a separate class of projects which are so large that they are considered in their own right. Early examples were the Ijssel Lake and the Delta Works. These are likely to have PKBs specially tailored to their requirements. But these authors still wonder to what extent it is right that these are dealt with separately, as against fitting fully into overall strategic planning. To what extent has the transformation of the Netherlands become "just" a scatter of big projects, airports, train lines, new stations and water projects, held together by little more than a form of words slotted into a national planning strategy every 10 or 15 years, and detailed a little by project-dominated sectoral strategies which are departmentally hedged in? Dutch experts debate the significance of the national strategies. Do the lines on the map mean much? Are the recent reports weakly conceptualised? Do they encapsulate much of the non-decision-making tendencies detected by Andeweg and Irwin in Dutch governing? Is the essence of the national reports keeping things vague enough to allow almost anything to happen subsequently? A project-oriented interpretation would say yes to many of these questions. A critical view might suggest that the big industrial lobbies in the Netherlands (now strongly linked to European and global counterparts) can pressurise strongly on projects and policy lines, and that the big national strategies may incorporate these pressures, rather than adopt a "rational" or general national interest perspective.

However, despite all these possibilities, I remain impressed by the force of debate around overall strategy making, much of it apparently thought through and long term, and not as far as I can detect really a cover for more project-based drives. As always, these are matters of balance and comparison. What is clear is that there is an ongoing tension in the Dutch planning system, a dialectic of more comprehensive and more project-oriented forces and approaches. This relates to the changes in political economy and the operation of states in a neoliberalising era, which can catalyse more project-oriented tendencies. In part, as is so often the case, the matter is temporal. There are moments for strategies and different moments for projects, each have their dynamics, and the challenge is to make them work together over long periods in reasonably coherent ways.

Speeding up procedures

Another way in which the infrastructure–spatial planning relation has changed is the drive since the early 1990s to speed up the process of infrastructure planning. It had been a consistent comment that planning and permitting procedures were too slow and complex (Mastop says since the 1970s, 2001 p.237). Central government ministries (especially VenW) saw their schemes obstructed by local authorities, who controlled permits, making some intrusive projects quite hard to get through at all, let alone quickly. This led first to the Tracéwet of 1993 (trajectory or route line law) and then to the so-called Nimby act of the following year. Wolsink (2004) explains that the latter was due to lobbying from the Waste Management Council, which was driving for a massive expansion of incineration plants that they feared the local authorities would block. These laws allowed central government to step in, impose routes and take over permitting. Apparently there was some lessening of timescales, but the "Nimby act" in particular was little used. It was argued that the Dutch tradition of trying to do things by negotiation ('polderen') dies hard. But excessive time and complexity was still seen as a problem, and so the new spatial planning act contains what Wolsink (2003) saw as even more drastic provisions for overcoming local opposition, with the powers given to both central government and provinces to intervene by ordinances or by their own plans.

The next step in the process was the appointment of a committee by the 2007 coalition government to examine ways of speeding up further. This committee, "Faster and Better", chaired by a businessman Peter Elverding, reported in summer 2008, and almost all its recommendations were accepted by the government. The essence of the way forward was to impose a much more ordered project management approach on the preparation of projects, with the in-principle decision front-loaded to the start of the process (the first two years), and then later stages also streamlined, without, the committee argued, cutting any rights possessed by citizens to be involved in or challenge the process. The process was directed at the easing of road planning procedures, but was to be widened to apply to all other major infrastructure sectors, with a team set up in VenW to manage this process to completion during 2009. This was overtaken by a further proposal to "speed up procedures" for building projects, the Crisis and Recovery Act, announced by prime minister Balkenende at the Christian Democrat Party conference in March 2009, and in effect from January 2010, to run for four years. The 2010 coalition agreement resolved to make the Act permanent, extending across most infrastructure sectors.

The Netherlands therefore shares in this international drive to speed up decision making. The measures appear less aggressive against public rights and less dedicated to extreme speed up than in the UK Planning Act of 2008. It was suggested that the effect of the Elverding recommendations would be to cut the period for developing projects from 14 to 7 years – apparently not too drastic a streamlining. A full review will be needed if and when the new system settles down, to see if the balances in the process have been maintained.

SECTORS AND SPATIAL PLANNING

What sort of variation can we detect across the infrastructure sectors in the Netherlands? Did some fit better with spatial planning and some worse? It has not been possible to cover all sectors in any depth here, so not all the evidence has been presented to substantiate any answer to these two questions. Much less has been said on energy, and nothing at all on waste. Waste infrastructure, and waste management as a whole, has been virtually removed from the national policy making zone by recent decisions. These have handed most powers to market processes, operating within EU regulation, once waste companies were given the right to trade material for waste incineration first across provincial borders (in 2003), and then internationally (in 2007), removing earlier provincial and national commitment to proximity principle approaches. So waste planning lacks teeth above the simple local permit level, and therefore there is no longer any policy sphere with which spatial planning may engage. This represents one end of a spectrum: one of no possible engagement or integration.

Energy is, as we have seen, more of a mixed case with significant steering that amounts to firm spatial planning in the case of the North Sea, a reliance on public ownership and centralised consenting (since 2004) for all the electricity transmission and gas transport systems, and a more localised and market flow for electricity production.

What was said above about national transport and water strategies shows that the linking in those cases was much closer. PKBs were widely used for key areas and decisions in the last two decades, and both played key parts in the NSS and other national level strategising, even if to a more consistent extent for water in recent years. So there are real differences between sectors, with the spectrum running from water to transport to energy to waste. For transport, the links were variable, with issues always at risk of escaping into departmental or sectoral decision-making silos. All parts of transport policy-making are in various respects more or less continuously within high politics – just thinking of decisions regarding railways, motorways, Schiphol and Rotterdam's port makes this clear. Such policy zones may well be taken over politically at ministerial or cabinet level, and predominantly within sectoral policy communities, and their future carved out as sectors, leaving only secondary matters to be subsequently squared with spatial planning requirements. It has been argued that is normal and will occur even in a system with a significant spatial planning capacity at national level, as the Netherlands has had, at least up to 2010.

CONCLUSIONS

The planning trajectory in the Netherlands in this field has been far from black and white over recent decades. On the one hand, the worth of a national spatial planning capacity has in my view been proven many times, through the coherence of responses in several fields over the years, whether on transport, water or energy. The ability to conjugate future needs in an informed and coherent way has surely made a difference in enabling valuable projects to be intelligently inserted into the country's fabric and used to link with the other prime streams of development. There is no doubt, as numerous Dutch scholars attest, that the capacity of national planning has been declining, above all because of the collapse since the 1990s of control over the location of new housing and therefore over urbanisation as a whole. If the 2010 coalition agreement is followed through, this decline looks set to continue, with a real risk to serious national-level spatial planning capacity, both in research and policy making. But for the moment, policy continues within the national strategising of the 2000–2010 period, and this should provide coherence to the big lines of infrastructure for years to come, if it is adhered to. In particular, if the NSS system endures, it will continue to allow the public conversation which enables the talking through of the national spatial imaginary: ideas of the country's territorial futures. This, it seems to me, is an extremely valuable mode of national deliberating democratic practice.

Looking from the other side, there are several areas where liberalisation, both structurally in the changing nature of the infrastructure industries, and politically, in the colour of policy making in recent years, has been causing the capacity of the Dutch model to be undermined. The opportunities that the existence of an NSS and articulated relations with infrastructure sectors offer had been only partially taken in the 2000s. This applies as much in transport areas as in energy, with any realities of green transitions hardly emerging at all. The same applies in the speeding up and centralising measures taken in the consents field, where business pressure has been evident in the last 20 years, although to a lesser extent than in the UK. Of course, this reflects the political balances within Dutch governments, and is therefore hardly a comment on the system. The collapse of several elements of the underlying Dutch political settlement recently has been bound to impact on this policy zone. But this weak delivery by national spatial planning in some fields does encourage disillusionment amongst its potential supporters, a disillusionment that is also obvious amongst Dutch planning commentators.

Part of the message is that full integration is never the plausible goal, but that deliberative intelligence and some coherence is quite viable, given good institutional design and political and ideological will. Signs of that will ebbing away in the Netherlands have been clear for some time, with infrastructuralisation and centralisation sapping spatial planning's strength to a problematic extent. Whilst Dutch planning fields have been subject to 30 years of both "ecological turn" and "liberal turn", the second has been consistently getting the better of the first during the 2000s.

More generally, we can reflect on what has been at the base of Dutch achievements in this area. The most evident constitutional and political foundations are important: consensualism has helped over the long-term of the last 50 years, a time-scale appropriate for seeing infrastructure planning in its full context. Equally, the insertion in a capitalist economic growth society has been fundamental to achievements and problems, interacting with the long-term geographical basis of the country and the big territorial imaginaries. The relatively deliberative and democratic formation of these imaginaries over these decades led to a broadly intelligent and equitable territorial politics, largely based on a strong commitment to planning at all societal levels. Strong elements of public ownership and funding supported this settlement; and since these have been reduced after the 1990s, the achievements have been less striking. Difficult project implementation, as in the new rail lines, has in my view owed more to misguided private–public partnership approaches than to poor strategic planning. Yet planning gets tarred by such problems.

In relation to strategies and projects, the message is complex. Much can be done with strategies, both comprehensive and sectoral, but these will be buffeted by the time pressures of politics, with project decisions taking on force and bubbling out of strategic confines on frequent occasions. There is nothing problematic about this, it is the norm of political as of all other existences. Both good strategising and good project intelligence are valuable and can support each other. No doubt any first-year business school student could echo this, and it applies just as well to the managing of major infrastructure and spatial planning.

It may seem a somewhat backward looking note on which to end this chapter, but the conclusion could be that outsiders may do best to gain inspiration from the "traditional" Dutch model, functioning probably at its best 10 or 20 years ago. Exactly when the "golden age" was can be contested, but certainly the pre-2008 assemblage of elements had many strengths.

CHAPTER 6
FRANCE

INTRODUCTION

France is a big country for a student of infrastructure. It is a heavyweight actor in the field, with a reputation for getting things done, for confident steering over long periods and for technological competence. Spatial planning also has well-known achievements in the fields of urbanism at all scales. So both sides of the equation have some independent weight and examination of the two separately, and of their linking, provides a critical case within the spectrum of European experiences. In fact, to an outsider there is an excitement in studying the French experience, because of the sometimes unexpected contours of change over the last two decades. Of course, this does not apply to the French observers, who are wearily familiar with these changes which have broken down stereotypes so slowly that they may not have noticed, until foreigners recite some old chestnut of "the French way of doing things".

This chapter takes broadly the same structure as that for the Netherlands. The first sections on government, infrastructure industries and the forces that generate infrastructure needs follow the same formulas. Later, in looking at spatial and sectoral planning and dealing with major infrastructure projects, the accents are very different. The overall common impression will hold: this *is* a country which does things differently, but perhaps not in the way that many might expect.

STATE, POLITICS AND INFRASTRUCTURE INDUSTRIES

State and governing

The French state is not what it was but it retains strength when compared to Germany or Spain, or in fact to what one would find in virtually any other European state. This double-sided reality permeates any discussion of France now. Insiders see decline, fragmentation and failed policy initiatives, whilst outsiders, usually taking a longer time-frame, see achievements. The old French Jacobin centralised state was a reality for several decades after 1945, and some of its structures, powers and mindsets have not been removed by the transformations of the last 30 years (Cole 2008, Cole et al 2008, Culpepper et al 2006). Both Gaullism and its liberal and socialist opponents believed, in different ways, in this strong state, and so a sort of consensus of action was possible from the 1950s through to the 1990s. The model rested on central state economic planning, based around the Commisariat General du Plan (CGP), which prepared five year plans from the 1950s to the abandonment of the 11th Plan preparation in 1993. The CGP was finally transformed into a central strategy unit in 2005, but had long lost its directing power. The existence of this central planning model, and the levers it controlled through the state ownership of all infrastructure industries (and at times of most banks), meant that real implementable spatial planning was possible, in a relatively integrated manner. This was the state model that had the confidence to construct the infrastructure systems for which France is famous: nuclear power systems, high-speed rail, motorways, hydraulic power and reservoir systems. These date in many cases to the period between the 1970s and 1990s, but their conception rests on an idea of the country which goes back earlier. In the case of high-speed rail, and, much more uncertainly, nuclear power, this momentum is still running.

But the erosion of this model began when it was at its height in the mid-1970s, with the cutting back of state power and budgets. Decentralisation of the structure of the state followed in the 1980s under Mitterand's governments. Both processes have continued ever since, with a second wave of regional and local reforms under the Raffarin government of the early 2000s, and more and more sell offs of state-owned holdings and civil servant redundancies since the 1990s, by governments of the left and right alike. This was joined in the same period by the creep of liberalisation, part forced on a not very enthusiastic France by the EU, part taken up from inside, to build up privately run national champions.

Decentralisation and liberalisation have formed a new sort of state, still with some recognisable features of big central ministries, but now with much smaller field services, more hived off or privatised agencies and semi-autonomous power centres like the gas and electricity companies and the motorway concession firms, and all or part private operations like Air France or Aeroports de Paris. The Ministere d'Equipement, which ruled much infrastructure investment, is folded into other shapes with the engineers previously in charge now being much weaker, and companies like SNCF making deals with city mayors rather than necessarily following central direction. The state is now a genuinely multi-levelled one. Central government shares power with the "collectivites territoriales", the 22 regions, 101 departments and innumerable (often cooperating) local governments, together emboldened by big powers and the lion's share of public budgets. This is without mentioning the EU, which has now permeated into the pores of French policy-making at least as much as in several other early members (Smith 2006).

This means that in governing terms everything spatial is by definition vertically shared. But not everything infrastructural is shared. Some remains centralised, but in different articulations: part liberalised and commercially driven. The task in analysing France is therefore to conjugate these two realities that are so different from 30 years ago. The neoliberalising of the economy and decentralising of the state have to be understood in terms of their combined impact, and in the context of the complex political geographies of France. And, to make things more difficult, there are limits to both: neither real central collapse nor fully competitive economy have materialised.

Provision of infrastructure

Public control, ownership and funding meant that most infrastructure industries had a simple form, with the big powers of EDF, Gaz de France, SNCF, and motorway, port and airport holdings dominating the "commanding heights" of the infrastructure economy. This only began to be removed in the mid 1990s, and privatisation remains much more incomplete than in the UK, and in several respects less than in the Netherlands and Germany. The water and waste industries are run by the big European companies: Veolia, Suez and SAUR are always powerful (Lorrain 2002, 2005). The motorway concession companies are now largely private, but all these services are run on the classic French concession system, where the central or other governments give concessions for long periods, but do not hand over basic control of the systems. EDF remains 85 per cent in state ownership, and effectively controls RTE, which manages the electrical transmission system. GDF/Suez is 35 per cent state owned, and still, with Total, runs the French gas system as an effective duopoly. Most ports and airports are in public ownership, though all but the Paris airports and the seven biggest ports are now controlled by local or regional consortia. The rail system is split between RFF controlling track and stations, and SNCF running most trains, but these remain public, and may stay that way in spite of the advancing liberalisation that is already causing significant incursions into SNCF's freight market. Voies Navigables de France, controlling navigable rivers and canals, is a public corporation. So although commercialisation and competition dominate the rhetoric, the government can still pull levers that are not so available in some other countries, particularly if it can concert this with the rest of the "lower" governmental system.

Of course, there is much more going on than this picture suggests. "Normal" state regulatory machinery on competition and separation has been set up for the energy and rail industries in recent years, and will doubtless be extended to all infrastructure sectors if liberalisation continues. Just as low-cost airlines were able to prise open the Air France monopoly during the 1990s, so change will begin in other sectors, and this affects all state and public action, with less scope for confident planning into the future. This is quite visible in SNCF's operation since the 1990s, when it started to prioritise high-speed rail as its best market, and set aside many other long-distance routes as unviable, and was happy to offload all regional rail services to regional management. Such "cherry picking" tendencies are well known in liberalising systems, and are undoubtedly reflected in the more competition-driven features of French infrastructure industries. Most capital investment is now provided by local authorities, the opposite of 40 years ago. So local authorities, especially in the big cities, lead the way in some infrastructure fields. But other forces work against this, and the central government still maintains investing, subsidising and concerting roles across all these industries.

FORCES GENERATING INFRASTRUCTURE NEEDS OR DEMANDS

France has a population of 64 million inhabitants, with an average density per square kilometre of 112 inhabitants. It is large (even if a citizen of the US or Australia might not say so). It lies in what is variously described as a turntable or cross-roads position in Europe (quite a few countries are in this position, although each one says this as a key fact, as if it affects no one else). This means it has a lot of through traffic, now including energy as well as normal freight goods and aeroplanes overhead. Its coastlines mean it has a strong maritime position, but with big differences between the south- and north-facing frontages. So its "basic" geography now has new meanings layered on top of it, through more intense global trading and travelling and relatively open borders mainly through the EU. These, overall, cause more pressure on the human and non-human ecosystems of its territory, including many parts of the land surface, the rivers, the coastlines and the airspace.

The urbanised geography is enormously uneven, a normal fact but with specific French features. Paris has always dominated (20 per cent of weight demographically and economically, give or take, depending on the boundary of the Paris region chosen), but it is not centrally positioned. Most major cities are far from Paris, as are most major industrial areas. These areas have been deliberately spread around the country by the planning of the post-war period, and the big metropolitan centres have equally been built up by the same mechanism. But these centres, and Paris, are now much "closer" to each other due to motorway and TGV investment, while other areas are still relatively remote from Paris and even from the half dozen metropolitan cities. Even so, the country is far "smaller" than even 20 years ago. There are one million kilometres of roads, 30,000 kilometres of railways, numerous ports and airports and a fair number of navigable rivers and canals.

Infrastructure systems were, until about the 1990s, mainly conceived within a purely French setting, whether transport, energy, water or waste. The same still applies to the last two, but energy and transport of all kinds are increasingly fitted within continental systems. This is causing big changes, and requires large investments.

All these features have facilitated some infrastructure investments and constrained others. The presence of the regional capitals helped TGV investment, and continues to push the next round. EU insertion has broadly the same effect, because France starts seeming like a country of continental corridors, mimicking the already existing national corridors (north–south, east–west) – SNCF TGV experts were instrumental in the EU TENs (Trans European Networks) programme. Other effects of EU insertion are on the long eastern border, especially where cross-border work is increasingly infrastructure-intense. Border cul de sacs will soon be a thing of the past.

Much of this could encourage spatial planning thinking, both in the past to push for national visions to tackle the very big distances and many isolation challenges, and now, given the massive implications of the continental geographies. I think they did have these effects, and to an extent still do, though given the liberalisation of most infrastructure industries, now in different ways. Of course, geographies are never determinant, but they do set challenges, especially ecological ones. France's climate and resource endowments are very variable, with consideration of wind, solar, river and tidal power now at the centre of planning, as against coal and iron in the past. All this gives great scope for macro spatial planning in the future.

So where does this geography and history leave infrastructure in recent years? Clearly no other country has the Netherlands' challenge of maintaining the country's shape, certainly not to anything like the same extent. Water is not the big issue that it is in some countries, though this is partly because of a complex and sophisticated system for managing water. Waste management has been managed down to the local level, as is now so often the case, with a relatively modest explicit spatial steering element. So the prime issues are connecting and powering.

France is a country marked by the transport and energy challenges of the last 40 years or so. The understandings of a modern high-growth and high-movement state have fuelled massive infrastructure creation in all areas of transport – motorways, high-speed railways, airports and ports – and in specific areas of power such as oil, gas and nuclear based systems, with power stations, transmission lines and pipelines being constructed on a very large scale. There have been ebbs and flows in different elements of this package, but the overall result has been highly distinctive. Until recently, as a centralised state France set the main parameters for the whole country from the centre. The most distinctive choices were electric power from nuclear, and a high-speed train system. The first is already mature and the big discussion in energy is whether to start planning for a new generation of nuclear power stations from the 2020s as the present set wears out, or whether the recently embraced drive for renewable sources will become the primary emphasis. President Sarkozy's decision in 2007 to go ahead with two nuclear stations appeared to have set the track to a renewed nuclear future, but time will tell whether the French state in its more plural form will be able to or wish to drive forward this massive programme. High-speed rail is not, at least on the surface, faced by any such doubts, with decisions in 2008 to continue the now 30 year old initiative for the next decades, giving the whole country access to the system. The third big infrastructure programme, creating the motorway system since the 1960s, was widely seen by the 1990s as running out of steam and no longer required. But although slowed, road building has not stopped, and it retains a large constituency, especially at local and regional level.

Meanwhile newer elements take the limelight. As everywhere, the emphasis is on using existing systems more effectively and on reducing demand. This was a central thread of the Grenelle (a national debate process, see below), and also runs through the national sustainable development strategy of 2010. These are intended to take the pressure off all new infrastructure, and especially off the most environmentally damaging energy and travel systems. But alongside this is the rather recent push behind renewable energy programmes, especially solar and wind. As in all countries, the drive behind infrastructure creation is now in part marked by low carbon concerns. These arrived relatively late in France, with the headline programmes only emerging since the early 2000s – the green movement having found it difficult to generate sufficient force to change government priorities. This means that this area is in flow at present, and is being driven forward with the passion of a recent convert.

Nevertheless the realities remain, of a high-energy and high-movement country, for which it is difficult to imagine being able to cut its addiction to existing systems, and which also wants some new ones. The present drive is most likely to be one of switching modes rather than cutting back power or mobility – from road and air to rail (and, marginally, to river and canal), from oil and maybe gas to renewables – with the infrastructure implications this has. Put simply, this means building the rest of the high-speed rail lines, and solar and wind systems, the former on land, the latter on both land and sea. So there are considerable planning challenges, but not ones which quite match the enormous transformations of the 1960s to 1990s.

But this does not make the challenges any less, simply because the sensitivity to big projects is undoubtedly much greater than two or three decades ago, making any such scheme a marathon of persuasion and consensus building. Much of the interest of this chapter will be in seeing how this is managed now in the new French governing system, rather than looking back to the undoubtedly effective big machine that built the present systems during those 40 years.

THE FRENCH PLANNING SYSTEM AND COORDINATING ARRANGEMENTS

Spatial planning at different levels

That "old machine" has not totally disappeared, but the new way in which things are done is very different in key respects. A top-down style is still visible in some particular circumstances, such as the offshore wind programme agreed in 2010 – as in all countries a very special spatial planning challenge given the absence of local and residential interests, meaning that old style corporatism can still have easier play. However, the future geographies and schemas are predominantly negotiated by different mechanisms than those that laid out the big systems decades ago.

French spatial planning builds its strength from the bottom upwards, with commune-level or cooperative systems forming the base of legally binding plans (Baron-Yelles 2008, Booth et al 2007, Ministere des Affaires Etrangeres 2006). Above those are, in many regions, the sub-regional schemas, the SCOTs (Schema de Coherence Territoriale), and, only functioning effectively in some regions, the SRADTs (Schema Regional d'Amenagement et de Developpement du Territoire: the plans of the 22 regional councils). In regions like Nord–Pas de Calais with now more than 20 years of serious regional planning, the SRADTs do have some force in negotiating infrastructure change, certainly in transport systems. Elsewhere there is little above the SCOTs up to the national sectoral schemas.

However, France has a powerful tradition of *amenagement du territoire*, which includes a strong literature that seeks to pin down the changing nature of the activity. These books do not agree precisely on the meaning of the term. Girardon (2006 p.3) calls it the way power organises its territory, Merlin (2007 p.7) something very similar but much longer: both very comprehensive activities. Part of its strength has been some elasticity, which can sometimes seem to include just about any public action for a place (including with any private or social actors). Jean (2008 pp.41–46) traces how semantic changes have happened since the 1980s, transforming "les mots de l'amenagement" from within. The key for my purposes is the accent on territory, space and place (to combine all current English-language fashions), especially in relation to the bigger scales. For *amenagement* thinking the region, and how the region is inserted in the whole country (in France, often the nation), is important. At any rate, having an indigenous and to an extent ingrained habit of thinking territorially affects all the processes described in this chapter.

There is no national spatial plan on Dutch lines. Up to the 1980s the general state planning system formed such a national strategy, given spatial form by the small but influential agency created for this purpose in 1962, DATAR (currently defined as Delegation interministerielle a l'Amenagement du Territoire et a l'Attractivite Regionale) (Alvergne and Musso 2008). This was formed to modify the five-year Plans in order to achieve geographical coherence. In its heyday it was effective in coordinating state and private investment to achieve macro geographical goals, above all the building up of big regional growth poles to rebalance the country, as well as channelling the growth of the Paris region, with large infrastructure and new-town programmes. From the 1980s DATAR was increasingly involved in managing the new dimensions of *amenagement du territoire*. These were part European, in coordinating EU regional funds, and part regional, in managing the post-1983 system of state: regional contracts (the CPERs). Part of both exercises was fire fighting: dealing with collapses of industries or whole regional economies. So DATAR found new roles, none of them so grand as national spatial steering, and with a heavily economic promotional slant in the 2000s. It changed its name to DIACT from 2006 to 2009, to mark a bigger stress on supporting competitiveness. But the old name came back, and although the consensus amongst observers I spoke to is that it remains weak, its presence may still make a difference.

This absence of national spatial strategising reflects the dominant, more liberal approach of the 2000s. But major attempts were made to create such a national-level system, with the Schemas de Services Collectifs (SSCs), completed in 2002, being a sectoralised form of national planning (Joignaux et al 2003, Pontier 2003). They were somewhat lower key than the national comprehensive strategy (the SNADT) legislated for in 1995 by the Gaullist minister Charles Pasqua, but were intended by the later Green Party minister, Dominique Voynet, to reinstate national direction for contemporary green purposes. Voynet did not favour the national schema, perhaps identifying such action with the mega project she had been campaigning against for years, the Rhine–Rhone canal, which was abandoned in 1998. However, the Socialist led coalition of 1997 to 2002 lost power and the sectoral SSCs were swept aside. The survivors of that phase were another nationally inspired planning instrument, the Directives Territoriales de l'Amenagement (DTAs), intended to concert all levels of public action for parts of the country with particularly large challenges, under the leadership of the regional prefect. The DTAs look like intelligent and coherent regional-level planning, but they were only carried out for seven regions in the end, and political support for this innovative approach fell away. They were renewed under the 2010 Grenelle 2 law, as DTADDs (Directives Territoriales d'Amenagement et de Developpement Durables) for sustainable development, but were given even less power over other types of urban planning, so their future may be no more rosy than before.

In most of France then, the strongest spatial planning is low down the system. But this does not remove the impact of two more elements which affect the spatialising of public policy: coordinating and governing arrangements, and national spatial imaginaries. I turn now to consider these two elements.

Central steering and coordination

The French state works via a combination of big pushes and continuous coordination and negotiation mechanisms. The latter mechanisms include the CPERs (Contrat Plan Etat Region), incorporating EU regional funds every seven years or so, as well as the everyday dealing with political notables spread across the governing geography of France, some of them often central government ministers. This is certainly coordination, but it may have little of the rational planning characteristics that planners might hope for, being of a more "pork-barrelling" nature. However, over longer periods, it may result in a rough-and-ready dividing up of spoils: a spreading around of infrastructure investment, for example, as political fortunes change and governments alternate.

The big pushes, which at one stage were partly played out in Plan processes, come from the top of government, reflecting its overall character. In the infrastructure and spatial field they were often articulated by key meetings of the CIADT/CIACT (DATAR's prime minister-led interministerial council) that resulted in big spending packages. So these reflect the work done by manifestos and coalition agreements in other countries, both of which can play parts in France too. DATAR has had a role in preparing the spatial balance of these packages, as in the Plan de Relance, passed to overcome the effects of the 2008 economic crisis. In the infrastructure and environment area, the most striking coordinating mechanism of recent years has been the Grenelle, running since 2007. Because of the innovative nature of this process, I describe it below in some detail.

The Grenelle de l'environnement – a political innovation

The Grenelle stemmed from the presidential election campaign of 2007: as so often, matters of real importance stem from the battlegrounds of real politics. One of the candidates, an ecologist and television presenter, Nicolas Hulot, was winning 10 per cent ratings in the opinion polls. He challenged the other candidates to commit themselves to a public debate process on how to meet climate change and related environmental challenges, if they won. All candidates promised to do so, and he then dropped out. Sarkozy appointed Jean-Louis Borloo to be effectively deputy prime minister and head of a new mega-ministry, and charged him with organising the Grenelle. Rather to the surprise of many observers, Borloo has seemed to take the challenge to heart, claiming the process is critical to meeting the revolutionary challenge faced by humanity. Sarkozy has generally given support.

This process has therefore, since 2007, framed most infrastructure policy in France. It is only one episode in the flow of state policy-making, and involves primarily national-level actors in the early stages. Many French observers have been sceptical, especially those most critical of Sarkozy. However, the groupings, which one might call the moderate green establishment – such as France Nature Environnement (FNE), a vast umbrella organisation of nature and broader environmental campaigners – joined in the Grenelle with energy once they had overcome their initial suspicions (FNE 2010).

Grenelle as process

The exercise is a sort of grand corporatism, with decision-making by five "colleges", made up of representatives of local and regional authorities, the state, environmental NGOs, employers and salaried workers. About 5 months' activity by working groups led to 3 days of round-table work to agree on 268 exact commitments. These were then endorsed in their entirety by Sarkozy, and the second phase consisted of 34 operational committees attempting to reach programmes for action. These reported by May 2008, with their conclusions again endorsed by the five colleges group. This core group, of 40 members, continues to meet with the minister every 2 months to ensure that the original commitments have not been lost, or if they are lost at least to find out why. The conclusions were also taken to the Parliament, in the form of the law Grenelle 1, adopted on first reading in both houses almost unanimously.

The law Grenelle 2, passed in 2010, swept up more key elements and has run alongside many other forms of implementation by a wide spectrum of actors: businesses, professions and particularly local and regional governments. The aim has been to "territorialise" the initiative, with DATAR heavily involved. Grenelle proponents argue that the initiative was never only Paris based, with widespread use of the Internet and many regional meetings during the early stages. However, it is clear that it is essentially a centrally directed project, and so the steps taken to get state field services and the complex French polity to take on the commitments have been critical. The second annual review in October 2010 summed up progress and challenges at that stage. One step was to make the five-college structure permanent, for implementing and monitoring the agreements (MEEDDAT 2010b). There are certainly problems in Grenelle implementation, but the process has not ground to a halt.

A related programme was a new sustainable development strategy, finalised in mid 2010 (Republique Francaise 2010). It took the environmental work from the Grenelle, and broadened this to include economic and social dimensions, with a strong emphasis on social equity. This superseded a first strategy of 2003–2008.

The Grenelle and the SNIT

The aim of the Grenelle at the highest level is to reduce greenhouse gas emissions by 20 per cent by 2020. Transport has a large part to play if there is any chance of achieving this. The instrument designed to deal with the infrastructural side of this effort is the Schema National des Infrastructures de Transport (SNIT). This was published in draft form in July 2010 (MEED-DAT 2010a), and revised following consultation in January 2011 (MEEDDAT 2011a). At the time of writing, it remained in a further revised, not finalised form. It deals with all infrastructure, on land, sea or for airports, and concentrates just as much on management and maintenance as on the construction of new infrastructure. It contains both general orientations on all policy areas, and a list of the main infrastructure projects seen as necessary. It therefore replaces previous forward-planning strategies such as the CIADT report of December 2003 (DATAR 2003). The law revises the basic French transport law of 1982, the LOTI (Loi d'orientation des transports interieurs), to give the SNIT legal basis, and requires that it is revised at least once every legislature.

The content takes on all Grenelle commitments, which include no more road capacity overall, except to eliminate congestion points, and safety issues or problems of local interest. Clearly this last phrase leaves many possibilities for retreat, some of which were reflected in the 2010 draft, which included 900 kilometres of further road building. The 2011 draft cut out some of these schemes, but some were treated as long-planned commitments, and the Plan de Relance of February 2009 included new road schemes. Even so the percentages of investments do remain heavily skewed to the Grenelle aims (see Figures 6.1 and 6.2), to create a modal shift from road and air to rail, including to raise freight by non-road and non-air means from 14 per cent to 25 per cent by 2022.

Many other freight elements are in the Grenelle law transport chapter, including more "rail motorways" (one scheme already crosses France, to take lorries off the roads and onto railcars), doubling the non-road freight part from French ports by 2015, more "sea motorways" (an EU idea), building the Seine–Nord canal during the period 2012–2020, and later the Saone–Moselle to Saone–Rhine link. One new airport at Nantes is supported for apparently

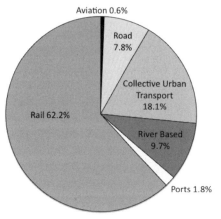

Aviation 0.6%

Road 7.8%

Collective Urban Transport 18.1%

Rail 62.2%

River Based 9.7%

Ports 1.8%

Figure 6.1 Modal split in Schema National des Infrastructures de Transport (SNIT). (Source: Ministère français de l'écologie, du développement durable, des transports et du logement, schéma national des infrastructures de transport, January 2011 draft)

Figure 6.2 Division of expenditure by mode, in SNIT January 2011 draft (Schema National des Infrastructures des Transport, MEEDAT January 2011 Table 1. Percentages are rounded to nearest whole number)

Investment categories	Development		Modernisation		Regeneration		Maintenance		Total	
	Million euros	%	Million euros	%	Million euros	%	Million euros	%	Million euros	%
Total	166000	64	59500	23	30500	12	4500	2	260500	100
Rail	103000	62	15000	25	25000	81	2000	44	145000	56
Waterways	16000	10	2500	4	4000	13	500	11	23000	9
Ports	3000	2	2000	3	–	–	–	–	5000	2
Telecoms	30000	18	17000	29	–	–	–	–	47000	18
Road	13000	8	22000	37	1500	5	2000	44	38500	15
Aviation	1000	1	1000	2	–	–	–	–	2000	1

environmental reasons, alongside some port extensions. Many urban public transport schemes are detailed. Above all the SNIT presses forward with new high-speed rail connections, including those not going through Paris but linking up regional capitals, building 2,000 kilometres more of LGVs (ligne(s) a grande vitesse) by 2020, and defining a further LGV programme for the long-term future of 2,500 kilometres (Figure 6.3 shows the main rail proposals. A similar figure exists showing rail freight schemes). The cost is naturally

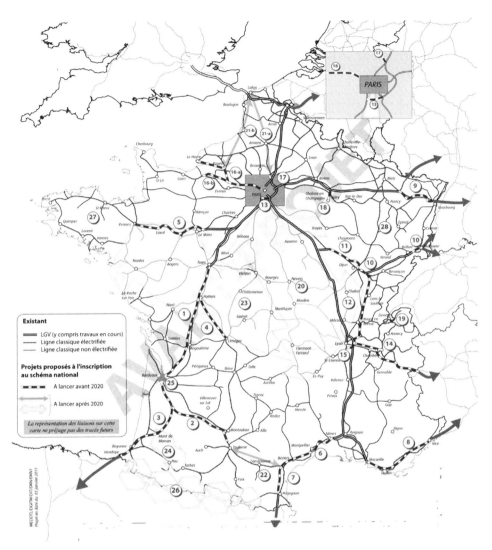

Figure 6.3 SNIT: Rail schemes proposed.
(Source: Ministère français de l'écologie, du développement durable, des transports
et du logement, schéma national des infrastructures de transport, January 2011 draft)

high: with 2,000 kilometres of LGV costing 55 billion euros and the Seine–
Nord canal costing 3 billion euros (Fremont 2008). Other elements include
the proposal for a "rocade", a rail ring 20 kilometres out from the Peripherique, around Paris, as the regional plan for Ile de France has proposed and
now detailed in the 2011 draft.

The SNIT is ambitious, trying to create a rational and multimodal plan
prioritising non-road and non-rail modes, and trying to make it implementable

in the long term. It may meet the same fate as previous such efforts, with just the "system friendly" parts of the transport agenda happening – normally those of road and air. But the drive is more concerted and, coming from a right-wing government, cannot so easily be attacked by the normal car and business lobbies.

But how far does this sectoral exercise, however multimodal, take spatial thinking into account? The last major campaign by DATAR in 2000 presented the polycentric net model as the ideal to move towards. Some signs of the polycentric idea can be detected in Grenelle objectives, but there is no explicit reference to overall spatial thinking. Any spatialising may depend less on DATAR input than on the "territorialisation" process now inherent in all French politics. However there is little sign, to my eyes, that the SNIT has been greatly changed by the political pressures on any French government to spread investment around. It has, so far, stuck closely to its Grenelle mission, which is an all-France one. As such it represents the "transport chapter" of a national spatial strategy, set by central goals, but no doubt put under the spatialising microscope of regions, localities and DATAR.

The new ministry

Alongside the Grenelle, the other big 2007 innovation was the restructuring of the central state machinery. Some regard this as a cover for large-scale cuts in staffing. One in two retirements in the new ministry are not being replaced, and the field services of the ministry are also being drastically rationalised, combining these units in parallel with the central mergers. Before the merger, there were two main ministries, Equipement, essentially for transport, and Ecologie, which dealt with a range of environmental concerns. Energy was in the Industry ministry. These are now all in the heavily-named ministry of Ecology, Energy, Sustainable Development and Territorial Management (MEEDDAT). The environment ministry had 700 staff, the new one has 7,000 staff. All will be in the tower at La Defense, where the Transport ministry has been for years.

Departmental change may invite scepticism, but no-one had tried to dismantle or transform the empire of the engineers, as observers tended to see the Equipement ministry. Sustainable development and responding to climate change are meant to be the core tasks of the new ministry, and planners are likely to see its integrating potential. The decree of 9 July 2008 laid out the new structure, which includes larger-scale spatial planning in the sub-direction of sustainable development, whilst urbanism (city-level planning) is in another division. Overall, little central capacity exists on planning in the new ministry. Probably DATAR is expected to deal with national and regional spatial dimensions. The DG (direction generale) for infrastructures, transports and the sea includes all transport work except that still in the separate civil aviation DG. One of the sections within that main transport DG deals with all transport infrastructure, specifically including that for airports, as well as the SNIT.

This was a radical reform. Its net effects depend on many factors, particularly on whether a slimmed-down ministry can really tackle the large number of new "dossiers" which have been handed down. Some sectoral lines, particularly transport and energy, do look promising, but there are many critics. It could in principle overcome some of the perennial problems of interdepartmental coordination, and it is clear that the Grenelle process has been used as an implement to this effect.

National spatial imaginaries

What about the role of spatial ideas? Some "old" ideas may have continuing effects such as those of the Schemas de Services Collectifs (SSCs), the DATAR work of the late 1990s under J-L Guigou (DATAR 2000). Some of the sectoral schemes may also have a cohering effect, given the importance of road and rail in structuring, combined with the implicit airport and port schemas. That is to say, as the debate on the TGV system has run on over the decades, this has served as a proxy or element of national spatial structuring, the balance of the nation's development and integration. In analogous ways, investment in ports and airports, and their land connections, may have the same effect. Road network decisions perhaps have a more incremental and often more localised nature, after the initial decisions of the 1950s and 1960s. The overall forms of sectoral planning will be in the minds of territorially attuned ministers and especially civil servants.

The Grenelle is notable for not having an explicit territorial drive, though its apparently collegiate preparation and continuation would have allowed access by numerous national spatial imaginaries in a more open way than perhaps in the past. The intermittent scenario work by DATAR would presumably have had the same effect, alongside the efforts by them to incorporate European factors into these. But it is not evident that this had much impact on the Grenelle process. The explicit work on the SNIT brings these aspects out into the open again, and so constitutes an important moment in any new "coming out" of the national spatial imaginary.

The substantive outcome is doubtless of a country making a systematic effort to de-centre itself since the 1960s, with regional growth poles, while balancing this with a continuing centralising policy that fits the airports and high-speed rail systems as they have developed. In part, this is about the size of France, where there is more room for the play of centrifugal and centripetal forces than in the Netherlands or even England. It is also due to the historical form of the state, the Netherlands being to some degree polycentric, and France having the dominating position of Paris. However, Paris's domination has never been so large as to automatically trump all alternative forces, as might happen in a smaller country. So, to some degree, the tension is built into the historical–geographical nature of things. This is given force by the democratic and pluralist form of French politics.

Overall a continuing tradition of national spatial thinking therefore exists, based on a mix of the old, the sectoral, and the continuing work by DATAR, with the recent boost of Grenelle work. This continues to give a sort of mental scaffolding for an implicit habit of national strategising, in and outside of government. The national spatial imaginary no doubt clusters round the two poles, creating more radial and more matrix/polycentric conceptions of French territory (and its insertion in wider Europe). This would give some sort of "match" between the substance of state policy and the imaginary, both with the same constant tension of the two poles, centralising and dispersing. This is therefore a less settled imaginary than that of the Netherlands, with less coherent and continuous debating, perhaps precisely because of the fault lines such debate has to continually negotiate, giving the grounds for consensus less room. However the rather strong commitment to a national future which lies at the core of the imaginary, powered by French nationalism, means that the risk of a breakdown in conversation is generally not too high. Up to the present, the ability to conjugate national, regional and local goals has permitted a roughly accepted double strategy.

THE SCOPE AND RANGE OF MACRO SPATIAL PLANNING AND THE RELATIONSHIP TO INFRASTRUCTURE PLANNING

What then are the processes affecting the dominant sectoral infrastructural fields? In broad terms three can be identified. First is the combined impact of general government policy-making, including the Grenelle and the SNIT as a kind of privileged sectoral planning. This we have already examined, noting its major impact and the fact that it does not explicitly adopt spatial rationalities. Second is the overall combined effect of *amenagement du territoire* type thinking, including the work of DATAR. Third is regional-level planning. Do either of these latter processes do any more to spatialise public infrastructure policy in some coherent way?

Territorialisation

Amenagement du territoire thinking contains the regional plan contracts, the CPERs, stressed by French observers as one of the lynchpins of the articulation of the French polity, a sort of reconciliation of the regionalisation and amenagement philosophies (Merlin 2007). Girardon says (2006 p.151) that the CPERs become "l'instrument essential de la coordination de la planification territoriale de l'Eat avec celle des regions" (or "the essential instrument for the coordination of spatial planning by the state with that of the regions"). The latest round of regional contracts and EU programmes was signed off in 2007, to run to 2013 (DIACT 2007a). At the beginning of each round the regional prefect prepares a statement of the state's objectives in each region, of course negotiated in Paris with all the ministries, and this becomes the base for the discussions with regional actors in the preparation of the contracts. DATAR leads the Paris end of the preparation, a long drawn-out national negotiation lasting two or three years. DATAR then has the role of vetting their implementation, and evaluating them later – until the next round starts. Elements of the 2007 CPERs provided national coherence. A number of themes are emphasised, especially that all the 300 "large projects" selected for the 2007–2013 programme must contribute to sustainable development and carbon neutrality. In addition a large emphasis on interregional projects is maintained, with a significant set related to river-basin plans: the Plan Loire and four more of the major rivers, plus smaller amounts for the five massif (mountain area) plans. However, transport is no longer within the CPERs, so their impact in that sector is negligible.

DATAR also acts to "territorialise" general policies (DIACT 2007b, 2008). So the Grenelle is being territorialised – that is, being taken down into regions and cities. The same happened to the Plan de Relance of February 2009. A CIACT was held to legitimise the dividing up of the cake of the special budget allocations, so that all regions could see what they were getting. The territorialising was clearly very careful, with each region getting a good share, no doubt according to time honoured rules of thumb. A map was prepared for every region showing all the transport investments, both from the Plan de Relance and other sources. Many other examples of territorialising could be given, such as the reorganisation of the armed forces that resulted in the closure of many bases. DATAR always has a hand in such policies, through its meetings each month with regional and city government notables, and so keeps an overview of the spatial impacts of state policies. It may not have the force to impose much "rationality" on these policies and redistributions, but it can talk directly to the prime minister or other ministers if necessary via its own minister.

DATAR is not what it was some years ago, but this does not sum up all the influence of amenagement, which almost certainly remains a deeper and wider force within political processes, acting through politicians, officials and even some executives in independent companies.

Planning by regions

The other channel is the planning carried out by regions. This now takes many forms, but varies widely across regions because all regional plans are voluntary and so are not prepared by all. The main spatial plan is the SRADT, as specified by the 1995 and 1999 laws. Other plans are for regional development and for sustainable development (most recently for energy and climate). But none of these form precisely the basis for the regional contracts and European funding programmes, so there is no absolute requirement for regions to align their long-term territorial thinking with that of the state, and so form what one might imagine as a shadow national plan.

In any case 22 regional plans, if they all existed and had compatible time scales, would not necessarily add up to something sensible. Salez (2008) sees the links in the regional systems as being quite weak, with SRADTs often not well linked to other regional programmes and finance. Gradually the region has become, just about, "chef de file", the leading authority, but this is precarious given the more extensive competences and budgets of both departments and communes, and intercommunal bodies (the regions have only 15 per cent of the total budget going to subnational authorities). Furthermore, some regions are small or have "bad shapes" and so lose power in that way. Salez, from the perspective of the European Commission, sees French regions as still too weak, in a clear comparison with German or Spanish cases.

A hybrid system

All this adds up to some sort of spatial development planning, one that necessarily reflects the sort of polity France now is. Girardon describes it as a hybrid system, between coherence and competition (2006, p.197). He argues that the state still has a leading role, acting both unilaterally in many fields, and in partnership. But he sees the system as undeniably complex now, made up of a plurality of actors and a diversity of territories, creating a dispersion and "eclatement" or "scattering" of efforts. He sees the regions and the EU as the key referents, with the state maintaining coherence between and within this system.

It is a thoroughly mixed dynamic, with no overall guiding steer, and has some similarities to the processes in federal states. Political power and especially economic power are determinant in the balance of forces at work: Subra's analysis of the geopolitics in play. A poorer region might have to scrabble for any infrastructure going, unable to launch any independent track to its future, and so effectively fitting in with at least some sectoral models handed down by the state. A rich and politically confident region might be able to negotiate especially fortunate infrastructure deals, perhaps bypassing the state to an extent by drawing on private and EU help. The Ile de France region should be in such a rich-region situation, but given its political importance it is a special case whose confident 2006 regional plan (SDRIF) was "called in" by the president (as is legislated for in this region – and only this region), and left on the shelf. So infrastructure for Ile de France comes in a separate box, with a strong state dominance (Subra 2007).

To illustrate this with a well known example: the mayor of Lille and the Nord–Pas de Calais region managed to ensure that the TGV from London to Paris went through Lille, and used this for a successful exercise in urban and regional boosterism (summarised in Subra 2007). Are we able to designate this as a wise piece of national strategic thinking, bolstering the fortunes of a region which had suffered most from deindustrialisation, and needed a new spatial insertion in the reconfigured core of Europe? Or do we interpret it as a sign that lucky and well-placed actors could distort the "rational" priorities of the national government, which would no doubt have chosen the direct route via Amiens without the pressure of Pierre Mauroy (mayor of Lille and ex prime minister)? French observers would say the distinction is meaningless, as the system is a seamless whole of such multiple pressures from above and below, confounding a simple analytical choice. The regions were given the competences of *amenagement du territoire* and economic and social development in 1982, and they would not be doing their job if they did not take initiatives of this kind.

So the above mechanisms have force in constituting some sort of spatial planning consciousness and outcomes, conjugating the sectoral and the territorial, however messily. This is a very partial set of mechanisms, nothing like the conscious if much criticised efforts of Dutch national planning, but equally more thought through and fought for than the absent national strategising that characterises the UK, in most respects.

This form is the only one "fit for" the current French polity, and the half neoliberalised and Europeanised condition of its political economy. But there is doubtless a lot of play in the system: political spaces which could be pushed differently by governments or other key players. The prospects are for an even looser and messier model, as liberalisation of infrastructure systems increases its pace (if this occurs, and the EU does not change its direction). At any rate the recent French model, of actually existing *amenagement*, has very interesting features.

PLANNING AND IMPLEMENTATION

The French government can still be quite attached to "planification": this has no spatial connotation, and simply means working out future requirements for any service, and how these may be met. It is sometimes referred to as desirable, as a complement or corrective to regulation or market decision-making, for example, in the Grenelle process, which calls for more planning for renewable energies and for improving waste management. This is no doubt argued for explicitly, because government has turned increasingly to the other two modes.

One interviewee said, only half in jest, that the French, unlike the Germans, do not plan. They make schemas, but these are only highly indicative, with no certainty at all of implementation, and no attached finance.

This gap between grand planning and action was stressed by academics as well. The complex process of the making of an infrastructure scheme might start with the pressure of an influential mayor, have to navigate the planning rationalities of numerous levels of state and non-state actors, go through several separated public-debate episodes, happen to reach the list of financeable projects at a lucky moment, and not be stopped at the last moment by any number of possible historical "accidents". Finding the money is now an extraordinary process of sticking partners together, with road and rail routes broken up into short stretches to facilitate this public-partnership world.

These trajectories towards (non) implementation vary by mode and by scale, so that one cannot suggest any one common path to implementation or otherwise. This awareness of both officials and academics of the "unplanned" nature of French infrastructure action is clearly to be taken seriously. It is certainly part of the story, as it would be in varying degrees in any country (Germany included).

The private monopoly power referred to above may affect state planning: in the motorway concession networks, in the Paris airports system and potentially in other areas if the privatisation of further parts of the infrastructure equipment of France progresses. The really powerful effects of such changes probably remain some years off, but already the balance of forces may be changing, so that the state is less able to set public objectives without considering the large payments necessary to persuade investors to do certain things.

Is planning in itself no longer very important? This may apply less in the water and energy areas, where there are still relatively unified bodies able to look long term and that are backed by the state in this task (Agences de l'eau, EDF and GDF especially). But in transport, it was suggested that schemes got into transport plans due to pushing by lobbies of one kind or another (mayors, regions etc) and then implemented, or not, by a whole range of pressures, above all financial and political, which have little to do with careful or rational planning or prioritising.

NATIONAL SECTORAL PLANNING AND INFRASTRUCTURE

Sectoral planning exists in all infrastructure fields: in energy and transport nationally, in water and waste lower down. All these can have "spatial spill-over" and so it is important to look briefly at each sector. We will see that, as in the Netherlands, there is a spectrum in the extent to which such planning is affected by wider spatial thinking and governing efforts. General sources on transport include Bernat and Ollivier-Trigalo 1997, Fremont 2008b, Ollivier-Trigalo 2002, 2007 and Seligmann 2005.

Ports

In the past, state spatial control was possible, because the state dominated investment in all the large ports and hinterland transport connections. But there has been only limited integration within the sector nationally, and little explicit linking to territorial planning at the widest scale. Thus, there has been a clear investment hierarchy, with Le Havre and Marseille treated as the national super-ports since the 1990s. But experts argue that this was nothing like a thought out national strategy, and was also not backed by clear terrestrial transport links (Cour des Comptes 2006, Debrie et al 2007, Fremont and Gouvernal 2008). The mindset that was ready to make big investment decisions on ports therefore lived on until recent years, but the mindset that planned to make this fit in an overall national territory did not. Furthermore, in recent years some degree of liberalisation and commercialisation has come into port management, and although public ownership avoids the extent of inter-port competition that one might see in UK or US cases, something implicit within French competition has been growing. This is related to the decisions to pass ownership of all but the seven "grands ports maritimes" to regional, local and chamber of commerce bodies, and to require the seven large ports to adopt the "landlord model" of port management, not employing workforces directly to run port services.

Airports

Some of the same picture applies to airports, which are still generally publicly owned, but now by different local, regional and chamber of commerce entities, except in the case of the Paris airports, which are in a stock market company but still majority state-owned. Competition emerged between regions to a certain extent, with localities subsidising many loss-making airports (Cour des Comptes 2008a, IAURIF 2003). So the strong corporatist hold of the Civil Aviation directorate in Paris, working closely with Air France and other aviation interests, has been weakening. Experts argue that there has been no clear national strategy and, as with ports, no strong ability to link with terrestrial interests, as rail investment took its own path. As with the ports case, the SNIT has now attempted to make these links key in deciding investment in future years, but this has not extended to any strategic decisions on the airports system. The SNIT land transport framing could give a firmer cross-modal coherence, but it depends on the cooperation of numerous, now semi autonomous, actors and what the central state can do to secure this.

Roads

The motorway programme was one of the big "successes" of the post war years, run as a well-oiled machine from the central ministry, if sometimes running up against local oppositions. This was clearly integrated in some sense with the territorial model of the country, probably most strongly in the years of high *dirigisme* when the greater part of the network was planned (Fayard et al 2005, Meunier and Quinet 2006). In recent years some planning exercises have sought to call an end to new building, including the SSC in 2002 and the SNIT in 2011, whilst others pressed on (for example, the CIADT/CIACT meetings of 2003 and 2005). The latest effort may have some success, but time will tell as to whether the formidable French roads lobby is finally halted. Road construction is classically sectoral, able to negotiate insertion at local and regional level over decades, tied in to some degree to regional plans, but also with a dynamic of its own.

Rail

The French rail achievement is world famous, and was based on the first adventurous development of a profitable route from Paris to Lyon opened in 1981, and then generalised through a national network plan in 1991, which has been driven forward by political pressures despite rising funding and local opposition difficulties. French critics note that the SNCF has increasingly planned its networks in separate ways, with parts of the high-speed network favoured, much of the traditional long distance network seen as disposable and the regional and urban networks maintained at the expense of local and regional governments, if paid for (Cour des Comptes 2008b, Varlet 2008, Zembri 1997). Again, there is a major element of national-level sectoralism driving decisions. In a very broad sense this fits in with state territorial priorities (indirectly or directly government pays for most investment), but SNCF's own interests, and that of the track authority, RFF, have an increasing role to play in key decisions (including station sites), with the two seen as poorly coordinated. Regional rail planning is seen by observers as much more successful, since its takeover by regions in 2003. In many regions this has led to a renaissance of rail planning, well linked in to wider spatial planning (Zembri 2004, 2005). So again, the story is mixed, with a very broad overall picture that connects to an idea of the country. In part, this is simply dictated by some unavoidable geographical realities such as the location of urbanisation (and therefore demand). However, rail planning autonomy and increasing fragmentation of the system weakens the overall sense of a national picture. There is a more positive picture at regional level, where more fully integrated planning has sometimes been able to hold sway.

Water

Major infrastructure investment in water schemes has been limited in recent years (Barraque 1998a, 1998b, 2000). Various projects of previous decades, such as those for the management of the Loire, were opposed by ecological campaigns and largely defeated. Only certain areas in the south are seen as having water-shortage problems, and so schemes for some modest reservoirs have been retained. In any case the management of French water has rested with six "Agences de l'Eau" since 1964, covering the big river basins, and these have been able to work in recent years with sub-national governments, especially the regions, to give a degree of coordination to measures, whether infrastructural or not. These agencies have been able to create the plans needed under the Water Framework Directive, with some oversight from the Paris ministry, largely proving the effectiveness of the institutional system and the ability to manage competing demands on water systems (Ministere de L'Ecologie et du Developpement Durable 2007). This may also reflect in part the long established public–private system of management, investment and ownership, which gives planning power to agencies and local authorities, but often gives investment to the corporate powers of Veolia and Suez. This is different from, for example, the more complex model in England, with a mix of economic and environmental state regulators, and private companies with full responsibility for systems in principle. But the presence of elected regional governments able to work with the water agencies may also have helped to integrate planning for water as a sector and for territories over recent decades. So, several elements have combined to allow some degree of effective operation, even if in the face of only moderate infrastructure challenges.

Energy

This, alongside transport, is the field with most controversy, if possibly not to the same extent as in some other European countries. It is run very much as a set of sub-sectoral policy zones, with the state preparing national plans for electricity and gas infrastructure systems. They are not binding, but set strong targets. These two programmes, the PIP for gas and PPI for electricity, do show areas of special concern (electrical fragility zones in Britanny, around Nice and in several border areas where transmission improvements are urgently needed), but this is not integrated with other *amenagement* issues, and DATAR appears to have been little involved in energy discussions in recent years. The regional spatial plans, the SRADTs, do not appear to dip into energy issues much either. Gas and electricity plans are then implemented by the monopoly or duopoly of firms in these two sectors, in both cases partly state-owned. Nuclear decisions are for the president and EDF, although with rising public opposition. Nuclear decisions are essentially debates on principles, as the sites for next generation reactors will be those that already exist, as in the case of the next two at Flamanville and Penly.

Though the 2002 SSC for energy tried to move state policy in this area to a more integrated approach, its efforts were largely limited to trying to promote renewables – with no great success. Planning for onshore wind has largely been seen as a notable failure (Jobert et al 2007, Nadai 2007).

Since government decisions in 2010, offshore-wind plans have taken a much more determined character. Accompanying the Grenelle commitments, the government led the identification of five offshore zones for wind farms, and published a strategy and a route map for contracting the construction and operation (MEEDDAT 2011b). The sites' identification was led by the maritime regional prefects, bringing in regional interests and stressing the economic benefits to French industry. The Grenelle is of course full of other energy commitments, but these are not directly spatialised. However, a new generation of regional plans is required under Grenelle 2, the Schema Regional Climat, Air et Energie (SRCAEs), to be prepared by 2012. The totals for renewable energy should, it is expected, add up to the required national totals, presumably (in part) under regional prefect guidance.

Overall, there is strong public involvement in the energy field, including the state-steered energy companies, with RTE, the electricity transmission firm, being an autonomous part of EDF. State planning continues, and the Grenelle is now regionalising this effort. More invisible links to the *amenagement* processes may well be present within the standard French territorially articulated polity, and so once planning momentum develops with the offshore plan and now the SRCAEs, there may be more integrated linking regionally, to supplement the national sectoral drive. The processes within the MEEDDAT, bringing energy together in one ministry for the first time with spatial planning and environmental issues, might facilitate this.

Waste

Management of waste is not given much emphasis within central government, with planning left very much to the local level. As in many other countries, issues are managed down to a combination of the big waste companies (Veolia, SAUR etc) and commune or conurbation level. The issue remains controversial, with FNE in 2009 calling for a moratorium on the construction of new incinerators, whilst the Grenelle called for an end to using contracts specifying minimum tonnages to be delivered to incinerators – clearly the base of the incineration industry. But any integration with spatial issues appears to be at the very local level, with traditional reliance on incineration no doubt offering the easiest path for hard-pressed municipalities.

Contrasts

Sectoral planning exists in all these fields in France, including strong national forms in road, rail and energy. In water and waste integration with spatial planning is probably greatest as most sectoral work in these fields is local or regional. In energy and transport the risk of silo decision-making is greater, given the weakness of national spatial planning, perhaps most strikingly so in ports and airports. However, we have seen the impacts of *amenagement* thinking coming out to some degree, most definitely in the post-2007 period with the Grenelle and SNIT, affecting the road, rail and river, and energy zones quite strongly. Here environmentalist drives have integrating effects, which are then to be territorialised in various ways by regional plans and pushes of various kinds. This is the French way now, a system of part-public part-private, part-central part-regionalised governance. This is really existing spatialisation and territorialisation, a complex process of considerable interest to outsiders.

PROJECTS, THE SYSTEM OF "DEBAT PUBLIC" AND THE SPEED UP ISSUE

Infrastructure planning in France is neither purely strategy led nor purely project led. In some fields the emphasis is more on strategy: in road, rail and energy. But some projects are so big as to escape, to a degree, large strategising. The obvious examples relate to Paris, especially its airports, and the two major ports schemes of Le Havre and Marseille. Whatever the force of a sectoral or more general strategy, projects matter, so decisions on projects matter in themselves. Infrastructure construction has been a big matter for public action in France, in its current mode since the 1940s, but it only started to generate big protest movements in the 1970s. Finally, in the early 1990s, one of the symbols of French progress, the TGV, was almost stopped in its tracks as the campaign against the route of the TGV Mediterranee found real force. This led quite quickly to a rethinking of the way in which big projects should be managed, and the most interesting element of this is the system of public debates.

Public debates

There have been public inquiry processes functioning in France for a long time, and these have been updated a great deal since the 1980s. Thousands of such inquiries take place throughout governmental levels each year. Via a two-stage reform, begun with the "loi Barnier" in 1995 and completed by the law of 2002, all projects over a certain size have the opportunity to come under a set public-debate procedure. The size thresholds are similar to the UK Planning Act 2008. A body was created, the Commission Nationale du Debat Public (CNDP), to manage the inquiries on each scheme if the CNDP saw a case for such an inquiry (CNDP 2007a, 2007b, 2008). The CNDP is an independent body, funded by the state, with presidents appointed by the government. The reason it is (I think) genuinely independent is that it does not make decisions. All it does is frame the debates. The developer has to organise and lead the case during a public inquiry that can take no longer than four months. Within two months the CNDP president for the inquiry publishes a report summing up the findings, but with no recommendation. Within three months the developers must then say what response they will make: go ahead as planned, alter, or withdraw the project. The CNDP normally also has some follow-up role, as a guarantor of the developer's commitments, though this is variable across presidents and cases. In part this is difficult, as the CNDP is a very slimline organisation, just five staff in the central secretariat supporting the three senior presidents, alongside a commission of 19 members meeting monthly, with other support appointed just for the duration of individual inquiries.

The function is to give a public space, normally very early in the project, to discuss the need, form and desirability of the project. About one third of the (over 50) projects so far have been withdrawn (two cases) or modified in major ways. Projects then have to go through all the normal stages of gaining public approval. So the procedure is nothing like the UK's 2008 Planning Act system. It might well speed up the overall process, by removing later blockages and confusions, but that is not the prime intention.

The system has real strengths, which have been built up gradually by innovative practice over more than a decade. I was struck by the commitment to doing everything possible to make a level playing-field for participants. Anyone wanting to participate can do so, and any body can get help to present its case during the run-up period to the inquiry. Leaflets presenting arguments are standard for big companies and small associations, published by the Commission. Fundamental issues of need are open for debate. Full details are written up each day, and participants are kept informed throughout, and then into the often long post-inquiry developments.

In other words, this is a radical experiment in participatory democracy, taken directly to the community or communities affected. It is unlikely it could now be abandoned – the strong French associational world would not accept this now, I was told. It is not purely linked to projects either. The Commission has made clear its readiness to organise public debates on wider issues, and has done this on some occasions: on nuclear waste policy in 2005, on transport developments generally in the Rhone corridor and on nanotechnologies. It offered to organise a governmental debate on energy in 2005, and the Grenelle in 2007, but (perhaps not surprisingly) the governments on both occasions preferred to hold onto control of these initiatives. But no doubt even the fact that such national debates took place owes something to the deepening of public debating experience in France led by the CNDP.

It is interesting that, although the invention in 1995 owed much to the Quebec system formed in 1978, no other body has copied the French system. This must say something about the political system in France, with its impressive combination of democratising energy and driving state power – both phrases may sound rather stereotypical and outdated, but compared to some countries, they may be appropriate. This power and energy threatened to collide from the 1980s and so generated this innovation.

The tensions in the system derive from the element of incoherence perhaps inevitably present in all democratic components (Saward 2003). Beyond local decisions (if such things can exist now) or small-scale isolated communities, representative democracy must rub against participatory democracy. The debates on the Flamanville and Penly nuclear power stations were boycotted by the Sortir du nucleaire NGO, given that it was clear that the government was not going to back out of the projects. Whilst the Commission did all it could to keep the debates open, in cases such as these, the tensions are clear. If a firm government strategy exists in a policy area which is already site specific the space for debate is reduced, though there may still be important issues and even reasons for participating to raise public consciousness.

There are other difficulties specific to all participatory democracy (Subra 2007). Expertise can be variable, on all sides, as can the quality of discussion. However, it can be argued that this might affect all political elements, representative institutions included. It is probably in the nature of all participatory democracy systems that some public debates will make more valuable contributions to a process than others. Clearly the French system is very inquiry heavy, with myriad processes over many years. The importance of the debate being early in the scheme process was stressed to me. This seems to be an essential point. But it could mean that schemes change or simply disappear later, with an overall waste of societal resources. And of course no system can resolve all conflicts by any means. The third airport for Paris was too thorny a problem, for example, and the conflict over the new Nantes airport was not solved by a public debate.

On balance, the system has great attractions. In particular, the detailed experience built up, and the commitment to proper management of the public sphere, seem worthy of emulation – in fact, perhaps some direct copying where appropriate. The system goes refreshingly against the winds of business and state speed up and slimming down. While this is no substitute for proper long-term planning and public governance, it could slot in as a valuable part of almost any public system.

To give one brief example: the public debate for the Charles de Gaulle Express rail link from central Paris to the airport was held in 2003. This is not typical, but interesting as an extreme case. The developer proposed one route, which was heavily opposed by many interests who promoted an alternative route. After a heated public debate process, the developer decided to adopt the route of the opponents, and the scheme is likely to be built by 2014 (see Figure 6.4). For French readers, Subra (2007) gives fascinating accounts of how public debates affect the existing geopolitical dynamics in France.

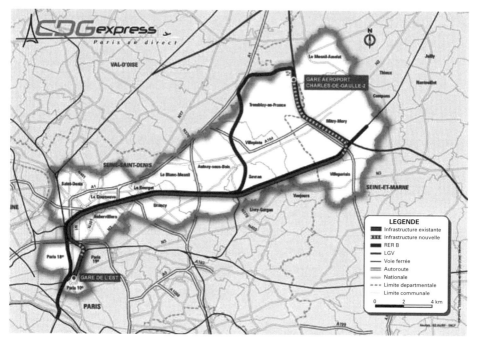

Figure 6.4 Charles de Gaulle Express showing chosen route after CNDP public debate, when developer chose opponents' alternative route, 2003. (Source: Ministère français de l'écologie, du développement durable, des transports et du logement webpages retrieved 24/11/2011)

Timing

In the UK, business has long insisted that slow state decision-making is a problem, and this led to the 2008 Planning Act. This is an issue that has been raised in France. For example, a lobby group called the Federation Nationale des Travaux Publics, through its website "Equiper la France", complained about the 10 or 15 year period needed to realise a project, and called for a national transport plan, as in Germany. So this lobby group's reaction was: better planning is needed. State officials did not seem to see slowness as a major complaint of business. It was widely understood that the public demanded very great care in deciding on projects, and that this would inevi-tably need time. This may reflect the continuing dominance of large groups like EDF or the big state role in road and rail construction, as against the more private-sector landscape in the UK. So it may change.

This suggests that calls for speed up increase as private power increases: as privatisation and liberalisation spreads. The Netherlands, perhaps half way between France and the UK in this sense, has a more generalised concern on timing, but still not the speed up calls experienced in Britain. The French system is undoubtedly heavy on consultation stages, a response in part to the enormous rise in the contestation of schemes from the 1980s onwards, as documented by Subra (2007). The French are very much aware of this conflict, and of the need to manage it carefully and intelligently. They therefore accept the need for time, and expect that developers will build this into their planning. Developers appear to accept this and do indeed cater for the necessary stages. This may be because they are still different sorts of developers from those in Britain, which may be drawing more on risky financing, acting speculatively, and be tied into complex international links, all elements which make long-term planning harder for businesses.

CONCLUSIONS

In France we see a fascinating dynamic balance. There is a coordinating and steering state with national ideas and national capacities, but with both the latter having been reduced in recent years. This is part of a model transformed by regionalisation and public debates and similar public engagement innovations – a re-articulated state with several dimensions of democracy. This permeates all decision-making on big infrastructure, and the various elements of territorial planning that exist. We should remember that France remains a unitary state, but one in a half-way-house to the federalism or quasi federalism of Germany and Spain. It is not necessarily a comfortable half way, one that almost demands steady innovation, and certainly struggles to take on the implications of the changing state form, the liberalising dynamics from within and without, and the pressures of business and environmentalism.

The landscape is tougher for new big infrastructure, something which is doubtless widely welcomed. France's big geography has been largely conquered by the post-war drives, even though this conquest is now seen as being in need of renewal or major change to encompass ecological or competitive purposes (depending on the viewpoint). So the emphasis is on maintenance, minor change, demand reduction and efficiency, thus reducing the pressure, it is hoped, on any infrastructure needed in future decades.

To sum up, the picture we have is:

- From above, a state which continues, in one shape or another to both prepare sectoral planning schemes (for roads, rail, electricity and gas at any rate), and to territorialise these and all other policy areas periodically, in a sense continuously; and
- From below, regions which adjust their idea of their future spatial development by taking into account the state's proposals, and the forces coming up at them from departments, cities, and perhaps sideways from other regions or neighbouring countries.

The following are areas that are valuable for learning or inspiration:

- Territorial articulation: the French blend of strategic thinking and up-and-down coordinating politics;
- Public control: keeping (rebuilding) state control of key infrastructure sectors, in one form or another (even if this is on a downward slope in France too); and
- Public debate: the value of continually constructing democratic approaches – the CNDP, the Grenelle – in very different forms.

CHAPTER 7
SPAIN

Spain is like France but more so, in several respects. It has retained some powerful central drives, but sits within an utterly changed polity, now federal or even potentially splintering. There are still all-Spain ideas and forces in several infrastructure fields, but the pressures that bend and restrain these are enormous. We are looking here at a story of stresses and strains, and of responding creatively to these: a picture that changes in front of our eyes. This feature of major change in the case countries in the last few years has been common to all the countries with the partial exception of Germany.

This chapter has the same broad shape as the other case studies, though nothing on national spatial planning, for reasons that will become obvious, and nothing on the project dimension. I did not find that there was any special innovation in the projects field, and this may reflect the fact that most interests have not seen it as a critical area. Certainly big projects can have difficulties and take time, but my impression was that, as in France, the national agencies and large companies are used to building this into their processes.

SPANISH GOVERNMENT AND INFRASTRUCTURE INDUSTRIES

The composite Spanish state

In the 1970s Spain swung from a highly centralised dictatorship to a decentralising democracy, one which has continued to pass powers downwards from Madrid to the 17 autonomous communities (which I will often call regions or CCAA for short). The central government retains considerable importance in financing much of the infrastructure investment and in leg-islating the ground rules for each sector, including rounds of privatisation and liberalisation (Chari and Heywood 2009). The regional governments have increasing force in this area, as they take over some financing, regulating and ownership roles, although their influence varies between fields.

The constitution is not precise on the division of powers, and this has left ample room for struggles between the centre and the regions, medi-ated by the constitutional court. In principle the division in Articles 148 and 149 gives most infrastructure roles to the centre, certainly where it can be argued that the transport, water or energy matters affect more than one region. Ports and airports are unambiguously in Article 149 (for the centre). But reality has not been so tidy, with change pushing the limits of inter-pretation that the present constitution can manage. This change has come since 2006, especially with new statutes for several CCAA, and most con-troversially for Catalonia (Keating and Wilson 2009). These statutes have some extraordinary clauses. Valencia stipulated that it must be awarded all the gains made by any other region in subsequent reforms (leapfrog con-stitutional reform). Andalucia and Catalonia both required allocation of state spending according to formulas, for Andalucia by population, for Catalonia by contribution to GDP (fiscal-struggle constitutional reform). The statutes also refer to water, with some regions explicitly rejecting any future transfers of "their" water.

Spanish politics is permeated by this vertical dynamic, with both left and right parties becoming, in part, regional baronies which must be satis-fied by any central government. Only one government since 1975 has had an outright right-wing majority, from 2000 to 2004 (though others were right-leaning coalitions) and that could not turn back the clock on decentralising pressures. This is backed by powerful sectoral policy communities: the "hydraulic" one is referred to by Moral (2000), others exist for roads, ports and airports, tightly linked to sections of the government in Madrid, to the regional governments and to the construction sector. Planning has no such policy com-munity, with the centre of gravity at the city or, at most, regional level.

Several ministries matter for infrastructure, with the public works or development ministry (called Fomento since 1996) responsible for trans-port, that for environment (now linked with agriculture) managing water and (minimally) waste, and energy being part of the Industry ministry. There is rel-atively little coordinating force across these three areas, apparently making the Spanish government a classically horizontally-sectoralised operation. Sectoral conferences joining the centre with the regional governments mod-erate this in many areas (Arbos et al 2009, Colino and Parrado 2009, Parrado 2008), joined since 2004 by a conference of presidents of all 17 communities along with the prime minister. The sectoral conferences are least functional in the areas of transport, water and energy, and there is a general expert opinion that these fields have seen major problems:

The problem with the central administration of the state (ACE) in Spain is that it does not really know what it is, where it is going, or what it "wishes" to be. The transformation of a centralized unitary system into a decentralized system, perhaps in evolution to a federal or a confederal form, leaves the ACE in some intermediate zone between its traditional superiority and new threats of marginality.

(Banon and Tamayo 1997 p.85)

Moral (2000) analyses the problems in water politics and ascribes the basic cause to "the incomplete restructuring of the Spanish State (in a nearly-federal way)" (p.3). Romero (2005) emphasises the "formidable problem of institutional coordination", with no culture of cooperation, no clear functioning of intergovernmental relations and no transparent and efficient financing system. He sees the sectoral conferences as a precarious mechanism (pp.64–66).

The Spanish state is "compuesto", composite, to use Colino and Parrado's phrase (2009), not specifically designed to be that way as in a federal system, but obliged to function as a real whole between the centre and regions. Practice has often fallen behind this reality and made coordination a struggle. This affects infrastructure especially because much of the currency of vertical politics is here, a fact that is particularly visible in transport or water fields, even if other areas may be more fundamentally important. This has been made stronger by coinciding with the era of competitive neoliberalising capitalism, whereby lower tiers of government engage in races to be the most attractive to global investors. Indeed, this is surely one of the forces fuelling the centrifugal process within the Spanish state.

Infrastructure industries

Infrastructure has long been big business in Spain. Figure 7.1 shows the high growth of spending since the mid 1980s, much of it fuelled by EU funding. Spanish infrastructure companies are now big players internationally. Though the collapse of the construction boom in Spain in 2008 cut back this growth, these corporations have been globalising and as a consequence are not dependent solely on Spanish economic trends. Privatisation came quite late to Spain, with the major changes after 1996 (Arocena 2006).

In transport, much remains public in rail and roads, though the latter has extensive motorway private-concession systems. Airports and ports remain in public ownership, but with ports already effectively controlled by regional governments, and airports being transferred in some cases under new statutes. The privatisation of Madrid and Barcelona airports was also being targeted for completion in 2012, as well as possibly some share of the rest of AENA, the airports agency. Energy has a few large private corporations, with Endesa and Iberdrola dominating in electricity, and Gas Natural in gas, but the

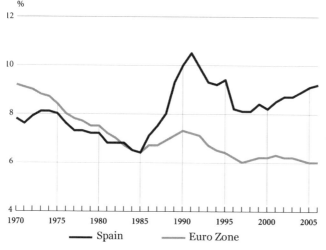

Figure 7.1 Growth in infrastructure investment (non residential construction) in Spain (higher line) and Eurozone 1970 to 2005. (Source: La Caixa, 2007)

transmission and transport systems are under public control. Water is mixed, with multinationals like Suez having much of the market, but also public companies providing services in many regions. However, the state, in the shape of the nine venerable hydrographic confederations, a national planning process and now much regional power, has overall control of the water field.

So, there is a thoroughly mixed economy in the provision of utility services and in infrastructure investment. This may tip towards more private control with the next central swerve to the right, but at present it is balanced between a powerful set of oligopolies and bodies that remain state controlled. However, those bodies are increasingly in regional government hands, which significantly affects the scope for wider links to territorial planning.

THE FORCES WHICH GENERATE THE PERCEIVED NEED FOR NEW INFRASTRUCTURE

Limiting demand and construction is not something that has gained much force in modern Spain. Many interests focus on catching up with the living standards of the rest of Europe, including high-mobility and high-energy lifestyles and economy. When the EU discussed energy and carbon reduction targets from the late 1990s, Spain was always allowed to increase its relatively low level per-capita emissions. Therefore, the fundamental source of infrastructure generation is easily found – a central growth imperative – with relatively little stress on environmental factors until the last decade or so, and very little emphasis on radical green objectives. Spain has had a lot of development, urban and infrastructural, in the last 30 years and, property crashes notwithstanding, this is unlikely to end in the short term. There is something to plan, should anyone wish to do so. Nevertheless, since the late 1990s some elements of the green agenda have been grasped, and so infrastructure like high-speed rail lines and wind farms are seen, as elsewhere, to be environmental pluses as well as motors of modern development.

Historical geographies

Here I look at two dimensions of the drivers in Spain: long-term geographical and historical character, followed by the ideas of the country. Spain is large, meaning that links between the highly dispersed urban cores have been weak. This is accentuated by the difficulty of the terrain in many areas, creating a broken up geography of small territories living rather autonomous lives, and with strong local and regional cultures. Before the development of the tourism territories of the last 50 years, Spain was a country of many small towns and a few strong cities, mostly on the coast, but with Madrid commanding the state from the centre of the peninsula. Madrid was very deliberately built up under the Franco regime, creating industrialisation in the region, and holding back the main Catalan and Basque industrial zones. This was a powerful and successful regional development policy. Arguably this dynamic, created under the dictatorship, has continued due to its own momentum since the 1970s, without any explicit policy. In the last half century coastal development has become more linear, particularly affecting large parts of the Mediterranean coastal zones, and the larger cities have all generated metropolitan zones – in the case of Madrid a massively expansive and expanding one, now occupying wide swathes of Castille (Juliana's Gran Madrid, the "ferropuerto" of Spain, 2009 p.205). But the essential separateness of the country's regions has not changed, and so all exchanges of resources become exchanges between these territories, whether water, energy, goods or people. Of course there is a much greater fluidity to this than in the past, with air travel having opened up connections to many people in a massive way, and high-speed rail and car travel doing the same to some extent. But it is still a segmented country, a set of islands. An interviewee referred to the 17 internal policy spaces of the country, referring of course to the political reality of the "estado de las autonomias", but this rests on at least 17 (probably 70 in fact) physical–environmental realities, which then infuse policy making, at regional as much as at all-Spain levels.

Juliana's discussion of current Spanish politics (2009) begins with a foreword by a Valencian geographer, J V Boira, who argues that geography is at the core of Spanish politics, much more so than in any other European state. He reels off a list of news items, making a powerful case that this is true, and that public debate is particularly dominated by infrastructure matters. This is at the heart of what could be called the hydraulic and construction state: paths chosen for over a century to try to build Spain's way out of backwardness.

This now includes a continental dimension, with ever more discussion since the 1990s of Spain's need to connect across the Pyrenees – we see this in the Plan Director de Infraestructuras (PDI) (Ministerio de Obras Publicas, Transportes y Medio Ambiente 1994), and it figures in the Plan Estrategico de Infraestructuras de Transporte (PEIT) (Ministerio de Fomento 2005) as well as all recent energy policy schemas. Secondary but important emphases are links with Portugal and Africa, especially in energy terms.

Very generally, Spain is an easier country to fit big infrastructure into, given its wide open spaces that are often near deserts and which tend to have low population density and little attraction for contemporary farming. Traditionally, and still to a significant degree, fitting in roads, rail, pipelines, electricity lines and wind farms has generated less opposition, especially well clear of big cities, than in northern European countries. But this varies with the configuration of infrastructure forms (linear, point), and the shape of "available" Spanish spaces: very spread out cities with big spaces in between and major coastal urbanisation (this last element can be a helpful feature for airports, some transport links and desalination plants etc).

Multiple territorial imaginaries

There are multiple mental maps at work in Spain, on many issues (water and energy, certainly), even if in transport areas there may be rather more agreement on the shapes of the future. This flows naturally from the presence of multiple radically-rooted and distinct standpoints, which do not go around with a same-centred map of the peninsular in their heads. On the other hand, within the big corporations (public and private) there is still a view of the whole territory that is based in the middle around Madrid, if perhaps it is less Madrid-centred than before. This perspective has not gone away.

I believe that "old plans" incorporating resilient ideas have had some continuing afterlives in Spain. I was reminded of the presence, in the early 1970s, of plans showing the development of certain major axes along the Ebro valley and along the coasts, not centred on Madrid, and how all plans since then seem to have had some sort of awareness of these axes, even if more stress has often been laid on the main radials until the last decade or so. The PDI maintained an emphasis on building up a more grid-like road structure, and this has now emerged in the rail plans. Water and energy planning is by no means predicated on a radial model, having to adjust to the evident reality of a very polycentric Spain/peninsular. So the memory of (in principle not at all valid) old plans, and the implicit spatial images residing in sectoral plans, both carry a sort of implicit national spatial imaginary through to the era of the "Spain of the autonomies" (a decentralised, formally unitary, but in reality fast if messily federalising state).

As in France, much of the same tension is visible. It is widely considered that the "default position" of the Spanish state is of an imaginary centred on Madrid, conceiving of the territory and its connections around a radial structure beginning or ending there. This seems to me to be a reasonable description for much of Spanish history up to the 1980s. The road and rail systems are strongly marked by this history, which clearly has an enormous historical inertia – a critical feature of all imaginaries, in that they cannot be easily reformulated by an act of the will, or at least not if they go too much against the grain of geo-history. However, other features are affected by quite opposite forces which go against this radiality, and these were in play throughout Spanish history. Perhaps the most critical is the absolute importance of the sea to Spanish economic and cultural development, meaning that core regions were precisely on the "edge" of the state, far from Madrid (Suarez de Vivero and Rodriguez Mateos 2002). Other features are the eternal importance of some big rivers, making them the centres of urban and agricultural development for millennia, and the nature of the mountainous relief, breaking up the country into regionalised blocs resistant to transforming and imposed radiality (much more so than in England or France).

These "non centralising" features have in a sense been revalorised in the post-Franco era, so that the force of lateral corridors and of grid patterns has begun to emerge in all its accidental and untidy complexity. The revalorisation has been multifaceted, driven by politics but running along economic and cultural tracks, and increasingly with a partly complicit Spanish state. So this has set up a dialectic with the continuing central economic and political power, which can still bask in the strength of the inherited infrastructure systems of road, rail and air transport. This is less the case with ports, water or energy infrastructures, which on balance favour the edges against the centre: the emerging Madrid super-region is rather a long way from most of these resources, perhaps one underlying reason boosting its fear of the break up of Spain. It should be emphasised that this super-region now occupies the whole of the central plateau, given the reconstruction of this core zone by road and rail, so that the central regions (including both Castilles and Extremadura, as well as Madrid itself) now can look more easily to Madrid, only an hour or two by high-speed rail from their provincial capitals. So the contraction of Spain's geography instigated through road and rail investments has had contradictory effects, which must feed into the competing spatial imaginaries. There is "core Spain" and lots of "non-core Spains". Both are powerful, and core Spain is more likely to speak with one political and economic voice than the others. So the imaginaries associated with both are likely to maintain power, perhaps in a rough-and-ready balance (unless the state breaks up).

The competition is not a simple division between a radial model ensconced in Madrid and a polycentric one flourishing around the peripheries. It is present within all regions, with many in Madrid committed to the polycentric idea of Spain, and many in the non-Madrid regions keen on maintaining excellent connections to the capital and so giving full investment value to radial work. Nevertheless the balance of perspectives does vary a great deal.

There is still a force which brings these competing ideas together, residing mainly in the central government's competences in most infrastructure sectors, through which it can hand out largesse to all regions (the Basque country and Navarre excepting, who collect their own taxes, and partly for that reason, are richer). But the most recent round of constitutional reform, through the revision of the statutes of the autonomous communities (regions), is reducing these competences, both by giving more tax-raising strength to many regions, and by handing over more infrastructural competences to some regions (intra-regional rail and smaller airports, for example). In due course the invisible fight of the imaginaries, which has taken place in the negotiation of each bit of infrastructure investment (whether airports, roads, rail or water), may become more visible, as regions express their own priorities with "their own" money.

THE SPANISH PLANNING SYSTEM AND COORDINATING ARRANGEMENTS

Spain is the only country studied here that effectively has no all-state planning arrangements (Gil Olcina and Gomez Mendoza 2009). The 1978 constitution gives all planning powers to the autonomous communities and lower government bodies. The centralising dreams of Francoist governments were firmly banished. When, in the 1990s, an effort was made under a powerful minister, Jose Borrell, to introduce some sort of central government steer, sections within the Public Works ministry were created to deal with planning and spatial policy. This included references to a Plan Nacional de Ordenacion in the revision to the 1975 planning law, and an attempt to promote the PDI, which was challenged as anti-constitutional, stepping on the rights of the autonomous governments (Farinos Dasi et al 2005).

The constitutional court did allow that the central government had the right to coordinate its infrastructural competences, as the PDI did, but this was the last time that a government has tried to bring together transport, water, waste and urban development issues in one document. A small spatial planning unit existed in the Environment ministry, the result of an attempt to introduce an environment-led coordination between 2004 and 2008 (under the minister Cristina Narbona, incidentally Borrell's partner). This led to a raft of work on sustainable development strategies and climate change responses, but nothing that was really able to challenge the hardwired sectoralism of Spanish central governing. The environment ministry was merged with agriculture in 2008.

Some sectoral planning has had wider effects, most obviously the PDI but also with the two transport plans of the successive right and left governments, the PIT of 2000 and the PEIT of 2005. The first was a simple road and rail investment plan, whilst the second was more ambitious, dealing to some degree with airports, ports and metropolitan transport investment, as well as discussing demand management. The PEIT set out broad guidelines for road and rail again, with rail investment planned to count for about 50 per cent of investment from 2005 to 2020. But the six plans intended to detail each mode were never published, and the integration with territorial and environmental issues was rather weak (Serrano 2009a). This reflected the sectoralisation within and between the ministries, with a traditional Fomento push for big new construction.

It is vital to note, however, that the 17 regional governments have power over territorial planning, which then guides the autonomous power of the municipalities over urbanism. At least it guides it in principle, even though municipal autonomy is exercised forcefully: the construction boom ending in 2008 was a powerful example of the failure of almost all regional governments to exercise strategic influence over the country's 8,000-plus municipalities. At any rate, by 2007 11 regions had strategies in place (Benabent Fernandez de Cordoba 2006, Moral 2008, also see Rodriguez 2010 for a recent overview). In some cases, such as the Catalan case I will look at later, this "ordenacion del territorio" has had some real impact and, as we will see, allows some coordination of spatial planning and infrastructure planning.

Several writers see a tendency in practice for central government sectoral planning to over-rule territorial planning within the regions. Benabent (2006) points out just one case where a region has a formalised procedure for involving the central government in its regional plan making, in Andalucia. An administrative lawyer also from Andalucia (Perez Andres 1998) brought out the depth of work on this area by lawyers around Spain. He chronicled the systematic tendency, as he saw it, for the central government to invade the regions' spatial planning powers in sector after sector: he details water, roads and ports for example. He argued for the more effective regulation of inter-administrative relations, to avoid the continual recourse to conflict resolution via the constitutional court. This should be a general law, specifying how the state and regions should act across all sectors, in order that they collaborate more effectively. He saw this as being similar to the procedures in Germany, where both sides have to involve the other in all planning exercises. Other-wise he saw the regions' spatial planning possibilities being much reduced by the sectoral planning of the central government. Whilst practice has, it seems, improved since 2004, these arguments doubtless still have weight.

Romero Gonzalez (2002, 2005) suggests that the central government responds to its inability to do any territorial planning by making national (sec-toral) plans in a centralised way, tending to exclude the views of regions in the process (also see Romero Gonzalez 2009). He refers to various plans of this kind (erosion, forestry, sustainable development), but is clearly thinking above all about the transport infrastructure plans and the national water plan (PHN). Moral (2008 p.4) makes this explicit for the case of water, pointing out that the strong water planning of the state bases itself not on territorial planning at all, with the 2001 PHN hardly referring to territorial planning issues. Moral refers to the "impossibility of an explicit formulation of a territorial model at state level" (p.8), and it is not clear if he is deploring this lack (an unlikely idea in contemporary Spain), or simply comparing it to the relatively strong water planning at that level. There has been some aspiration to a more active role centrally in recent years, and real efforts were made in the preparation of several strategies after the PEIT to develop an approach that was more environmentally sympathetic (Serrano 2009b chronicles some of this).

Such integrative thinking is pushed, in part, by the integrating requirements of the EU water directive, hence by forces outside the normal play of Spanish politics. Others push similarly for a more cooperative model in territorial matters, such as the group of academics and professionals calling for a "new culture of territory" in May 2006, and who awarded their first prize in February 2009. This manifesto is notably vague when it comes to saying how this may be done, suggesting differences between those in favour of more centralising or more decentralising paths. However, the manifesto does say clearly: "the state administration cannot avoid considering the territory as part of its responsibilities", calling for a revision of the land and planning law: the ley del suelo (Nueva Cultura del Territorio 2006).

All commentators agree that Spain's "big planning" is very limited. As Farinos Dasi et al (2005) put it:

> In Spain, the process of decentralizing political power and the unfinished process of constructing a composite state have made it impossible to set up institutional mechanisms to coordinate strategic spatial planning policies.
>
> (Farinos Dasi et al 2005 p.219)

The way things actually work out in each sector at each time depends on political circumstances at the two levels: the personalities of ministers and overall party philosophies. The looseness of the framing leaves open a wide play for different practices, even if it is becoming increasingly the norm to try to consensualise strategies and approaches in the key areas I am looking at.

CATALONIA – A REGIONAL CASE, IF AN UNUSUAL ONE

It is clear that the central–regional link, and the operation within regions, is critical in Spain. Each region is different, and as I know Catalonia much better than other parts of Spain, I present here a brief study of how this region (or nation, as many citizens would say) deals with infrastructure planning, alongside its spatial planning. It should be noted that the period studied largely relates to the period when the Generalitat (the Catalan government) was run by a left–green coalition, from 2003 to 2010. This put a far stronger emphasis on planning than the right-wing governments before and since. As such, the exceptionalism is doubled, with planning having a higher profile in Catalonia than in most of the 16 other regions, and being given far more resources during those years.

"Infrastructuralism" arrived in Catalonia in 2009, with the agreement of the Pacte Nacional per a les Infraestructures (Generalitat de Catalunya 2009). This was developed by the department of territorial policy and public works, primarily by the transport divisions rather than the spatial planning sections. However, it was signed by government ministers as a whole and by some political parties, business organisations and trade unions. This had a strong Catalanist politics, particularly stressing the historic deficit perceived in financing infrastructure: it was partly a lobbying instrument. The Pacte has relatively little spatial content, though with many lists of specific projects. So we need to look more closely at spatial and sectoral planning processes to find out how well these link together.

Catalans have a strongly independent understanding of their position within Spain: a competing all-Spain imaginary, against what they see as a Madrid centred and radial idea. Several interviewees argued this: the stress on Madrid Barajas airport as the intercontinental hub (unfairly excluding Barcelona), and on the radial bias of the high-speed train, which has excluded the two transversal routes that are equally critical to vertebrate Spain: the Mediterranean axis and the Ebro axis. It was finally conceded in the transport department that the first of these had been given European-category importance, committing action sooner rather than later by both French and Spanish governments (and perhaps eligibility for EU funds). But this was seen as too late and too little. These examples are then usually followed by discussions of bad management by other Spanish bodies such as Renfe's trains and the confederations dealing with water shared with other regions. Finance usually follows after this, arguing that Catalonia subsidises the rest of inefficient Spain (as argued in the UK by London and the South East). The Pacte stresses this dimension (Generalitat de Catalunya 2009 pp.16–18, 31–32). A central government view would point to the recent investments in many elements of Catalonia's infrastructure, including high-speed trains, local trains and the airports, and the quite advantageous financial deal struck in 2007. So it is not clear how far Catalan resentment fits the more recent polycentric understandings in Madrid, at least in some sectors.

In fact the Catalan government actors I interviewed did not report great difficulties in dealing with Madrid ministries, with each sector able to come to agreement with their professional colleagues: road planners negotiating routes and deals across administrations, and similar experiences in rail and energy planning. Even an independent Catalonia would have to work out how to use much of its water with Aragon and other neighbouring regions, and the Generalitat has a firm seat at the water confederations tables. Of course, there is conflict. The minister argued that the Generalitat can win arguments because it has the municipalities already on its side, and so can present a good deal to central government with a pact already agreed. An example was the setting of the high-speed train route through Catalonia. The central government imagined a service with very few stops, whilst the Generalitat wanted more, to achieve its own territorial goals. Fomento planners pointed out that this is always the stance of subnational governments. In the case of Catalonia, a rich region, negotiation could be supported by sharing the financial burden of investment. So a more "territorially friendly" model has resulted, with more urban areas served, without great loss of journey time. This is the normal give-and-take of political perspectives, perhaps reflecting somewhat different mental maps, but not showing deep chasms of difference. Certainly each case has to be negotiated through and the hard cases take up the energy of politicians, probably more than that of civil servants used to smoothing the everyday paths of cooperation. The absence of any overall schema, as would exist in the Netherlands or Germany, makes such case-by-case approaches inevitable, and means that integration with spatial planning always remains a matter of negotiation, not something set in advance or overall. The Pacte of 2009 was an example of how this negotiation is orchestrated, at the most general level.

The minister in the introduction to one plan said that "our obsession with planning continues". The tripartite government elected at the end of 2003 managed to pursue a perhaps unique (for Spain) package of territorial and sectoral planning. By 2010 a complete set of sub-regional plans had been approved for Catalonia, alongside plans for public transport, road and rail infrastructure, ports, airports, cycling, and many county or growth-town plans, as well as the enormously important coastal protection plan rushed through in 2005 (Departament de Politica Territorial i Obres Publiques 2006a, Esteban 2006, Nello 2010). This has been done without revision of the General Plan for Catalonia of 1995, which is generally regarded as weak. This was because it was sensibly decided that if this revision took priority, the plans with most bite might never get done. So the general plan revision will be done later. In the meantime the sub-regional plans were framed with a set of general criteria, a demographic and economic model, and the transport plan.

How far is the sectoral integrated with the territorial? The answer is a lot, but with weaknesses. The territorial plans focus on few issues, protecting open land, fixing transport infrastructures, and marking urban development zones. They do not deal much with water, energy and waste issues, which are seen to be only conditioning in long-term and complex ways, and not really structuring change in the medium term. As such, the integration with those three sectors is not great, even though in the case of water there was some consideration of water issues in territorial plans, before the opening of the desalination plants in 2009, which have in a sense let all Catalonia off the integration hook by providing extra water quantities previously undreamed of (Agencia Catalana d'Aigua 2009).

The case of transport planning is more critical. The prime transport plan (PITC, Departament de Politica Territorial i Obres Publiques 2006b) became an input to all the territorial plans, with the exception of the metropolitan Barcelona plan, which was allowed to work out its transport investment side by itself. Planners argued that they had had an input to the PITC, so it already incorporated an idea of the spatial model of the country. This seems reminiscent of the leapfrogging idea of the Dutch on sectoral and spatial interlinking. Nevertheless it was also clear that some "independent" sectoral planning was carrying on as always, with the road planners probably pursuing their schemes to some extent as before, and the airport planners putting together a very strongly growth-oriented plan, approved in 2009, which would send Catalonia's aviation carbon emissions on a long-term upward course, and takes no notice of the capacity of high-speed rail to cut aviation demand massively. For rail there was more interlinking, given that the two big schemes emerged out of spatial planning (in the case of the metropolitan orbital route) and out of the clearly held idea of a future polycentric country, for the transversal railway linking the secondary towns of Catalonia without passing through Barcelona. This idea of "polycentric Catalonia" was the prime theme of the state secretary in charge of territorial planning in the ministry, himself previously a geography academic (Nello 2007a, 2007b). He came into government with this very clear idea, and it chimed with the needs of the government to present a new direction. Polycentricity naturally links sectoral and spatial planning, and so is a highly convenient and simple mental map with which to steer things in a relatively integrated way.

The combined political and administrative push since 2004 has served to improve the integration of transport and spatial planning. The Catalan statute of 2006 gives extra competences in the areas of airport and rail infrastructure, so there may be good prospects for carrying the plans forward in an integrated manner. But how far such autonomous community integration can "add up" to a wider cross-Spain picture is more doubtful. The model of the cumulative making of a jigsaw for the peninsula relies on the pieces already having harmonious patterns. Competition between the different parts of Spain has been somewhat restrained by state-wide governance, in the case of ports and airports, and by the planning and funding of rail and road infrastructure. In the absence of such central steering, it is clear that great differences might accumulate between different regions (or nations). For some purposes good subnational integration may be sufficient. But infrastructure sectors are largely those where spillover effects are systemic.

NATIONAL SECTORAL PLANNING AND INFRASTRUCTURE

There are some big sectoral stories in Spanish infrastructure: high-speed rail's explosion in very recent years, after the Madrid–Seville one liner of 1992, the surge of wind farms in the last 10–15 years and the ongoing tangles regarding water given two massive droughts since 1990. I concentrate on these parts here, and especially on water, which has the complex fascination of a theme at the core of the country's future and as an idea in itself. This means leaving most energy, road, port, airport and waste issues out of detailed discussion. Sectoralism is common (another good example would be the road sector, see Rubio Alferez and Borrajo Sebastian 2009). Some brief contrasts are given in Figure 7.5 at the end of the chapter.

Wind power

It will be clear by now that spatial planning is subordinate to sectoral planning at the national level: at least we have seen this is so in explicit and formal terms. Here I explore this theme of explicit and implicit frameworks through the three headline examples. One is easily disposed of. Wind power has come up from below, as has all power generation since the end of centralised planning in this field. Developers and local or occasionally regional governments have promoted wind farms within the national support given since the late 1990s by feed-in tariffs (Szarka 2007). Regional governments have in some cases undertaken some indicative planning, but as in many countries in Europe, wind power has emerged in a more hit-and-miss way, finding its spaces (Martinez Montes et al 2005). Trajectories are doubtless different in each of the autonomous communities, but the case of Valencia is showing how difficult the role of spatial planning can be (Moragues-Faus and Ortiz-Miranda 2010). Here a Wind Energy Plan was passed by the regional government in 2001, designating 15 areas. Most of these were heavily contested, and the whole issue ended up in the courts, meaning slow progress on the ground in most designated areas. In this case at least, the proactive spatial planning approach, designating precise zones for investment, has not been very successful.

Of course, the grid connections still need planning, and this has benefitted from the national support which gives it priority alongside the feed-in tariff regime. So there are spatial planning elements, but there is, as far as I can see, no wider idea of how much wind energy should materialise where. This is consistent with strong liberalisation, which has had force in the wind farm area, as investment is not as massive as in conventional power stations for example.

High-speed rail

In the case of high-speed rail lines, the matter is more complex. Rail has long been the poor relation next to roads (Figure 7.2). But a consistent line of advance has been present since the PDI in 1993 (Figure 7.3). It can be argued that this represents a commonly understood, and in a sense "obvious" geography of the peninsula, connecting the urban cores, subject to some complications of cost, terrain and so on. This schema has then moved

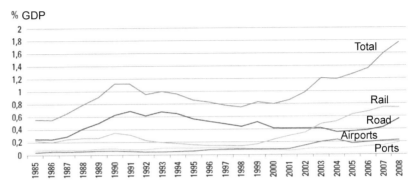

% GDP

Figure 7.2 Investment by the central state and its agencies on four transport sectors as percentage of GDP, 1985–2008, from yearbooks of Ministerio de Fomento. (Source: Fundicot, 2009)

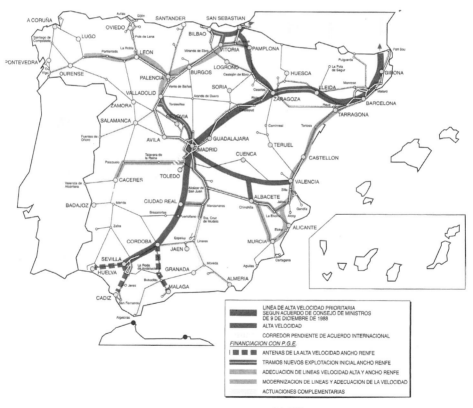

Figure 7.3 Expected long-term action for rail network in PDI.
(Source: Ministerio de Obras Publicas, Transportes y Medio Ambiente, 1994)

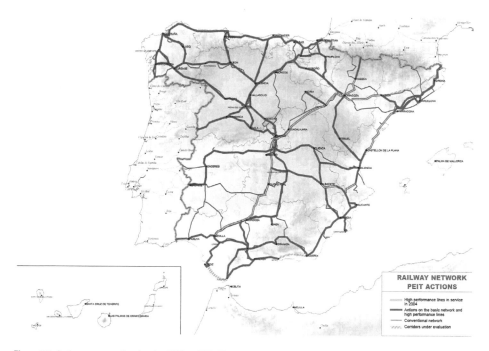

Figure 7.4 Actions proposed under the PEIT to 2020. (Source: Ministerio de Fomento 2005)

to execution largely by the power of regional politics, generating commitment from successive governments, each one keen to support regional power bases, whether of their party or the opposition. Successive ministers have driven forward lines to their home areas in Valencia, Andalucia and Galicia, bringing a fast link to Madrid from "mi tierra" (my homeland) has been irresistible to Spanish politicians, central and local, and looks set to continue to fuel the investment, whatever economists or critics of other kinds may say, and whether or not public money can be found in the short term. The minister in 2000–2004, Alvarez Cascos, promised that no provincial capital would be more than four hours by rail from Madrid. As the minister Magdalena Alvarez put it in 2008: "we are weaving Spain with cables of steel" (El Comercio 2008). Station locations and routes are then negotiated within this drive, often with very weak linking to territorial planning considerations (Ribalaygua et al 2002, Urena 2002, 2006).

Sometimes new links do not work: the Toledo to Albacete line had to be closed not long after opening due to a lack of passengers. I rather doubt that much would be different in the impossible situation that Spain had a national spatial strategy. So the implicit idea of the country does matter, and at the same time the continuing force of politics is the basic driver. Certainly, this is not territorial planning and not a rationally schemed consideration of public investment: of the choice of modes, of the trade offs with port and airport investment and of the best way to link the high-speed rail network to the conventional network (which is in some cases being allowed to decay). The imaginary is much more vague and looser than that, but it does frame decisions, incarnated every now and then in specific maps, in the PDI, the PIT of 2000 and the PEIT of 2005 (Figure 7.4). So, it is sectoral planning, of a kind, set within this very general spatialised framing.

Water planning and spatial planning

The case of water is not so easily described (Arrojo 2006, Candela et al 2008, Lopez Pineiro 2006, Moral 2006, Sauri et al 2009). The PHN required by the 1985 water law was finally approved in 2001, which is testimony to the difficulty of water policy in Spain. A first draft had been issued in 1993 under Borrell's period as minister, and in fact water formed part of the PDI. This had been effectively a national water infrastructure plan, drawing up an all-Spain picture of water resources for the first time, and proposing to rectify once and for all the perceived imbalances afflicting the country: part wet and part dry. This involved massive water transfers as well as continuing the programme of reservoir construction: an average of 20 reservoirs a year were being constructed in Spain from 1950, adding to the 270 already existing by then. The most controversial element was the transfer of water from the river Ebro to the south and to more northerly parts of Catalonia, but many other transfers were proposed. Revisions cut down the transfers by the time of approval in 2001, but left in the Ebro transfer. The Socialist government then removed this element in 2005 and began a new programme with more emphasis on water conservation, and also promoting desalination plants as the new answer to localised shortages. There are different views on how far this is a really deep seated reform, with some commentators seeing the hydraulic machine as still being intact, with 100 reservoirs still in the planning list, and cheap and wasted water still the norm (Arrojo 2008, Moral 2008, Naredo 2008). Generally it has not been possible to challenge the underlying unsustainability of the development model "requiring" the water works (whether for farming or urban development): in other words to make the water–spatial planning link.

This relates to the deeply problematic play of local and regional politics in the water area. Newspaper commentaries by water experts noted the heavy political battles underway over water in 2008–2009 (Estevan 2008, Prat 2008, Wendling 2008). The 2004–2008 drought set one region against others even more than usual. Catalonia saw itself as being crucified by other regions which had water available (these regions in fact answered that they were just as much in crisis), and in general one feature of water battles is that the historic nationalities call as much for solidarity in this case as other poorer regions call for it in relation to financial transfers (Moral 2000 p.18). So, there is no easy play of losers and winners, especially in drought periods:

that is, much of the time. Water cuts up the Spanish political landscape in its own original ways, which one might have thought would strengthen the hand of central government: the honest arbiter above regions. But this works only up to a point.

Arguments about water works are arguments about the relationships between territories: ecopolitics in the purest and classical sense. Moral (2008) draws this out by discussing experiences in the Canaries and the Balearic islands, where the understanding of carrying capacity is naturally quite advanced, leading to more or less effective attempts to stem development, tourism and anything else which will further stress water and other hyper-scarce resources.

There is a fundamental misfit of the governing institutions in relation to water. The post-1993 phase in water politics stems from a frontal collision between hydrological planning in its historic form and the equally historic maturing of the state of the autonomies (as Moral makes clear in his periodisation of the recent years, 2008 pp.26–30). Most commentators (for example, the administrative lawyer Embid Irujo 2008) are clear that water-basin agencies remain the key to water planning, and that the state must adapt to make these work, essentially by incorporating the state institutions (central, regional and local) into the bodies which run the basins (for now the confederations), in such a way as to make water sense in themselves, and so as to make the right links with territorial planning. In general terms, this means giving the regions more say in the confederations.

Territorial planners are perfectly aware of the need to plan areas taking into account water issues, and, the other way around, to design water policy by thinking of the urban or other expected developments. This is explicitly written into regional plans in some regions, including the Basque country and Andalucia. But traditionally water policy has been a more powerful sector than "ordenacion del territorio", and in many areas this dominance continues.

In a sense the PDI and the 1993 PHN were attempts to make links between the two fields, showing how the development of Spain would be conditioned by the development of new infrastructure, including that for water. Water in the shape of the PHN was to be used to "vertebrar Espana" (or "structure Spain", to use the common metaphor – see, for example, Naredo 2006, p.24): that is to say, to give underlying skeletal support to a development model, in the same ways as road, rail and air transport systems structure a country. These national planning exercises may have laid out a sort of continuing template, for Spain overall, but in the field of water this mentality has been fundamentally challenged. Because it was based on a highly growth-driven and "concrete-driven" idea of the country, this one linking attempt (the PDI with the PHN adhering to it) probably had only confusing effects.

Since then, a national idea of future spatial development has not really existed. The underlying idea still dominant in Spain is the growth drive, which is therefore content with no hydro–spatial planning link. In a sense, when that link is made, we will know the growth drive is being challenged. The desalination investments (along with many other factors) have put off that moment. So there is little sign of a new, coherent way of dealing with all-Spain (which here are largely all-Iberia) questions. The thinking is still about water problems as a "limit to growth". Furthermore, climate change is not yet the forcing element: for example, a recent article used an energy analysis against desalination plants, pushing back to transfers as being better for climate change progress (Gil Diaz 2008). As with every other debate, water refracts issues in a contested way.

Spain therefore has a government and governing structure not easily suited to make sense of the water conundrums, and, partly because of this and partly for other historical reasons, finds it very hard to make integrated efforts to bring water and spatial planning together. The new water-culture movement has clearly shifted some parts of the "technical" considerations, but has been unable to change the "deep politics" of water issues (to interpret a bit of commentary from Arrojo 2008). In particular, water remains tied up with rural and agricultural politics, and some see more change coming from the new EU agricultural regime than from the water zone: how these two work together is being closely watched (Garrido and Varela Ortega 2008, Moral 2008). The calls in Spain for a "new culture of territory" to go alongside the new culture of water are beginning to have effects in some regions.

These matters remain continuously important. The urbanisation boom of the decade or more to 2008 meant construction in many of the most water-poor regions of Spain, which are now supported by major investments in desalination plants. Spanish agriculture's most profitable areas are mostly supported by irrigation, which can cause long term damage to ecosystems and to future farming prospects. As such, the long-term basis of Spain's economy relates to water issues, causing enormous political pressures around water decision-making, and around urban planning decisions. It is possible that the end of the construction boom may allow some reprieve, helping the development of both regional plans and basin plans.

CONCLUSIONS – PROBLEMS AND REAL MODES OF FUNCTIONING

The weak link between infrastructure planning and spatial planning

Each sector of infrastructure is planned with few considered or explicit links to territorial issues, beyond that which is essential to all basic planning, fitting in with existing geographies and with expected demand. In some sectors (ports, airports, waste) all-Spain planning simply does not exist in an explicit form. On others (rail, road, water, energy), far more developed planning is present at central government level, whether in statutory plans or high-level strategies. These cite objectives, one of which is normally about the properly balanced development of the whole country. So, in a sense, these plans do have an overall territorial objective. Implicitly this does go quite a long way, structuring the overall form of policies. But in no case is this made explicit, at least since the days of the PDI, whose philosophy was developmentalist: growth for all, with a subsidiary emerging discourse of (light) environmentalism (Diaz Zoido 1994). The reasons for the territorial–sectoral gap can be summarised as follows:

- The *lack of constitutional powers for the central government in territorial planning*. In principle, central government has no right to think territorially and to set up a territorial planning role as Borrell did in the mega ministry.
- The *sectoralism of Spain's central ministries* and even of the directorates within each ministry. This appears stronger than in the Netherlands and France, with less effective mechanisms to combat it.
- The *weakness of collaborative mechanisms with the regions*, often referred to as a constitutional design failure, in a weak Senate role, and with the absence of formalised mechanisms of interaction.
- The *persistence of powerful policy communities*, which are linked to the corporation powerhouses of the Spanish economy, the foundations of the political economy behind several decades of economic growth and internationalisation. The character of the Spanish state's central administration reads across all too easily to the political economy of the big corporations, in construction, energy, water and telecommunications, alongside the banks which are linked to them and often share control, most with headquarters in Madrid.
- The *political dynamics of Spain*, which has been shifting more of the bones of power to the regions. Spanish politics is a battleground, and this area lies in the midst of the smoke, or to change the metaphor, sits right on the fault line of the earthquake zone. *Spanish politics is territorial politics*, much more so than in the Netherlands or the UK (even taking into account the non-English parts), and even more sharply than has become the case in unitary France. *The Spanish state is a regionalised state*, but a rather incompletely regionalised one, with few clear federal type ground rules.
- Academics have long seen the fight over scale as a critical element of the fight over state forms (Jessop 2002, Swyngedouw 1997): *scalar politics matter*, especially in Spain. They form the daily bread of the main passions at play. So when a new domestic policy direction is under construction, such as sustainable development or a climate change strategy, the central Spanish administration has to struggle mightily to ensure its wishes have real effect around the

country, even assuming it is internally united on this area – something that is rarely the case in most governments.

Qualifying elements have been identified in this chapter, including the planning processes within the water, transport and energy sectors, and the regional coherence secured in some parts of Spain by bringing territorial and infrastructural elements together to some degree. The development of democratic governing traditions in each autonomous community over nearly 30 years means that Spain is equipped with an effective regional government system, which can in principle be the foundation for working on the most critical areas of infrastructure policy, conservation and demand management, as well as pushing transitional investments for renewable energy and local and regional public transport. Adaptation to and taking advantage of the EU has been quite impressive too, and is another valuable part of the governing capacities developed. So, there is a wealth of planning and governing potential in certain dimensions.

Real workings – long run and implicit mental models, with heavy contestation

Given planning weaknesses, how do things really work? We must go back to historical geography and mental maps. One interpretation is that the whole territory of Spain rests on an enduring base of urban nodes and of corridors, most of which go back centuries, and which have constituted the basis for all planning and individual project-making of the last 50 years and more. The present functioning of the country, its watering and travelling and fuelling, was largely set up during the twentieth century, but on the foundations of those nodes and corridors. There are exceptions, above all the explosion of some urban areas, particularly around Madrid, on the tourist coastlines and on the islands. The road and rail investments since the 1970s have reinforced this structure, with the most recent high-speed rail campaigns arguably giving even more centrality to the big regional capitals. To an extent, big all-Spain planning has its own historical logic, which hardly needs explicit talking through. In the twentieth century one territorial paradigm or trajectory dominated: growth, modernisation, development and "catching up". With this base, "Spain" has always been able to grasp and act on the "big geography" of the peninsula. The limits of this idea would be in thinking about major transitions, to adjust this long-enduring base to transformed ecological processes. A low carbon society would need such extensive changes that only large challenges to implicit ways of imagining the geographies would begin to offer paths to surviving. Big and explicit planning would be needed.

In Spanish circumstances, it is necessary to consider what was lying behind approaches to planning in several of the sectors. This might then show an implicit territorial framework with which policy makers were working, even if this was not explicitly clear in some approved strategy. It is valuable to excavate implicit national framings, given that these are much more common than explicit ones. In Spain, in particular, the territorial sharpness of so much politics may encourage thinking in this direction: implicit politics matters a lot, and it remains implicit *because* it matters a lot. As such, the implicitness is strongly selected for. Fuzziness is at a premium in the sort of continuous maneuvering for position formed by the interplay of the central and regional.

I would hazard that there are central mental maps for the sectors for the primary all-Spain actors:

- *Ports*: not at all clear. Essentially following past trajectories, that are rather limited in linking to full logistic chains, intermodally, but a stress nevertheless on wider international positioning in Mediterranean and Europe.
- *Airports*: at first bipolar Madrid and Barcelona, with Madrid the global actor, and regional airports with essentially international tourist roles. Later gradual regionalisation, with liberalisation and spread of low-cost airlines, so more multi-centric.
- *Roads*: radial and main corridors to early 1990s, grid universal motorway structure after that, but subject to more regional negotiation (i.e. a looser mental map).
- *Rail*: based on a model of big-city Spain, seen within a European network, though in 2000s gradually taking on intermediate cities (most provincial capitals), thus leaving "holes in the doily": gaps which risked falling out of the rail net.
- *Energy*: at first stable with power stations as nodes, established cross-Spain networks, from 2000s becoming more fluid with large increase in gas supply (three or four ports as nodes) and more wind energy. Both leading to more multi-centric idea of the country: less radial and more grid-like with extra lines to be built to provide extra security. Portuguese, European and African connections getting more important.
- *Water*: early on the classic emphasis of dry (south and east), and wet (north and west) division, with long-distance transfers built into the image. Later moderating of this to reduce transfers, with dependence on localised desalinated production, so more micro and regionalised approach: more negotiated. Old idea still powerful of a water-threatened territory, heavily ecologically challenged and very hard to resolve, and even added to by biodiversity and climate challenge issues.
- *Waste*: hardly at all a national idea (perhaps inevitably), but transposed to the regional scale where issues are fought out over local versus sub-regional solutions, and big infrastructure versus behavioural-change approaches.

Figure 7.5 Sectoral planning and the degree to which it is linked to all-Spain and regional spatial planning. (Source: own elaboration)

	How much sectoral planning at all Spain level	How far linked to wider spatial planning	Relationship to spatial planning in regions
Transport as a whole	Several strategies but mostly on road and rail systems	Limited, only through underlying common ideas	In some regions, planned alongside regional government spatial plans
Ports	Only informal control via oversight of port masterplans	No explicit spatial links	In some regions, planned alongside regional government spatial plans
Airports	Strong hold via investment and central role in airport masterplans	No explicit spatial links	Important political area, rather than a primarily spatial matter
Roads	Strong steer through finance and regular strategies	Largely sectoral considerations	Normally tied into roads plans for regions, though those may link to wider spatial plans
Rail	Strong steer through finance and regular strategies	Largely sectoral considerations	Tied into territorial plans where this is working in regions
Water	PHN as base for national strategy	Not explicitly tied in at all	Few territorial plans put strong emphasis on water
Energy	Little on generation, strong planning on transmission and transport	No sign of this	Worked out sectorally with all regions
Waste	No national planning	Not at all	Planning is primarily at regional level, or locally

On this basis, several tendencies are visible:

- In almost every sector a shift to more polycentric mental ideas, probably less bipolarity than before as Madrid–Barcelona duo relativised;
- In some areas less structuring overall, looser mapping, leaving more space for negotiation with regional and private actors; and
- In some sectors Europeanisation having some significance.

There are other dimensions, such as energy security, or water threat, which do not fit neatly in the three more cross-cutting trends.

These postulated implicit maps broadly cover the whole of Spain, and have an idea of the coherence of this territory – this is clear in the thinking of those concerned with rail and road networks, with energy systems, and, to an extent, water planners (who are obliged to work on EU directive lines for water basins, not by regions) and airport planners, who remain important allocators of investment in some cases (with some scope it seems for cross-subsidising). The major difference from around 25 years ago is that this view, modulated though it is, now meets the solidly settled views from at least 17 other centres of power. A rail planner in Andalucia will have a quite different take on what is needed from one in Castilla la Mancha, even though their territories adjoin, and each will be different from that of the Madrid ministry and of the main infrastructure agency/company AGIF. Each will have different agendas for high-speed rail (how many stops, where, what routes), for conventional rail and for local systems. This was clear in the Catalan case study. Hence the dominance of the central mental map is challenged from several directions.

So we come back to contestation and democracy, with the interaction of three levels of government, and elections occurring at some point or another almost continuously. This creates a complex set of force fields, working diagonally, up and down. Of course other powers work as well, above all business power, partly through mass media. But much comes down to the working of the electoral democracy. Some regions may be closed oligarchies, but even then there may be a rich associative tissue. In some sectors or subsectors there tends to be a strong response: with waste incinerators and intrusions into urban areas, for example. But new roads, rail lines and wind farms have tended to be accepted, and even expansions to airports, as in Madrid and Barcelona in recent years, have been relatively uncontested – not that there have not been objections, but the weight of public opinion has not been on that side.

CHAPTER 8
GERMANY

INTRODUCTION

Germany sits in this panorama of approaches to guiding major infrastructure in a rather paradoxical way. An outsider would see Germany as a highly planned and regulated country. This could be expected to include the approach to the arrangement of infrastructure systems at all levels. And this might be expected to be particularly the case given Germany's fame in engineering and high technology fields, able to stand alongside countries like Japan, the US and France. In some respects this expectation is fulfilled. Germany is a country equipped with high-quality infrastructure systems in most fields, whether for transport, energy, water or waste. At least to the view of the outsider, it is not a country which needs to agonise too much about critical infrastructure gaps. In recent decades much has been built to deal with any incipient gaps. But, it is not a country which finds these decisions especially smooth or easy to take, certainly in some fields. In some ways, infrastructure plays to German worries about its governance systems. It is interesting to look at this concern, in the midst of relative success, as well as what this stems from and how the country responds. This then provides the context for the relationship to spatial planning. As we will see, that relationship is also not easy in some dimensions.

These frictions and struggles relate in part to factors that we have seen in other cases, including the transitions to a more liberalised and Europeanised regime of governance (Streeck 2009). But they also have features which are peculiarly German, including the process of reunification and the nature of German federalism. It is this combination of more general and quite specific infrastructure dynamics which makes the German case especially interesting – interacting with as always the particularities of the ways Germany does spatial planning. As ever, this chapter is a continuous blend of needing to understand planning processes, at all levels, and the wider processes of governing and economy. This is challenging, as in other cases, and I can expect again that German readers will find my perspective rather different from the one they would tend to have.

GERMAN GOVERNMENT AND INFRASTRUCTURE INDUSTRIES

State and government

Federalism dominates any discussion of this field (Green et al 2008, Jeffery 2003, Schmidt 2003). Germany is the only formally federal state I am studying, and only one other case would have been available to me in Europe: that of Austria. While I described Spain as semi- or proto-federal, the differences are important. Germany has been constitutionally federal for over 60 years: time enough to evolve ways of managing policy in all areas. This is a process of continuous change, but one based on past-accumulated practice, with a powerful constitutional court having autonomy within its own developed traditions. Since reunification in 1990, one major reform package has been passed (Federalism 1) and a second one is still under discussion (Jeffery 2008, Scharpf 2008). The general drift of these packages is to confirm the shifting of the balance of power towards the 16 federal states, or Länder, away from the federal or central government.

In the fields of planning and infrastructure, the key features of the system are as follows (Pahl-Weber and Henckel 2008):

- Spatial planning is primarily the domain of the Länder, and of the municipalities, whose rights are also protected in the constitution. The federal government only has residual or indirect powers in this area. Municipalities are in a strong position, not necessarily having to follow regional plans, though their plans should not be in contradiction to those. Regional planning is highly variable, with different forms and weights in different states, and with regions sometimes lacking identity and political weight. In addition, much is left to the project level, with all levels of planning not necessarily covering infrastructure issues fully.
- The federal level has powers in some infrastructure sectors, above all road, rail and waterways, but has much less influence in others, where the Länder have most competences: ports, airports, water and waste. The 2011 energy law gives the federal level direct input to some electricity transmission planning for the first time. But all

sectors have elements of shared power, so cooperative federal practice is, in principle, the norm. Finance and political salience give federal force even in areas where they may appear to lack constitutional strength, but this is rarely unfettered.

- Germany is certainly in the consensualist (and of course federal) camp under Lijphart's framework, and powerfully so. Germany is a "polycentric polity" (Goetz 2003 p.21), based on cooperative federalism, although competitive federalism has a strong constituency in the rich and powerful southern states of Bavaria, Baden-Wurttemberg and Hesse. Political scientists have long debated the risks of logjams and stalemates within the federal system, and this can certainly be seen to be present in some infrastructure fields, where slow and tortuous decision making is absolutely common. Decision-making has to be based on the majorities in the Bundestag (lower house) and the Bundesrat (upper house representing the federal states), in effect requiring a continuous "grand coalition" governing machine, covering most major parties. Only for a few years in the 1980s did one party, the Christian Democrats, hold overall power in both houses. However, the stalemate anguish of political observers is not necessarily shared by many social interests, who may be very happy with the glacial rate of progress, giving ample time to debate dubious schemes or wasteful projects and reach fuller societal consensuses. Business interests on the other hand have sometimes been less content, complaining, as in other countries, about the costs of democratic complexities and delays to investments.
- Within the federal government, ministries are strong, so silo effects are significant. This partly reflects the almost universal presence of coalition governments, with portfolios handed out to different parties. The environment ministry, for example, dealing with water, waste, renewable and nuclear energy, might be held by a Green or Free Democrat, whilst the economy ministry is held by another party, with other political positions. This complicates the character of German federalism, by setting up tensions within each federal government.

Infrastructure provision

Some changes to the infrastructure industries have been similar to those in other countries, but some are specific to Germany. Privatisation in the transport sectors has been uneven. For rail, DB has been a formally commercial company since 1994, but with all shares still held by the federal government. It acts much like many globalising corporations, buying firms in aviation, road and other sectors around the world, with only 40 per cent of its turnover apparently now from rail operations in Germany (Engartner 2010).

It still dominates rail in Germany, and manages all infrastructure (as DB Netz AG), but freight services are already diversifying, and this is expected to gradually spread to passenger services after 2012. Roads remain in public ownership and operation, with only sporadic and usually unhappy use of toll and contract systems. Planning and financing roads is a joint federal and Länder matter. Ports are mostly public, with the city-states of Hamburg and Bremen in the leading positions, though each has created ports agencies for everyday management in the last decade. Airports have been privatised or quasi-privatised (Frankfurt, for example, is still publicly owned but run completely commercially by Fraport), but many key airports, including those of Berlin and Munich, remain in joint federal, Länder and sometimes municipal hands. So, the transport sectors, whilst working often in highly commercial styles, retain many public levers for steering.

Energy industries have never been under state control. Gas and electricity have strong players like RWE and EON in dominant positions, in charge of much generating and gas-importing capacity. The transmission of electricity is divided between four companies, with full separation from the generating arms of these companies being forced through by the EU and the German competition authority (Bundesnetzagentur) during the 2000s. The wind generation, solar and biogas industries have many small companies, as well as investment by the big corporations, especially in the emerging offshore programme. There remain many of the local Stadtwerke companies in municipalities, where the local authorities run power, water and waste services, and, in fact, some have recently bought privatised concessions back. These are represented by a national industry body (the VKU) lobbying for their interests, alongside the multinational power of RWE and EON. So, there is a rather more fragmented energy landscape, compared to the position in France, Italy or even the big oligopolies of Spain, the UK or the Netherlands. This affects energy infrastructure planning.

Water and waste show similar features, with the Stadtwerke sector holding its own in many areas, alongside big corporations taking over many contracts. As such, a mix of profit and not for profit pressures is present, with less overall commercialisation and internationalisation than in the energy sectors.

As a whole then, the provision of utility services is in a mixed economy, with significant public control in some sectors, commercial norms fairly generalised, and powerful private or semi-private companies in key positions in some cases: DB, RWE, EON most obviously. Federal control is rarely absolute, with the waterway sector being an exception, where the federal agency (WSA) plans, finances and manages the entire main-river and canal network. At the same time, Germany is a country gradually in transit to a liberalised and Europeanised infrastructure-provision model, and this has affected all planning and decision-making processes in the most recent period.

FORCES GENERATING THE PERCEIVED NEED FOR NEW INFRASTRUCTURE

Germany is a large country with a traditionally big appetite for connections, both within the country and wired into its continental neighbours and the rest of the world, by air and by water. It is a big energy user too, though recently energy consumption is levelling off somewhat. It has big modern infrastructure provision, some going back to the nineteenth century, but for the most part from the massive reconstruction and renewal effort of the decades after 1945. This means that there is a high standard of provision in all sectors, in international terms. Investment continued after the post-war drive, with nuclear power stations appearing in the 1970s, and motorway construction continuing through to 1990. Reunification sparked another enormous round of investment, as eastern Germany was raised to the standard of the west in all the major infrastructure sectors except energy, where weaknesses remain, particularly in grid systems. This has dominated the two decades since 1990, an era which made infrastructure-planning high politics. It is a process that is now beginning to come to an end, with 12 of the 17 "German Unity" projects announced by Chancellor Kohl in 1991 virtually completed, and most of the rest nearing completion. Just the rail link from Berlin to Nuremberg, in a section through mountainous terrain, is likely to take until at least 2017. Investment in rail and, to a lesser extent, road has continued in the west, but overall is in decline. This is joined by the new renewables sectors, especially wind power, largely in northern and eastern Germany. Another factor generating pressure on German infrastructure systems is its position as "European transit land number one". On top of the heavy north–south transport flows, the east–west flows have built up enormously since 1990. To this are added increasing amounts of energy flowing across borders and through the country, whether in pipelines or by electricity transmission.

On the other hand, this picture of a big infrastructure machine must be moderated by remembering that Germany has long been a country with high ecological aspirations. The power of the green movement since around 1970 shows no sign of declining, with Green Party representation in the federal government from 1998 to 2005 and in many Länder governments since the 1980s, including most recently a Green prime minister in traditionally conservative Baden-Wurttemberg. This means that major questions are often asked as to the need for any new infrastructure, to a greater extent than for the other large-country cases of France and Spain. Opposition movements to reservoir construction were already in full force in many regions in the 1950s (Blackbourn 2006), and the fights against nuclear power since the 1970s have impeded its spread in many Länder, as well as the finding of waste deposit sites, and have continued to press for the phase-out of existing stations by the 2020s, with no political parties committed to a new round of construction. In 2011, following the nuclear crisis in Japan, the government reversed its position of 2010, when it had intended to extend the life of existing stations, and proposed to close these by 2021 – a challenging target, given the complexities of energy goals. The encouragement of renewable energy has been consistent since the 1990s, and energy conservation is increasingly a top priority in federal spending and regulation. Support for public transport has in part a green base, with rail and local public transport schemes seeing continued federal funding, which also supports port investment. So not all green pressure is anti infrastructure-investment, but is often about encouraging the most ecologically favoured modes.

Germany's geography is polycentric, with no city or region dominating the federation. This goes back in part to the late unification of 1870, which brought together many autonomous cities and principalities or as in Bavaria, a kingdom, none wishing to lose all power to Prussia and Berlin. This has had a range of effects, which distinguish the country from many others in Europe. It encourages the mentality of aiming to give equal treatment to all parts of the country, a goal embodied in the constitution, the Grundgesetz of 1950. Federalism cements this polycentricity institutionally, formally dispersing power, with some sort of veto powers held by the bigger Länder, and a strong tendency for Länder to group together for particular goals: the eastern ones to press for continued preferential financial treatment, given their relative poverty, the northern ones to support their port economies, and the southern ones to fight to retain more of their tax wealth. Reunification was in a sense just a variation on this theme, with a shared assumption that the east must be brought up to common standards, however much this would cost.

All this sits within the evolving debates on what to do about the big imbalances in the country between a thriving south, an uneven north west and a struggling north east, which is lower on every possible indicator despite billions of post-reunification funding over 20 years. The consensus on keeping equal conditions gradually becomes more brittle. But this reality means that the part of the country with spare capacity and spare energy is emptying out, with shrinking cities the most discussed theme in German planning. As such, the renewable energy output in the north has to be transferred to the south if this overall linking between settlement and infrastructure cannot be corrected. This is the real macro social-economic-environmental spatial planning issue of Germany.

This geography and politics affects the national imaginary which may lie behind debates on the future shape of the country and long-term transitions. On the one hand there is probably a shared all-Germany sense, to a much less contested degree than in Spain, stemming from shared histories, endeavours and cultures. German nationalism, whilst not seamless, is strong, and so gives cohesion alongside an enduring commitment to internationalism and Europeanism. This gives a basis for all action at the federal level, such as the reunification drive. On the other hand, this imaginary can only go so far, with strong commitment to more fragmented understandings of the country, the "Heimat" sense of the local homeland like the "pays" of France, with this also adding up to loyalties to Länder to some extent, even when these were artificial constructions of 1945–1950 (or 1990). So the imaginary may be a shared one across Germany in many ways, but one of a rather pixelated or regionalised variety, giving only so much hold for any wide-scale strategising or debating of futures. The insertion within a European consciousness is important too, as I discuss in a later section.

So, the infrastructure challenges emerging from this set of pressures are mixed. There have been big pressures over decades to connect the country, whether by road, rail, sea or air, internally and externally, and to give it full power-systems, and this was extended to eastern Germany after 1990. That meant that a need for new or modernised infrastructure was generated, but this was held back by the force of ecological consciousness and politics, which questioned the need for new water or power or transport investments, and wondered about the scope for demand management. Sometimes this green view also encourages new rounds of infrastructure investment, so it is unlikely that anyone can conceive of Germany as a country with "finished infrastructure". On the contrary, policy makers envisage much new investment, with wind power on and off shore expected to expand massively over the next two decades, alongside solar power, and the accompanying grid and storage systems needed to make these work. Competing conceptions would be for new nuclear, coal and gas investment. It is true though that infrastructure investment in the transport, water and waste fields is more likely to take minor or updating forms, aimed at lower carbon systems rather than changes involving large new infrastructure systems. In that sense there may be less of an infrastructure planning challenge than in some other countries from now on. However, that is assuming that the current cross-party agreement, or at least rhetoric, on low carbon futures continues. Road and aviation travel remain buoyant, and this could generate new demand for building in those fields.

THE GERMAN PLANNING SYSTEM, NATIONAL SPATIAL PLANNING AND INFRASTRUCTURE

The weight of spatial planning in Germany is at local and federal state level, not with the central government or Bund (Farber 2005, Gust 2007, Henckel et al 2010). That is a critical factor when studying the relationship of the spatial planning system and the various sectoral planning or investment efforts in the infrastructure sectors. It means that the areas which have most force are, by and large, those least apt for steering big decisions about spatial matters on a macro scale. Of course this varies, as some Länder are large and already contain within their borders critical spatial distribution options, certainly in sectors like waste, renewable energy generation and, to an extent,

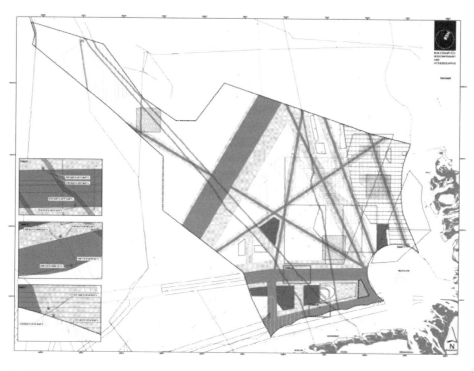

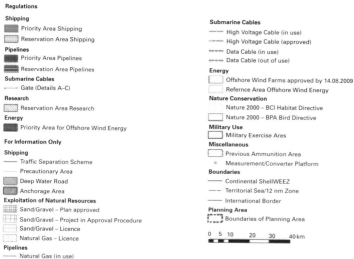

Regulations

Shipping
▓ Priority Area Shipping
▒ Reservation Area Shipping

Pipelines
▓ Priority Area Pipelines
▒ Reservation Area Pipelines

Submarine Cables
←— Gate (Details A–C)

Research
▓ Reservation Area Research

Energy
▓ Priority Area for Offshore Wind Energy

For Information Only

Shipping
—— Traffic Separation Scheme
—— Precautionary Area
▒ Deep Water Road
▓ Anchorage Area

Exploitation of Natural Resources
▦ Sand/Gravel – Plan approved
▦ Sand/Gravel – Project in Approval Procedure
☐ Sand/Gravel – Licence
▨ Natural Gas – Licence

Pipelines
—— Natural Gas (in use)

Submarine Cables
～～ High Voltage Cable (in use)
～～ High Voltage Cable (approved)
✳✳ Data Cable (in use)
✳✳ Data Cable (out of use)

Energy
☐ Offshore Wind Farms approved by 14.08.2009
☐ Refernce Area Offshore Wind Energy

Nature Conservation
☐ Nature 2000 – BCl Habitat Directive
☐ Nature 2000 – BPA Bird Directive

Military Use
☐ Military Exercise Ares

Miscellaneous
☐ Previous Ammunition Area
▫ Measurement/Converter Platform

Boundaries
—— Continental ShellWEEZ
--- Territorial Sea/12 nm Zone
—— International Border

Planning Area
▢ Boundaries of Planning Area

0   5 10   20   30   40 km

Figure 8.1 Plan for German part of the North Sea.
(Source: Bundesministerium für Verkehr, Bauund Stadtentwicklung, BMVBS 2009c).

water management. But for some sectors, such as energy transmission and transport, big transport systems and for some water issues (which often cross Länder and even country boundaries), the Land and lower levels of planning are less appropriate. My account here concentrates on these supra-Länder levels, mainly the role of the federal government. This may seem eccentric, given the arrangement of German spatial planning and the realities of a strongly federal state. There is, I am sure, much more to say from within Länder practice, which I did not have the opportunity to study in any depth (see, for example, Pahl-Weber 2010). But for the really large infrastructure issues, some emphasis on the all-Germany scale can I think be justified.

The 1965 spatial planning law, revised several times since then (most recently in 2008), gives plan-making powers primarily to the Länder, in cooperation with lower authorities for regional planning within Länder, and to local authorities, for binding land-use plans (Aring 2010, Sinz 2005). In fact the 2008 revision of the law weakens the Bund further by no longer requiring states to follow the principles of spatial planning laid down by the Bund – although so far states have not taken advantage of such latitude. Durner (2009) gives a strongly critical account of the missed opportunity that the revision represented, with sectoral planning likely to be left even more dominant than before. The revision does give an option for the Bund to make spatial plans for "Länderubergreifenden Standortkonzepten" (location concepts dealing with more than one state), specifically including ports and airports, but it remains uncertain as to whether this power will be used, and it is explicitly stated that this has no binding power over Länder spatial planning. Otherwise the only cases of federal spatial plans are the marine ones for German territorial waters in the North Sea (see Figure 8.1) and Baltic Sea, of 2009, mostly made by the BSH, the federal agency for sea and shipping (BMVBS 2009c). This shows what the Bund can do when it has clear powers and no Länder directly affected, although even here the coastal states control the first 12 miles, and so exercise real influence via their own plans: even marine planning is a joint endeavour.

Otherwise the role of planning at Bund level is to offer some overall framing by means of a range of soft instruments. The most important ones are as follows:

- Research and intelligence, based on the work of the BBSR, the research agency of BMVBS (the Transport, Building and Urban Development ministry). This includes the spatial planning reports produced every four years (Lutter 2005).
- Perspectives or Leitbilder-type exercises, undertaken irregularly since the 1970s (Aring and Sinz 2006a, 2006b, BMVBS 2006a, 2006b, Knieling 2006, Sinz 2006, Staats 2006). These are produced not by the government directly, but by the MKRO (Michel 2005), the mechanism bringing together all spatial planning ministers

of the Länder with the BMVBS (such bodies exist in all sectors, as a key part of federal functioning). Main meetings are normally annual, but there are committees, including one on transport and infrastructure.

- Liaison with other ministries in their sectoral planning. This is given weight by the fact that several sectoral laws have "spatial planning clauses" whereby they must ensure that their schemes fit in with relevant spatial planning proposals. These would be predominantly those at Land or lower levels.

None of this work is easy, as the federal spatial planning presence is quite small, since 1998 no longer enshrined in a ministry with the word planning (Raumplanung) in its title. There is a strong tendency to split up government at federal level, with the large ministries communicating but not necessarily cooperating fully. The spatial planning section is in one part of BMBVS, whilst key transport decisions on the federal transport plan are in other sections, as are road and rail planning, and ports and airports policy, with the whole operation divided between Berlin and Bonn (Dienel 2007). The BBSR is also in Bonn. But the interest of the current German system is in seeing the scope and potential of "light" high-level spatial planning. This has a very particular character, just as the French DATAR model does, and is quite different in character from the (traditional) "heavy" Dutch high-level system. For Germany, it naturally fits the federal system, and so particular features would not play across directly to non-federal countries, but some of the overall principles can have wider relevance.

The key is the force of data, debate and dialogue, in relation to underlying imaginaries, and so the degree to which wider all-Germany understanding may infuse both the everyday realities of Land and lower-level spatial planning and the force of sectoral planning. We will discuss these aspects in the following sections.

Does federal spatial planning have adequate strength?

Almost certainly the German system is, in some senses, too light to have serious effects in most circumstances. In the terms of one German analyst, the system depends on relatively weak instruments in a pyramid of planning responses, with federal work largely in the monitoring and information-based modes, and Land and regional planning more like "co-regulation" (Einig 2008 p.35). The joint impacts of market-led thinking and the natural decentralised tendencies of German government mean that federal policy-makers cannot go beyond some fairly limited statements in the Leitbilder documents. Schmidt-Eichstaedt (2001) considers federal spatial planning "a relatively weak instrument, especially when compared with sector planning", with the main useful elements in the informal parts considered above. The debates

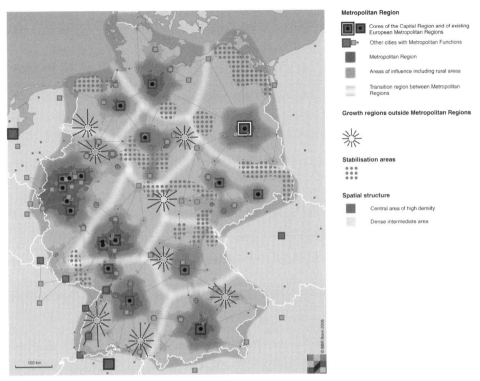

Figure 8.2 One of three Leitbilder in 2006 Concepts and Strategies for Spatial Development in Germany. (Source: Bundesministerium für Verkehr, Bau und Stadtentwicklung, BMVBS 2006a)

leading up to the 2006 Leitbilder (see Figure 8.2) revolved around equity (the goal of maintaining equal living conditions) and the drive for spatial competitiveness, as the core of modern policy-making for Germany. This brought these issues out into the open, and was a basis for a compromise between the two positions, in which holding to some sort of equitable principles was doubtless important for the overall framing of German planning. This was a much looser framing than the post-unification documents of 1993 and 1995, which contained transport elements for the whole of Germany, above all linking to the Germany Unity projects within and connecting to eastern Germany. However, the continuous presence and background work of the MKRO does provide further input, with many short reports on infrastructure issues passed at the annual meetings.

Arguably more important is the federal planning report, published every four or five years and debated in parliament, providing detailed understanding of spatial trends (BBSR 2005). In fact, the spatial observatory process is continuous, so surveys of trends can continuously inform work at Länder levels and below, as well as inform sectoral planning. This research capacity reaches well beyond the BBSR, with a network of connections considerably stronger than in most European countries, including that around the Akademie für Raumforschung und Landesplanung (ARL), which is a learned society bringing together all those involved in German planning, including in the universities. Recent studies at the ARL include some on infrastructure issues and on transport planning at the macro, including European, level (Hesse 2010, Tietz and Huhner 2011). This is the kind of work that DATAR has, on occasion, carried out or coordinated or that the Dutch planning agency has done routinely, but which is largely absent in many other countries (certainly in England).

But how far can such light touch approaches influence the big issues of future transport systems and energy systems and how these relate to the changing demographic and economic trends within Germany? Dutch "performance theory" might be optimistic that such a framing and intelligence-sharing role is as good as it gets, and that it can provide as much framing power as is needed in an era when national-level planning in particular no longer has instruments or mindsets which can lay out big long-term patterns or directions. I am more sceptical about the possibilities that the German federal approach can really have much steering power, if one is talking about large spatial choices that would have to have some integrating force and the highest-level of political backing. But I do think that the German approach, evolved to fit the restraints inherent in a federal system, is one worthy of study, and possibly emulation in countries where stronger approaches may always seem impossible.

Länder and regional-level spatial planning

How far can integration at the "real" levels of planning make up for this relative weakness federally? The levels at which this might be able to work are either in the Land level plans, or in the regional plans below these. I was not able to find a comprehensive study of the position of infrastructure within Land level plans (though Goppel 2005 has a good overview). Some years ago Kunzmann concluded that "state planning is not subordinated to federal spatial planning" (2001 p.157), although he did note that "its role as a long-term clearing instrument for securing rights of way for infrastructure corridors should not be underestimated" (p.163). Here I have had recourse to a rapid examination of just three plans at this level (for Berlin–Brandenburg, which is a two Länder joint exercise, for North Rhine Westphalia, and for Lower Saxony). This is far from conclusive in answering the question, but from this evidence it appears that there are problems in this level being able to take on this integrating infrastructure/spatial planning role. Generally the plans have only broad principles on large infrastructure, with some exceptions such as high-speed rail in the North Rhine Westphalia plan of 1995, and airport issues in all three plans (with strong growth plans, despite equally strong green rhetoric). What infrastructure content there is, above all transport, is linked to some degree to the core settlement and open space determinations of the plans – most strongly in the Berlin–Brandenburg case, where one goal is access to middle and upper tier urban centres in set times (60 and 90 minutes travel). There is often a clear wish not to tread on any regional-planning toes by going into transport, water or energy detail. The plans do pick up on federal-level framing of the times they were produced, including the 1993–1995 and 2006 Leitbilder, but this is somewhat light too. In some areas, there is very full adoption of sectoral plans, most obviously the BVWP decisions (see section of BVWP).

In terms of sectoral examples, the new Berlin airport in Brandenburg has been the subject of intensive work within the new spatial planning process during the 2000s, which led to a new state plan in 2008 (Gemeinsame Landesplanungsabteilung Berlin–Brandenburg, 2006 and 2008c, Gordijn 2008). The airport was related to development patterns and transport links, with special plans detailing the airport area itself. But this is perhaps a special case: one that is especially controversial, and as an infrastructure under public control, amenable to public steering. In Brandenburg too there has been some wind-farm planning, mainly at regional level, as has occurred in a number of Länder. This is based on the scope given in the 1998 planning law revision to designate priority areas. In other areas one has the impression more of silo effects at state level, with road planning having its own dynamic, and, at least on the surface, not much sign of linking to overall energy strategies.

The difficulty of course in all Land-level planning, however well integrated, is that issues across states, as many certainly are in the transport and energy fields, may not be treated effectively. In water there is an institutional mechanism to deal with this (river basin planning), and the consensus on the Water Framework Directive round of planning (2000–2009) is that this has led to sound planning for the river basins, including working across international borders, as is very often required (Moss 2003, 2004, 2011). This is helped by the fact that the water sector does not require large amounts of new infrastructure, but is predominantly management planning with, according to practitioners, less need to coordinate in any intricate way with higher-level spatial planning. But in transport and energy, as we will see, such mechanisms as there are do not necessarily work this well.

Most Länder have a regional tier, dividing Länder into areas perhaps the size of English counties or French departments: 105 in Germany as a whole. What scope does this have to provide the necessary integrating glue? Clearly there are problems as stated above, that there are many issues which straddle numerous regions, so integration capacity could only go so far at this level anyway. But recent studies at the BBSR (Einig 2008, 2011, Domhardt 2007) have established that even within these limitations, regional planning has not, by and large, been dealing with infrastructure issues effectively. This varies across sectors, but the study found that the regional planners normally either accepted what was in sectoral plans, without much sign of reflective adjustment or consideration of adjustment (merely, say, writing in a road project), or simply omitted infrastructure issues. Regional plans have been the great hope of German spatial planning in the last 20 years, and have doubtless played a major part in determining settlement and open-space protection patterns across the country, overcoming some incoherence resulting from each local authority going its own way within the often generalised schemas of Land-level plans. But this progress does not appear to have fed into more sophisticated infrastructure planning.

A documented exception is the regional wind-zone planning (Ohl and Eichhorn 2008). The federal building act designates wind turbines as "privileged projects": that is, their development is normally permissible where there are no conflicting public interests. Länder may then delineate priority areas (Vorranggebiete), where wind projects take priority over other land uses, and also suitability areas (Eignungsgebiete), where wind power is feasible, with the effect that other areas are excluded. Combining both instruments tends to concentrate development in a few areas, as against early schemes more spread around the regions. Ohl and Eichhorn argue that the effect now is more to restrict future possibilities than enable them, so this raises issues about the spatial planning approach in Germany in this area. Nevertheless, outside observers have seen this model as valuable, giving local scope to guide development (IEEP/RSPB 2009).

NATIONAL SECTORAL PLANNING AND INFRASTRUCTURE

The next question is whether the sectoral planning in each area does the job of linking spatial and infrastructural development effectively, by taking into account the guidelines available from spatial planners at each level. As always, this is not an easy question to answer in the absence of extensive studies over many years of many plans, their making and their fates. But my overall understandings are presented here, starting with the transport sectors.

Road, rail and waterway – the BVWP

The main instrument in the transport planning field across all Germany is the federal transport plan, the Bundesverkehrswegeplan, BVWP (BMVBW 2003, Bosch and Partner et al 2010, Heuser and Reh 2010, Peters 2007, Rothengatter 2005). This was invented in the high planning era of the 1960s, has continued to be revised at roughly ten-yearly intervals and has maintained some continuity in methodology, with the last plan still dominated by cost–benefit techniques redolent of decades ago. The BVWP lays out needs for

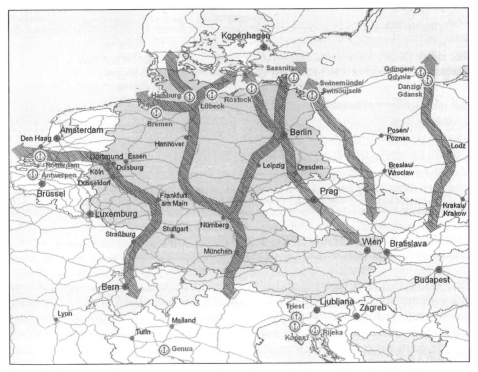

Figure 8.3 Alternative north–south routes in central Europe. (Source: Heinrichs and Schmude 2010 p. 69)

the coming decades, and schemes of road, rail and (since the last plan in 2003) waterway investment intended to meet those needs. The plan is then followed by laws for each sector, giving more detail and leading to the annual budget allocations which drive the investment forward. Work has begun on the preliminary stages of the next plan, scheduled for 2015, although much of the last plan has not actually reached implementation, and so there is not much sense of urgency in preparing the next investment round. The last two decades have been dominated by the German Unity projects, which were prior commitments to a subsequent BVWP: not cost–benefit (etc) derived, but resulting from an open admission of wider political goals, of an imagined future "joined up" country. In this case we see very clearly the working of broader shared imaginaries, as against technical planning exercises based on the assessment of submitted project lists.

Since the 1990s the technique of making the plan has evolved, with the project based approach still at the core, but with further assessment environmentally and with spatial planning criteria added to the standard cost–benefit analysis (BMVBW 2002). Nevertheless, analysis of the 2003 plan does not suggest a major change in the approach, and critics continue to argue that the plan still constitutes a machine for generating road and rail projects, mainly those put forward by the Länder and by DB. Scholl and

Seidemann (2010 p.22) say that "Germany, despite the BVWP and subse-quent detailing investment plans, is a long way from a national transport strategy" (my translation). An ARL study of the north–south freight corridor down the Rhine valley considered that the BVWP was incapable of dealing with the wider spatial challenges, seeing cross-border issues, or understand-ing the big strategic challenges, as against gaps in the existing networks (Heinrichs and Schmude 2010). Figure 8.3 shows the big thinking outside government on macro corridors. All this says that the plan follows a traditional transport planning approach, suffering from the absence of insertion within a comprehensive spatial planning approach. Being based on the extrapola-tion of existing transport flows, compared to current network capacities, the bigger questions of transitions to new sorts of systems are not tackled. The current federal government puts its faith in electric cars and technological fixes rather than behavioural change.

Ports and airports

The impact of transport sectoralism is increased by the absence of consider-ation of port and airport issues in the BVWP. The absence is not surprising as the Bund has no direct competence in these sectors. It has tried rather gin-gerly to engage with this problem, with a freight plan dealing with all modes in 2008 (Federal Government 2008), and port and airport strategies prepared within the federal transport ministry in 2009 (BMVBS 2009a and 2009b). These provide a valuable source of data, and their preparation has brought port and airport operators together to consider all-Germany issues. The ports strategy essentially presses for growth and investment across the key ports, including a particular emphasis on inland ports to satisfy Green demands for using all possible ways to take traffic off roads. But in the absence of the will to steer national economic activity and fully coordinate investment, the ports plan had to remain aspirational, though with some federal funding to prime port cooperation. Individual ports press on confidently (Hamburg Port Authority 2007).

The airports strategy entered a very difficult area, and was not a con-sensus document, but the perspective of the Bund. Since the 1990s Länder and cities have been competing in some areas to build up secondary airports using low-cost carriers (Muller-Rostin et al 2010). The Bund takes a dim view of much of this activity, and tries to limit by means of persuasion the (in its view) excessive spread of new airports, some of which are not well served by public transport (in fact there are only half a dozen new ones at most, with one or two such as Frankfurt Hahn being significant). Länder now have to consult the Bund on any airport expansion proposals, but all decisions remain constitutionally with the Länder. The airports strategy (perspective would be more accurate) recognises two airports – Frankfurt and Munich – as the key hubs of the system, five more as the key international airports, and another

15 as having international roles. The strategy states that no new airports are needed, and for the moment this approach is holding. But given the absence of the possibility of genuine multi-modal planning, it is difficult for the Bund to do more than this: well short of any genuinely integrated approach to movement within the country as a whole.

So there is some contrast within the transport field, with a stronger instrument for road and rail (but not necessarily one integrated with national spatial change in a broader way), and weaker approaches necessary for ports and airports, allowing strong play to competitive regionalism or localism (though with the federal government holding some cards relating to finance and political or cooperative persuasion). All modes are growth areas, and governments at all levels have tended to go along with or encourage this growth direction. This has resulted in massive new investment in eastern Germany, and significant if selective expansion elsewhere, including in some smaller and some larger airports and in the big ports of Hamburg, Bremen and Rostock, and the creation of a brand-new deep-water port, the JadeWeserPort (promoted by the states of Lower Saxony and Bremen, Hamburg dropping out of the grouping in 2001). After the end of the German Unity projects, this dynamic will slow, but probably not come to a halt. Even *considering* a slow down in mobility growth would seem to be a tough challenge for the German polity.

Energy

Liberalisation has been extensive since the 1990s in the electricity and gas sectors (oil of course having already been in the open market for many decades). There has never been any generalised energy planning in Germany (Gust 2005, 2007, Hinrichs-Rahlwes and Pieprzyk, 2009). The main push from recent governments has been to implement EU policies on unbundling and opening markets, alongside security concerns, which support both gas negotiations with Russia and support for renewables and energy saving. But the challenges can be seen in Figure 8.4, which shows the concentration of renewables in northern Germany. The nearest thing to energy planning has been the work of the German Energy Agency, dena (dena 2005, 2010a, 2010b). Its 2005 study showed the change required in electricity grids given large onshore wind investment (and, to a lesser extent, biomass and solar generation). The dena 2 study, published in 2010, also dealt with offshore wind and with more long-term factors to 2025. It pressed for a massive investment in the grid system and constituted a powerful intervention on the whole German electricity system, considering generation, demand management, transmission and storage together.

However, neither of these studies constituted government policy. Ultimate responsibility lies with the four grid companies covering Germany, and the generators operating on the electricity market. It has been realised

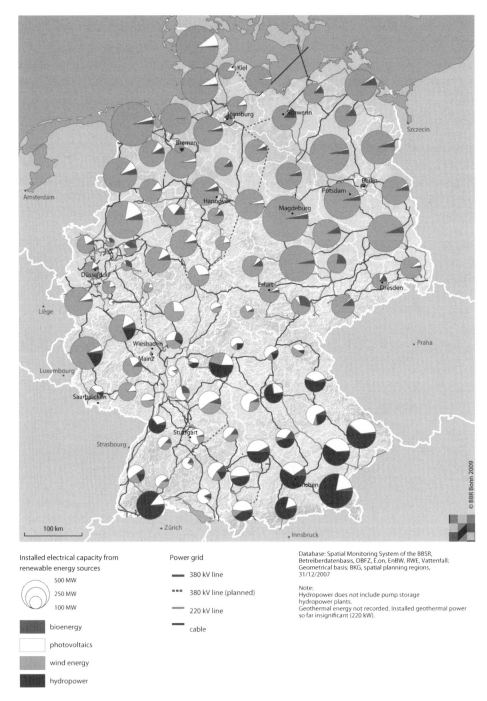

Installed electrical capacity from
renewable energy sources

500 MW
250 MW
100 MW

bioenergy
photovoltaics
wind energy
hydropower

Power grid

— 380 kV line
--- 380 kV line (planned)
— 220 kV line
— cable

Database: Spatial Monitoring System of the BBSR,
Betreiberdatenbasis, DBFZ, E.on, EnBW, RWE, Vattenfall;
Geometrical basis: BKG, spatial planning regions,
31/12/2007

Note:
Hydropower does not include pump storage
hydropower plants.
Geothermal energy not recorded. Installed geothermal power
so far insignificant (220 kW).

© BBR Bonn 2009

Figure 8.4 Renewable sources (mainly wind) dominate in some north German regions.
(Source: BBSR Research News, 2010/1 p. 7).

for some time that this may leave gaps in the investment, and a number of measures emerged during the 2000s to encourage investment. One required the grid companies to promise to connect all new wind capacity, onshore and offshore, and a 2009 law (EnLAG) identified the 24 projects selected in dena 1, that were essential to improving the transmission of the new energy coming onto the grid in northern Germany, down to the big consumption areas of southern Germany. The projects identified in the law were to benefit from somewhat lessened administrative requirements, given overall federal support, though all the normal procedures appear to have been retained.

However, following the nuclear crisis in Japan, the German government introduced a new approach to dealing with the planning of the critical grid connections (Bruns 2011). Under two laws passed in 2011, the parliament will approve a national plan for Energy Infrastructure Demand, giving the list of transmission lines to be taken into the new procedure. Then the law on accelerating grid development allocates the planning (examining corridors, dealing with all consents) to the Bundesnetzagentur. This was quite a radical shift, taking powers from the states to the federation, and placing them within a body with no spatial planning history, overseen by the economy ministry.

So, change is underway to address the challenges of switching to a renewables-based economy. Up to 2011 there had been rather juddering progress in energy liberalisation in Germany, in which the prime companies have not been too keen on competition, with the state taking a rather weak line of least resistance. But in 2010, an overall Energy Concept was produced (BMWi/BMU 2010), confirming the push to renewables. There remains scope for more effective linking to spatial planning issues, as called for by some academics (Tietz 2005, 2007, 2011). An action research project showed consideration of how to plan for a range of renewables, not just wind, at regional level, picking out best practice around the country (BMVBS 2011), so trying to press this scale of action further.

Water and waste

The water sector is one where, as mentioned above, the new investment is not significant and so linking to spatial planning has not been a major issue in the new generation of plans under the Water Framework Directive completed by the 2009 EU deadline (BMU 2006). In any case the institutional framework chosen, under the Directive guidance, is one that requires extensive and sophisticated coordination between Länder and adjoining states and so can benefit from developed and well-resourced German planning capacities. There has long been widespread support for good-quality water systems and rising ecological quality, and the willingness to pay for this. Linked to the absence of any generalised supply problems, this makes the sector reasonably manageable in itself.

The waste sector is, as in my other cases, one that is planned for at the regional level, with good practice increasingly dealing with it by means of metropolitan cooperation, sometimes brokered by the Land ministry (Niedersachsisches Ministerium fur Umwelt und Klimaschutz, 2010a, 2010b, Priebs 2011). The link to spatial planning is there, certainly in places like the Greater Hanover authority, which brings together the waste planning and spatial planning for a large number of local authorities around Hanover since the creation of this wider body in 2001. The switch away from landfill is being managed, as in the Netherlands, with wide-scale resort to incineration as well as recycling, and the survey at federal level of recent plans suggested that no more provision of any sorts of waste facilities was needed, meaning that the waste planning challenge had been met.

Sectoral planning and spatial planning contrasts

It is clear that there are processes to link up sectoral work and spatial dimensions, including spatial planning clauses, the ROV instruments (see below), state spatial plans, and regional planning. But this works better in some sectors than others, either where the challenge is more localised (waste, some renewables) or where it is very firmly framed institutionally (water). By contrast, big systems in energy and transport, the latter crossing all modes (ports, airports and terrestrial) are less adequately linked, with sectoralism and sub-sectoralism present, and the federal government struggling to provide clear steering at the macro territorial level.

PLANNING AND INFRASTRUCTURE PROJECTS

Germany is a country which prepares policy carefully and over time, and although business complains of slow procedure as elsewhere, there have been rather uncertain moves towards speed up. The two main examples in Germany, up to the changes in 2011 described above for power lines, have been the one limited to the reconstruction effort in the Eastern Länder (of December 1991), and a law that applied to the whole country in 2006 (the Infrastructure Planning Acceleration Act). The aim of the latter was to shorten the planning process period by more than two years, for energy and transport projects alike. This was to be achieved by procedural simplifications, particularly by ensuring that only the top federal court had jurisdiction, to try to stop projects being stuck in a series of cases at each step up the judicial system. Though the grand coalition partners approved the act, both economic and environmental critics were vocal, arguing either that it did not go far enough, or that basic rights were infringed. It has been suggested by the BUND environmental group that the law had had little effect by 2009, partly because the top court had too few resources to deal with all the cases. At any rate, a further law was passed in 2009 specifically aiming to speed up the approval of transmission line schemes, listing 24 schemes where, in principle, support should be given, showing continuing worries about the difficulty of getting approval of these schemes.

Projects are prepared years in advance, whether by government bodies or large companies, and the time to get permissions is doubtless taken for granted, even if the frequent opposition of citizen groups is resented by developers. One of the processes used by most Länder since the 1970s is the Raumordnungsverfahren (ROV), under which any large projects have to be checked against the relevant spatial plans. Where the project is exceptionally large, like the (later abandoned) magnetic rail scheme from Hamburg to Berlin, the ROV may be carried out by the federal government, but normally it is the work of the Land planning ministry.

German planning history of the last decades has been marked by famous struggles over controversial projects, such as that on the Gorleben nuclear waste repository (still not progressed), the extension of Frankfurt and Munich airports (both eventually went ahead) and most recently the Stuttgart 21 rail station and rail-links project. These project battles then resonate across the country, and no doubt slow similar schemes if the difficulty of getting permissions is shown in an emblematic case. A short account of the contemporary Stuttgart case will give some idea of the way this works.

The rail station redevelopment in Stuttgart was related to the arrival of the high-speed line in the city, and also connected to plans to link the airport to the long-distance rail system. It was the main survivor of a set of "21" schemes developed by DB and presented in 1996, most importantly for Munich, Frankfurt and Mannheim. (The new Berlin central station completed in 2006 was a rather special case.) Stuttgart 21 had strong support from many elite interests in the Baden-Wurttemberg capital, and cross-party support, with federal and Land governments ready to put in large sums on top of DB's investment. The scheme was also a property development project for much of this part of central Stuttgart, as, like most of the "21" schemes, it proposed to put the new through station underground (the existing station is a dead-end line). This undergrounding was to free up lots of development space, for houses, offices and parks. Gradually opposition built up to the scheme, which was seen as too expensive and intrusive by local Greens, and linked to dubious political–business connections of the main promoters. A widespread distaste for the behaviour of DB since its commercialisation has been another feature in the attacks on the scheme (Engartner 2008, 2010, Esser and Randereth 2010). Perhaps surprisingly, the opposition gained widespread popular support, and was one factor in sweeping the Green Party to power in the 2011 Land elections.

So, a scheme that might appear to an outsider as an important example of public transport improvement, perhaps shifting modal behaviours away from the still hegemonic car, became a symbol of wasteful and corrupt politics. At the time of writing the dispute about the scheme rests with yet another review of the project, commissioned by the new Green/SDP Land government, and a referendum. This followed a 2009–2010 review under which the mediator said that there was much wrong with the scheme, but that it deserved, in major part, to go ahead. The possibly successful challenge to the scheme in its current form is encouraging opposition to other, more "normal", development schemes across Germany, and boosting Green electoral chances. It is possible that a large and enormously complex scheme which took two decades to prepare will be abandoned, or at least see major revisions. It is this sort of challenge that has repeatedly opened up debates about infrastructure in Germany, although very unevenly. It seems to show that even the most supported and prepared schemes can be stopped in their tracks, and that the role of project and infrastructure developer is not necessarily an easy one in Germany. Germans are sometimes full of doubts about new development, and the processes involved are not the key issue, it is the real essence of change and modernisation which often comes under the spotlight. Time will show how the case develops.

EUROPEANISATION OF HIGH-LEVEL GERMAN SPATIAL PLANNING?

German spatial planning has been highly conscious of European issues, certainly since the transformations of 1990. Due to its central position the country has many international borders, and energy, water and transport planning all have obvious international linkages at their core. Much BBSR work, and many MKRO meetings, have been dominated by European issues, probably to an extent greater than any other country and certainly greater than any other large state. Groupings of Länder are especially active here too, such as those of northern Länder with port interests, or those gathered in the Scandria project with EU funding. For example, in Berlin–Brandenburg a strong European spatial planning section is involved in this project, promoting the significance of the north–south corridor from Scandinavia to Italy and the Adriatic (Gemeinsame Landesplanungsabteilung Berlin–Brandenburg, 2008a, 2008b). This is partly a marketing and economic development tool, and partly a bid for transport resources with the federal government or for TENs (Trans European Networks) recognition within EU strategising (the 2008b document makes the link quite explicitly to these transport goals, p.11 para. 8.4). This is in conjunction with the eastern German states, and is typical of much recent political and strategic work, where Länder with some perceived common interests work and lobby together in defined areas. Scandria runs from 2009 to 2012 and has a strong freight dimension. This builds on earlier cooperative work in the wider region by Berlin–Brandenburg, shown, for example, in the Berlin declaration of 2007 on the same corridor. Such a "wide focus" planning and initiatives programme of this kind will surely affect the reworking of the BVWP in due course, probably into much broader paths than in the past.

The EU is increasing its role, indirectly, in major-infrastructure spatial issues, via its revised TENs drive (McGowan 2009). In Germany up to the present, TENs probably had its normal style, taking advantage of EU support for projects desired anyway. The case of the Fehmarn Belt, a bridge from Germany across the Baltic to Denmark, is an interesting if untypical example. The project was agreed in 2007 in time for gaining matching EU TEN funds, but nearly all the costs will be covered by Denmark (at that time, Germany was to only pay 800 million out of 5.6 billion euros, Peters 2007 p.14). So, here a project may go ahead because of the TENs programme, when otherwise very low German enthusiasm for the scheme would never have promoted it: a clear case of European space building, which will, in the long-run, shift north German geography. In the energy field, work in the European electricity and gas organisations is surely feeding back into German thinking on energy already, as will cooperation in the North Sea marine-planning cooperation process.

So, a degree of Europeanisation does already appear to be at work, constituting a dimension above the perhaps weakening federal scale, though its reach and significance are still unclear, and will remain so until further progress has been made on the TENs revision in 2011–2012. Until now the impact may have been marginal, literally, mostly working at state borders. But this emergent governance and framing is definitely something to keep under review in the near future.

CONCLUSIONS

The picture in Germany is a mixed and complex one – a conclusion that may be starting to sound familiar. I suggested earlier that this is a polity in transition to a more liberalised and Europeanised regime, politically and economically. This intersects with the established implications of German federalism. On the one hand there are big principles and drives at work which frame action on major infrastructure: the still powerful idea of equal conditions across German territory, the related drive at reunification that has become a decades-long territorial and infrastructure project set and the osmosis and irruption of green principles across all fields, even if sometimes rhetorically rather than substantively. The federal government has, upon these bases, given considerable leadership in several fields, whether coordinating rail or road investment, pushing (rather less effectively so far) electricity transmission investment, planning for the northern seas or pressing for waterway investment. On the other hand, the relatively weak federal spatial planning machinery has only been able to give a rather broad framing via research and persuasion on many issues, being required by federalism to keep its distance in several sectors, and being unable to coordinate the transport field to full effect. The flip-side of this is the relatively effective and democratic systems ruling at Länder and municipal level planning, which can innovate on demand management and urban ecological projects. Good government at this level can make an enormous difference, even though this has not been the focus here. Equally, the commitment to, in most cases, careful planning and open decision-making, gives a chance in projects to reach a full consensus under the glare of continuous electoral pressure. Bad projects have a fair chance of being stopped, despite some efforts to impose speed up regimes in recent years. Even after the 2011 energy laws, there is nothing systematic like the moves initiated in the UK in the 2008 Planning Act. All of this reflects the cooperative federalism and respect for law still flourishing in Germany, despite the emergence of competitive boosterism as in all countries in recent years (Peters 2007).

The net result is of considerable interest, with constitutional, legal, democratic and ideological or ethical features to the fore in this discussion of how the system deals with challenges. The commitment, so far apparently cross-party, to long-term ecological transitions in the face of climate change, makes the country especially interesting. As the dominant European state with these objectives, Germany becomes a critical case to try to negotiate a path, democratically, to new systems, including infrastructure systems. It is not clear yet that the will is really there, with slow movement in the energy field and continuing addiction to the car culture (Zeller 2007). But change seems marginally more likely than in any other country. Now that the post-reunification phase is drawing to a close, the need to grapple with and formulate a new national imaginary is probably coming into focus. Can German federalism find this focus, or is the polity shifting to more fragmented approaches? Will European determinations come to be the mode of moving forward, and if so will that mean a much less ambitious approach to transition than would be the case within the national framing? It is unlikely that either liberalisation or Europeanisation have run their course, and there are naturally other critical forces at play, including the drive for competitiveness and the force of ecological thinking. As such, the new era cannot yet be seen with the clarity required to answer the above questions.

CHAPTER 9
"TRADITIONAL" PLANNING FOR MAJOR INFRASTRUCTURE IN THE UK

This chapter and the next look at the way major infrastructure was planned up to the very recent past, and then at the flurry of reform in the last five years or so. After introducing the UK context, the different infrastructure sectors are surveyed, in their "traditional" mode, in this chapter. Chapter 10 examines the reforms process and emerging prospects, as well as looking at some important projects, of the past or in prospect.

UK GOVERNMENT AND INFRASTRUCTURE INDUSTRIES

The composite UK state

British government and the British state have changed significantly since the late 1990s (Bogdanor 2009). Devolution of powers to Scotland, Wales and Northern Ireland has been the most important element of these changes, at least for the purposes of this study. Certainly policy and politics had long been distinct within these countries or regions (Macdonald and Thomas 1997), with separate departmental systems based in Belfast, Cardiff and Edinburgh and each having their own Secretary of State with a seat in the Cabinet. But broadly speaking legislation on most primary policy-areas covered all parts of the UK. The legislation of 1998–1999 changed the situation fundamentally, with the creation of new institutions (a Scottish Parliament and Welsh and Northern Ireland Assemblies), and the transfer of varying amounts of law-making powers. Flinders (2009) calls this "bi-constitutionalism", with a majoritarian model more centralised than ever before in England, and more consensualist and innovative polities evolving in the rest of the UK. He regards the hybrid settlement as being unstable for a unitary state, having no coherent constitutional principles behind it. He finds further features, including low trust in the political class and no skills in big constitutional and framing thinking, that impede moving forward on such principles. These circumstances impinge, I believe, on the possibilities of thinking about UK futures, including geographies, and so are relevant to infrastructural imagining.

Scotland gained primary legislative powers in planning, giving them full scope to bring in new systems, within the inherited traditions of law and practice. The Welsh and Northern Ireland Assemblies were given only secondary legislative powers, but this already gave some room for adapting processes. Wales was given primary legislative powers in some areas, including planning, in 2010, and this was expected to result in due course in a Welsh Planning Act, possibly making the system there more distinctive still. Scotland had already taken advantage of its situation with the passing of a fresh Planning Act in 2006. All this meant that when the UK passed Planning Acts, in 2004 and 2008, these applied mainly to England, with variable application to Wales and Northern Ireland, and only occasional implications for Scotland.

In the field of infrastructure, UK legislation continued to cover many important areas, treated as reserved matters. This included aviation, regulatory regimes in energy, water and telecommunications, as well as regulation of parts of the rest of the transport systems, on ports, roads and rail. All three devolved territories had their own territorial waters, but a wider UK marine space gave the UK government the senior position in marine planning, alongside the position of the Crown Estate as "owner" of the sea bed. So, the infrastructure regimes remained under mixed control, in spite of continuous pressure from Scotland which sometimes resulted in something approximating joint management of some of these areas.

Taking the planning and infrastructure features together, this therefore produced a new and more complex geometry of power compared to that before 2000. Previously, the UK government in London controlled all of the most important regulatory and financial levers for the whole of the UK, even though highly significant detailing and at times policy making could rest with the Scottish Office or Welsh Office. This meant that, had the government possessed an overall idea for the evolution in spatial or sectoral terms for the UK and its various parts, it had the tools to execute that idea, insofar as these existed in the relevant era of more-or-less state intervention, powers and finances. After 2000, the government in London could still order what was to happen in some fields, but it no longer possessed the full spread of sectoral controls, and had relatively little direct say on the spatial planning arrangements outside England. In that sense the situation had some similarity with Spain, with its fuzzy and evolving uncertainties, and shifting of power relations between the centre and the devolved administrations. However, there are clearly big differences from the Spanish constitutional position, and from the balances and numbers of administrations. Some of the dynamic of Spanish change was due to there being many regions, with a pressure to catch up for the slower ones, as well as very uneven regional powers. The UK is simpler, with only the UK government, Scotland and Wales as the key players, with Northern Ireland being an even more unique case.

Just as in other countries, the internal arrangement of the government is significant. At certain periods there have been super ministries including most powers in the infrastructure field – this was so in the early 1970s, and from 1997 to 2001. But fragmentation or departmental specialisation has been the norm, with departments for or including transport, energy, water and waste, sitting alongside those with more comprehensive ambitions for planning and the environment, business and the economy. "Joined up thinking" was a mantra of the Blair governments (Bogdanor 2005), and UK governments have always had a range of instruments to try to make this happen: cross departmental committees, Cabinet committees, central policy units and financial control wielded by the Treasury, among others. These have rarely had very strong integrating effects, with the constant complaint of regional and local policy-makers that central government operated above all sectorally, by silo government, impeding lower-level efforts to produce comprehensive area-based policy approaches (Haughton et al 2010).

Between 2004 and 2006 the government, primarily driven by the Treasury, promoted reports in key infrastructure fields, on planning and transport (Barker 2006, Eddington 2006). These were intended, alongside the contemporary Energy Review, to give overall steering to those areas of the economy seen as critical to long-term futures, and served very much as integrating cross-government mechanisms. These led on to the institution of Infrastructure UK in 2009, which itself contributed to the first "National Infrastructure Plan" in October 2010 (HM Treasury 2010).

Infrastructure industries

The net result of varying phases of the nationalisation, privatisation and centralisation of utilities from the early twentieth century was, by the mid 1970s, that the state achieved a strong position in the ownership and control of infrastructure industries in the UK. This included public ownership of all gas and electricity systems, of the largest airports and most ports, of all rail and road infrastructure and of all rail-service provision, and of the great majority of water and sewerage systems. The main airlines were state owned. Waste services and infrastructure were mostly controlled by local authorities, as were many bus services. Central government was in a stronger position in most areas than in some European countries where municipal ownership was greater (particularly in Germany). The Treasury therefore exerted considerable control over the finances of most of these providers, taking money from profitable operations, and restricting funds to most other sectors most of the time.

This changed in the 1980s under the Thatcher government's privatisation programmes, so that, by the 1990s, almost none of this institutional architecture remained. Rail privatisation followed in 1994, leaving only roads in full public ownership across a whole sector. Public influence in some other areas, through municipal ownership of some airports or ports, or trust ownership of some ports, remained, but with much reduced force, and strongly affected by the generalised spread of commercial cultures and competition across sectors. However, at the same time as privatisation, extensive regulatory machinery was created in each sector (Helm 2004a). By the 2000s the most important were bodies managing the economic and social side of energy (Ofgem) and water (Ofwat), the Environment Agency (managing environmental aspects of water and waste), the Office of Rail Regulation and the Civil Aviation Authority, a venerable survivor from 1971. All these bodies were charged with regulating the now private industries in order to achieve a mix of competitive and public-service goals (the latter being a varied set of environmental and social factors). Other specialist bodies were also in play, such as the Competition Commission and the Health and Safety Commission. So, regulation was extensive and far more intricate though probably less significant than the steering that existed before privatisation. The previous public bodies had been charged with social, environmental and efficiency goals, in different ways in different periods, under the overview of ministers, and had stronger instruments to achieve these goals.

Some differences remained between different parts of the UK. Water and sewerage services were not privatised in Scotland in 1990. The Welsh water company converted itself into a non profit-making enterprise in 2000, contracting out its operational work to private companies, but not being obliged to make returns to shareholders, as were the English companies. However, differences in the transport and energy sectors were limited.

FORCES GENERATING THE PERCEIVED NEED FOR NEW INFRASTRUCTURE

A collection of forces, some of them driving in different directions, set the scene for how much and what sort of new infrastructure is seen as needed in Britain. In the fields of ideas and lobbying there has been little consensus. Environmental interests broadly advocate demand management, by energy saving and reducing the need to travel, though at times arguing for investment in certain renewable energy systems or preferred transport modes. Business interests tend to argue for investment across the board, supported by engineering lobbies. But in the field of action the companies running the utility sectors in the last two decades since privatisation have tended towards "asset sweating", rather than large amounts of investment (Helm 2004a). There are exceptions in some sectors at certain times, such as the "dash for gas" in power station investment in the 1990s, investment in new sewage and some water systems to meet EU standards, or the expansion of airports to meet rapid growth in demand. Governments have swayed around these differing emphases, at different periods promoting more one tendency or another. Most of the time governmental reluctance to invest public money has been a common feature since the 1970s. Exceptions to this have been rail infrastructure investment since about 2000, including, in the case of the London Underground system, through attempts to bring in private finance.

Historical geographies

Underlying this picture is, as always, a unique geographical–historical set of features and challenges. Some reference to Ireland makes sense in this context:

- The islands are close to but separated from the European mainland, one much the largest (Britain), one smaller (Ireland).
- The edge-of-continent position is always important, and European Union membership has been one factor in generating more pressure on the regions facing the continent in recent decades, including the pressure to create the Channel Tunnel link and associated infrastructure since 1994.
- Two sovereign states exist in these islands – the UK and the Republic of Ireland – complicating decision-making on major infrastructure issues in certain ways, and providing different vantage points on future needs.
- Distances are rarely very long between main centres on these two main islands, but significant enough to give separation and friction from journey times, with separate labour markets and significant cultural differences.
- Distances are not long enough overall to encourage large domestic aviation or high-speed rail investment, though both have some plausibility between London and northern England and especially Scotland. Distances have suited first normal-speed rail investment and then motorway systems.
- The islands' positions have meant most freight has always come in via ports, giving these economic importance, and their locations significance in the generation of transport systems. Historically this has given some balance to investment and geography, with all parts of Britain seeing importance at different periods as ports – east and west coasts (both north and south), and the English Channel ports system, with the latter having prime importance for naval defence.

- Energy systems have swung between different indigenous sources (wood, coal, oil and gas in the North Sea), and imported fuels (oil, uranium and in the most recent decades, coal and gas). These have been highly significant in the generation of infrastructure systems. Most recently they have encouraged port investment for large-scale coal imports, pipeline construction for bringing in gas, and electricity links to support international electricity trading. Renewables energy investment, only significant in the last decade or so, changes the geography again, with both onshore and offshore wind power, and possibly solar power, increasing in importance, especially with regard to changing demands on the electricity grid.

- Water has rarely been a limiting determinant or force in geographical change or placed big pressure for recent infrastructure investment, though the drier south of England has affected recent discussions on urbanisation. However, industrial decline has reduced this potential effect, leaving domestic and agricultural demands as dominant in southern England.

- Waste sinks have not been a major challenge, given the use of seas and rivers historically, and the many landfill sites created by industrialisation processes in most parts of urbanised Britain. Most recently landfill use has been changing via policy, and some challenges emerge with infrastructure for incineration plants.

- The urban structure shows the force in England of a mega primate city, London, dominating southern England and to an extent the whole country, though Scotland has counterweights in Edinburgh and Glasgow, bolstered by long distances.

These features of course work together. They generate some well-known macro contrasts, such as those between the different cultural cores of the four parts of the UK, and within England between the North and South. The first has led to a gradual differentiation of the UK polity, as described above, whilst the latter has had no such effect, with the only real attempt to promote English regionalisation after 1997 being unsuccessful. Later discussion of changes and pressures in each sector will bring out how some of these geographical–historical factors play out in particular cases. As always, neither histories nor geographies are in any sense determinant, but they do give a template on which debates and struggles are played out in each era, as we will pick up in a few illuminating cases.

Multiple territorial imaginaries

Several fractures run through the UK, alongside the cohering features that have maintained the existence of the state. One is at the highest scale of the UK, reflected in national struggles over many centuries, and especially visible since the 1970s. The dominant tendency since that time has been towards centrifugal movements between the four parts of the UK. The north–south divide within England has been equally prominent during this period, in part because of lesser attempts since about 1980 by governments to tackle its underlying causes. Then there remain locally based imaginaries, focused on the living spaces of cities or counties competing with the larger regional, macro-regional or national framings. All these give some grounds for competing national imaginaries, not just with the long subaltern nationalisms of "not-England", but also viewed from non-southern regions or regional capitals. However, these alternative imaginaries have had to compete with a powerful London or south-east-centred idea of Britain, holding on to the cultural capital of empire, monarchy and other institutional props of the UK state in its heyday (Allen et al 1998, Amin et al 2003).

Who wins in this tussle of ideas of the country? Does such a tussle really exist? We will try to find some evidence for answering these questions in the discussions of sectoral planning below, these being the main sort of planning or strategising in recent times. What do big, relatively recent, cases – for example, the motorway system, the Channel Tunnel and high-speed link, the proposed high-speed route from London to the north and proposed or actual airport and port investment – show about the way in which leading powers imagine Britain? How far is the UK spatial imaginary fractured, and how does this affect the understandings of how large infrastructure might be fitted into the existing geographical base? How far is the weight of path dependency bound to limit scope for any innovative approaches to energy and movement and production transitions?

THE UK PLANNING SYSTEMS AND COORDINATING ARRANGEMENTS

Project approvals

Up until the 2008 Planning Act, the UK planning system treated major infrastructure essentially like other development. Because of its size certain things applied automatically to it, such as an Environmental Impact Assessment on each project. Equally, any development the size of a power station or airport extension would necessarily be subject to a public inquiry, although until 2002 there was no definition of "major inquiries", with matters having developed informally. The only alternative used occasionally was the Hybrid Bill, taking the issue through Parliament, but this tended to be seen as not giving enough scope for public debate. On rare occasions, when a major project became the object of deep contestation at public inquiries – such as the Sellafield nuclear processing plant (1977–1978), the Sizewell nuclear power station (1983–1985) or the Heathrow airport Terminal 5 (1993–1997) – the full weight of legal and debating machinery would be deployed in the glare of media attention. These were the *causes celebres* for commentators on the long drawn-out nature of decision-making in Britain, though similarly lengthy processes were quite common in various European countries, especially where strong environmental and developmental pressures clashed. At any rate, the procedure came within the normal town and country planning legislation, starting with applications to local authorities, even though normally schemes of this size were effectively taken within the decision-making processes of ministers.

Major infrastructure schemes also had to go through various sectoral permitting processes, with the relevant government ministry (energy, transport, or environment normally) responsible for allowing relevant orders. This was also criticised by businesses who, after privatisation, were now having to negotiate the development of schemes from outside the public sector. The Transport and Works Act of 1992 was intended to streamline this process, cutting out some of the complexities of procedures, but still leaving quite a number of separate steps. For controversial schemes, the planning part was likely to be the most time-consuming and risky element, as it was determined in public, unlike most of the orders procedures in ministries which, while subject to all due process, were only occasionally exposed to much public scrutiny and debate.

Strategic planning in Britain

Until the devolution processes of 1999 no part of the UK had had anything like a national spatial strategy. For Northern Ireland, Wales and Scotland that then changed, and all three have had high-level spatial strategies since that time. We will look later at how these interact with infrastructure planning. England has remained without such a strategy, with at most sectoral planning approaches being present at this level. It should be noted that the series of national policy guidance, known as Planning Policy Guidance, or Planning Policy Statements, which existed from 1988 until 2012, were not directly spatially oriented. They stated policy that was to apply to any part of England: general principles with no implication for location. Of course these, like other policy instruments (for example, regional policy or urban regeneration policy) did indirectly affect what happened where, by bolstering protection or development policies which came into the relevant lower-level plans. But this effect was indirect, and could not take on any conscious spatialising role (Tewdwr-Jones 2002).

Subnational planning, mainly at the level of the eight English regions (nine with London) has existed at various periods since the 1960s (Glasson and Marshall 2007). In certain ways this did incorporate infrastructure-planning issues, although this was never its main *raison d'etre*, which was the management of urbanisation and land-protection policies. Particularly once the Regional Spatial Strategies were made statutory in 2004, infrastructure departments and companies did engage more fully with regional planning in the English regions (the London Plan already had a major infrastructure element in its first statutory version in 2004, given the greater powers and coordination in London). This included the initiatives in 2005 and 2009 to coordinate investment in the regions – the Regional Funding Advice offered to government by all the regional actors – which began to give some coherence to some parts of transport decision-making. There was also work by the RDAs pressing fresh transport approaches (Ecotec and Faber Maunsell 2004) and by the regional planning bodies looking at England as a whole, from their perspectives (Arup et al 2005). The more powerful single Regional Strategies being worked up in 2009–2010 might have gone further with this process, but all work, and any possibility of judging long-term impacts was brought to an end by the 2010 government, abolishing all regional-level governance in the Localism Act of 2011. Many judged that the English regions had great potential to progress environmental and investment coordination (Payne and Reid forthcoming), but government departments often remained reluctant partners, and this regional level was not able to become a prime field for steering large infrastructure during this phase – probably even less so than in the 1960s–1970s period.

In England we are therefore dealing primarily with an *absence* of spatial planning at the most relevant level, so the question is how this affects the approach to deciding on infrastructure. To get answers to this, we will need to look at each infrastructure sector in some detail, and much of the rest of this chapter deals with this task. In the following chapter we will move on to examine the arrival of new systems in all parts of the UK from 2000 onwards, and see how these impact on, or are likely to impact on, major infrastructure development. This may appear to make the survey in this chapter of purely historical relevance. However, the processes at work until virtually the present day (at least in England) are of interest in themselves, and will form a contrast with the emerging systems, as well as with those in other countries. In addition, the new systems may not bring about changes as big as some hope for. Significant underlying continuities are to be expected.

NATIONAL SECTORAL PLANNING AND INFRASTRUCTURE

At most Britain has relied on the sectoral planning of infrastructure. In fact very often this has been sub-sectoral planning. It has been said that it has long been a truism that there has never been transport policy in Britain, only policy for transport modes (Tolley and Turton 1995 p.339). The same could often be said in the energy field. This is not to say that there have not been moments when more integrated approaches to both fields have been attempted,

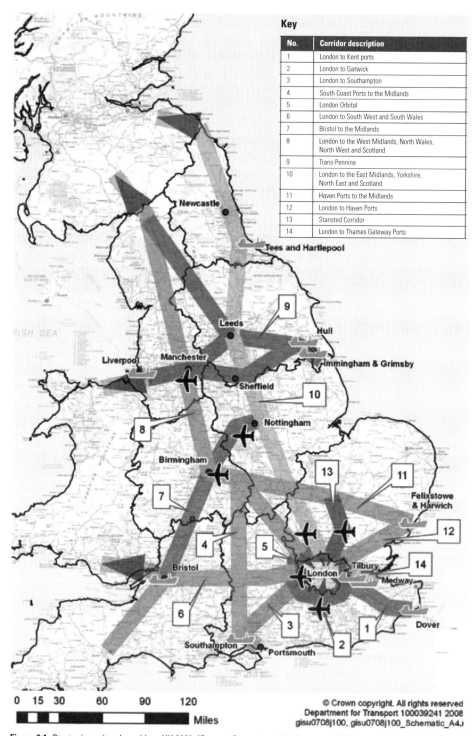

Key

No.	Corridor description
1	London to Kent ports
2	London to Gatwick
3	London to Southampton
4	South Coast Ports to the Midlands
5	London Orbital
6	London to South West and South Wales
7	Bristol to the Midlands
8	London to the West Midlands, North Wales, North West and Scotland
9	Trans-Pennine
10	London to the East Midlands, Yorkshire, North East and Scotland
11	Haven Ports to the Midlands
12	London to Haven Ports
13	Stansted Corridor
14	London to Thames Gateway Ports

0 15 30   60   90   120   Miles

© Crown copyright. All rights reserved
Department for Transport 100039241 2008
gisu0708j100, gisu0708j100_Schematic_A4J

Figure 9.1 Strategic national corridors UK 2008. (Source: Department for Transport 2008)

principally by the Labour governments of the 1940s, 1960s and 2000s. At one moment, in the production of the 1965 National Plan, this even had aspirations to become a comprehensive economic plan led by government. However, the National Plan had a very small spatial component, which was left to subsequent regional planning processes, and so the elements on transport and energy were equally general, discussing global investment rather than locations. In any case the Plan was largely laid aside after a year or two. Transport White Papers in 1968 and 1998 (DETR 1998) were important milestones in policy development, but still treated modes separately, with little integration of ports or airports policy, for example. Energy White Papers of the 1970s and 2000s were equally generalised, setting the broad frameworks for state or private investor strategies, which contained the spatial detailing.

This tendency to highly sectoralised policy-making was reinforced by administrative arrangements, whereby the ministries were split up by modes or fuels. In the transport ministry the tilt to road building was stark until quite recently: of 13 under secretaries in 1987, 11 dealt with road building and road transport (Hamer 1987). A transport strategy directorate was set up in 1997, but this struggled to reduce the silo effects (Glaister et al 1998, 2006, Headicar 2009, Turton 1999). Eventually there did emerge, following the Eddington report (2006), a more concentrated drive to link up transport strategising. This was marked by the TASTS (Towards a Sustainable Transport System, DfT 2007b) and DASTS (Delivering a Sustainable Transport System, DfT 2008) processes, which sought to synchronise investment planning into the far future, laying out new cross modal planning cycles and presenting "strategic national corridors" (Figure 9.1). Though this was an early stage of strategic thinking, it was perhaps the first time since the 1940s that a more comprehensive cross-modal view of both freight and people movement was being examined, if this time primarily for England.

Given these tendencies to split up policy making, it is appropriate to survey the strategic approaches by the seven sectors examined by this book, before returning to some wider reflections.

Ports

Ports were mainly publicly owned, in one form or another, up until the 1980s, and so government influence over their development could in principle be significant. There were periods of strong public intervention in the 1960s and 1970s, when the government sought to rationalise the number of important ports, merging port authorities and linking this to regional planning in key areas such as the Solent/Southampton and in northern England. A government report recommended making a national ports plan at the start of this period (Ministry of Transport 1962), in order to relate port investment to the needs of UK industry, but this proved too much for the Conservative government of the day. So investment was directed in line with regional plans and policy, but only according to broadly sketched principles rather than a national strategy.

From the 1980s such a strategic approach was regarded as wrong, with privatisation intended to create a competitive system that would determine investment without government involvement. The role of the planning system was then limited to considering individual port applications and to making decisions according to normal principles. This had in fact been in process in some key cases since the 1970s, when one or two private ports, most notably Felixstowe on the east coast, were able to break through against the traditional ports and become leading container ports. This occurred outside of government policy, due largely to the fact that Felixstowe was not unionised, and meant that later on government had to fund land transport investment in order to provide adequate road, and to an extent rail, links for the massive freight movement generated.

By the late 1990s the booming import trade to Britain, especially from east Asia, meant that pressure was growing on port capacity, primarily in southern England (RSPB 1997). This generated several planning applications for large new ports or port extensions around 2000, for new facilities in Southampton, London and the Harwich/Felixstowe area. This set off a public debate as to whether the government should be operating a free-market approach, as it had done since the 1980s, or whether wider social or environmental considerations should come into play. NGOs, grouping the campaigns against the port expansion schemes within Portswatch, argued that there should be strategic criteria guiding investment to areas with the most environmental capacity or social need, including to the north of England (Portswatch 2003). The government countered with support for market choice by the industry, subject to the consideration of details on each application. Eventually, by 2005, all four applications had been decided, with only one refused: Dibden Bay by Southampton, which was seen as too environmentally damaging. The other three were approved, though subject to some significant conditions requiring the supporting of investment in transport links and environmental compensation. Whilst the government then admitted in 2005 that some review of policy would be desirable, this never happened. The draft National Policy Statement (NPS) in late 2009 simply reiterated the case for port investment meeting rising future demand, and provided no spatial guidance, arguing that this must be left to the market (DfT 2009).

This then is a clear case of movement from an era of some public intervention, in part steered by regional planning considerations, to the dominance in the last 30 years of non-planning principles, or at least only the most localised planning (Pinder 2008). The net result was highly significant and responded, inevitably, to the changing trade patterns of this half-century or more (Beresford and Pettit 2009). In the 1950s the ports of London and Liverpool dominated most trade sectors, though there were quite a number of other significant ports spread around the UK. By 2004, south-eastern

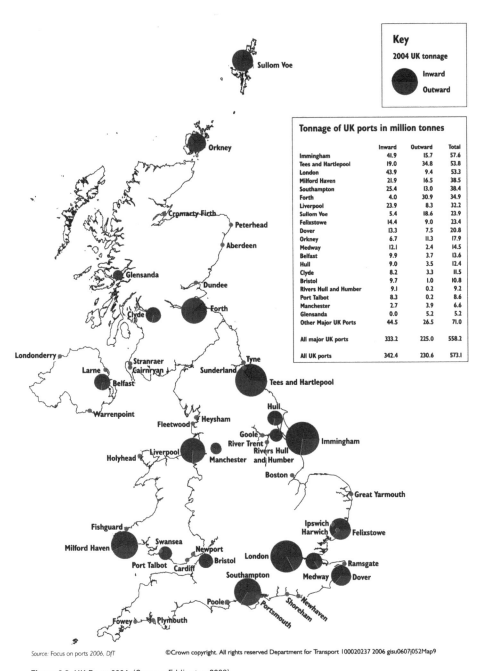

Key

2004 UK tonnage

Inward

Outward

Tonnage of UK ports in million tonnes

	Inward	Outward	Total
Immingham	41.9	15.7	57.6
Tees and Hartlepool	19.0	34.8	53.8
London	43.9	9.4	53.3
Milford Haven	21.9	16.5	38.5
Southampton	25.4	13.0	38.4
Forth	4.0	30.9	34.9
Liverpool	23.9	8.3	32.2
Sullom Voe	5.4	18.6	23.9
Felixstowe	14.4	9.0	23.4
Dover	13.3	7.5	20.8
Orkney	6.7	11.3	17.9
Medway	12.1	2.4	14.5
Belfast	9.9	3.7	13.6
Hull	9.0	3.5	12.4
Clyde	8.2	3.3	11.5
Bristol	9.7	1.0	10.8
Rivers Hull and Humber	9.1	0.2	9.2
Port Talbot	8.3	0.2	8.6
Manchester	2.7	3.9	6.6
Glensanda	0.0	5.2	5.2
Other Major UK Ports	44.5	26.5	71.0
All major UK ports	333.2	225.0	558.2
All UK ports	342.4	230.6	573.1

Source: Focus on ports 2006, DfT   ©Crown copyright. All rights reserved Department for Transport 100020237 2006 gisu0607j052Map9

Figure 9.2 UK Ports 2004. (Source: Eddington 2006)

ports were dominant in the most vital sector, container traffic, with London, Felixstowe, Dover and Southampton testimony to the tilt to a heavily consuming southern import economy (Figure 9.2). Humber, north-eastern and Scottish ports were important in other sectors of bulk trade, as well as Milford Haven in west Wales for oil and gas. So real spatial shifts had occurred, in part steered by public decisions and investment, in part responding to Britain's deindustrialisation and reorientation to consumption. This was not consciously planned in relation to other factors nationally, though in places regional planning did have some role in links to the hinterlands and transport systems of ports. So there was little scope for any link to some overall idea of the economic and environmental nature of Britain, with the incremental evolution of responses being paramount – responses increasingly set by the mainly globalised corporations which owned British ports: policy for a globalising economy, free of integrated governing.

Airports

Airports policy was in some respects more planned from above (Graham 2008, Sealy 1976, 1992). Airports, like ports, were largely in public hands until after 1986, when the BAA portfolio was sold off, including the three main London airports and the larger Scottish airports. Municipally owned airports were also gradually privatised, though Manchester airport remains municipal. Strong regulation was present, directly by the ministry and then in the shape of the Civil Aviation Authority from 1972, which controlled airport expansion, the use of landing slots and much else. As such, the airports industry has been publicly steered to a significant extent. Individual planning projects have been the most evident focus of public and political action. Decisions on airport expansions have been high profile, with one of the most famous UK planning exercises resulting in the choice of a site for a third London airport in 1973 (Roskill 1971), and struggles over expansion at Heathrow, Stansted and Manchester involving large campaigns and large public inquiries (Mander and Randles 2009). The building of the second runway at Manchester was opposed, unsuccessfully, by "eco warriors" in the early 1990s, whilst the similar project by BAA to expand Stansted was fought, so far successfully, by an alliance of very well resourced local residents, under the Stop Stansted Expansion campaign in the 2000s (Griggs and Howarth 2004, 2008). The proposal to expand Heathrow by means of a fifth terminal led to an eight-year process, with about half of this taken up by a public inquiry and the rest by other elements, above all political decision-making by ministers. Opponents of planning procedures made this the core of their campaign, despite the fact that it was completely atypical: one of the few cases of such long-running decision-making in post war history. The terminal was approved, and opened in 2008, thus showing the normal European pattern of up to two decades to implement such controversial projects.

What about the relationship of airport development to government sectoral policy? There was a continuous pull between more strategy-led and more hands-off approaches. For most of the period, the most important decisions were about the London airports, which dominated and still dominate in demand terms, so research and analysis tended to focus most on this question. Three policy-making episodes have taken place since the 1970s. The White Paper of 1978 (Department of Trade 1978) sought to set up some sort of hierarchy of primary and secondary airports, with Heathrow, Gatwick, Manchester and Prestwick as international hubs, and seven more B category airports where services should be concentrated, a choice which fitted ideas of prioritising investment. The 1985 White Paper (Department of Transport 1985) only retained one element of the 1978 priority system, maintaining support for Manchester in the "first division", and, most importantly, included the decision to privatise BAA (with the biggest airports), and encourage local authorities to sell their holdings. The 2003 White Paper sought to return to a more planned approach, to meet the expected high growth of demand to 2030. It identified airports to be expanded, including a raft of regional airports that had boomed on the low-cost carrier wave since the 1990s, and expansion of Stansted and Heathrow, subject to meeting environmental conditions. So it represented a long-term planning approach, but only partially linked to spatial planning considerations, primarily at the level of regional policy goals (supporting non-southern areas) and pressing for more environmentally sound land-side transport links, to be achieved by local and regional planning.

So how far can the infrastructure built over these decades be seen to be responding to wider strategic visions, and how far are they just emerging from the bottom up, from each airport operator? The answer is mixed. Sectoral planning was significant, prioritising London and Manchester as centres, and taking expansion decisions within the frame of White Papers, even if these were produced somewhat irregularly, and with varying research bases (the most comprehensive being in 1976 and 2003). But it can be seen that this largely matched market demand in any case, and so was predominantly trend-based planning, fitting in expansion regionally or sub-regionally, rather than challenging growth or wider locational geography. There were full debates in the 1976 episode about how far growth could be pushed up from London to the Midlands or even north, and the same recurred in 2003, but on each occasion there was limited enthusiasm for these options, which were seen as largely impractical. The post-1990 low-cost carrier boom showed how localised decisions could boost previously weaker centres, as well as give enormous pushes to the existing bigger airports – neither resulted from the outcome of national strategies, except in as far as the 1986 White Paper clearly hoped for market-led expansion. So, overall we see a half planned, half market-driven sector. But such planning as there was did not respond overall to wider spatial considerations. In a similar way to the ports case, there is a response to the underlying geography of economic change, with the richer southern businesses and residents enthusiastically adopting flying from the 1960s and driving expansion. This may be seen to fit the power of the southern-based national imaginary – of the naturalness of the overwhelming investment in aviation being around London. The balancing or contesting element of the expansion of other airports too, for example, the consistent national support for Manchester, shows another idea of the country, but in a subsidiary mode.

Roads

All modes of transport have seen big changes in the last half century, but that of roads has doubtless had the biggest impact on the whole nature of living in the UK. All existing roads have been improved, many trunk roads widened to dual carriageways, but the creation of the motorway system was the most dramatic infrastructure development of the twentieth century. This system was in part the result of international learning, with visits by roads engineers to Germany, the European innovator, in the 1930s. These visits resulted in schemes by various lobby groups in the late 1930s (Figure 9.3), detailing what had been much earlier calls for the creation of a new and separate system for cars (Plowden 1971). These were picked up by transport ministry officials during the war, and resulted in the first official strategy maps. Lack of funding and, to an extent, government enthusiasm held back progress till the early 1950s, but the shape of the system was more or less set at that time, and the first major road, the M1, was opened in 1959 (Baldwin and Baldwin 2004, Drake et al 1969, Starkie 1982). The motorway construction era ran on until the 1990s, with ups and downs due to increasing opposition in the 1970s, periods of more promotion of public transport investment, and spending cuts. This created a full national network, if it did not quite include every link desired by engineers or lobbies. It was far the biggest programme of infrastructure construction, running over four decades and riding out the occasional slow-downs. It was almost completely government funded from taxation, with just one toll road, the M6 toll road built in 2000–2003, bringing in another financing model. So, it is important to consider what thinking and ideas lay behind the overall achievement and the form that it took.

On one level, British settlement geography has not changed massively during the last century, with some interregional shifts leaving the north as a whole and most cities a bit emptier, many rural areas fuller, and the belt stretching up from the south west to Lincolnshire the main zone for new urbanisation (Fullerton 1982). Economic geography has changed rather more dramatically, cutting manufacturing zones and boosting office and service areas, especially in southern England. But the motorway system was designed in its broad outlines in the 1930s and 1940s, and fitted the idea of the country then. Even a redesign in 1970 would doubtless not have shifted

Figure 9.3 Motorway proposals 1938, as proposed by County Surveyors Society.
(Source: Baldwin and Baldwin 2004)

the positioning of the main axes much, with regional policy still supporting investment in the much less congested north. A redesign in 1990, if creation of the system had begun then, might well have thought of less investment in the north and more in the increasingly congested south. At any rate, it can be argued that the system responded to a straightforward idea of the country and its expected vehicle flows at mid-century. This was a decidedly unimodal idea, hardly (as far as one can tell in reading transport policy and motorway histories) related at all, at least explicitly, to other transport modes such as rail and ports. The roads' engineers and enthusiastic ministers who oversaw the system's creation from the 1950s were simply set on creating it, regarding motorways as being the essential counterpart to the adoption of cars and lorries as the main elements of movement. An effective network within the engineering community functioned to link up national, regional and county levels, securing approvals and land, led from London but well articulated downwards and with the construction industry gaining the contracts.

So there was no need, viewed from this perspective, for any linking to any other imaginary or spatial thinking. The principle was set once the die was cast to build a system in 1955, if not earlier. Routing decisions required local judgements and dealing with battles in localities, but these rarely set back construction, though they did make going much further with the programme increasingly difficult by the 1980s and 1990s. It may be that too much linking to any wider imaginary would have held back progress and generated doubts about the wisdom of the overall strategy, and whether this was what was wanted overall for the country. Motorway programmes internationally do appear to have this feature of insulation from wider understandings of countries, no doubt backed by such wide political support that this can work very effectively, until opposition towards the ends of programmes eats into this political consensus. By that time the bare bones of the system exist, with most places linked in or nearly so. This also appears to apply in countries with rather more planned approaches like France, Germany and Spain. Even in the Netherlands the motorway system may be largely a unimodal creation, based on "commonsense geography", the forces of demand speaking by themselves, rather than linked to national physical planning.

Rail

Railways in Britain have clearly had a dramatically different history from roads in the last 50 years (Haywood 2009, Henshaw 1991). The story is largely one of decline and contraction, although there has been large-scale modernising investment at certain periods, in the 1950s, 1970s and 2000s in particular. Only one significant new line has been built, the Channel Tunnel Rail Line (CTRL), opened in two steps in 2003 and 2007. This is for high-speed trains linking to the continental high-speed network, and was important in showing that a new line could be built in Britain, a century or more after the last major lines were finished. But it indicates that the creation of major new infrastructure in this sector has been very much the exception, compared with all the other sectors examined here.

Therefore the issue was largely how decline was planned, or more generally how the future of this transport mode was strategised. The moments that stand out in this history are the Beeching Report of 1962 (which recommended the closure of large parts of the rail system), the privatisation of the whole system in 1994, separating track (under one company) and train services (which were split into a number of separate operating companies) and an element of revival in the 2000s, in which state investment in modernising infrastructure has been significant, and in which more forward-looking strategic thinking began to emerge from about 2005 onwards. The first two of these key moments were treated very much unimodally, with implicit assumptions that railways were not, in most circumstances, key to the country's future. Decisions were not placed within an overall strategy for the future of person and freight movement around Britain. There had been other moments when, as mentioned above, transport policy had been treated in rather more integrated ways, but these were rare. Another exception has been some more integrated planning within the metropolitan areas, under arrangements made in the 1968 Transport Act, and to an extent in London, with GLC (Greater London Council) and GLA (Greater London Authority)/Mayor of London coordination able to plan across modes. The critical decisions of Beeching in particular were carried out almost totally on the basis of economic calculations of recent travelling trends, and not linked to spatial or other considerations. The majority of the report's proposals were implemented by the 1970s. So decline was a very much sectoralised operation: it may have been set within some wider idea of a switch to a road based movement system that political leaders had, but it is hard to see what imaginary future this was part of. The difference between this and the confident modernising thinking and investment in Japan and France, during the same period, is striking.

Privatisation followed the same model, expecting investment to be forthcoming on the criteria of profitability within the sector, without making the complex links to other modes and the mix of cross-subsidy involved. In effect, there was no strategy, just an "in principle" resolution to pass the decisions on to companies. When this turned out to be flawed, with the collapse of Railtrack (the infrastructure body) and the continued public support for train operations, the government responded with major infrastructure investment, and, eventually, with a more strategic approach. This was part of the moment referred to above, of TASTS and DASTS (also DfT 2007a), when government began to look forward with long-term planning across modes (or at least across road and rail). The last Secretary of State under the Labour governments, Lord Adonis, became a passionate advocate of rail and especially of a new high-speed rail line from London to the north. This project, called HS2, is being supported at present by the post-2010 government, though on a very long time-scale seeing implementation in the 2020s and 2030s. So, this third key moment has a different character from the previous ones, at least on the surface. Some of the enthusiasm for more planned and visionary approaches seen in many other European countries seems to have filtered across to political leaders and possibly parts of the wider public debates. Whilst there is clearly still no national spatial strategy with which a rail strategy might link, there is probably some underlying idea of a national space visible within the ongoing debates about HS2 in a way not seen before, certainly since the 1940s. We will return to this in the next chapter.

The rail sector is therefore another story of unimodalism, until the very recent past. It seems to have been largely remarkably detached from any wider thinking about the nature of the country and how it works, separated off as a technical or economic subsidy issue, or an ownership and organisational issue, rather than a critical part of real territorial functioning. This has to be qualified as above, that at metropolitan level there has been far more linking to planning in an integrated manner, facilitated by the institutional innovation of Passenger Transport Authorities since 1968, and the (fitful) support given to these by government funding. Whilst this has not produced the outburst of investment in trams or train systems seen in many continental cities, it has shown capacity to plan in a more integrated way, when the opportunity is given, with midland and northern conurbations gaining some new systems. Largely though, in line with what we are seeing as a common pattern in British transport policy, there has been a determined construction of space and institutions to block such opportunities, from the 1950s onwards. Each mode is separated, a deliberate construction, with real continuing impacts: an impressive motorway system, a declining railway and market-driven ports and airports sectors. This is the top political framing – meta-governance – of infrastructure thinking and creation, not a "natural" policy-making flow. The (non) intersection is in some ways critical in blocking radical long-term thinking, by separating off real choices into limited silo zones. Territory matters, and there are gains in bringing it in – as we will see that it has been, to some good effects, in the devolved post-2000 administrations.

Water

Water infrastructure investment is a receding image to a large extent. The expansion of water storage by means of reservoirs became increasingly contested from the 1950s onwards. These had been largely carried out by local action: cities negotiating arrangements with their catchments, near or far, to build reservoirs and pipelines. In 1963 a national Water Resources Board (WRB) was set up and one of its last acts, before abolition in 1974, was to publish a large-scale water strategy calling for a range of new infrastructure to meet the rising demand that British industries and households had been exhibiting for some decades. This strategy was later seen as overblown, constituting the high point of what came to be called the "supply-fix" mentality of the water engineers who dominated the industry (CPRE 1993). Proposals included the development of estuary schemes, groundwater schemes, enlarging existing reservoirs and building new ones, as well as water transfer schemes. Such schemes did not disappear, but the force of central guidance was much reduced for many years. A Central Water Planning Unit in the Department of Environment survived till 1979, and a National Water Council with advisory powers through the 1980s, but neither pressed strongly for national-level responses (Parker and Penning-Rowsell 1980).

In 1977 the Labour government did propose in a White Paper to set up a National Water Authority (Department of Environment 1977). This was to prepare a broad national strategy, coordinating the work of the Regional Water Authorities (RWAs) created in 1974, as well as to carry out research and data collection, overview investment and abstraction licensing, and in general provide a more consistent approach to water policy-making. However this never progressed. The new regional bodies were already showing their strength, and did not want much national steering. In three of the fields I am looking at, there has been a moment when the creation of such a national authority has been considered (where it did not exist already, as it did effectively for energy, rail and roads). But in all three cases such a route has not been taken, with other regulatory or governance solutions being adopted for ports, airports and water.

Hanna's account (in House 1982) makes it clear that a real debate on how to deal with water issues ran through the 1970s. Had the predictions of the WRB and of several RWAs been right, then avoiding large-scale new supply-schemes would have been difficult. What happened was that the collapse of industrial demand, a certain degree of conservation in several fields, and new and cheaper ways of regulating supplies, particularly by regulating the use of rivers, all put off most of the major investment needs. The detailed consideration of estuarine schemes, with or without inland reservoirs and transfers, could be left on the shelf. This was not a result of planning or great foresight, but some sort of incremental adaptation by the RWAs to their often-constrained financial situations.

The privatisation of the RWAs in 1990 set up a new regulatory framework, with an economic/social regulator (Ofwat) and the Environment Agency taking over the tasks managed from 1987 to 1995 by the National Rivers Authority (NRA). The NRA did still consider the scope for big supply schemes (NRA 1992, 1994), but the Environment Agency progressively moved away from that approach. In 2006 it issued a short report entitled "Do we need large-scale water transfers for south east England?" in a response to the drought that was affecting the UK. The answer, after a quick analysis of the costs of likely west to east or north to south transfers, was no: no need at all. After listing six possible schemes, the Agency said:

> We believe that some new reservoirs will be required in south east England, though we do not think that all of those proposed will prove necessary. Water companies must work together to explore all the options and to build strong cases for any proposed reservoir development.
>
> (Environment Agency 2006 p.15).

The Agency's 2009 strategy suggested that it wished to avoid the need for any new schemes (Environment Agency 2009). Large new reservoirs were still not ruled out, with a few schemes being proposed in England. Six of these were in water companies' plans in 2004, all in the stressed south: for example, by South East Water at Clay Hill in Sussex, or by Thames Water near Abingdon. A public inquiry into the Abingdon scheme in 2010 resulted in a rejection of Thames Water's Water Resources Plan, of which this was the cornerstone. This was an inquiry under the water regulatory and investment process, not one under the Planning Acts, showing the complexity of public steering of water policy. The ministry has tended to be a bit more guarded than the Agency, sometimes supporting the idea of some new investment (for example, Department of Environment 1996). But on balance, since the 1990s, the hopes of water companies to increase supply in southern England have been given limited encouragement.

Therefore there are two tracks evident in water planning and its links to spatial planning in this 40 or 50 year period: one national, one regional. The nearest thing to a national water plan was at a time (1973) when integrated big spatial planning was already challenged, and so the strategy had little to integrate into. As in some other fields, the scale was shifted for a few years to the regional scale, with some integrated planning progressing in the 1970s, resulting in some "successes" for the "supply-fix" approach (though in a case like Kielder in northern England, this was rather more a memorial to the difficulties of integrated forward planning, as the expected demand never materialised due to northern deindustrialisation). A decade of no planning at either level followed.

The last two decades have again seen activity at the national level, but this is increasingly focused on avoiding infrastructure development of any kind, and therefore little interaction with spatial planning has been necessary. As always, this requires a different sort of spatial planning, related to demand management and to connecting the ecological bases of current and new development. At the regional level tensions have been different, with intense debate around regional strategies and the water implications of development. Sophisticated working arrangements between the Environment Agency, regional planning bodies and water companies developed during the 2000s in several English regions, giving a firmer set of evidence for the 2005–2008 round of Regional Spatial Strategies. This was to provide help for the placing of new urban development, seeing the implications for managing demand, and possibly for new supply arrangements. The linking up of planning in the two fields at this level was developing at this time, although whether that filtered up to the national level in substantive terms and in action is more questionable.

Energy

Energy-infrastructure investment has never gone away in the manner that has tended to occur with water. Energy is seen as more critical, by governments and by business, and although the role of the state has been highly contested, the issues have always been in the public view. There are two eras in which very different relationships to spatial steering have existed. The first ran from the Second World War to the end of the 1980s, when most of the energy industries were owned by the state and were therefore guided in whatever was considered as being in the national interest in each period. This applied to coal, gas and electricity industries, but not to oil. The second period began around the end of the 1980s, when all the sectors passed to private ownership, in most cases to become part of foreign-controlled corporations, and where a regulatory machinery, centred on Ofgem, has been critical to the operation of each industry. The network parts of the gas and electricity sectors are under one company: National Grid (a profit-seeking corporation, but one expected to fulfil some public tasks). Supply-side solutions have always dominated over conserving energy, or creating a built environment that would minimise new supply needs. This is continuing in the era when low carbon is finally being considered by UK governments.

Fuel and power policy, or energy policy as it came to be known from the 1960s, was part of the "commanding heights" of the economy, and at various periods had its own ministry – most recently since 2008, as the Department of Energy and Climate Change (DECC). Energy policy was normally conceived sectorally, with little attempt to examine the links to urban change or regional policy – though in the regional planning exercises of the 1960s or 1970s, energy issues did sometimes surface, for example, in the planning of the arrangements for North Sea gas and oil. Normally the decisions were internal to the industries. For example, from the 1950s new power stations tended to be constructed near the coal-fields, not near the consumption centres, for transport reasons (Hills 1984, Humphrys 1982). At first nuclear power stations were to go away from coal field areas, thus in the south, though with some spreading around to the north from the late 1960s, coastal locations being preferred, given Britain's absence of rivers big enough for cooling functions. Although elaborate search methodologies were deployed by the Central Electricity Generating Board, Helm (2004a) sees the choices as being more incremental, slotting into zones of least resistance, and later where companies already owned sites, given the lack of consensus on energy policy which remained the norm. North Sea oil and gas investment followed the "natural" geography. The national gas grid built in the 1970s, without too much fuss it seems (Roberts and Shaw 1984), reflected patterns of maximum demand, with the flow running from the east-coast arrival points to the zone of big energy use, along a line from London to Manchester. That line is the backbone for other sectors of course: motorways, rail and the electricity grid. In that sense there is an "obvious" awareness of the geography of the country, just as was expressed to me in Spain. But that obviousness tends to be challenged each time a paradigm is fundamentally changing, whether in industry, settlement, energy or transport.

All this was decided by government, even though in the case of North Sea oil it was normally in conjunction with the oil multinationals (Mackay 1984). So this was nothing like a private enterprise gas and oil rush. The effect was clearly to transform the energy geography, meaning that the country faced eastwards for several decades for its core energy-base, just as it had previously looked into its coalfield heartlands for a century or more, as well as (for a generation or more) to more remote global oil sources. The privately-run oil industry, it may be noted, was the most "market oriented" part of the geography, with its refineries mostly based near the largest areas of demand in the south-east of England. However, this was in part "distorted" by regional incentives which encouraged some refineries to other areas, with 70 per cent of new refineries after 1960 being located in Development Areas (Humphrys 1982 p.298). But these had some market sense too, with the big markets at that stage for steel plants or other heavy industry in the north-west, midlands and south Wales. Britain's geography is distinctive in that sense, with most industrial markets less than 100 kilometres from navigable waters.

So we see already in the pre-1990 period how "constructed" the geography was by the underlying political economy, allied to other features of the UK's economic geography, with explicit spatial aims coming a poor third in power of causation (above all regional policy, often melded with the Labour government's electoral instincts). We may generalise by saying that the energy geography of Britain before the early twentieth-century (above all before the forming of the Central Generating Board in 1926), with coal the key agent, was formed by market forces. Since the 1920s/1940s, this has not been so. This served to preserve both the energy geography (coalfield cores) and the economic and demographic geography to a degree, as it stood at the end of the most marketised era, say in the 1920s. Continuing public control through a period of big change, the 1960s to 1980s, allowed this to be maintained in a way that might have been quite different under a privately-owned regime. North Sea oil and gas came to cover over the collapse of coal under the Conservative governments between 1979 and 1997, aided secondarily by the nuclear plants of the 1960s and 1970s. All this was facilitated by the global oil market, constructed since the 1950s with Britain as an active participant, which fed into Britain's decades as an oil (and gas) power. These are the determining coordinates of the constructed spatiality or energy geography.

Since 1990 the dynamics of investment, regulation and government policy have been very different. Given the long life of most energy infrastructure, this does not mean that everything has changed. Precisely the massive investment in the decades before 1990 meant that, as Helm has stressed, this has been largely a period when the inherited assets could be "sweated". This meant that the inherited geographical elements could to a large extent be "sweated" too, not requiring any large-scale reorientation of the country, as had occurred regularly through the period of the 1950s to 1970s.

Helm's account of the history of UK energy policy (2004a) gives several examples of the way in which the new regime impacted on the spatial structure of energy, without this ever being a deliberate aim of policy. Generators were given permission to build new power stations by the regulator, who wanted above all to encourage new entrants. This allowed the rush to gas, spreading new generation around haphazardly in a way that Helm judges to have "led to significant inefficiency in locations of new plant" (p.136). In effect the grid company was obliged to connect whatever the generators created. This was also a result of differing regulatory systems for electricity and gas, giving different pricing signals: as Helm says, the effects of institutional design are now cemented into our energy systems (pp.279–280). Another example was how generators created new ports facilities for coal, when the fuel supply market was liberalised in 1993. Again this was an institutional design effect, Helm argues, from the failure to create competition in electricity early on (pp.177–178). The effect was to allow the switch to globalised coal sources, with massive impacts on the geography of the remaining British coal industry.

Each country has an energy-space economy, which goes through periods of stability and radical change. In Scrase and MacKerron's terms (2009), the lock-in achieved from earlier rounds of investment was working forcefully, and to the advantage of new owners. Helm would refer to the position in the "capacity cycle", with excess capacity in the 1980s and 1990s meaning that different forms of governance were not critical, given the overall (constructed) availability of power (2004b pp.16–17). He sees this as changing through the 2000s and being a major element in the change of energy paradigm.

Some saw energy policy as dead after privatisation – there was no energy ministry from 1992 to 2008 at any rate. But recent policy for energy has been a fast-moving zone, with five White Papers in six years, following the general absence of such strategising for decades. The 2003 White Paper (DTI 2003) first raised low carbon to a major policy concern, that of 2007 (DTI 2007) brought nuclear power back into being a primary governmental goal, developed in a White Paper just on this issue in 2008 (DBERR 2008), whilst the two 2009 White Papers on a low-carbon transition strategy and on renewable energy rushed the agenda forward to much more ambitious transitional programmes (DECC 2009a, 2009b).

Several areas of development had real significance for planning, hence the ever closer intertwining of energy policy and planning concerns from 2006 onwards, in dramatic contrast to their only passing acquaintance, normally case by case, over several decades. These included:

- The designation of wind-farm zones off three coastal areas, and the sale of options by the Crown Estate, from 2003 onwards. This was one of the Maritime Management Organisation's main tasks after its establishment in 2010.
- Building of Liquefied Natural Gas (LNG) terminals, most importantly at Milford Haven (open in 2009 and a connecting pipeline to England), but also in Essex and Anglesey.
- Nuclear power stations, even if their impact was intended to be moderated by simply developing existing sites. This was widely seen as the critical drive for the planning reforms.
- Nuclear-waste site search. This rose to the front of the policy queue after the report of the Committee on Radioactive Waste Management (CoRWM 2006), and the White Paper on the issue in 2008 (DECC 2008).
- Tidal barrage schemes, with the Sustainable Development Commission giving cautious support for a Severn Estuary scheme in 2007 and the government consulting on the options for the Severn, carrying out a feasibility scheme in 2009–2010, and discussing the options for other areas (Morecambe Bay and Solway Firth, for example). The Severn estuary scheme was abandoned by the government in October 2010.
- Discussion of smart grids for electricity, and more widely the appreciation of the need for extensive change to the national grid, given the need to connect up wind farms and other renewables and to replace a rapidly ageing system that had largely been "sweated" by its private owners for 20 years. Government convened a DECC-Ofgem Electricity Networks Strategy Group (ENSG 2009).
- Even transport and land use issues seem to have returned to the agenda, with the Committee on Climate Change (2009) referring rather vaguely to the potential for integrated land-use and transport planning (pp.11 and 26).

All this suggests that the spatiality of energy policy is resurgent in the UK, as it could potentially be on the continent. But this has not led to much spatialised energy policy-making, in England at any rate. Attempts were made to insert renewables policy within RSS (Regional Spatial Strategies) processes in the 2000s, but this had limited success, with policy there remaining largely localised and responsive. Only on offshore wind was government spatial planning more confident, showing (as usual) the specificity of this zone, free of normal political pressures and with a distinct political economy of ownership (the state in the shape of the Crown Estate being the prime mover).

So, we may conclude that energy planning has always been sectoral, and largely sub-sectoral, with little explicit account being taken of spatial factors. However, with the change of paradigm, or of challenges, this situation began to generate big tensions given the privatisation of control, the lack of a national consensus on energy and the force of local opposition. So planning at all levels is more in the energy front-line, in a way that for various reasons it was not in previous periods of change. The situation is extremely challenging for any government to manage.

Waste

Infrastructure for waste treatment, whether landfill sites, recycling or treatment centres, or incinerators, is a good example of how the governmental framing of the issue results in an initial scaling of decisions, and then a "natural" linking (or not) to spatial planning possibilities. In Britain waste issues were localised until the 1990s, both in overall policy and for planning, with continued adherence to a traditional waste to landfill system (Blowers 1992). Until PPG10 (Planning Policy Guidance Note 10) was finalised in 1999, Davoudi and Evans say that "the location of waste disposal sites was determined in the context of a national policy vacuum" (2005, p.26). This changed, with new regulatory structures and privatisation of the industry giving new dynamics, and hard EU targets looming for 2012 and 2020. This institutional and economic reconfiguration combined to generate a search for new systems with a new geography.

Government's first thoughts in the draft waste strategy in 1999 were to push strongly for a dramatic growth in incinerators, meaning 130 new ones around the country (DETR 1999b, p.25). This was toned down somewhat in the final strategy (DETR 2000), given widespread criticism. The 2007 strategy (DEFRA 2007) was less insistent on incinerators, giving only a range of scenarios in an appendix, and targets of 25 per cent of municipal waste by 2020 for energy recovery, including anaerobic digestion (as against 34 per cent by 2015 which had been suggested in 2000). Apart from wishing to encourage anaerobic digestion, it proclaimed itself technology neutral, saying that the best mix depended on circumstances. The strategy put considerable emphasis on both the planning side, including RSSs and local plans, and the financing and facilitation side, with the Waste Infrastructure Development Programme (WIDP) given a major role, and Private Finance Initiative (PFI) funding the preferred model for supporting new plants (NAO 2009, WIDP 2006).

The spatial planning component worked largely at county (and unitary) level, framed by regions. Regions allocated waste quantities to authorities, who then decided what to do about the "capacity gap" left by these allocations and the need to reduce landfill. Since 1997 this has generated a stream of proposals for large new infrastructure, which is largely contracted for by the big companies: a few arms-length municipal operations remain, like the Greater Manchester company. So, the essential theatre is sub-regional, but in interaction with the ministry, which controls the PFI credits which are essential for most schemes to have a chance of going ahead. The regional layer worked variably, according to a comprehensive study of Davoudi et al (2005), but appears often to have left the tough decisions to local authorities. The new guidance, PPS10 (ODPM 2005, 2006), said that apportionment was to follow a rational process, with attempts to maximise the extent to which sub-regions dealt with their own waste (with other factors coming in too: so this was qualified, as was regional self containment). PPS10 also said that the RSS should show "the broad locations where the pattern of waste management facilities should be accommodated" (ODPM 2005 p.9). This rather vague wording identified the difficulty in this planning area, given that localities rarely wish to welcome waste treatment plants.

This left the issue at a level, unlike almost all other infrastructure sectors, where integration with the rest of spatial planning was at least plausible. The local and the sub-regional are the levels in England where such integration could traditionally work, however messy it could sometimes get in terms of formal statutory planning and of integrating with central government programmes. In principle, government could have taken a more leading role in this sector, but the political costs argued against this. Letting the councils carry the task, and just adjudicating on the inevitable appeals, was easier. This was a created structuring of spatial decision-making, not something "natural". The whole privatisation and regulatory dynamic spelt out a sort of retreat. But EU policy and environmentalism demanded other responses. Spatial dimensions were caught in the middle. There was a sort of spatial policy from the early 1990s onwards: reduce landfill, keep relatively local, allow large private firms to run and leave to sub-regional bodies (all of these effectively closed off certain spatial options). But how those worked out was complex and uncertain: far from a spatial strategy. So, all the battles about the location of waste treatment plants were localised.

An alternative national view might be to go back to first principles, as some of the background scenario work for the 2007 White Paper did, and then consider appropriate scales of action, costs to society and levels of control. This might challenge the present structure, which is a sort of public–private partnership arranged around local and central government. This might reconfigure the system spatially, and could have a radical affect on the sorts of infrastructure seen as appropriate and on the ways of obtaining and running them.

CONCLUSIONS ON THE "TRADITIONAL" PLANNING OF MAJOR INFRASTRUCTURE

Two levels of analysis have been attempted here. One is to understand how the infrastructure industries were managed "on the surface", whether in the mainly publicly-owned era or in the years after the 1980s. This showed a norm of managing within tightly bounded frameworks, stopping even considerations crossing from say road to rail or coal to renewables, let alone to spatial planning concerns. Figure 9.4 gives a bare summary of the account. Sectoral planning's nature meant that there was little stimulus from those sources for forming a clearer idea of the country, which allowed the perpetuation of a fuzzy and contested national spatial imaginary. The aspiration, especially after privatisation, was to leave investment to the market or at least to the experts who knew about demand and technical matters. Transport policy, energy policy, water policy: all these were to be avoided if possible, even though politicians periodically sought broader ideas in order to address the problems that bubbled up. Spatial considerations came in by the side door, as afterthoughts. The absence of any national spatial planning required such denial or absence of linking. At times regional planning did do something to fill the gap, but rarely in an effective way, with real powers rarely concentrated at that level. More localised coherence was possible in some cases: in metropolitan transport planning and in some cases in county waste or renewables energy planning. But this localised level was too low for many purposes, certainly the big framing of energy and transport systems.

The other level examined here has been the underlying spatial or geographical construction of policy zones, which sits underneath the changing infrastructure systems. This constructedness of the spatiality of each sector has been harder to pin down here without presenting lengthy case studies. The full resistance, in England at any rate, to any sort of higher spatial framing, necessarily fixes most infrastructure decisions as project decisions, like those on ports and often airports, and refuses the scope to consider in relation to other big investment choices, or big regional development options. This fits neatly with a commitment to a private-competition based economy, and so has been especially powerful since the 1980s. But it also describes the siloised systems of government which have been the norm since the 1940s, where each ministry has power within its own field, without the need to consider what this might do for broader territorial developments (in the style of DATAR or Dutch national physical planning). At times utilities have been involved in more integrated approaches, as in the regional planning wave following the 1965 National Plan, but this was very much the exception.

Reflections on the UK's geography are relevant to this constructedness. A "traditional" British geographer like Fullerton (1982) made much of the shape and size of Britain. This meant, he argued, that different modes fitted variably into this "small" island, such that rail was not very comfortable

Figure 9.4 The links between infrastructure sectors and spatial policy and planning.

Sector	Clear spatial policy	Link to integrated spatial thinking	Links to town and country planning
Roads	Yes, connecting of whole network to key urban and economic areas.	None explicit at all, purely unimodal.	Only at local and subregional levels, via links to strategic and local planning; a little linking in recent regionalist round.
Rail	Not really, spatially drifting, though reduction of network had a spatial analysis, to retain only core urban links.	Very little, unimodal, except at subregional metropolitan level since 1968.	Little, though some attempts in conurbation areas and in recent regional work to make links.
Ports	Some national and regional thinking about spatial balances up to 1979, not at all since.	Very little linked to other modes, at least since 1960s, though some roads/ports key routes do get noticed.	Mainly local case by case, with national support for expansion, in case of appeals.
Airports	Sometimes white papers did give overall spatial policy (1947, 1978, 2003). But also depended on two zone structure (London and the rest) and often very incremental.	Rather unimodal, though some thought regionally in 1970s and 2000s.	Mostly case by case, though some linking via the big white paper strategising phases.
Energy	Some spatial policy within each sector, little linking between them, though some overall coherence during the publicly controlled era. National equal access and pricing policy an important overall spatial norm.	Only implicitly linked into economic geography, as part of overall economic policy, but largely within its own sector.	Case by case, but public bodies during publicly controlled era drove strongly, with power on their side rather than on that of planning system.
Water	Locally set until 1970s, regional since, with national spatial direction never practically adopted, despite occasional national consideration.	Only partial linking into regional thinking on economic geographies, in 1970s and again in 2000s.	Case by case in earlier period, little development in last 30 years, so rarely an issue.
Waste	No, localised arrangements, though recent policy on finance and cooperation across subregions has spatial implications.	No linking to wider development issues, though regional policy making in 2000s in some cases connected to other regional concerns.	Case by case, despite attempts via regional policy mechanisms in 2000s.

(Source: own elaboration)

with the shorter distances, road was extremely well adapted, and air was always going to be limited internally. The number and diversity of ports was a natural result of geography, though not one conducive to meeting European competition. Internally, he refers to the "axial belt" of the country, being a strip from Lancashire to Kent, 400 kilometres long and 120 kilometres wide, containing most people and economic activity, and generating most freight movement. All these conditioning inheritances clearly do influence the imaginary and implicit ideas of policy makers in each sector. But, taking the long view, they are all socio-economically constructed, with policy makers far from being free agents.

The question then is: Which of these two dynamics is the one with more impact on what really happens? Is the underlying construction what really matters, taking in the political economy and constitutional considerations, or is the evident power of unimodal or subsectoral decision-making enough to focus on? No doubt it is important to understand both. The dominant tendencies (meeting growth expectations, following demand, taking paths of least political resistance) created a spatial path-set which the unimodalism then fits and cements by policy decisions. The underlying drives and the sub-sectoralism of governments have been complementary parts of the spatial governance regime for infrastructure-making in Britain. Planning is, as always, only a part of the whole mechanism set. We may expect in the next chapter to take much of this baggage with us into the future, as we examine the 2000s reforms to that planning component, and to a certain extent to other elements.

CHAPTER 10
NEW APPROACHES TO MAJOR INFRASTRUCTURE PLANNING IN THE UK

We have seen how the "traditional" approach to planning major infrastructure worked in the UK up to the early 2000s. This chapter switches to the most recent period, looking mainly at change in England, but with shorter studies of the new regime in Scotland and the situations in Wales and Northern Ireland. This will be complemented by a scan of a few large projects of recent importance. The chapter will finish by returning to the question of the role of national imaginaries in thinking about infrastructure systems, and how this may affect planning or strategising at this scale.

THE 2008 PLANNING ACT SYSTEM

The 2008 Planning Act introduced a new system for dealing with major infrastructure projects, or "Nationally Significant Infrastructure Projects", NSIPs, as the Act called them (Duxbury 2009, Moore 2010). This applied to England and, for certain sectors and for larger energy and harbour projects, to Wales. It had very little application to Scotland, and none to Northern Ireland. The system was for all projects over certain thresholds, essentially including new development on a large scale in all the sectors examined in this book. The system contained three main elements. One was relatively uncontroversial: an attempt to simplify the consents regime, so that developers could meet the majority of different regulatory requirements with one application. The other two elements are shown in Figure 10.1. The strategic part is a new system of National Policy Statements (NPSs): sectoral policy documents

Figure 10.1 The two main elements of the infrastructure planning system
formed under the 2008 Planning Act

Element of 2008 system	Function	Form of operation	Progress of implementation	Prospects under post May 2010 government
National Policy Statements	To set main strategic guidelines to be taken into account by IPC.	Drawn up by sectoral ministry (energy, environment or transport), debated by parliamentary select committee, and approved by government.	6 Energy NPSs published in draft in November 2009, and in revised form in late 2010. Ports NPS published in draft in November 2009, revision awaited. Waste Water NPS published in draft in November 2010. Other NPSs, on national networks (road and rail), and hazardous waste, expected 2011–12.	New government accepts the 2008 system, although expects to alter guidance on other parts of national planning, possibly with national planning framework. Parliament will now approve all NPSs by votes.
Infrastructure Planning Commission	To take decisions, once NPSs are approved, on all infrastructure projects above certain thresholds. Time limits for decisions will apply, normally a maximum of 6 or 9 months from the submission of schemes.	Project applicants have to conduct one round of consultation, and the IPC a second, prior to (if necessary) hearings. IPC consultation phase includes the submission of local impact reports by local authorities. Decisions are by panels or single commissioners depending on nature of project.	Chair, deputy chairs and 36 commissioners appointed by spring 2010. Co-located with Planning Inspectorate in Bristol. First formal application submitted in August 2010.	IPC will be abolished and incorporated in Planning Inspectorate as Major Infrastructure Planning Unit. Final decisions will be made by minister, not Commission, once legislation is revised, by late 2011.

(Source: own elaboration)

intended to spell out government's view of the need for new infrastructure investment, and how to judge conditions for approval. This was then to be the guide for any decisions in that field for the coming years, until the NPS might be revised. The NPSs were to be worked up by the relevant sectoral ministry, and then consulted on publicly and via the relevant parliamentary Select Committee. After revision they would then be issued by government. So, this part built on the White Paper approach used, for example, in the Aviation 2003 document, but giving this greater force as the prime guide on principle for the relevant sector, and having far more detail to help decision making. As such, it was in several respects a novel regulatory instrument.

The second part, and the one which aroused most controversy, was the creation of an Infrastructure Planning Commission (IPC). This would receive applications for permission to build all schemes over the thresholds, manage the consultation process (including public examination where needed) and make final decisions within the framework of the NPSs (where these exist and are up to date). Developers had to prove they had already carried out pre-application consultation to a proper standard before applications would be accepted. A maximum of six months was allowed for the IPC to examine applications, with another three months after this to issue decisions. The IPC was indeed formed, and by the fall of the Labour government in May 2010, had recruited 36 Commissioners and set up an administrative base alongside the Planning Inspectorate. This was therefore quite a strongly innovative approach, emphasising independence of government and arms-length decision making. Always in the past elected ministers had made final decisions on schemes – this principle was now abandoned. The Commissioners were appointed by government, but the principle was to be that they were independent after their appointment.

In 2010–2012 this system was modified by the Conservative–Liberal Democrat government: both parties had criticised the 2008 Act. The 2011 Localism Act now removed the part they most disliked: the decision-making by the IPC. So the IPC was abolished and inserted into the Planning Inspectorate as a National Infrastructure Directorate. Final decisions, based on National Infrastructure Directorate advice, were to go back to ministers. Other changes included the need to have parliamentary approval of NPSs, intended to give them greater legitimacy. Many observers saw these changes as leaving most of the 2008 changes intact, even though the principle of ministerial approval was constitutionally and politically important. The limited extent of the changes reflected the basic consensus in the major parties about the need to streamline the system, despite the disagreement about details. To understand how this consensus was constructed, we need to look at how the Act came to be, before looking at the two components in a little more depth.

THE PROCESS OF REFORM IN THE UK GOVERNMENT

The lead up to the infrastructure planning reforms

After 1945 the publicly-owned utilities were privileged in planning terms, and only gradually from the 1960s did difficulties begin to emerge in planning major projects (Marshall 2010a). This did not lead to very pressing calls for planning reform, with a general assumption that the normal system of public inquiries was there to deal with the struggles over both principles and siting, whatever the outcome in one case or another. Some planning experts did argue for a more effective national framing of major infrastructure in the 1980s (Bruton and Nicholson 1987, Nuffield Foundation 1986) and this formed a minor key of planning debate through to the political reforms arguments of the 2000s.

The major key was provided by business pressure. In 1992 the Confederation of British Industry (CBI) published a report worked up with the Royal Institute of Chartered Surveyors (RICS), called "Shaping the nation". The RICS published a similar report (1992), which also suggested a "national land-use strategy interlinked with a transportation strategy and a statement of national long term objectives", and wanted the Departments of Environment and Transport to merge (RICS 1992 p.16). However, the RICS report was essentially about transport. The CBI's was an interventionist call for a much more strategic and national-led approach to infrastructure planning. They pointed to greater French efficiency in dealing with the Channel Tunnel and its links. The report saw delays and uncertainty as major inefficiencies, and that these increased risk. This theme of risk is one that returns again and again during the 1990s and 2000s.

The CBI then called for a national policy framework, led by a cross-departmental annual national-policy paper, costed by the Treasury and guaranteeing available capital. They wanted integration of land use, transport and environmental policies, and national strategies including roads, rail and air transport. They also recommended more use of Special Development Orders by government for specific projects – effectively an override system, which governments had rarely wished to use. Here we are seeing business pushing for a more coordinated central government role. Already the view on public inquiries was that they should not have to discuss need once the national policy was in place – the continuing refrain for the next 15 years.

The presence, in already considerable force, of "infrastructuralism" is clear: the word infrastructure recurs frequently in the 1992 CBI report, and the sense of lost millions due to planning costs and delays is already in full flow: "*major infrastructure and business projects are not well catered for in the absence of clear strategic guidance and this results in avoidable costs both to business and the nation*" (p.6). A later report (CBI 1995) showed a similar perspective, though with a stronger marketising orientation and significant worries about cuts in the roads programme. A full European comparative study examined transport planning problems, and decided that a long-term coordinated strategy was the way forward that looked 20 years ahead, similar to the view of 1992. The strategy should identify key transport corridors. Growth was the key, and much of the undertone of the approach, as ever since with the CBI, is to press on with more roads capacity. By 2000 the CBI manifesto, designed to keep up the pressure on the Labour government, was unambiguous in its phrasing on planning: "The planning system is seen by business as a barrier to competitiveness ... The government should ... urgently and radically improve the speed and transparency of the planning process. For major infrastructure projects, the time taken to hold enquiries must be radically shortened" (CBI 2000 pp.22–23). A later paper (CBI 2005) pressed the need for national policy statements, again to get away from lengthy inquiries, and was very critical of planning as a barrier.

The reform process began to gain momentum after 1997. From their first weeks the Blair governments were concerned about the time taken in deciding on major infrastructure. One of my interviewees explained that in May 1997 the Prime Minister Tony Blair had asked the ministry containing planning for urgent proposals to speed up the planning system at national, regional and local levels. The responding memo dated 4 July 1997 offered various ideas on how this might be done. The section of the memo on major infrastructure sketches out three elements which the department considered would improve matters:

- Improve public inquiry procedures;
- Make more use of parliamentary procedures, broadening the approach of the 1992 Transport and Works Act; and
- Publish more explicit national planning-policy guidance and national policy statements on the need for projects of national importance, such as airports, roads or prisons.

Already in 1997 we see both sides of the New Labour approach to the question. Firstly, politicians were already worried about the issue, and we may reasonably assume (I believe it would be hard to extract this evidence now) that the CBI or similar business bodies were behind the pressure: Blair himself was not known for ever having had a personal interest in planning. Secondly, civil servants already had a menu of possible responses, which were those that had in one way or another been under discussion since the mid 1980s. In all likelihood, when left to themselves the civil servants inclined towards a light-touch mix of all three elements, which is in effect what came about in 2005. This resulted in a detailed speeding up of public-inquiry procedures and pressure being applied to other departmental policy-makers to make explicit sectoral planning statements, of which the Airports White Paper was the only one to have a really spatialised approach. However, the parliamentary route is also present, so this situation did not emerge from nowhere in 2000–2001.

During the first term of government this did not result in practical action in this area (DETR 1999a, 1999b). This changed in 2001, when a reform to the procedures for deciding on major projects was proposed, moving to decisions by Parliament (DTLR 2001a, 2001b). This was attacked by environmental, legal and parliamentary interests, and was dropped from the wider planning-reform package (House of Commons Procedure Committee 2002,

ODPM 2002). No coherent story-line had been created by that stage, with only a push from the Prime Minister, and limited support around government. Planning bodies did not really oppose this or the 2007 initiative, with the Royal Town Planning Institute being broadly supportive, perhaps seeing this as a move towards its hoped-for national planning framework (RTPI 2006, also see TCPA 2006). But wider planning scepticism was considerable.

However, the New Labour agenda, increasingly driven from the Treasury, now had a fixed idea that major infrastructure reform was needed. Two major inquiries in 2005–2006, led by Kate Barker (previously of the CBI) and Rod Eddington (previously head of British Airways) concluded from planning and transport perspectives that a reform was now possible, by setting up an "independent" planning body to make decisions, beyond the immediate political sphere (Barker 2006, Eddington 2006). Equally importantly, the energy review of the same year decided that nuclear power stations were needed to fill the prospective energy gap, and that planning reform was critical to this as well as to other progress on renewable energy (DTI 2007, Kelly 2008). In this way the three key departments (business, finance and transport) were lined up for a planning reform, and the matter was taken out of the hands of the department in which planning sat (still unconvinced of the need for a root-and-branch reform, having successfully promoted other approaches since 2001), and worked up in the Cabinet Office. The practical details quickly emerged in a planning White Paper (HM Government 2007) and the nature of the reform was fixed. Opposition to the bill was significant in the environmental movement, but limited elsewhere, and the government was able to push through the White Paper proposals more or less intact (Newman 2009).

National policy statements

Since the 1980s planning commentators had discussed the merits of either a national planning framework of some kind, or of strategies for particular sectors (airports etc). The former was resisted by governments throughout, but the latter was pursued, if fitfully, mainly by the tried and tested means of White Papers. The 1997–2010 governments were quite keen on this sectoralised approach, and after the collapse of the 2001 reform initiative in this area, planning officials again advocated sectoral efforts. These did emerge in the 2003 aviation White Paper, and to a more limited extent in the roads, rail and energy sectors, but were resisted completely on ports. By 2006 the lack of enthusiasm for such spatially attuned strategies was clear, with only the airports one taking this form: identifying and deciding on each airport across the UK. Other White Papers in these years were all-UK documents and not spatialised. The aviation White Paper did not show that approach to be very effective, with some key elements contested heavily since 2003, especially for the London airports. The key decision in the 2008 system was that the

NPSs would be the preserve of sectoral departments, with the ministry including planning having very little role in their production, beyond sketching out a route map for their drafting, consultation and completion. This meant that any principles of spatial coordination (or perhaps other sorts, financial, for example) were largely lost. The contrast with the relative forcefulness of spatial planning in the UK's devolved administrations in these years is sharp.

This form of implementation of the NPS principle has had important effects. There has been a gradual retreat in the number of sectors to be covered, with NPSs for airports and water now unlikely (DCLG 2010b). That for airports will be replaced by an "aviation framework document" by 2013, for which a scoping report was issued in 2011 (DfT 2011). It is significant that even an instrument such as an NPS that is departmentally controlled is being resisted by ministries, moving back to lighter and more politically malleable policy tools. The drafts of the energy and ports NPSs issued in November 2009 indicated that their guidance was intended to be noted not only by the IPC, but also by local authorities and the Planning Inspectorate for cases falling below IPC thresholds, and, where relevant, by the Marine Management Organisation. The UK had gone within a year or two from having one spatial planning regime (that of the Town and Country Planning Acts) to three, with the marine and IPC regimes added. This surely leaves scope for uncertainty over the coming years, as the validity of NPSs and any other national planning frameworks is argued out. Effectively, sectoral ministries have become sort of spatial planning agencies, without the ministry containing planning being able to give a strong steer on the evolution of these regimes. These are unexpected consequences, not worked through by the Barker and Eddington processes which gave birth to the Act.

Another critical feature of the NPS process as it evolves is how non-spatialised the documents are. So far the only one that identifies sites is that for nuclear power. None of the others discuss even general locations, and that for ports argues explicitly against such an approach. It is unlikely that the national networks (road and rail) NPS could be despatialised in this way, and the implicit play across to the (absent but perhaps partially imagined) national planning framework will become visible, even if its implications will doubtless be resisted by government. That is to say, an implicit national imaginary may come into a sphere of public visibility and debate, and cause major political difficulties for governments.

A further, vital feature was raised by critics of the energy NPSs in the consideration in the parliamentary select committee (House of Commons and Climate Change Committee 2010). This related to the fact that there was no way of judging how far proposals coming forward would relate to the government objectives under the 2009 Climate Change Act. The energy NPSs encouraged the development of generation by most fuels, without prioritising, meaning that the IPC cannot use the low carbon issue in its deliberations. There could be a flurry of gas power stations, for example, removing the need for low carbon investment, as in the 1990s. This is surely another destabilising issue that will effect the working out of this institutional innovation, unless the present government simply removes the climate change goals. Government had taken little notice of the points of critics in the final energy NPSs laid before Parliament in June 2011, so they are seen by many planning and environmental interests as problematic: but in the energy field they are set to dominate decision-making in the immediate future.

Together these features mean that the NPSs will move in a contested and possibly contradictory force-field over the coming years. Whilst they may, in some cases, give the much longed for national certainty on principle and so give a firm basis for decisions, it is equally likely that they will be caught up in complex and sometimes politically difficult tensions. That does not necessarily mean that their invention was unwise, but that they may not provide the desired solution.

The Infrastructure Planning Commission

The IPC was a child of the idea that politicians cannot be trusted to decide in many difficult areas – the 1997 handing over of interest-rate decisions to the Monetary Policy Committee was a sign of New Labour's support for this sort of thinking (Hay 2007). In the Barker and Eddington reports the insistence on the need for an "independent" system of planning decision-making explicitly connected to the Monetary Policy Committee experience, and to the creation of "independent" central banks. The major Treasury input to both reports makes this connection unsurprising. It is a little ironic that the most strongly neoliberalised parties in the UK have (in this one small policy area) gone against this line of thinking, which spawned numerous policy initiatives under Conservative governments in the 1980s.

There are other interesting features of the IPC experience. For example, their commitment to transparency has been striking (with all correspondence published immediately), and not necessarily to the liking of some businesses. This might give the stimulus to pioneer some of the policy dialogue forms discussed in Chapter 6, under the Commission Nationale du Debat Public (CNDP). Again, the law of unexpected consequences may hover over this governance innovation: May developers find this process more challenging than the old one?

WIDER DEVELOPMENT OF INFRASTRUCTURE POLICY IN THE UK AND ENGLAND

The 2008 Act was not the only initiative in relation to infrastructure in these years. Infrastructure UK was set up in late 2009, bringing together the Treasury's public–private partnership support unit (Partnerships UK) and other elements from the emerging consensus in the Brown government that a more strategic view of national infrastructure matters was needed, related to the Barker and Eddington reports drive. This had been pressed by several influential bodies: the Confederation of British Industry since the 1990s, the Institution of Civil Engineers with its State of the Nation reports each year through the 2000s (for example, ICE 2009), and the Council for Science and Technology, a government advisory body (CST 2009). The latter was particularly concerned about resilience and interrelations between infrastructure industries following the 2007 floods, when major power collapses due to flooding were only just avoided. There was thus a forceful blend of pressures acting on government, and this must be one factor explaining the confirmation of the role of Infrastructure UK by the new Chancellor of the Exchequer in the June 2010 budget. But the core philosophy is that "economic infrastructure" (as against "social infrastructure": the welfare state's schools and hospitals) is the key to economic growth.

Infrastructure UK's chief executive was previously head of Partnerships UK. It has an advisory council led by the chairman of Rio Tinto and made up of seven private sector representatives from companies including Carillion, E3G, 3i Investments, Arup Group and National Grid. Thus it is a mix of PPP (Public Private Partnership) companies and infrastructure businesses, (with the balance to the first) and the Permanent Secretaries of six government departments: the Treasury; Environment, Food and Rural Affairs; Transport; Energy and Climate Change; Communities and Local Government; and Business, Innovation and Science. The council meets quarterly and its role is described as follows: "Infrastructure UK is focused on enabling of greater private sector investment in infrastructure, and the improvement of the Government's long-term planning, prioritisation and delivery of infrastructure" (HM Treasury 2010 p.47).

In October 2010 the government published the first National Infrastructure Plan, worked up by Infrastructure UK. This was a fairly lightweight "Plan", primarily committing to a number of important infrastructure projects, and referring across to proposed regulatory reviews. But it did adopt some sort of planning approach: "Government's key role is to specify what infrastructure is needed, to identify the key barriers to achieving that investment and to mobilise the resources, both public and private, to make it happen" (HM Treasury 2010 p.7).

A significant four-page accompanying note published a few days after the Plan was headed Infrastructure Planning and Prioritisation. It presented a methodology, working on common planning assumptions (economic, demographic etc), examining investment needs across sectors and identifying constraints. This was a Treasury approach to bring together infrastructure concerns, perhaps forcing DECC, DEFRA and Transport ministries to think about making long-term policy for each sector, and in part stemming from the work on NPSs carried out in each of those departments. Probably the New Labour approach to policy making, which began to take on a more analytical edge with the Barker and Eddington reports, carried through to this work, and brought with it a new respectability for planning approaches.

The Plan referred to the regulatory reviews underway in energy, water and elsewhere, showing that now the links between finance, regulation and planning were being made. It also had support from a Cabinet committee chaired by the Chancellor of the Exchequer, with representatives of all the key infrastructure ministries. So, it showed that the government remained interested in the infrastructure field, and that the more integrated approach emerging in the previous three or four years would continue, though probably not with much spatial planning emphasis. It was due to be revised in 2011 (HM Treasury 2010).

SCOTLAND – ANOTHER PATH

One other highly distinctive approach has been evolving in the UK over the same years, in Scotland (for detail see Marshall 2010b, key references include Lloyd and Purves 2009, Purves 2006, 2008, Vigar 2009). This is marked above all by the making of a National Planning Framework (NPF), first in non-statutory form in 2004 (Scottish Executive 2004), then as part of a reformed overall planning system under the 2006 Act, with NPF2 finalised in 2009 (Scottish Government 2009a). This is intensely infrastructural, with both editions full of discussion on transport issues, and the second one leading with energy developments. The net effect is that, in terms of page length, half of NPF2 is about infrastructural issues. This may in fact seem almost imbalanced. More of the first NPF had been on more standard planning issues of settlement policy and regeneration. It would appear at any rate that a major effort was made to work closely with the transport and energy parts of government (both in separate departments in Glasgow, not Edinburgh where the ministry containing planning is located). Given that work was underway at the time on a major review of transport (the Strategic Transport Projects Review, Transport Scotland 2008), following on from the more general National Transport Strategy (Scottish Executive 2006), such close working was clearly essential. Equally, a wave of policy making on energy, especially on renewables and offshore wind, was advancing, effectively leapfrogging beyond NPF2 (Marine Scotland 2010, Scottish Enterprise 2009, 2010, Scottish Government 2009b).

What is more, it was decided to incorporate a list of national developments into NPF2 that were, it was held, linked to the overall national spatial strategy (see Figure 10.2). For these developments, as for those shown in the UK NPSs, the principle of development was seen as having

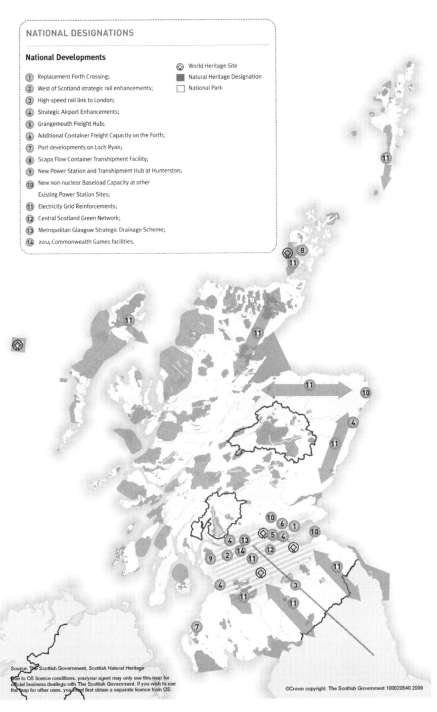

NATIONAL DESIGNATIONS

National Developments

World Heritage Site

1 Replacement Forth Crossing;

Natural Heritage Designation

2 West of Scotland strategic rail enhancements;

National Park

3 High-speed rail link to London;

4 Strategic Airport Enhancements;

5 Grangemouth Freight Hub;

6 Additional Container Freight Capacity on the Forth;

7 Port developments on Loch Ryan;

8 Scapa Flow Container Transhipment Facility;

9 New Power Station and Transhipment Hub at Hunterston;

10 New non-nuclear Baseload Capacity at other Existing Power Station Sites;

11 Electricity Grid Reinforcements;

12 Central Scotland Green Network;

13 Metropolitan Glasgow Strategic Drainage Scheme;

14 2014 Commonwealth Games facilities.

Source: The Scottish Government, Scottish Natural Heritage

Due to OS licence conditions, you/your agent may only use this map for official business dealings with The Scottish Government. If you wish to use the map for other uses, you must first obtain a separate licence from OS.

©Crown copyright. The Scottish Government 100020540 2009

Figure 10.2 National designations in Scottish National Planning Framework 2, 2009. The arrows refer to electricity transmission line requirements, the numbers to individual projects. (Source: Scottish Government 2009a)

been established by NPF2, which had been debated in parliamentary committees, though not approved by Parliament (like most national strategies it is approved by the Cabinet).

This therefore contrasts with the UK approach. It stemmed from some of the same concerns with problematic decision-making, in this case with difficulties concerning the completion of the M74 Extension in the early 2000s in particular. But it was tackled in a much more planning-friendly culture, which appears to be quite at ease with broad spatial strategies. This applies across most parties, with NPF1 produced by a Labour-led coalition, and NPF2 by a Scottish Nationalist Party (SNP) minority government. By combining the 14 major projects with a spatial strategy the Scottish system takes a quite different path, with the NPF representing the whole bundle of NPSs, and the "in principle" support then leaving decisions with the normal planning machinery with no hint of an IPC-type body. This approach is supplemented by an active strategic approach to projects, with central ministries working intensively on wind farm issues with local authorities, for example. Other elements include a more strategic use of Strategic Environmental Assessment, with an SEA unit established in-house within the government.

This is not to say that the Scottish approach can necessarily be held up as a success story, or certainly not yet. Environmental interests remain very unconvinced in some cases, with a campaign against one national project at Hunterston for a coal power station making some progress via legal challenge at the time of writing. There were also doubts about the need for the second Forth road bridge, although this had the unanimous backing of the main parties, and the contract for construction was signed early in 2011. It was due to totally overshadow all other public infrastructure investment for a decade or so, at a cost of between £1.5 and £2 billion. However, the justification is essentially economic, and this can be seen to fit with the main NPF drive, even though climate-change rhetoric would point to other uses of this funding. At any rate, most of the 14 national developments appear to be less controversial.

The NPF system, and particularly this element of linking it to big projects, is still evolving. It remains to be seen whether this particular solution stays as a central element in NPF3. My own judgement is that this way of linking projects may not be fully effective. NPF2 presents the 14 projects as if they follow from certain criteria, and are fully justified by the overall spatial strategy. However, this is not terribly convincing, and it is clear that – quite understandably – the political choices of ministers are behind the project list. During the very extensive public consultation on NPF2, the original nine proposed national projects were extended to 207, which were then assessed against plan criteria. These were subsequently cut back to those that were regarded as of genuinely national importance: just 14, a judgement essentially made by ministers.

At any rate, the over-riding decision in Scotland, common to NPF1 and 2, to include infrastructure planning within a national planning framework, has strength, and may well offer a contrast to the difficulties around NPSs in England. The consensus across the three major parties in Scotland is quite different from that of the (different) three major parties in England. Infrastructure and spatial planning are as ever caught up in contrasting state projects. The SNP in particular takes a special interest in energy infrastructure, relevant to its vision of an independent Scotland, and it is here that the biggest differences may be played out over the next decade or more. A government can hardly have a bigger state project than its own independence, and territory remains core to state form. National imaginaries come out of hiding in this sort of historical juncture, and the links to state projects and the construction of territory become a bit more visible.

WALES

The newly devolved government in Wales was keen on strategy making, perhaps in part reflecting its lack of tax or law-making powers. Alongside a statutory Spatial Development Scheme, and an overarching governmental strategy (called One Wales in 2008), was the Wales Spatial Plan. This was first produced in 2004, and updated in 2008 (Welsh Assembly Government 2004, 2008). This does not have a strong infrastructure emphasis, and has a distinctly fuzzy character (Harris and Hooper 2004, 2006). It has a strongly decentralised approach, providing rather more detail at the level of the six Spatial Plan Areas than at the all-Wales scale. This very strategic approach, based on general principles, colours Welsh policy-making as a whole. It is very careful not to tread on the toes of any interests, spatial or sectoral, and is keen to emphasise the integrated nature of decision making, facilitated by numerous cross-cutting governing mechanisms within the Government and the Assembly. The lack of firmer strategic content contrasts with the Scottish approach, which is ready (on infrastructure at least) to give stronger steering.

On climate change, energy and transport the Plan is about principles, leaving more specific content to the set of sectoral strategies of the Assembly. In one case these include spatially-specific guidance, the Technical Advice Note (TAN) 8 on wind-energy locations (Welsh Assembly Government 2005). This carried out an exhaustive technical and collaborative study of the country to find wind priority areas, which were then designated, with instructions to the local authorities to detail them and ensure development could progress (Cowell 2007, 2010). The results have been mixed, with some areas steering investment successfully, but opposition breaking out elsewhere. In the Europe-wide discussion on the most effective and fair approach to wind-farm planning, there is still no agreement as to whether this strategic approach, of which TAN 8 is perhaps the best known and best prepared example, can be effective, in the face of the sort of resistance common across the continent. In 2011 the TAN 8 regime was coming under considerable pressure from campaigns against new power lines for renewables in mid-Wales, with ministers emphasising that current targets were maximums, with no possibility of wind farms outside TAN 8 areas.

An inquiry into Planning in Wales in 2010–2011 raised many questions about the effectiveness of the strategic planning arrangements in Wales, partly looking forward to the new possibilities given by the next round of devolution, which is to give the Assembly powers to design more domestic policy, including on planning, and so heralding a Wales Planning Act (National Assembly for Wales 2011). One issue was the role of the IPC in Wales, where all energy schemes over 50 MW are decided by the IPC (or, with its abolition, by the UK Secretary of State). The Assembly hopes to be given powers in the 2008 Planning Act areas, allowing full control over infrastructure decisions, or at least as much as Scotland has (aviation is not devolved to any of the three administrations). A Wales Strategic Infrastructure Plan (WSIP) was being drawn up in 2011, largely following in the paths of Infrastructure UK and the Scottish Infrastructure Investment Plan (Scottish Government 2008). It was to have a primarily economic orientation, but links to the Wales Spatial Plan were not clear yet. It will be interesting to see which policy instrument has greater strength. It seems likely that the usual tussles between the more sectoralised approaches (such as the WSIP), and the aspirations to overviews (as in the Wales Spatial Plan), are alive and well in Wales as elsewhere. This is surely the stuff of authentic democratic politics, and reflects the normalisation of Wales' government. It also reflects a very different approach to self-government, largely accepting collaboration with England (for example, with adjoining English regions in the period up to 2010) rather than aspiring to independence. Again, basic mindsets affect the approaches to thinking about these big territory-forming questions.

NORTHERN IRELAND

Northern Ireland's Regional Development Strategy (RDS), Shaping our Future, was approved in 2001 (Department of Regional Development Northern Ireland 2001). A draft revision was published in January 2011 (Department of Regional Development Northern Ireland 2011). Both are examples of integrated spatial development strategies and therefore address, to varying degrees, the infrastructure challenges affecting this part of the UK, and also link these to challenges affecting the whole island. These cross-border or whole-island issues have been in particularly strong focus since 1997, as continuing progress was made towards a "normalising" of relations between the Republic and Northern Ireland. Devolution also brought different constitutional and political possibilities, although the devolved government (the Northern Ireland Assembly) has only functioned sporadically: most consistently since 2007. The 2001 Strategy contained much more on transport infrastructure issues than on energy. The draft revision of 2011 was more focused on climate change and therefore on energy issues, and is slightly more specific on renewables and grid extensions, with the region aspiring to a high wind-energy future. However a Regional Transport Strategy was being drafted at the same time, and the RDS was rather vague on transport issues. Overall, the linking of settlement and infrastructure issues was not that strong, probably due (in part) to the complexities of Northern Ireland politics, whereby ministerial portfolios had to be shared out across the political spectrum, making integration hard. As always, political and institutional factors infuse planning's scope and potential.

HOW MUCH DIFFERENCE MAY THE NEW SYSTEMS MAKE?

I mentioned in the last chapter that there may be more continuity with the past than the designers of the new arrangements wished for. How far have the processes changed, and how might substantive realities be affected? On the first, the changes are real, in both England and Scotland: new procedures can alter the balance of advantage for different interests. These are not fully liberalising reforms – the idea that projects of this size and significance could be somehow freed from public decision-making is implausible. But they could make the path by which businesses gain approval easier in some cases, and thus the job of opposing interests (of whatever kind: "dark green", purely local "self interested" opposition, etc) harder. This could happen under both system-changes. Under the NPS and IPC (then the Planning Inspectorate/ National Infrastructure Directorate) route, which some cynics see as primarily being designed to secure nuclear power approvals, opponents may find arguing against matters already approved in Parliament much more demanding than the more open format of the public inquiry system. The same applies in Scotland, where the NPF has the legitimacy garnered from many years of public and technical working. On the other hand, the process changes are going to acquire much of their impact in use. I have referred to possible unintended consequences, whereby the new systems may give more hand-holds for opposition. Certainly the IPC procedures are demanding for businesses, with a lengthy pre-application obstacle race, and a drive to achieve as much common ground as possible before the more official IPC stage. Some of this can be altered if it looks too "over engineered" to developers, but so far a commitment to transparency and (apparently) taking note of public views is built into the process. In Scotland the 14 national designations are proving a learning process for opponents, with some big projects (such as the Second

Forth Crossing) very hard to mobilise against, whilst that at Hunterston for a coal fired station does not seem to have had its legitimacy enhanced by inclusion in NPF2.

In both cases the commitment to forward planning and thinking may be as important a change to the process, with the institution and maturing of Scottish national planning a possibly critical tool in continuing "national conversations" and developing a national civic culture (Peel and Lloyd 2007). The NPSs are a far less imaginative and interesting instrument in this respect, which do not seem to be as open to democratic and critical development (although this is dependent on how contestation and politicisation develop over the coming years). The general principle that future need in all these sectors should be explicitly debated may still be a step forward, which could at some point lead to at least more openly-considered sectoral planning by governments.

Any judgements on substantive effects must be speculative of course, given that NPF2 is from 2009, that the system for England has not even been "finally" legislated for, and that only two schemes had come forward at the time of writing for consideration by the IPC. As indicated above, I have doubts that these processes will necessarily make it easier to get schemes through than under the old system where heavily contested (which may well be the majority of schemes now). In all probability, developers will get a firm answer more quickly than before, as the system, certainly in England, should cut down some administrative time though not, following the abolition of the IPC, necessarily political decision-making time. So, in England, the effect may not be as considerable as might have been expected, with the same judgements required of developers as to the direction in which the process is really likely to go – NPS backing notwithstanding. In Scotland a somewhat more consensualised and much more integrated governing approach may have more effect, although mechanisms other than the NPF, such as the informal coordinating efforts of the energy department with local authorities on wind power, may be just as significant. This sort of approach, like that of TAN 8 in Wales, is in principle somewhat easier for a government "closer" to the people, and much tougher for a now ruthlessly centralised London-based government for England.

So the unexciting conclusion is that, although the process changes are significant and highly distinctive on the substance, it must be a matter of waiting and seeing. The key actors in infrastructure planning of this kind are an array of societal interests, not just governments and developers. The UK certainly forms a good laboratory for such waiting and seeing, with the English and Scottish approaches very different in principle, even though both have some centralising and forward-looking features. A third model might emerge, if Wales gets full control of its planning affairs, at which point it will be interesting to see which of its two neighbours' models it inclines towards, if either. A third way might be just to stay with the pre-2000s system: taking projects on their merits through a public inquiries system. However, this would be unlikely to fit the tenor of these infrastructuralist and climate changing times.

PLANNING AND INFRASTRUCTURE PROJECTS

Big project struggles

Experience in each country with just a few key projects provides the material for debate and argument about infrastructure planning. This has been very much the case in Britain, in part because most projects have been relatively invisible to anyone except the particular industries involved and locally interested parties. It is only with large and controversial projects that the issue comes into the public view, and it can then be used to construct particular storylines or discourses. Sometimes this will be more about the substance of the scheme and sometimes matters of process will be brought to the front of the discussion. The famous or iconic schemes will vary between countries and periods, with waves of (non) controversy swirling around issues and sectors and countries.

Nuclear power stations

In Britain the biggest struggles of the early or mid-twentieth century were about creating reservoirs (Sheail 1986), whilst in the 1970s and 1980s the two most famous inquiries were about nuclear power, for the Windscale (later renamed Sellafield) nuclear reprocessing plant in 1977–1978, and for Sizewell B nuclear power station in 1983–1985. Both schemes were approved, but the issues out in the public sphere gave a good airing to anti-nuclear arguments, which were given further support during the privatisation of the electricity industry in 1990, when it was found that the nuclear part of the industry was not saleable under the regulatory system prevailing at the time as it was loss-making. Therefore there is a critical interaction of project decision-making and perspectives on the whole sector. Clearly in the nuclear case this interacts with a worldwide opposition movement intertwined with fundamental questions about security and nature, and marked by periodic accidents of a dramatic kind. The absence of a consensus on energy futures in Britain since the 1970s has left the governments of each period exposed on nuclear issues, in a way that has not normally affected other sectors. The planning system has been a major vent for the playing out of these issues, although since the 1990s the biggest investment has been in gas-fired power stations, an issue not generating much controversy. A striking feature of the nuclear planning history is that, wherever the first generation stations ended up, that is where the follow-on stations go, given the lesser opposition expected in these areas and existing company stakes: a sort of frozen geography (Openshaw 1986). A planning application for Hinkley Point C nuclear station was submitted in late 2011, so the dynamic is in full flow.

Airports

The next sector to come into the headlines was airport expansion, with struggles and long inquiries for the expansion of Manchester and Heathrow airports. The Heathrow Terminal 5 experience has already been mentioned, as providing the ammunition needed by those wishing to streamline the planning system. Industry perspectives saw the time taken as indicating government inefficiency. Those conducting the inquiry took another view, saying that the planning applications were not well prepared (with late changes coming in throughout the process) and that considering the circumstances the time had been needed for a fair and open treatment (House of Commons Procedure Committee 2002). Opponents in this case, as in the most important case in the 2000s, Dibden Bay port, argued that only because the scheme was so potentially damaging did the inquiry need to take so long. They argued that the developers in both cases should have been aware of the massive environmental damages likely, and that they bore prime responsibility for imposing expensive and unwanted inquiries on the public purse (Levett 2007a, 2007b). The airport schemes were approved, and Dibden Bay rejected, but four other schemes were not, including London Gateway (Figure 10.3), which is now being constructed. It is interesting to note that the only way in which a major airport scheme has been blocked has been politically, where top government decisions resulted in the abandonment (for the time being) of the Heathrow and Stansted schemes in 2010. It seems unlikely such abandonment would have occurred via a public inquiry if such political switching had not intervened. Again the geography is distinctive: airports were sited in the early and mid-twentieth century quite near cities, often with urbanisation surrounding them in due course, and that is where

Figure 10.3 London Gateway port, projected image before construction.
(Source: Port of London Authority webpages, retrieved 24/11/2011)

they have stayed, multiplying their impact and traffic by factors of 10 or 100. New sites are hardly ever attempted: more frozen geography.

So, again this was a highly controversial sector, in which public debates were deeply implicated with the top-level issues of the day: climate change and the massive growth of air travel over the preceding years. As in the case of nuclear power, the project cases were wrapped up in these wider debates. This was what infuriated industry representatives who argued that, given government support in these cases, it was wrong that projects should have to go through the discussion of principles. However, until the 2008 reforms for England, this was clearly the way the planning system was inclined to deal with the issues: case by case, taking local circumstances into account. Planning lawyers discussing the challenge of reforming the system in the early 2000s returned time and again to the difficulties of removing this basic feature of the UK planning system (Lindblom and Honey 2007, McCracken 2009, Purdue and Popham 2002, Robinson 2009, Thompson 2002). Some argue that it is still by no means certain that NPSs will remove the tendency to debate the spectrum of issues. The nuclear power NPS is very determined to remove the location issue from debate, by specifying each of the eight sites for future nuclear stations. But so far other NPSs are not so spatially specific, so it remains to be seen if the principle and location dimensions can really be separated.

Past and future possibilities

The Severn Barrage

The Severn Barrage scheme has been promoted for several decades, but never made any headway. It proposed a tidal barrage across the Severn Estuary, which has one of the most powerful tidal resources in the world. In its larger variants, it would generate around 8–9 GW of electricity, estimated at 4.4 per cent of the UK electricity supply in 2007. The early 2000s Labour governments returned to the issue in its energy policy making, and in 2007 the Sustainable Development Commission (SDC), an independent "environmental watchdog" of government, recommended progressing work on the scheme, though with rather a lot of caveats about public debates and involvement (Sustainable Development Commission 2007). This set off another round of studies, which might or might not have culminated in some action if the government had not lost the 2010 election. As it was, amidst the deep expenditure cuts of 2010 the scheme was abandoned, or at most left for reconsideration in 2015.

This is therefore by far the largest single UK renewable resource that has never got beyond the drawing board. It has always been under great pressure from the natural environment lobbies, particularly the powerful Royal Society for the Protection of Birds (RSPB). The enthusiasm of some engineers and "deep green" advocates was never matched by a wider movement promoting the need to use all available renewable resources in Britain. So the country (British society as a whole) took on ideas of being a coal, gas or oil country through the twentieth century, but never moved (or was never obliged to move) to greener ideas of managing territory. National imaginaries of countryside protection and nature could always trump talk of "deep green" progress. There was no sign of this changing during the 50 years the barrage was promoted by minority voices, and if anything the likelihood of implementation receded over these years. As the SDC pointed out, the scheme had a long payback period and would probably only work as a public-sector investment – something problematic since the 1980s.

High-speed rail

A second field, high-speed rail, illustrates the wavering flows around big schemes in Britain. Only one short section of line has materialised in Britain, the Channel Tunnel Rail Link (CTRL). It runs from the place the Channel Tunnel emerges near the English coast to London, a distance of 108 kilometres, and was opened during different stages in 2003 and 2007. It was, in effect, a public–private partnership scheme, needing to be rescued repeatedly by state funding, given the reluctance of private finance. The scheme suffered considerable attacks for its potential damage to the Surrey and Kent countryside during the planning stages, but determined government leadership and payment for lots of tunnels and related measures secured a more-or-less acceptable route in the end. It was renamed "High Speed 1", when pressure began to develop for creating a second route, HS2, from London to the north of England (and possibly Scotland). This emerged from work by the Strategic Rail Authority, the short-lived body charged with guiding British rail planning and development from 2001 to 2006. The idea was picked up again in the policy-making work in the Department for Transport from 2007, and particularly by an enthusiastic minister, Lord Adonis, from 2008. Before the Labour government fell, a White Paper was published (DfT 2010), detailing a proposed route from London to Birmingham and, in broader terms, routes for a Y-shaped scheme branching off to Manchester and Leeds, and possibly on to Scotland (Figure 10.4). Some criticism emerged regarding the way in which this was promoted without clear links to the rest of the rail system, and without establishing what complementary measures would be needed to give advantages to northern England (Wenban-Smith 2009).

The London to Birmingham section is the part now in public play, with the post-2010 government picking up the scheme and arguing for its importance, in part to take market share from domestic aviation, and so supposedly taking pressure off the expansion of London's airports. During the year or two since discussion on detailed routes began, massive opposition has built up to the scheme along the majority of the route, especially through

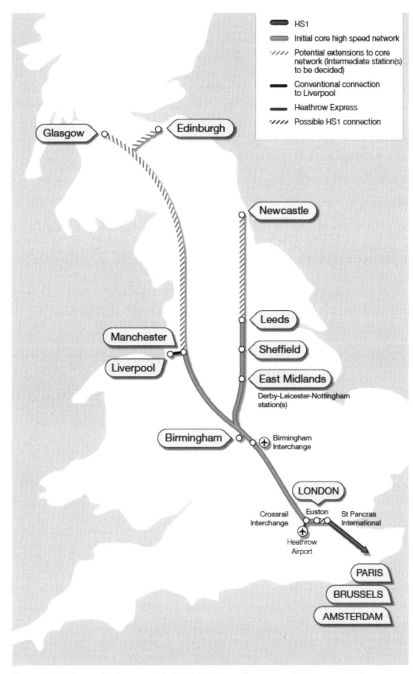

Figure 10.4 High-speed rail proposals in UK 2010. (Source: Department for Transport 2010)

the solidly Conservative and wealthy zone of the Chiltern Hills, in Bucking-hamshire. Progress, if it occurs, is planned to be slow, with the scheme being promoted through Parliament by Hybrid Bill during the period to 2015, and construction not taking place till after 2017 (or many years later for the northern sections). This displaces the considerable public cost, estimated at £17 billion, to the far future, as well as displacing some of the political cost. The Hybrid Bill approach may have been taken in the hope that this will gen-erate less chance for opponents to make themselves heard, as against the use of the 2008 Planning Act machinery (as modified in 2011). It would place the responsibility widely on the government and parliament as a whole, and was the relatively tried and tested approach used for CTRL and for London's Crossrail underground line.

Wind energy
Whilst the future of HS2 hangs in the balance of political and public sup-port and opposition, one sector of infrastructure investment suffers these pressures with every individual scheme – wind energy. Only in Wales has a strategic planning approach to onshore wind been taken, which has had some success, but has not proved to be a comprehensive solution. In Scot-land, Northern Ireland and England, planning has been essentially reactive. In Scotland government did finance a wind-speed study, and the RSPB com-missioned research on less acceptable areas from their perspective, giving some basis to companies in their planning. In England some county authori-ties sought to plan for renewables from the 1990s, but found it hard to gain acceptance for areas regarded as fit for investment, as became common in German planning. The government then pressed for wind and other renew-ables to be included in Regional Spatial Strategies from the early 2000s, but again regions found it hard to go beyond pressing general principles. Some did translate targets for wind generation to their regions, but apportioning this was again a politically-demanding task that was generally avoided in the 2005–2008 round of RSSs.

The result is that onshore wind has struggled to establish itself almost everywhere in England, with all schemes individually fought through the planning system and the courts. Progress has been greater in Scotland and Northern Ireland, in part because of the lower population densities, and in the use in some areas of community-led approaches. The contrast with Ger-many, Denmark and Spain has been drawn many times. The mix of reasons for this is the subject of continuing debate. Countryside protection attitudes and imaginaries appear to account for much of the answer, alongside (com-pared with Germany) much lower support for "deep green" values. These feed back into the difficulty the planning and governing system has had in providing strategic leadership on the issue, leaving full play to localism, not something seen in many other sectors: road building since the 1950s, power station construction (most recently in the nuclear power NPS), or in the much easier zone of offshore wind, where the UK and Scottish administrations have been forging ahead strongly since the mid-2000s.

This subtle construction of spatiality is something that has been critical in many of the cases examined here, such as in the waste sector, where central governments have been happy to leave the issue to localities while setting highly demanding targets. In this case, as in renewable energy, these targets are set at EU level. So the planning question has a very determined spatial shape: the need being set at the highest level and the task of implementing passed to almost the lowest level. This system of spatialised non-responsibility is evidently a recipe for myriad local struggles. The outcome depends on attitudes locally, and within local or regional governments (where these exist). The sort of halfway-house developed in Scotland, where the energy department in the government attempts to share responsibility with local authorities and developers may ease implementation somewhat, though even there it is no guarantee of easy progress. It is not hard to see why governments turn to "easy fixes" like fossil fuel sources (coal, gas, oil) and, if that fails, to top-down nuclear imposition. Like energy saving, the implementation of renewables in Britain always threatens to be a low priority, given variable public budget-support, and gaining from little invested political capital. Planning is caught up in this wider panorama of half-heartedness, which also affected the tidal barrage options over the decades. Project approval is never a free-standing issue, but is a constructed element related to the flow of policy. Whilst its particular design is important, that is only ever one part of the whole setting of policy and decision-making.

CONCLUSIONS — PROBLEMS AND REAL MODES OF FUNCTIONING

Firstly we may note some underlying national spatial tendencies:

- Growth is the headline of all policy sectors: common to all sectors, and therefore with definite spatial implications;
- Growth is variable, and in a more marketised era tilts infrastructure development towards southern England;
- State regimes are very variable in modifying the extent of this marketised era, sometimes pressing less marketised principles, such as rebalancing national economic productivity. This then redirects the budgets of private infrastructure companies, in some sectors;
- In each period these tendencies fit into a historically mature society and territory, variably inhabited, and responding differently to dynamic economic change. Clearly this strongly limits spatial options; and

- Process changes are emergent after these major substantive regime changes, with speed up and major planning reform not materialising until the 2000s. This was based around two particularly problematic sectors for the marketised growth regime, airports and nuclear power stations. The first has clear spatial implications, enabling more development in the south.

The explicit link between infrastructure planning and spatial planning is weak in England, and stronger in the rest of the UK, particularly (but only very recently) in Scotland. This has meant a consistent history of separated working, little integrated with spatial planning at the larger scales, with partial exceptions during the two high points of regional planning in England, between the 1960s and 1970s, and the 2000s. It is not yet clear if reforms in the 2008 Act centring on England will make a big difference to this silo system. So far the National Policy Statements seem as separately drawn up as ever, if anything reinforcing the traditional tendencies to highly sectoral approaches contained within single ministries. Whether the processes led by the IPC/Planning Inspectorate's National Infrastructure Directorate will be able to make more effective links to strategic and local planning remains to be seen. In my view, the project stage was never especially problematic in the UK system, but there is still scope for improvement.

A continuous theme, especially evident in Chapter 9, was the way in which the underlying dynamics of change were constructed in each sector, forming the "obvious" geographies emerging in each period. I argued that the national imaginaries were never made very explicit in Britain, partly because they have been so contested, between the four parts of the UK, between different regions, and down to localities. A dominant south-east and London-centred view has always had most power, and this has often been able to impose the spatial structuring appropriate to its own national image: the anchor around London, an axial belt running up to the less important midland and northern centres, and the areas beyond being protected where possible to serve as farming and recreation space. But this imaginary was never brought out or argued out, as happened in more conscious ways in the Netherlands and France, and in much more conflictual and/or "from-below" ways in Spain and Germany. This left space for the individual sectoral processes analysed here, with no admission of the broadly dominant mind-model suggested above. The political and electoral geography naturally carried ways of deciding the investments and policies in each period: largely southern-centred but with periods in which other emphases were added, mainly during the Labour governments. All these gaps are problematic, if the challenge is to think about long-term transitions affecting all living in the country in fundamental ways. We will come back to these basic issues in the concluding chapter.

PART III
Conclusions

CHAPTER 11
CONCLUSIONS

This final chapter will bring together some important themes, which were raised in the first four chapters and were encountered in various forms during the country studies. These are grouped in three sets. The first reflects on the larger framings within which the infrastructure development issue has been examined and relates this to wider theoretical considerations. The second focuses more on planning and how spatial steering may be understood, both by explicit planning and by more constructed and indirect mechanisms. The third considers the ways in which the planning of major infrastructure might be done better, and what conditions would be necessary for such improved policy-making and action.

It is worth remembering that, on most current judgements, very large future investments in infrastructure will be needed in Europe during this century (quite apart from the, much more dynamic, rest of the world). ENTSO-E's (European Network of Transmission Operators for Electricity) 2010 Ten Year Network Development Plan estimated a need for 42,000 kilometres of new power-lines in Europe, many linked to renewable-energy investments. Whilst energy is expected to be the largest growth field at the moment (storage facilities, new electricity generation, undersea cables and gas pipelines all add to the picture), predictions of a growing need for waste facilities in some countries, and of new high-speed rail lines still being planned in France, Spain and maybe the UK, suggest that other sectors will also figure under these assumptions of growth and current policy drives.

The geographical placing of such investment matters. Corridors become important, often across sectors, where new transport and energy links are to be pushed through already heavily-loaded strips such as the Rhine valley. So, planning is important at the continental scale, as the recent phase of EU work on the big scale networks has begun to recognise. It may not be *the* critical barrier it is sometimes presented as, but the combined effect of contextual changes, including political economic (profit-making companies more concerned about delays, funding and regulatory demands) and political ones (more public opposition to proposals), has tended to promote planning to an equal status alongside finance and regulation in some sectors and cases.

THE BIG PICTURE – MAJOR INFRASTRUCTURE DEVELOPMENT IN THE EARLY TWENTY-FIRST CENTURY

A new regime was gradually formed from the 1980s onwards, whereby the prime actors in several infrastructure sectors came to be private companies, with states and the EU taking on important new regulatory and financing roles. The companies are often very large multinationals, often European, though with some US and Asian presence. This changes the economic and political force-field, with these companies, individually or in association, able to exercise major power over national and EU-level governing. They are far from homogeneous however, with big differences between the still (in effect) state-directed rail, electricity transmission and gas transport companies, and the much more autonomous areas of many ports, airports, waste and other energy fields. These powerful commercial sectors sit alongside the still largely public systems of provision for roads and in some water, waste and transport sub-fields.

In the global view, Braithwaite (2006) sees this as a globalisation of a US model of regulatory capitalism, in which regulation created large businesses in the early twentieth-century, which then went out to "corporatise" the world. Braithwaite argues that regulation in the wider sense is now a shared endeavour of states, business associations (in the international chemical industry, for example) and civic society, particularly international NGOs. So he sees a public–private hybridity at the core of the system. This intersects with the debates (see Moran 2006, for example) on the degree to which regulatory capitalism has national styles at its base, or is seeing a convergence of models to one more like that seen by Braithwaite. A common half-way house is that globalisation has indeed made countries more exposed to international economic forces, but that this is highly variable and that states often choose to use their room for manoeuvre in very different ways (Marsh et al 2008). We have seen this in the case studies, with each country's domestic context giving quite varied responses to the internationalisation of infrastructure industries and regulation, within certain EU-defined parameters. The country studies would not support a characterisation based on "varieties of capitalism" (whether based on two, three or even more European variants), but fits better with something like the approach of Crouch (2005), who sees each state as recombining elements and ideas within its own historical traditions and current political options. Certainly there are similarities between some of the cases, for example, the elements of top-down national steering remaining in Spain and France, but these are outweighed by large and very country-specific differences. This can then support the images of "variegated neoliberalism" discussed in recent geographical debates (Brenner et al 2010). The issue of convergence in the governing of infrastructure across European states, whether pressed by neoliberalising forces or combined with pressures of climate change and citizen activeness, is harder to answer at this stage. But some convergence, from very varied positions, is surely occurring, and this would then tend to affect planning approaches.

The vast structure of sunk capital, mostly created by public corporations in the half-century before 1990, is now "locked-in" to a largely but by no means completely commercial system. This idea of lock-in has been common in recent years, especially in discussions of the dependence on carbon-based energy systems: referring to technological dimensions. These are vital, largely constituted by big systems reflecting the high industrialism of the twentieth century, with reliance on extensive, universally-based provision networks covering most of each national territory. But it is worth also emphasising economic and governance lock-ins. These might be seen as less long-run and more subject to political change. But the paths set by political-economic decisions since the 1980s can be seen as being just as determinant as the inherited hard-built forms for several decades into the future. Mitchell (2008) called this the Regulatory State Paradigm, and argued that it had tied all UK energy policy-making to quite limited paths, with governments frozen in its ideological headlights since at least 1990. The attempts, now nearing fruition, to construct Europe-wide, market-based, energy and transport systems broadly follow the same paradigm and have had a profound impact on the drive behind changes to infrastructure systems, particularly to creating standardised systems that link up across the continent. The water and waste fields are not affected in the same way, though they are driven by Europe-wide norms and strategising processes.

This is not so far from the concerns of planning as it may appear. Planning responds to these several dimensions of lock-in. Those who, during the height of the post-2008 economic and financial crisis, discussed the need for a reorientation towards "ecological investment", in infrastructure as much as in industry as a whole, were aware of the difficulties in engineering this (Jackson 2009). Both the corporate structures discussed above, and the elements of the emerging "Macquarie model" of global infrastructure financing, would be likely to clash with shifts to slower and lower rates of return for such ecologically bent infrastructure investment. It is difficult to imagine localised energy and production/consumption systems having a good fit with the provision structures outlined above, but quite easy to see the very different planning challenges which such switches could generate.

This brings us back to the issue of the generation of the need for infrastructure. This is typically seen as the filling of gaps, whether geographically or sectorally – particularly by business lobbies. Certainly there has been a continuous building up of more and more advanced and energy-hungry networks, creating the "material integration" of countries (Verbong and van der Vleuten 2004), with several infrastructure fields sometimes generating key network nodes or hubs (Dutch mainports being obvious ones, but most countries have such nodes that are perhaps less obviously linked to public policy). This is seen as progressing to the continental scale by EU policy makers and lobbies, creating parallel continental nodes and key channels of movement. This remains fossil-fuel driven, across all infrastructure sectors, with new electricity generation still largely focused on gas and coal power stations, for example. So, in a commercial investment world need is in part just taken to be demand, however rhetorically steered by low carbon or other non-commercial discourses.

But need is contested, as any developer of infrastructure knows, all round Europe, even in many less rich or developed areas. There is no consensus in most countries about the overall need for new investment, and even where there is some agreement, this may not extend to agreeing where the investment should go. Current research programmes, such as that in the UK Infrastructure Transitions Research Consortium (ITRC) or proposed by the European Investment Bank (EIBURS) seek to pin down need using objective scientific techniques, but much social-scientific wisdom would doubt the prospects for such approaches – especially if funders are expecting one "correct" answer.

Given contestation, sweating existing assets, locations, geographies and systems therefore becomes the norm because, being already there, they cannot be resisted easily. Nature and heritage protection in specific places are at the heart of much resistance, rather than wider debates on the progress of welfare or planetary health. Instruments to help local protection are at hand for this purpose, many being promoted and validated by the EU.

It is far from clear what sort of threat this contestation might pose to the mechanism of capital accumulation. Harvey (1982) argued long ago for the importance of infrastructure (one part of fixed capital) as an outlet for surplus capital, especially during economic crises. There may be an urge for such outlets in the present period, which may be blocked to some extent by the "sensitivities" of democratic European countries. Certainly business interests fear that such blockage is occurring, and this has generated the push for reforms at EU level and in some national cases. We are back then to the purpose and functioning of investment and the role of regulation, including spatial regulation in planning, within overall state objectives. The proliferation since around 2000 of "Infrastructure Canada/UK/etc" type bodies suggests a collective urge on the part of richer capitalist states to manage the infrastructure investment process in more agile ways. This is more noticeable in the most liberalised, mainly English speaking, countries. But support for public–private partnerships, of which this is one variant, is much more widespread. The relationship between the functioning of the system and the infrastructure is an issue that connects to the sort of economic growth that is seen as valuable (Jackson 2009). We can imagine "infrastructure coefficients" of quite different forms from those existing (how much infrastructure needed per unit of well-being, say). Less and different consumption may mean less trade, less need for new ports and airports, less or no need for new electricity-generating capacity and so on. Many consider that this would be a revolutionary challenge to the nature of capitalism's movement, removing capital accumulation as the main motor of societal change. What follows here works just within current parameters, though much of what is said would also facilitate movement to more radically changed futures.

We will now move on to the specifics of planning and spatiality, having set these within their wider realities – which as I have tried to argue throughout, is critical for understanding planning's meaning and possibilities. Planning should facilitate this linking to context. A big project should be able to present a challenge such that alternative framings can emerge: of need, of appropriate geography and of political economic framings such as ownership, regulation and cost. Recent and current national and EU reforms often try to close down these sparking forces from particular sectors or projects – potentially to the detriment of long-term intelligent governance. This book is intended to support connecting and the chance to challenge.

PLANNING, SPATIALITY AND GEOGRAPHICAL IMAGINATIONS

Planning major infrastructure is difficult and may well be getting more difficult – a trend that may be becoming more generalised around Europe. The last statement is not based on any extensive work, which would require the study of far more countries, and cases within each country, than I have been able to do here. However, anecdotally, there does appear to be evidence of such increasing problems with getting construction permits in the sectors examined, as has long been the case with most of the countries surveyed here (least so in Spain, where motorway, rail and wind-farm building was able to surge forward even within the last decade, although it has experienced problems in some sectors, such as water and waste, and in many individual cases).

Here a number of dimensions of this experience are explored in concluding form:

- What sector and country variation has been detected?
- How has strategising been used, and how has it helped, if at all?
- How has project planning been managed?
- "Behind planning", how has the spatiality of sectors been constructed, and how far have spatial imaginaries been critical to this?
- How has planning related to the generality of conflict in this field?

What sector and country variation has been detected?

There are differences between countries, as implied above, with Spain demonstrating some slightly easier planning paths than elsewhere, but the overall picture is that major infrastructure projects have been controversial throughout Western Europe in these decades. Nevertheless, beyond this basic generalisation, the differences constitutionally, politically and in details of planning systems and associated regimes of governance, make the experiences of each country quite distinctive. Sectorally, there have been less struggles around water simply because, beyond Spain, there have been rather few large infrastructure schemes, except for the upgrading of sewage treatment plants, which generally do not cause planning problems. Port schemes have been contested in England and the Netherlands, perhaps less elsewhere, but these, which might have been accepted rather easily 40 years ago, are no longer easy development fields. Otherwise, almost all transport and energy subsectors have been contested, and often required complex planning processes. So, all countries have had the opportunity and some incentive to develop strategic and project oriented approaches to these fields, with varying results.

Naturally all countries have procedures to deal with projects, but the extent of wider strategic framing is far more variable. That extent is a critical factor defining national approaches. There appears to be some convergence in planning approaches towards less national strategising, whether comprehensive or sectoral, matching the tendency towards the more market-based political economy observed above. The retreat in the Netherlands from national planning may be especially significant. But there appears to be a perhaps equally important tendency to switch decisions on planning major infrastructure to outside normal town and country planning machinery. This has happened in England since the 2008 Planning Act, and in 2011 in Germany in relation to critical power-line projects, as well as in the work by the EU, which is very rarely linked to spatial planning concerns. Of course, this has always happened to some extent, for example, in water plans or transport plans, but the tendency for the economic ministries to be those most heavily involved in recent initiatives is striking.

How has strategising been used, and how has it helped, if at all?

National comprehensive spatial planning appeared to help in progressing major schemes where it has been used, but as this is limited to the Netherlands, in terms of decades of practice, this is not a strong base for wider generalisation. The experience in Scotland is too recent to draw conclusions from, though signs are similarly promising. So, the arguments remain more from the observation of these two cases, and the absence elsewhere, than from a really clear empirical base. But there are supporting cases. One is the distinctive *amenagement du territoire* and national economic planning of France, which for decades gave broad directions for infrastructure and an integrating effect perhaps equal to the very different Dutch system. Others are the regional planning carried out in federal or semi-federal states, which has some of the same integrating impact, from the cases viewed in Berlin–Brandenburg and Catalonia, though the size of the states limits this effect for the larger systems like gas and electricity transport, high-speed rail, and ports and airports.

The arguments for comprehensive spatial planning are well known, at least to planners: that looking comprehensively at territories allows more intelligent decisions to be made, in this case at the macro level, relating big infrastructure systems to the long-term dynamics of settlement, production and movement. The play across regional and national levels to related policy areas, for example, to regulatory systems for energy or transport, should also allow integrated steering. But such comprehensive planning is rare, and becoming rarer. Politically it is surely demanding, obliging politicians to support one geographical model over another, benefiting some interests more than others. So attention has been given in the book to sectoralised planning.

Such sectoralised planning is more complicated. It may be strongly or weakly spatialised: most countries have had this in some form or another at some time, although it too has declined under the force of neoliberalisation in most sectors. Broadly speaking, it has clear functional strengths, laying out say the electricity grid or the motorway network in a manner that is integrated with regional and local planning to some degree, given the consultation with authorities at those levels. There will also be consultation with other ministries, at least in formal terms. However, the very sectoralness has impeded integration. Time after time the pressure was for silo decision-making, whether the White Papers for aviation occasionally emerging in the UK, the rather light federal ports and airports strategies in Germany, or the all-Spain road and rail plans. The French SNIT underway in 2010–2011, dealing formally-speaking with all transport modes, went the furthest in trying to link these. Through being debated in public and by negotiation with DATAR and the regions, it could, it would appear so far, be integrated to some degree with other spatial concerns. Nevertheless it was essentially driven by high-level national concerns, not based on spatial structuring logics, even though the rail lines on the maps are likely to be powerful instruments of long-term spatial transformation. So the SNIT had some similarities to the eminently sectoral device invented by the UK 2008 Planning Act, the National Policy Statement (NPS), for energy and some transport sectors, managed by the relevant ministry with rather little coordination or input from the spatial planning section of government. At the time of writing, only one NPS was spatially oriented, to identify eight nuclear power station sites expected to need high-level backing from Parliament. That for national transport networks may be expected to be more like the SNIT.

The contrast of this sectoral strategising with the Dutch system remains clear. There the electricity network schema or the plans for ports or airports have had to be tied into the national spatial strategy, simply because they are planning system documents in which the opinion of the minister responsible for planning had a high degree of authority. In the absence of such integrated national-level strategising policy making in other systems often stays at a project level, with implicit prioritising by investment plans: for example, the amount of state funding to Madrid or Barcelona airports, or to Marseille or Le Havre ports, but with no explicit link to any national strategy. In the UK, with largely private funding outside the rail and road infrastructure systems, such spatial prioritising becomes taboo, although all sorts of steers then come in via back-door or local means, where expansion becomes impossible in one locality but not another. The denial of wider system and externality effects in such market-facing arrangements makes the decision to press neither single nor integrated strategising an explicit choice. I will return shortly to this issue of the constructedness of spatial choices "beyond planning".

How has project planning been managed?

Permits for big projects are always the key issue, for proponents and opponents. A range of processes and public inquiry systems have existed in each country, with increasing ammunition available from EU systems introduced since the 1980s. In controversial cases, especially nuclear power stations and airports, and sometimes road and rail schemes, these gave opponents the space to make their cases and mobilise public opinion. Until recently, and still in several countries, such space has been seen as democratically healthy. However, the concern about lengthy permit processes has been widespread amongst business interests, in the UK since the 1990s, and elsewhere more recently. It can be argued that the planning of projects was adequate in most cases, giving planning its usual role to balance interests, as these were expressed regarding a specific case. However, the "jamming up" phenomenon, whereby opponents delayed and blocked schemes desired by governments or business, has generated diverse reform reactions. The CNDP system in France, set up in 1995 to counter problems in getting transport-route approval, allowed public debate in the localities years before a proposed scheme, with no decision from the inquiry manager, only an airing of arguments and a summary. This has strengths in promoting deliberative governance, the venting of conflict, and the possible movement, over time, to consensus views. Poor or damaging schemes may be altered or even abandoned. However, the CNDP has not been copied as it is perhaps seen by business and business oriented governments as being too open and democratic.

The Dutch and now the Scottish systems seek to link large projects to the national physical strategy. The Scottish system is still a work in progress. The Dutch model allows several stages for the really large projects (above all the mainports). This again, like the French arrangements, gives lots of space for working through the conflicts of interest that all large infrastructure schemes contain within them.

However, the leading edge of reforms is represented by the most neoliberalised case, the UK, with the Infrastructure Planning Commission set up under the 2008 Planning Act. Though the principle of arms-length decision making by an "independent" government-appointed agency was rescinded by the post-2010 government, the basic model of a speeded up and simplified system is one that may well be copied. The Dutch and German governments had already introduced "speed up" laws since the 1990s, although from highly variable bases, and in 2011 the German federal government proposed to take over control of big energy schemes, in a way reminiscent of the UK Act. It is much too early to say how these streamlined approaches to project decision-making will turn out for different interests. Many observers did not see the planning systems in these countries as being especially in need of reform, fearing that these changes would mainly benefit schemes around which there is not societal consensus. However, the next five to ten years will reveal the actual effects. Some observers predict little change, arguing that schemes take so long for a complex mix of financial, regulatory and planning reasons, and that reforming the planning element of the package may not alter the basic dynamics of development. Shifting the locus or arena of project consenting may not always result in faster or more pro-development decisions.

"Behind planning" – constructing the spatiality of sectors and the influence of spatial imaginaries

High-level (normally national) spatial planning rarely exists, yet decisions on large-scale infrastructure are taken, with some understanding of the countries they deal with in the minds of those taking the decisions. A focus of this account has been on these framing ideas, which can be seen as parts of national spatial imaginaries. Alongside this background idea of territories is the way in which policy fields are constructed, to filter out some dimensions and emphasise others. This was studied more in the English cases, where the history could be treated more confidently (due to my own understanding of

UK history from within), than in the European cases. But the same applied in other cases, for example, to the way in which waste policy making in the Netherlands was constructed to cut out spatial treatment, beyond certain broad rules about what waste could be traded or pass across provincial or national boundaries, and what targets were set by EU directives. Together these constructed no-go lines for the spatial planning of waste, effectively leaving choice to municipal and market actors, within these framings. The same sort of process was examined in the UK, where road and rail policies were built over decades within certain limiting frameworks, to stop consideration, normally, of any comprehensive approaches to transport or mobility. Road infrastructure was seen as a capacity problem built up largely from below, whilst rail was seen as the management of decline and closure until at least the early 2000s. All these were considered without relation to ports or airports. This was the construction of the silos discussed above, with or without explicit strategies, with or without openly geographical or spatial formulations.

How did these constructed regimes interact with the underlying ideas of countries? In the case of the Netherlands, this was continually worked and reworked, on the basis of multiple historical and contemporary imaginings and material realities. The different infrastructure sectors were just parts of this overall discursive realm: some more out in the open, some less so. However, given the intensiveness of Dutch governing practice and democratic deliberation (especially through parliamentary processes), all of these entered into the mix, as recent debates on transport projects, on water policy, and on energy (wind, gas and so on) show. The National Spatial Strategy was a lynchpin, but formed only part of a much wider, deeper and more continuous national geographical conversation. In England (and, pre-devolution, the UK), there is no such "out in the open" discursive realm. Debate sometimes focuses on elements of such a national imaginary when it deals with the north–south divide, or the pressures on the south-eastern part of England from house building or other types of development. Observers argue that there is an implicit pro-southern England policy permanently in place, an "unwritten spatial constitution" (Wray 2010). There is no way to indicate the precise nature of any such national spatial imaginary, other than by tracing policy initiatives and spending that vary over decades, alongside the expressions of policy makers in White Papers or similar government pronouncements, most of which are not phrased in geographical terms, at least not at national or regional levels. So, the constructed policy zones referred to above, such as the creation of the motorway system or the management of the decline of the rail system, are taken without wider spatial moorings. This is a gap in democratic government, and could easily be one element at the heart of the escalating contestation of major infrastructure schemes. With no opportunity to argue out competing national imaginaries and their spatial dimensions, it is perhaps not surprising that many citizens orient themselves towards project opposition.

This relates to the treatment of subnational governance of all kinds. In Germany, France and Spain, the territories are articulated by means of representative governmental structures. Decisions on infrastructure are generally made within this structure, sharing goods for regions across the particular forces dominant at the time: the gains or losses made within a delicate and intricate horse-trading system. This tends, certainly in the French and Spanish cases, to lead to a "coffee for all" tendency, spreading things seen as desirable (transport infrastructure, reliable energy systems) across all territories over time, and avoiding decisions on things seen as unattractive (nuclear waste depositories and water storage or transfer systems, for example). This is hardly a top-down idea of the countries, though that lurks in the background in all three cases, partly as folk memory, partly as continuing loyalty to an idea of the nation. This is rather different to the more centralised structure in England, where regions have never had much force, even in the two periods of regionalisation, and where local authorities are mostly small enough to be disregarded (mayoral London now being an exception). So, two-way territorial articulation plays a lesser part in the "balancing" of a national dynamic in the English case, making the national imaginary even more invisible to everyday observation.

The construction of aspatiality and hidden spatiality described for sectors above is related, it has been argued, to the varied exposure and deliberation on national spatial imaginaries. Planning is expressed within these constitutional, sectoral and imaginary frames: the more siloised and the less openly debated, the less scope there is for effective integrated planning. Scotland since 2000 has been an example of bringing territorial development in as a building block of a national civic culture, so that citizens have some idea of the future options for the development of transport and energy sectors, within a discussion of the country's overall possibilities. This is very much a work in progress, and conditioned by varying positions on nationalism and much else. But the contrast with England, where no such open development process has really got going in recent decades, is stark.

How has planning related to the generality of conflict in planning major infrastructure?

Planning is widely seen as a societal process about the mediation of conflict between competing interests. Much planning theory of the last two decades has roamed around these areas of consensus and conflict. The survey here has often found that heavy contestation is at the heart of the major infrastructure field of planning, whether in Spain, focusing above all on water and the national hydrological plan (showing conflict can thrive on strategies, not just projects), in Germany, on rail schemes like Stuttgart 21, in Britain, on the high-speed rail line HS2 or in the Netherlands, in Maasvlakte 2. In France, this conflict was one motive leading to the setting up of the CNDP.

It is this element in particular that has pushed the emphasis towards dimensions of democratic governance at all levels, and to the scope for deliberative democracy as well as good local and regional government systems. As theoretical work on agonism has stressed, this will not necessarily lead to an easy resolution, or to answers satisfactory to all interests. But it does support mediating and learning approaches, which can, in the shorter or longer run, lead to more intelligent results, because they are exposed to deeper societal involvement. As Barry and Ellis (2011) stress, this can most valuably lead to a widening of debate and options, connecting up to issues at higher-levels: confronting low carbon itself, for example, rather than only arguing over the local wind farm. There are all sorts of complexities here, which would benefit from further analysis, including the effect of battles lost by opponents, which later alerted decision-makers to similar risks and perhaps better results elsewhere, or the way multi-stage decision making can play out in an individual long-running case.

WAYS TO IMPROVE MAJOR INFRASTRUCTURE PLANNING

Institutional design is a famously difficult task, especially when drawing on international studies of widely differing systems. De Jong (2008) studied approaches to dealing with transport infrastructure and set up a grid of factors affecting different approaches. But this raised, as he made clear, difficult questions about how far anyone might pick-and-mix from the factors. The same applies here: certain approaches may appear to be consonant with values seen as both important and effective in their functioning, but it may be impractical to suggest importing them to different countries, in some incoherent mish mash, like mixing quite distinct recipes in making a meal. So, what follows is at most indicative of the areas that are worth looking at. I will suggest a sort of ABC of the elements and principles I see as important, without trying to specify how these can be combined in any concrete time and place.

It has been suggested that there is an "infrastructure turn" in spatial planning, at least in the case of Australian metropolitan planning (Dodson 2009). I believe, as discussed above, that the increasing emphasis on infrastructure development is indeed widespread, though it does not necessarily take the form observed by Dodson, whereby city planning becomes more of an engineering job, fitting in relevant transport equipment above all. My view is that a great deal of major infrastructure development is likely to be unnecessary, and that what is needed can be planned better. The infrastructure turn can be better managed.

The general principles will not be surprising: integrated spatial planning at the right levels would be the key to better major infrastructure development. This should be publicly led by democratically elected governments, not in the hands of private infrastructure companies (an increasing tendency, as the example of the strategic planning by Peel Holdings in north-west England in 2011 demonstrates). This should be particularly effective in showing where no new development was needed, by thinking about the real objectives of policy. Those should, arguably, be about long-term wellbeing, not about maximising mobility or making growing amounts of energy available. I have spent little time on the issues of demand management, but tend to take it as read that in the long-term planning can do a great deal to promote the cause of demand reduction or appropriate management, so cutting the need for most new infrastructure, especially the largest.

Beyond this integrating principle, it is necessary to look at the different "levels" of framing and policy.

A) The framing of major infrastructure

I am impressed by the importance of the broadest and highest-level public debate on all infrastructure sectors. The examples of the Grenelle in France, the continuous public contestation on energy in Germany, on water and transport in the Netherlands or on water in Spain suggest that this can give a backcloth and publicly understood context to all policy and planning. Of these only the Grenelle is comprehensive, although the Dutch national spatial strategising, alongside other national steering, has traditionally had a powerful public integrating effect. Without this, issues are in a vacuum, whether of sectoral or silo form, or of individual projects. The latter constructions are those that appear to be preferred in many recently neoliberalising polities or political economies, but they are not conducive to subsequent good practice at levels B and C.

The message here is therefore about the importance of big-scale political and institutional dimensions for this field – something well understood by wide-angle political thinkers, but forgotten at times by planners and those working at the coalface of local action. This is without touching on the future approaches to financing and the ownership of infrastructure provision. Here I would echo the recommendations of Whitfield (2010), to move away from the public–private partnership model promoted in recent decades, towards much more transparency, clear public funding and a comprehensive approach to treating social, economic and low carbon considerations together. His formulas could give effective spatial planning for infrastructure much better chances, even though formally they are well outside the bounds of planning in the normal sense.

B) Strategies and major infrastructure

The Dutch and Scottish systems can be taken, in my view, as good models, however exceptional and internationally eccentric. Comprehensive spatial planning does not solve all problems, or wipe away conflicts in projects or over big value questions. But it does allow a level of democratic consideration across territories (even if in these two cases they are somewhat smaller ones), giving the chance to see interrelations that are so critical in creating intelligent long-term social and economic policy, as much as long-term energy and transport transitions. Sectoral strategies, though often of value, particularly if widely framed (like the SNIT), always risk missing out the key connections, and being restricted to simple "predict and provide" responses to growth pressures. There may be a few high-speed rail lines, but they may not be integrated into the classical rail network – considering all transport as a whole, the French and Spanish systems have run these risks (Zembri 1997) more than the (admittedly much smaller scale) Dutch approach. To some extent sectoral strategies may be tied in to spatial considerations, particularly by the play of territorially articulated politics. Countries with strong regional and local governments can press for linking up at those levels and so influence the big sectoral plans in that way: Catalonia's planning in the 2000s gave good examples of how that can work. So, regional and strategic planning can do something to integrate the infrastructural silos, if fitted into effectively functioning vertical and horizontal political structures.

Here the emphasis is still on wider comprehensive intelligence and planning. There can be value in "light" national-level planning as in Germany, if backed by good research and coordinating mechanisms, and certainly in the central agency role exemplified by DATAR, able to make effective connections in its heyday. So, there is a sort of ladder of valuable practice, which might look like this, running from best first:

1. Comprehensive spatial planning strategies at the national level, which both knit together sectoral programmes to some degree, and give a framework for the most important projects.
2. Lighter linking mechanisms, using research and intelligence to inform, persuade and coordinate, working in with the articulated polities that all three of my big country cases have been. That is, territorial power politics can be modified by understanding effects, having mediating bodies like DATAR to hold the ring in as sophisticated a manner as possible.
3. Sectoral strategies in each area, in well-articulated forms, as in the Water Framework Directive round of water planning, again working in with the articulated polities as above, where regional and local planning can provide integrating glue, and adjust the sectoral strategies accordingly.

C) Projects planning

Worst practice can be exemplified by the English case in the 2000s, where port projects were considered individually, on the basis of the market deciding locations and priorities, with planning just responding to local circumstances.

Moving away from this points us towards improvements, where major projects are considered in their wider contexts. This may be within national strategies, as above, and use the French approach praised here: a national commission for public debates, far in advance of formal permit procedures, exposing the project to maximum public deliberation within a process made genuinely independent of all government, business and special-interest pressures. There are many hints of this in wider planning or public-policy literature on how this can be advanced, building the public sphere in water planning as described by Hall et al (2007), for example.

Reforms in England (the IPC) and in Germany (the proposed energy planning processes) may also move in this deliberative direction, despite the main goals of the initiators. The point should be to argue through real conflicts and find the areas of common ground, if they exist. This may require a lot of work: a recent working group in Germany to examine the issue of integrating renewable energy into the electricity grid, including building new lines, brought together diverse interests for nearly two years, and issued a first set of recommendations (Forum for Integration of Renewable Energy 2011). This sort of mediating and policy work requires resources, but may find ways to avoid endlessly repeated local conflicts around power lines. If seeking common ground causes delays, or obstructs developments, planning may well be doing its job: stopping societally dubious schemes. Institutional design should enable this. So, good practice in projects planning, as well as benefitting from the suggested approaches in A and B, should in itself aspire to incorporate good democracy. This may not need more time – although that is highly dependent on how the whole framing of policy has been moving. At any rate time is not necessarily the main issue for the generally massive infrastructure and sometimes state-connected development companies typically investing, as their planning is long-term and tied to related and often more important financial and regulatory issues.

AN EXAMPLE – ENGLAND

Finally, this will be made more concrete, via a brief discussion of England. Many calls were made for more planned approaches to infrastructure development in England in the last decade (CST 2009, ICE 2007, RTPI 2006, TCPA 2006), but the government chose to create individual sectoral instruments (National Policy Statements) hardly linked to mainline planning concerns and processes. The UK government consistently rejected the idea of a national spatial framework for England matching those then emerging for the other parts of the UK. The National Infrastructure Plan, which appeared in 2010, was more a general policy document coupled with a projects list, than anything like a plan. For example, at the time the Severn Barrage proposal, cautiously promoted by the previous government as an energy option, was simply discarded without a coherent linking to energy policy and options for the long term. Project decision-making (for a subset of large projects) was taken away from local authorities and normal town and country planning – but the subsequent move back to ministerial decisions means that change in reality is not as great as intended. What might be better than all this for England?

A better system would need many changes, a set of ingredients, not just one or two big measures. The roots of some of the following points may be discerned in the European cases.

- An independent understanding of infrastructure need should be built up, based on real research. A study in 2008 looking at UK energy futures (MacKay 2009) was remarkable for being perhaps the best work on how to shift to low-carbon systems – but was done by a single enthusiastic physicist, not by a government body or programme. MacKay's work made clear the hole at the centre of energy policy making, with complex issues unaddressed on both need and supply sides, within the UK's geographical possibilities. A large programme on Infrastructure Transitions funded by a government research council was begun in 2011, and may start to close the gap. The reliance on the shaky claims of professional and business lobbies in recent years has meant that all UK policy has been highly contested, across most of the fields examined here. A continuous research capacity is needed.

- There should be proper coordination of public policy on the financing, regulation and planning of infrastructure. This began to emerge with the establishment of Infrastructure UK, but the first National Infrastructure Plan only made small steps to a serious integration of these elements – given the limited research base, and the heavily ideologically-driven foundations within the Treasury (market principles trumping any other possible goals), this was not surprising. But the principle of coordination was, it seems, accepted. The next steps would be to move from a reactive approach, whereby each development company presents proposals, to the government giving a stronger framework in each field, and indicating ways to travel along these paths. Clearly this is not in sympathy with present political economies, but in the absence of far more determined and sophisticated green fiscal and regulatory policies, it is impossible to imagine how relatively rapid transitions to sustainable systems might be achieved otherwise, in transport, energy or other infrastructure fields.

- National Policy Statements should be coordinated with each other and with overall geographical goals for England and to an extent for the UK (Sustainable Development Commission 2011). It is true that this is close to calling for a spatial plan for England, which would be desirable but is currently highly unlikely. But at least on certain criteria it would be possible to coordinate across the ten or so NPSs, rather than letting these emerge from each ministry with very little play across to general government goals as is currently the case. Such criteria could include the need to reduce demand in the relevant area, the cumulative impact on carbon reduction and the effect on rebalancing the economy sectorally or geographically. A light criteria-based mode is no doubt more plausible in England than any more developed planning. Final approval by the ministry containing spatial planning functions, the Department of Communities and Local Government, rather than by the sectoral ministry, could help to give integrating coherence.

- Project decisions should be tested early on by a Public Debates Commission. This would indicate early problems, and discuss both general need and locational questions, but, like the French CNDP, have no decision-making power. Cost should not be an issue, when one considers the enormous expected cost of infrastructure investment. Some estimate £400 billion to 2020 – one nuclear power station alone costs £10 billion. The real cost of bad decisions on major infrastructure (making something that is not needed, building it badly or in a poor location, for example) is therefore truly large, dwarfing by factors of thousands any possible costs of better planning processes. Such a Commission would be independent of the NPS system and project consenting process. But project consenting should as far as possible take on similar deliberative colours, without needing to set up long-running public inquiries. There have been clear signs that the IPC has been moving in this direction since it was set up in 2009. Once inside the Planning Inspectorate, it is to be hoped that it retains and accentuates this open and public-facing approach. After the removal of the inquisitorial elements of old-style public inquiries, the goal of the IPC to reach decisions (or pass these to the minister) within 12 months should be quite possible. Furthermore, the Public Debates Commission should already have removed some of the less plausible or desirable schemes early on. The planning skills of balancing and mediating would be critical to the stages of project-consideration functioning effectively, probably more so than those of lawyers, who typically dominated the public inquiry system.

CODA

Some paths of infrastructural use and development are firmly locked into the economic and social functioning of Europe. In the short term, other paths are locked out. Even in the medium term of two or three decades, much is excluded – the essential elements of water systems would be very expensive to change, and the same applies to lesser degrees in some transport and energy areas. Over years, more options could in principle be opened up, through mixes of technical and political innovation. These are on EU agendas and those of most countries, in weaker or stronger form, primarily related to an unstable mix of low carbon and economic growth objectives at present. Geographical lock-in is part of the present overall system set, governed by the way in which the varied systems have been created over many years. Everything from metropolitan system functioning to continental and global connectivity is entwined in the nature of these geographies, with vast capital stocks tied up in each location or each business flow. Ideological lock-in is similarly critical, as Mitchell's UK energy study showed (2008). All these elements constitute powerful barriers to sustainable transformation, interacting with the current political and economic conjunctures, in varying forms of crisis. The suggestions for change in this chapter are admittedly not strong forces against these realities: Davids against very large Goliaths.

Nevertheless planning could be an instrument that can be used to unlock the paths to future change. Naturally, it is also part of the set of lock-in mechanisms, given the tendency for interests of nearly all kinds to support existing arrangements, for all sorts of more individual or more collective reasons. Planning is not by nature either primarily part of the problems or part of the solutions. But it could be used, at a host of scales (from local to continental) to enable transitions which would be more intelligent, efficient and faster than those that might emerge (if they ever would) without any planning. It is because of this potentially pivotal role in enabling transitions, as well as more mundane demands around the business pressures to invest and valorise massive capital systems, that planning is so much in the spotlight in the discussion of major infrastructure. I have argued here that it needs to be incorporated into the wider development of democratisation essential for any equitable and effective long-term transitions to more sustainable ways of life.

The major infrastructure planning question is not a technical one: of how to get so many kilometres of electric or high-speed rail line built, or so many kilowatts generated. It has to be tied up into the core debates of political and societal change – as planning, when effective, has tended to be in the past in tackling issues of urbanisation, countryside protection or other historically central challenges. That is a message of this book: the necessity to connect and integrate discussions in this planning field with the issues of basic values. This means that such debates will always be conflictual and contested, which is the normal sign of proper societal functioning. All institutional design should aim to facilitate this opening out of discussion, not closing down to powerful economic or political special interests. In this book I have put the emphasis on the democratic working of national states in enabling these tasks, whilst not excluding the importance of the EU, regional and local levels. It is time to put the spotlight of planning work back on this national scale, and press for much more adequate spatial planning competences at that level. At present, neoliberalising ideas are unfortunately moving in the other direction. But those concerned with planning, from many perspectives, need to put the case for accountable, well-researched and intelligent action at this level: properly articulated with subnational democratic structures. I believe this applies to all the cases I have examined here, and may be appropriate to many other nations, in Europe and beyond.

REFERENCES

Agencia Catalana d'Aigua (2009) *Water in Catalonia*, Barcelona: ACA.

Allen, J., Massey, D. and Cochrane, A. (1998) *Rethinking the Region*, London: Routledge.

Alterman, R. (ed.) (2001) *National-Level Planning in Democratic Countries*, Liverpool: Liverpool University Press.

Altshuler, A. and Luberoff, D. (2003) *Mega-Project: The Changing Politics of Urban Public Investment*, Washington, DC: Brookings Institution Press.

Altvater, E. (2005) *Das Ende des Kapitalismus wie wir ihn kennen*, Munster: Westfalisches Dampfboot.

Alvergne, C. and Musso, P. (2008), *Les Grands Textes de l'Amenagement du Territoire ed de la Decentralisation*, Paris: La Documentation Francaise.

Amin, A., Massey, D. and Thrift, N. (2003) *Decentering the Nation*, London: Catalyst.

Anderson, B. (1991) *Imagined Communities*, London: Verso.

Anderson, V. (1991) *Alternative Economic Indicators*, London: Routledge.

Andeweg, R. and Irwin, G. (2005) *Governance and Politics of the Netherlands*, Basingstoke: Palgrave Macmillan

Arbos, X., Colino, C., Garcia, M. and Parrado, S. (2009) *Las Relaciones Intergubernamentales en el Estado Autonomico: La Posicion de los Actores*, Barcelona: Institut d'Estudis Autonomics, Generalitat de Catalunya.

Aring, J. (2010) 'Bundesraumordnung', in Henckel, D. et al, *Planen – Bauen – Umwelt. Ein Handbuch*, Wiesbaden: VS Verlag, pp. 86–89.

Aring, J. and Sinz, M. (2006a), 'Neue Leitbilder der Raumentwicklung in Deutschland', *disP*, 165, 43–60.

Aring, J. and Sinz, M. (2006b) 'Neue Leitbilder der Raumentwicklung: Ein Impuls zur Modernisierung der Raumordnung?', *Raumforschung und Raumordnung*, 6, 451–459.

Arocena, P. (2006) 'Privatization policy in Spain', in Kothenburger, M., Sinn, H. W. and Whalley, J. (eds), *Privatization Experiences in the European Union*, Cambridge: MIT Press, pp. 339–364.

Arrojo, P. (2006) 'Planificacion hidrologica y sostenibilidad, nuevas claves en materia de gestion de aguas', in Cuadrat Prats, J. M. (ed.) *El Agua en el Siglo XXI*, Zaragoza: Institucion Fernando el Catolico, seminar paper of 2003.

Arrojo, P. (2008) *Luces y Sombras de una Legislatura Historica en Materia de Gestion de Aguas*, Fundacion Nueva Cultura del Agua, Panel Cientifico-tecnico de seguimento de la politica de aguas, Convenio Universidad de Sevilla – Ministerio de Medio Ambiente.

Arts, G., Dicke, W. and Hancher, L., (2008) *New Perspectives on Investment in Infrastructures*, Amsterdam: WRR.

Arup, Regional Forecasts and Oxford Economic Forecasting (2005) *Regional Futures: England's Regions in 2030*, London: Arup.

Aschauer, D. (1989) 'Is public expenditure productive?', *Journal of Monetary Economics*, 23, 177–200.

Baldwin, P. and Baldwin, R. (eds) (2004) *The Motorway Achievement, Volume 1: The Motorway System*, London: Thomas Telford Publishing.

Banon, R. and Tamayo, M. (1997) 'The transformation of the central administration in Spanish intergovernmental relations', *Publius*, 27, 3, 85–114.

Barker, K. (2004) *Review of Housing, Final Report*, London: HM Treasury.

Barker, K. (2006) *Review of Land Use Planning, Final Report*, London: HM Treasury.

Baron-Yelles, N. (2008) *France, Amenager et Developper les Territoires*, Paris: La Documentation Francaise (Dossier No 8067).

Barraque, B. (1998a), *Water Policy Formulation in France, Water21 Phase 1 Report*, December 1998, Brussels: European Commission, DGXII.

Barraque, B. (1998b) *Le Ministere de l'Environnement et les Agences de l'Eau*, unpublished paper.

Barraque, B. (2000) 'Les demandes en eau en catalogne: perspective europeenne sur le projet d'aqueduc Rhone – Barcelone', *La Revue d'Economie Meridionale*, 191, pp. 357-370.

Barry, J. and Ellis, G. (2011) 'Beyond consensus? Agonism, republicanism and a low carbon future', in Devine-Wright, P. (ed.) *Renewable Energy and the Public*, London: Earthscan, pp. 29–42.

Baudelle, G. and Peyrony, J. (2005) 'Striving for equity: Polycentric development policies in France', *Built Environment*, 31, 2, 103–111.

BBSR (2005) *Raumordnungsbericht 2005*, Bonn: Bundesinstitut fur Bau-, Stadt- und Raumforschung.

Becher, B. and Becher, H. (2002) *Industrial Landscapes*, Cambridge: MIT Press.

Beck, U. (1992) *Risk Society*, London: Sage.

Benabent Fernandez de Cordoba, M. (2006) *La Ordenación del Territorio en España. Evolución del Concepto y de su Práctica en el Siglo XX*, Seville: Universidad de Sevilla.

Beresford, A. and Pettit, S. (2009) 'A geographical perspective on port performance in the United Kingdom 1999–2007', in Notteboom, T., Ducruet, C. and de Langen, P. (eds) *Ports in Proximity*, Farnham: Ashgate.

Bergmeier, M. and Muller, W. (2010) 'Neubaustrecke Rhein-Main – Rhein-Neckar: Engpass im Korridor de Nord-Sud-Transversale', in Hesse, M. (ed.) *Neue Rahmenbedingungen, Herausforderungen und Strategien fur die Grossraumige Verkehrsentwicklung*, Hanover: ARL, pp. 40–55.

Bernat, V. and Ollivier-Trigalo, M. (1997) *Transport Policy in France*, working report in Project TENASSESS work package 6, May 1997, Paris: INRETS.

Blackbourn, D. (2006*) The Conquest of Nature: Water, Landscape and the Making of Modern Germany*, New York: W W Norton.

Blowers, A. (1992) 'The political geography of waste disposal', in Clark, M. Smith, D. and Blowers, A. (eds) *Waste Location*, London: Routledge, pp. 227–247.

BMBau (Bundesministerium für Raumordnung, Bauwesen und Städtebau) (1993) *Raumordnungspolitischer Orientierungsrahmen*, Bonn: BMBau.

BMU (2006) *Water Resouce Management in Germany*, Bonn: BMU.

BMVBS (2006a) *Concepts and Strategies for Spatial Development in Germany*, Berlin/Bonn: BMVBS and BBSR.

BMVBS (2006b) *Perspectives of Spatial Development in Germany*, Berlin/Bonn: BMVBS and BBSR.

BMVBS (2009a) *Flughafenkonzept der Bundesregierung 2009*, Berlin: BMBVS.

BMVBS (2009b) *Nationales Hafenkonzept fur die See- und Binnenhafen*, Berlin: BMBVS.

BMVBS (2009c) *Raumordnungsplan fur die Deutsche Ausschliessliche Wirtschaftszone (Nordsee, Ostsee)*, Berlin: BMBVS, Hamburg: BSH.

BMVBS (2011) *Erneuerbare Energien: Zukunftsausgabe der Regionalplanung*, Bonn: BMBVS/BBSR.

BMVBW (2002) *Federal Transport Infrastructure Plan 2003, Basic Features of the Macroeconomic Evaluation Methodology*, Berlin: BMBVW.

BMVBW (2003) *Federal Transport Infrastructure Plan 2003*, Berlin: BMBVW.

BMWi/BMU (2010) *Energiekonzept fur eine Umweltschonende, Zuverlassige und Bezahlbare Energieversorgung*, Berlin: BMWi.

Bogdanor, V. (ed) (2005) *Joined-Up Government*, Oxford: Oxford University Press.

Bogdanor, V. (2009) *The New British Constitution*, Oxford: Hart.

Booth, P., Breuillard, M., Fraser, C. and Paris, D. (eds), (2007) *Spatial Planning Systems of Britain and France*, Abingdon: Routledge.

Bosch and Partner et al, (2010) *Erarbeitung eines Konzepts zur "Integration einer Strategischen Umweltprufung in die Bundesverkehrswegeplanung"*, Hanover: Bosch and Partner GmbH.

Bowen, J. and Leinbach, T. (2010) 'Transportation networks, the logistics revolution and regional development' in Pike, A., Rodriguez-Pose, A. and Tomaney, J. (eds), *Handbook of Local and Regional Development*, Abingdon: Routledge, pp. 438–448.

Braithwaite, J. (2006) 'The regulatory state?' in Rhodes, R., Binder, S. and Rockman, B. (eds) *Oxford Handbook of Political Institutions*, Oxford: Oxford University Press, pp. 407–430.

Braudel, F. (1973) *Capitalism and Material Life 1400–1800*, London: Weidenfeld and Nicolson.

Brenner, N. (2004) *New State Spaces*, Oxford: Oxford University Press.

Brenner, N., Peck, J. and Theodore, N. (2010) 'Variegated neoliberalization: geographies, modalities, pathways', *Global Networks*, 10, 2, 182–222.

Breukers, S. and Wolsink, M. (2007) 'Wind energy policies in the Netherlands: Institutional capacity-building for ecological modernisation', *Environmental Politics*, 16, 1, 92–112.

Bruns, E. (2011) 'Energy infrastructure planning in Germany and the UK', note produced for research visit to Oxford in June 2011.

Bruton, M. and Nicholson, D. (1987) *Local Planning in Practice*, London: Routledge.

Bryson, J. (2004) *Strategic Planning for Public and Not for Profit Organisations*, San Francisco: Jossey Bass.

Calderon, C. and Serven, L. (2004) 'The effects of infrastructure development on growth and income distribution', World Bank Policy Research Working Paper Number 3400, September 2004.

Candela, L. et al (2008) 'An overview of the main water conflicts in Spain: Proposals for problem solving', *Options Mediterraneennes*, 83, 197–203.

Caplan, D. (2005) 'Ontario's infrastructure revival', *Infrastructure Journal*, winter 2005, 23–29.

Castoriadis, C. (1987) *The Imaginary Institution of Society*, Cambridge: Polity.

CBI (Confederation of British Industry) (1992) *Shaping the Nation*, London: CBI.

CBI (Confederation of British Industry) (1995) *Missing Links*, London: CBI.

CBI (Confederation of British Industry) (2000) *Manifesto: Towards 2010*, London: CBI.

CBI (Confederation of British Industry) (2005) *Transport Policy and the Needs of the Economy*, London: CBI.

CBI (Confederation of British Industry) (2011) Investment in infrastructure would kick-start UK growth – new CBI/KPMG survey, Press release, 9 September 2011, www.cbi.org.uk/media-centre/press-releases/2011/09/investment-in-infrastructure-would-kick-start-uk-growth%E2%80%93new-cbi-kpmg-survey/

CEC (Commission of the European Communities) (1997) *EU Compendium of Spatial Planning and Policies*, Brussels: CEC.

CEC (Commission of the European Communities) (1999) *European Spatial Development Perspective*, Brussels: CEC.

Cerny, P. (2006) 'Restructuring the state in a globalizing world: Capital accumulation, tangled hierarchies and the search for a new spatio-temporal fix', *Review of International Political Economy*, 13, 679–695.

Chari, R. and Heywood, P. (2009) 'Analysing the policy process in democratic Spain', *West European Politics*, 32, 1, 26–54.

Clark, G. and Root, A. (1999) 'Infrastructure shortfall in the UK', *Political Geography*, 18, 341–365.

CNDP (2007a) *Les Cahiers Methodologiques*, Edition 2007, Paris: CNDP.

CNDP (2007b) *Rapport d'Activite 2006/2007*, Paris: CNDP.

CNDP (2008) *Debat Public sur la Refonte de la Station d'Epuration Seine Aval, Compte Rendu*, Paris: CNDP.

Cole, A. (2008) *Governing and Governance in France*, Cambridge: Cambridge University Press.

Cole, A., Le Gales, P. and Levy, J. (eds) (2008) *Developments in French Politics 4*, Basingstoke: Palgrave.

Colino, C. and Parrado, S. (2009) 'Análisis de la práctica y la dinámica de los procesos formales e informales de las relaciones intergubernamentales', in Arbos, X., Colino, C., Garcia, M. and Parrado, S. *Relaciones Intergubernamentales en el Estado Autonómico: Actores*, Barcelona: Institut d'Estudis Autonòmics, pp. 135–296.

Committee on Climate Change (2009) *Meeting Carbon Budgets: The Need for a Step Change. Executive Summary*, London: Committee on Climate Change.

Coombs, G. and Roberts, C. (2007) 'Trends in infrastructure', in *Economic Roundup Summer 2007*, Canberra: Australian Government, The Treasury.

CoRWM (Committee on Radioactive Waste Management) (2006) *Managing our Radioactive Waste Safely*, London: CoRWM.

CST (Council for Science and Technology) (2009) *A National Infrastructure for the Twenty First Century*, London: CST.

Cour des Comptes (2006) *Les Ports Francais Face aux Mutations du Transport Maritime: l'Urgence de l'Action*, Cour des Comptes, Paris: La Documentation Francaise.

Cour des Comptes (2008a) *Les Aeroports Francais Face aux Mutations du Transport Aerien*, Paris: La Documentation Francaise.

Cour des Comptes (2008b) *Le Reseau Ferroviaire: Une Reforme Inachevee, une Strategic Incertaine*, Paris: La Documentation Francaise.

Cowell, R. (2007) 'Wind power and "the planning problem": the experience of Wales', *European Environment,* 17, 291–306.

Cowell, R. (2010) 'Wind power, landscape and strategic, spatial planning – the construction of "acceptable locations" in Wales', *Land Use Policy*, 27, 222–232.

Cowell, R. and Owens, S. (2006) 'Governing space: Planning reform and the politics of sustainability', *Environment and Planning C*, 24, 403–421.

CPB (Netherlands Bureau for Economic Policy Analysis) (2006) *Scenarios to 2040 (Welvaart en Leefomgeving)*, The Hague: CPB.

CPRE (1993) *Water for Life*, London: CPRE.

Crouch, C. (2004) *Post-Democracy*, Cambridge: Polity.

Crouch, C. (2005) *Capitalist Diversity and Change*, Oxford: Oxford University Press.

Culpepper, P., Hall, P. and Palier, B. (eds) (2006) *Changing France*, Basingstoke: Palgrave.

Cunliffe, B. (2008) *Europe Between the Oceans*, London: Yale University Press.

DATAR (2000) *Amenager la France de 2020*, Paris: DATAR.

DATAR (2003) *CIADT Decembre 2003*, http://territoires.gouv.fr/ciadt-du-18-decembre-2003, accessed 29/2/2012.

Davis, P. (2008) 'Infrastructure takes a knock in downturn', *Financial Times*, 24 November 2008, 9.

Davoudi, S. and Evans, N. (2005) 'The challenge of governance in regional waste planning', *Environment and Planning C*, 23, 4, 493–517.

Davoudi, S., Evans, N. and Smith, A. (2005) *Regionalisation and the New Politics of Waste: A National Overview*, Leeds: CUDEM, Leeds Metropolitan University.

DBERR (Department of Business, Enterprise and Regulatory Reform) (2008) *New Nuclear*, London: DBERR.

De Bruijn, H. and Dicke, W. (2006) 'Strategies for safeguarding public values in liberalized utility sectors', *Public Administration*, 84, 3, 717–735.

Debrie, J., Gouvernal, E. and Slack, B. (2007) 'Port devolution revisited: The case of regional ports and the role of lower tier governments', *Journal of Transport Geography*, 15, 455–464.

De Jong, M. (2008) 'Drawing institutional lessons across countries on making transport infrastructure policy', in Priemus, H., Flyvbjerg, B. and van Wee, B. (eds) *Decision-making on Mega-Projects: Cost-benefit Analysis, Planning and Innovation*, Cheltenham: Edward Elgar, pp. 304–32.

Dena (2005) *Planning of the grid integration of wind energy in Germany onshore and offshore up to the year 2020* (English summary, March 2005), Berlin: Dena.

Dena (2010a) *Kurzanalyse der Kraftwerksplanung in Deutschland bis 2020 (Aktualisierung)*, Berlin: Dena.

Dena (2010b) *Integration of Renewable Energy Sources into the German Power Supply System in the 2015–2020 Period with Outlook to 2025*, Berlin: Dena.

Departament de Politica Territorial i Obres Publiques (2006a) *Criteris de Planejament Territorial*, Barcelona: DPTOP.

Departament de Politica Territorial i Obres Publiques (2006b) *Pla d'Infraestructures del Transport de Catalunya*, Barcelona: DPTOP.

DCLG (Department for Communities and Local Government) (2010a) *The Community Infrastructure Levy, An Overview*, London: DCLG

DCLG (Department for Communities and Local Government) (2010b) *Major Infrastructure Planning Reform – Work Plan*, London: DCLG.

DECC (Department of Energy and Climate Change) (2008) *Managing Radioactive Waste Safely*, London: DECC.

DECC (Department of Energy and Climate Change) (2009a) *The UK Low Carbon Transition Plan*, London: DECC.

DECC (Department of Energy and Climate Change) (2009b) *The UK Renewables Energy Strategy*, London: DECC.

DEFRA (Department of Food, Environment and Rural Affairs) (2007) *Waste Strategy for England*, London: DEFRA.

Department for Regional Development Northern Ireland (2001) *Shaping our Future. Regional Development Strategy (RDS) 2025*, Belfast: DRDNI.

Department for Regional Development Northern Ireland (2011) *Shaping our Future. Regional Development Strategy (RDS) 2025. 10 Year Review, Draft*, Belfast: DRDNI.

Department of Environment (1977) *The Water Industry in England and Wales: The Next Steps*, London: DOE.

Department of Environment (1996) *Water Resources and Supply: Agenda for Action*, London: DOE.

Department of Trade (1978) *Airports Policy*, London: HMSO.

Department of Transport (1985) *Airports Policy*, London: HMSO.

DETR (Department of Environment, Transport and the Regions) (1998) *A New Deal for Transport: Better for Everyone,* London: DETR.

DETR (Department of Environment, Transport and the Regions) (1999a) *Modernising Planning. A Progress Report,* London: DETR.

DETR (Department of Environment, Transport and the Regions) (1999b) *A Way With Waste: A Draft Waste Strategy for England and Wales,* London: DETR.

DETR (Department of Environment, Transport and the Regions) (2000) *National Waste Strategy 2000 for England and Wales,* London: DETR.

DfT (Department for Transport) (2007a) *Delivering a Sustainable Railway,* London: DfT.

DfT (Department for Transport) (2007b) *Towards a Sustainable Transport System: Supporting Economic Growth in a Low Carbon World,* London: DfT.

DfT (Department for Transport) (2008) *Delivering a Sustainable Transport System,* London: DfT.

DfT (Department for Transport) (2009) *National Policy Statement for Ports*, draft, November 2009, London: DfT.

DfT (Department for Transport) (2010) *High Speed Rail,* London: DfT.

DfT (Department for Transport) (2011) *Developing a Sustainable Framework for UK Aviation: Scoping Document,* London: DfT.

DIACT (2007a) *Les Contrats de Projet Etat-Regions*, Paris: La Documentation Francaise.

DIACT (2007b) *Diact, une Administration de Mission a Vocation Interministerielle au Service des Territoires*, Paris: DIACT (leaflet in French and English).

DIACT (2008) *Annual Report 2007*, Paris: DIACT.

Diaz Zoido, R. (1994) 'El medio ambiente y la politica territorial: ejes de la reestructuracion del "ministerio de obras publicas, transportes y medio ambiente"', *Revista de Obras Publicas*, 3300, 7–12.

Dienel, H.-L. (2007) 'Das Bundesverkehrsministerium', in Scholler, O., Canzler, W. and Knie, A. eds, *Handbuch Verkehrspolitik*, Wiesbaden: VS Verlag fur Sozialwissenshaften, pp. 200–214.

Dodson, J. (2009) *The 'Infrastructure Turn' in Australian Metropolitan Spatial Planning*, Brisbane: Griffith University, Urban Research Program, Research Paper 25.

Domhardt, H.-J. et al, (2007) *Festlegungen zum Verkehr in Regionalplànen*, Werkstatt: Praxis Heft 48, Bonn: BMBVS/BBSR.

Drake, J., Evans, D. I. and Yeadon, H. L. (1969) *Motorways,* London: Faber and Faber.

DTI (Department of Trade and Industry) (2003) *Our Energy Future – Creating a Low Carbon Economy,* London: DTI.

DTI (Department of Trade and Industry) (2007) *Meeting the Energy Challenge,* London: DTI.

DTLR (Department of Transport, Local Government and the Regions) (2001a) *New Parliamentary Procedures for Processing Major Infrastructure Projects*, London: DTLR.

DTLR (Department of Transport, Local Government and the Regions) (2001b) *Planning: Delivering a Fundamental Change*, Planning Green Paper, London: DTLR.

Duhr, S. (2007) *The Visual Language of Spatial Planning*, London: Routledge.

Duhr, S., Colomb, C. and Nadin, V. (2010) *European Spatial Planning and Territorial Cooperation,* Abingdon: Routledge.

Dupuy, G. (1991) *L'Urbanisme des Reseaux: Theories et Methodes*, Paris: Armand Colin.

Durner, W. (2009) 'Das neue Raumordnungsgesetz', *NuR*, 31, 373–380.

Duxbury, R. (2009) *Telling and Duxbury's Planning Law and Procedure*, Oxford: Oxford University Press.

Ecotec and Faber Maunsell (2004) 'Surface infrastructure of national economic importance (SINEI): A study for England's regional development agencies', January 2004.

Eddington, R. (2006) *The Eddington Transport Study: Main Report*, London: HM Treasury and Department for Transport.

Edensor, T. (2002) *National Identity, Popular Culture and Everyday Life*, Oxford: Berg.

Edwards, P. (2003) 'Infrastructure and modernity: Force, time, and social organization in the history of sociotechnical systems', in Misa, T., Brey, P. and Feenberg, A. (eds) *Modernity and Technology*, Cambridge, MA: MIT Press, pp. 185–225.

Einig, K. (2008) 'Regulierung offentlicher Daseinsvorsorge als Aufgabe der Raumordnung im Gewahrleistungsstaat', *Informationen zur Raumentwicklung*, 1/2, 17–40.

Einig, K. (2011) 'Fachplanungskoordination durch Raumordnungsplanung', in Tietz, H. P. and Huhner, T. eds *Zukunftsfahige Infrastruktur und Raumentwicklung*, Hanover: ARL, pp. 85–116.

El Comercio (2008) 'Estamos cosiendo Espana con cables de aciero', Interview of Pedro Luis Gomez with Magdalena Alvarez, 11 May 2008, www.elcomercio.es/gijon/20080511/politica/estamos-cosiendo-espana-cables-20080511.html, accessed on 29/2/2012.

ENSG (Electricity Networks Strategy Group) (2009) *Our Electricity Transmission Networks*, London: ENSG.

Embid Irujo, A. (2008) 'La politica de aguas y su marco juridico', Fundacion Nueva Cultura del Agua, Panel Cientifico-tecnico de seguimiento de la politica de aguas, Convenio Universidad de Sevilla – Ministerio de Medio Ambiente.

Engartner, T. (2008) *Die Privatisierung der Deutschen Bahn*, Wiesbaden: VS Verlag fur Sozialwissenshaften.

Engartner, T. (2010) 'German rail reform: Railway policy aligned for the capital markets', *International Journal of Public Policy*, 6, 1/2, 73–86.

Ennis, F. (ed.) (2003) *Infrastructure Provision and the Negotiating Process*, Aldershot: Ashgate.

Environment Agency (2006) *Do We Need Large-scale Water Transfers for South East England?*, London: Environment Agency.

Environment Agency (2009) *Water Resources Strategy: Water for People and the Environment*, London: Environment Agency.

Esser, C. and Randerath, A. (2010) *Schwarzbuch Deutsche Bahn*, Munich: C Bertelsmann.

Esteban, J. (2006) 'El programa de planejament territorial: Continguts i metode', *Espais*, 52, 14–24.

Estevan, A. (2008) 'El gen del trasvase', *El Pais*, 14/2/2008, El Pais.com.

European Round Table of Industrialists (1984) *Missing Networks*, Brussels: ERT.

EZ (Ministerie van Economische Zaken) (2008) *Energy Report*, The Hague: EZ.

Faludi, A. (2000) 'The performance of spatial planning', *Planning Practice and Research*, 15, pp. 299–318.

Faludi, A. (2010) *Cohesion, Coherence, Cooperation: European Spatial Planning Coming of Age?*, Abingdon: Routledge.

Faludi, A. and van der Valk, A. (1994) *Rule and Order: Dutch Planning Doctrine in the Twentieth Century*, Dordrecht: Kluwer.

Faludi, A. and Waterhout, B. (2002) *The Making of the European Spatial Development Perspective – Not a Master Plan!*, London: Routledge.

Farber, G. (ed.) (2005) *Das Foderative System in Deutschland: Bestandsaufnahme, Reformbedarf und Handlungsempfehlungen aus Raumwissenschaflicher Sicht*, Hanover: Akademie fur Raumforschung und Landesplanung.

Farinos Dasi, J., Romero Gonzalez, J. and Sanchez de Madariaga, I. (2005) 'Structural problems for the renewal of planning styles: The Spanish case', *European Planning Studies*, 13, 2, 217–235.

Fayard, A., Gaeta, F. and Quinet, E. (2005) 'French motorways: Experience and assessment', in Ragazzi, G. and Rothengatter, W. (eds) 'Procurement and financing of motorways in Europe', *Research in Transportation Economics*, 15, Amsterdam: Elsevier, pp. 97–106.

Federal Government (2008) *Freight Transport and Logistics Plan*, Berlin: Federal Government.

Finger, M. (2005) 'Regulation', in von Weizsacker, E., Young, O. and Finger, M. (eds) *Limits to Privatization*, London: Earthscan, pp. 291–297.

Fischer, F. (2003) *Reframing Public Policy: Discursive Politics and Deliberative Practices*, Oxford: Oxford University Press.

Flinders, M. (2008a) *Delegated Governance and the British State*, Oxford: Oxford University Press.

Flinders, M. (2008b) 'Public/private: The boundaries of the state', in Hay, C., Lister, M. and Marsh, D. (eds) *The State*, Basingstoke: Palgrave Macmillan, pp. 223–247.

Flinders, M. (2009) *Democratic Drift*, Oxford: Oxford University Press.

Florence Forum (2010) '19th Electricity Forum, Draft Conclusions', pp. 13–14 December 2010.

Flyvbjerg, B., Bruzelius, N. and Rothengatter, W. (2003) *Megaprojects and Risk*, Cambridge: Cambridge University Press.

FNE (France Nature Environnement) (2010) *Grenelle de l'Environment : Bilan de'Etape de FNE*, Paris: FNE.

Forsyth, P., Gillen, D., Mueller, J. and Niemeier, H. M. (eds) (2010) *Airport Competition: The European Experience*, Farnham: Ashgate.

Forum for Integration of Renewable Energy (2011) *Plan N: Recommendations for Political Action*, Berlin: Deutsche Umwelthilfe.

Fremont, A. (2008a), 'Conclusion', in Jean, Y. and Vanier, M. (eds) (2008) *La France, Amenager les Territoires*, Paris: Armand Colin.

Fremont, A. (2008b) *Les Transports en France*, Paris: La Documentation Francaise (Dossier No 8066).

Fremont, A., Franc, P. and Slack, B. (2009) 'Inland barge services and container transport: The case of the ports of Le Havre and Marseille in the European context', *Cybergeo*, article 437.

Fremont, A. and Gouvernal, E. (2008) 'Public and private interests and the balance between local and national claims: the French experience', in Musso, E. and Ghiara, H. (eds) *Ports and Regional Economies: The Future of Port Clusters*, Milan: McGraw-Hill.

Frey, R. (1972) *Infrastruktur*, Tubingen: Mohr.

Frey, R. (2005) 'Infrastruktur', in Akademie fur Raumordnung und Landesplanung *Handworterbuch der Raumordnung*, Hanover: ARL, pp. 469–475.

Friend, J. and Hickling, A. (1987) *Planning Under Pressure: The Strategic Choice Approach*, Oxford: Pergamon Press.

Fullerton, B. (1982) 'Transport', in House, J. (ed.) *The UK Space,* London: Weidenfeld and Nicolson, pp. 356–425.

Fundicot (2009) *Cambio Global. Espana 2020, Programa Transporte*, Fundicot: Madrid.

Funnell, W., Jupe, R. and Andrew, J. (2009) *In Government We Trust*, London: Pluto Press.

Garrido, A. and Varela Ortega, C. (2008) 'Economia del agua en la agricultura e integracion de politicas sectoriales', Fundacion Nueva Cultura del Agua, Panel Cientifico-tecnico de seguimento de la politica de aguas, Convenio Universidad de Sevilla – Ministerio de Medio Ambiente.

Gaudin, J.-P. (2004) *L'Action Publique,* Paris: Sociologie et Politique, Sciences Po.

Gemeinsame Landesplanungsabteilung Berlin-Brandenburg (2006) *Gemeinsames Strukturkonzept Flughafenumfeld Berlin Brandenburg International (BBI)*, Potsdam: Berlin-Brandenburg.

Gemeinsame Landesplanungsabteilung Berlin-Brandenburg (2008a) *Spatial Development in the Baltic-Adriatic-Development Corridor*, Potsdam: Berlin-Brandenburg.

Gemeinsame Landesplanungsabteilung Berlin-Brandenburg (2008b) *Regional Development in the Baltic-Adriatic-Development Corridor: Chances and Potentials of Spatial Economics*, Potsdam: Berlin-Brandenburg.

Gemeinsame Landesplanungsabteilung Berlin-Brandenburg (2008c) *Airside meets Landside. Beitrage zur integrierten Entwicklung des Hauptstadt Airports BBI*, Potsdam: Berlin-Brandenburg.

Generalitat de Catalunya (2009) *Pacte Nacional per a les Infraestructures*, Barcelona: Generalitat.

Giddens, A. (1998) *The Third Way*, Cambridge: Polity.

Giddens, A. (2009) *The Politics of Climate Change*, Cambridge: Polity.

Gil Diaz, J. L. (2008) 'El factor energetico en la gestion de los recursos hidricos: Aproximacion al uso del analisis del ciclo de vida', *Ingenieria y Territorio*, 82, 86–93.

Gil Olcina, A. and Gomez Mendoza, J. (eds) (2009) *Geografia de Espana*, Barcelona: Ariel (chapter on la ordenacion del territorio a distintas escalas, pp. 595–618).

Girardon, J. (2006) *Politiques d'Amenagement du Territoire*, Paris: Ellipses.

Glaister, S., Burnham, J., Stevens, H. and Travers, T. (1998) *Transport Policy in Britain,* London: Macmillan.

Glaister, S., Burnham, J., Stevens, H. and Travers, T. (2006) *Transport Policy in Britain* (2nd edn), London: Macmillan.

Glasson, J. and Marshall, T. (2007) *Regional Planning*, Abingdon: Routledge.

Gnest, H. (2008) *Entwicklung der Uberortlichen Raumplanung in der Bundesrepublik von 1975 bis heute*, Hanover: ARL.

Goetz, K. (2003) 'Government at the centre', in Padgett, S. Patterson, W. and Smith, G. (eds) *Developments in German Politics 3*, Basingstoke: Palgrave, pp. 17–37.

Goppel, K. (2005) 'Landesplanung', in Akademie fur Raumordnung und Landesplanung *Handworterbuch der Raumordnung*, Hanover: ARL, pp. 561–573.

Gordijn, H. (2008) 'Airport growth versus urbanization', in Gemeinsame Landesplanungsabteilung Berlin-Brandenburg, *Airside meets Landside. Beitrage zur integrierten Entwicklung des Hauptstadt Airports BBI*, Potsdam: Berlin-Brandenburg, pp. 16–22.

Graham, B. (2008) 'UK air travel: Taking off for growth?', in Docherty, I. and Shaw, J. (eds) *Traffic Jam*, Bristol: Policy Press.

Graham, S. and Marvin, S. (2001) *Splintering Urbanism*, London: Routledge.

Gramlich, E. (1994) 'Infrastructure investment: A review essay', *Journal of Economic Literature*, 32, 1176–96.

Green, S., Hough, D., Miskimmon, A. and Timmins, G. (2008) *The Politics of the New Germany*, Abingdon: Routledge.

Gremion, P. (1976) *Le Pouvoir Peripherique*, Paris: Seuil.

Griggs, S. and Howarth, D. (2004) 'A transformative political campaign? The new rhetoric of protest against airport expansion in the UK', *Journal of Political Ideologies*, 9, 2, 181–203.

Griggs, S. and Howarth, D. (2008) 'Populism, localism and environmental politics: The logic and rhetoric of the Stop Stansted Expansion campaign', *Planning Theory*, 7, 2, 123–144.

Gust, D. (2005) 'Energiepolitik', in Akademie fur Raumordnung und Landesplanung *Handworterbuch der Raumordnung*, Hanover: ARL, pp. 207–213.

Gust, D. (ed.) (2007) *Wandel der Stromversorgung und raumliche Politik*, Hanover: Akademie fur Raumforschung und Landesplanung.

Habermas, J. (1989) *The Structural Transformation of the Public Sphere*, Cambridge: MIT Press.

Hajer, M. and Wagenaar, H. (eds) (2003) *Deliberative Policy Analysis: Understanding Governance in the Network Society*, Cambridge: Cambridge University Press.

Hajer, M. (2009) *Authoritative Governance: Policy-making in the Age of Mediatization*, Oxford: Oxford University Press.

Hall, D. (2007) 'Decision-making and participation: The Watertime results', *Utilities Policy*, 15, 151–159.

Hall, D. (2009) *Infrastructure, the Crisis and Pension Funds*, London: PSIRU.

Hall, D. (2010a) *Waste Management Companies in Europe 2009*, London: PSIRU.

Hall, D. (2010b) *Waste Management in Europe: Framework, Trends and Issues*, London: PSIRU.

Hall, D. (2010c) *Why We Need Public Spending*, London: PSIRU.

Hall, D. and Lobina, E. (2010a) *Water Companies in Europe 2010*, London: PSIRU.

Hall, D. and Lobina, E. (2010b) *The Past, Present and Future of Finance for Investment in Water Systems*, London: PSIRU.

Hamburg Port Authority (2007) *Focus of Dynamic Growth Markets: Prospects and Development Potential for the Port of Hamburg,* Hamburg: HPA, Ministry of Economics and Labour, Free and Hanseatic City of Hamburg.

Hamer, M. (1987) *Wheels Within Wheels*, London: Routledge and Kegan Paul.

Hanna, L. (1982) 'Water supply' in House, J. (ed.) *The UK Space,* London: Weidenfeld and Nicolson, pp. 226–241.

Harris, N. and Hooper, A. (2004) 'Rediscovering the "spatial" in public policy and planning: An examination of the spatial content of sectoral policy documents', *Planning Practice and Research*, 5, 2, 147–169.

Harris, N. and Hooper, A. (2006) 'Redefining the "space that is Wales": Place, planning and the Wales Spatial Plan', in Allmendinger, P. and Tewdwr-Jones, M. (eds) *Territory, Identity and Spatal Planning*, London: Routledge, pp. 139–152.

Harvey, D. (1982) *The Limits to Capital*, Oxford: Blackwell.

Harvey, D. (1985) *The Urbanization of Capital*, Oxford: Blackwell.

Harvey, D. (1989) 'From managerialism to entrepreneurialism: The transformation in urban governance in late capitalism', *Geografiska Annaler*, 71B, 418–434.

Harvey, D. (1996) *Justice, Nature and the Geography of Difference*, Oxford: Blackwell.

Harvey, D. (2005) *A Brief History of Neoliberalism*, Oxford: Oxford University Press.

Harvie, C. (1983) *The Rise of Regional Europe*, London: Routledge.

Hay, C. (2007) *Why We Hate Politics,* Cambridge: Polity.

Haughton, G., Allemendinger, P., Counsell, D. and Vigar, G. (2010) *The New Spatial Planning*, Abingdon: Routledge.

Hayes, B. (2005) *Infrastructure: A Field Guide to the Industrial Landscape*, New York: W W Norton.

Hayward, J. and Wright, V. (2002) *Governing from the Centre,* Oxford: Oxford University Press.

Haywood, R. (2009) *Railways, Urban Development and Town Planning in Britain: 1948–2008,* Farnham: Ashgate.

Headicar, P. (2009) *Transport Policy and Planning in Great Britain,* Abingdon: Routledge.

Healey, P. (1997) *Collaborative Planning,* Basingstoke: Palgrave.

Healey, P. (2007) *Urban Complexity and Spatial Strategies; Towards a Relational Planning for our Times,* London: Routledge.

Healey, P. (2010) *Making Better Places,* Basingstoke: Palgrave.

Heinrichs, B. and Schmude, K. (2010) 'Der Verkehrscorridor Ostsee-Adria durch Ostdeutschland im Wettbewerb der Nord-Sud-Korridore', in Hesse, M. (ed.) *Neue Rahmenbedingungen, Herausforderungen und Strategien fur die grossraumige Verkehrsentwicklung,* Hanover: ARL, pp. 66–80.

Helm, D. (2004a), *Energy, the State and the Market: British Energy Policy since 1979,* Oxford: Oxford University Press.

Helm, D. (2004b) *The New Regulatory Agenda,* London: Social Market Foundation.

Helm, D. (ed.) (2007) *The New Energy Paradigm,* Oxford: Oxford University Press.

Helm, D. (2009) 'The challenge of infrastructure investment in Britain' in Helm, D., Wardlaw, J. and Caldecott, B. *Delivering a 21st Century Infrastructure for Britain,* London: Policy Exchange.

Henckel, D. et al (2010) *Planen – Bauen – Umwelt. Ein Handbuch,* Wiesbaden: VS Verlag.

Henshaw, D. (1991) *The Great Railway Conspiracy,* Hawes: Leading Edge.

Hesse, M. (ed.) (2010) *Neue Rahmenbedingungen, Herausforderungen und Strategien fur die Grossraumige Verkehrsentwicklung,* Hanover: ARL.

Heuser, T. and Reh, W. (2010) 'Die Bundesverkehrswegeplanung', in Scholler, O., Canzler, W. and Knie, A. (eds) *Handbuch Verkehrspolitik,* Wiesbaden: VS Verlag fur Sozialwissenshaften, pp. 225–251.

Hillier, J. (2002) *Shadows of Power,* London: Routledge.

Hills, P. (1984) 'Planning for coal: Issues and responses' in Cope, D., Hills, P. and James, P. (eds) *Energy Policy and Land-use Planning,* Oxford: Pergamon, pp. 21–68.

Hinrichs-Rahlwes, R. and Pieprzyk, B. (2009) *Ausbauprognose der Erneuerbare-Energien-Branche fur Deutschland,* for REPAP 2020 and BEE Bundesverband Erneuerbare Energie.

Hirschman, A. (1958) *The Strategy of Economic Development,* New Haven: Yale University Press.

HM Government (2007) *Planning for a Sustainable Future,* London: CLG, DEFRA, DTI, DfT.

HM Treasury (2010) *National Infrastructure Plan,* London: HM Treasury.

Hobsbawm, E. (1962) *The Age of Revolution: Europe 1789–1848,* London: Weidenfeld and Nicolson.

Hobsbawm, E. (1975) *The Age of Capital 1848–1875,* London: Weidenfeld and Nicolson.

Hood, C. (1998) *The Art of the State,* Oxford: Clarendon Press.

Hopkins, R. (2008) *The Transition Handbook: From Oil Dependency to Local Resilience,* Dartington: Grenn Books.

House, J. (ed.) (1982) *The UK Space,* London: Weidenfeld and Nicolson.

House of Commons Procedure Committee (2002) *Major Infrastructure Projects: Proposed New Parliamentary Procedures,* London: House of Commons Procedure Committee.

House of Commons Energy and Climate Change Committee (2010) *The Proposals for the National Policy Statements on Energy,* London: House of Commons Energy and Climate Change Committee.

Hughes, T. (1983) *Networks of Power: Electrification in Western Society 1880–1930*, Baltimore, MD: Johns Hopkins Press.

Humphrys, G. (1982) 'Power and the industrial structure', in House, J. (ed.) *The UK Space*, London: Weidenfeld and Nicolson, pp. 282–355.

IAURIF (2003) *Aeroports et Territoires, Les Cahiers d'IAURIF 139–140*, Paris: IAURIF.

ICE (Institution of Civil Engineers) (2009) *State of the Nation: Low Carbon Infrastructure*, London: ICE.

ICE (Institution of Civil Engineers) (2010) *State of the Nation: Infrastructure 2010*, London: ICE.

IEEP/RSPB (2009) *Planning for Onshore Wind*, London: IEEP and RSPB.

Iglesias Perez, C. (1994) 'Una vision general del Plan Director de Infraestructuras', *Revista de Obras Publicas*, 3333, 7–13.

Irwin, A. (1995) *Citizen Science*, London: Routledge.

Jackson, T. (2009) 'Recovery without growth?', *Renewal*, 17, 3, 43–56.

Jackson, T. and Marks, N. (2002) *Measuring Progress*, London: New Economics Foundation/Friends of the Earth.

Jacobs, M. (1991) *The Green Economy*, London: Pluto Press.

Jean, Y. (2008) 'De l'etat amenageur aux nouveaux territoires de l'action publique', in Jean, Y. and Vanier, M. (eds) *La France, Amenager les Territoires*, Paris: Armand Colin.

Jean, Y. and Vanier, M. (eds) (2008) *La France, Amenager les Territoires*, Paris: Armand Colin.

Jeffery, C. (2003) 'Federalism and territorial politics', in Padgett, S., Patterson, W. and Smith, G. (eds) *Developments in German Politics 3*, Basingstoke: Palgrave, pp. 38–59.

Jeffery, C. (2008) 'Conclusion. Groundhog day: The non-reform of German federalism, again', *German Politics*, 17, 4, 587–592.

Jensen, O. and Richardson, T. (2004) *Making European Space*, London: Routledge.

Jessop, B. (2002) *The Future of the Capitalist State*, Cambridge: Polity.

Jessop, B. (2008) *State Power*, Cambridge: Polity.

Jobert, A., Laborgne, P. and Mimler, S. (2007) 'Local acceptance of wind energy: Factors of success identified in French and German case studies', *Energy Policy*, 35, 2751–2760.

Jochimsen, R. (1966) *Theorie der Infrastruktur*, Tubingen: Mohr.

Jochimsen, R. and Simonis, U. (eds) (1970) *Theorie und Praxis der Infrastrukturpolitik*, Berlin: Duncker and Humboldt.

Joignaux, G., Ollivier-Trigalo, M., Rigaud, P., and Zembri, P. (2003) *Analyse Comparative des Schemas Multimodaux de Services de Transport: Alsace, Nord-Pas de Calais, Rhone Alpes*, (Les collections de l'Inrets 246), Paris: INRETS.

Juliana, E. (2009) *La Deriva de Espana*, Barcelona: RBA Libros.

Keating, M. (ed.) (2005) *Regions and Regionalism in Europe*, Cheltenham: Edward Elgar.

Keating, M. and Wilson, A. (2009) 'Renegotiating the state of autonomies: Statute reform and multi-level politics in Spain', *West European Politics*, 32, 3, 536–558.

Kelly, B. (2008) 'The Planning Bill: Implications of the proposals for a new regime for major infrastructure for democracy and delivery', *Journal of Planning and Environment Law*, 13, supplement, pp. 1–12.

Kern, F. and Smith, A. (2008) 'Restructuring energy systems for sustainability? Energy transition policy in the Netherlands', *Energy Policy*, 36, 4093–4103.

Knieling, J. (2006) 'Leitbilder und strategische Raumentwicklung. Planungstheoretische Einordnung und Diskussion der neuen Leitbilder fur die deutsche Raumentwicklung', *Raumforschung und Raumordnung*, 6, 473–485.

KPMG (2009a) *Bridging the Global Infrastructure Gap: Views from the Executive Suite*, London: KPMG.

KPMG (2009b) *The Changing Face of Infrastructure: Public Sector Perspectives*, London: KPMG.

KPMG (2010) *The Changing Face of Infrastructure: Frontline Views from Private Sector Infrastructure Providers*, London: KPMG.

Kunzmann, K. (2001) 'State planning: A German success story?', *International Planning Studies*, 6, 2, 153–166.

La Caixa (2007) 'Infraestructuras', *Informe Mensual 302*, May 2007.

Le Gales, P. (2005) 'Reshaping the state? Administrative and decentralization reform', in Cole, A., Le Gales, P. and Levy, J. (eds) *Developments in French Politics 3*, Basingstoke: Macmillan, pp. 122–137.

Le Gales, P. (2006) 'The ongoing march of decentralisation within the post-Jacobin state', in Culpepper, P., Hall, P. and Palier, B. (eds) (2006) *Changing France*, Basingstoke: Palgrave, pp. 198–222.

Le Gales, P. (2008) 'Territorial politics in France: Le calme avant la tempete?', in Cole, A., Le Gales, P. and Levy, J. (eds) *Developments in French Politics 4*, Basingstoke: Palgrave, pp. 156–171.

Leunig, T. and Swaffield, J. (2008) *Cities Unlimited*, London: Policy Exchange.

Levett, R. (2007a) 'A White Paper for planning growth', *ECOS*, 28, 2, pp. 79–81.

Levett, R. (2007b) 'Deconstructing Barker, a report for CPRE on the Planning White Paper', London: CPRE.

Levinson, M. (2006) *The Box*, Princeton: Princeton University Press.

Lijphart, A. (1999) *Patterns of Democracy*, New Haven: Yale University Press.

Lindblom, K. and Honey, R. (2007) 'Planning for a new generation of power stations', *Journal of Planning and Environment Law*, pp. 843–862.

Lloyd, G. and Purves, G. (2009) 'Identity and territory: The creation of a national planning framework for Scotland', in Davoudi, S. and Strange, I. (eds) *Conceptions of Space and Place in Strategic Spatial Planning*, Abingdon: Routledge, pp. 71–94.

Lopez Pineiro, S. (2006) 'Politica y aprovechamiento del agua en Espana: El Plan Hidrologico Nacional', in Cuadrat Prats, J. M. (ed.) *El Agua en el Siglo XXI*, Zaragoza: Institucion Fernando el Catolico, pp.47-56.

Lorrain, D. (2002) 'Capitalismes urbains: La montée des firmes d'infrastructures', *Entreprises et Histoire*, 50, 5–31.

Lorrain, D. (2005) 'Infrastructure and private firms: The institutional challenge (a socio-economic view)', *The ICFAI Journal of Urban Policy* (Hyderabad), fall 2005.

Lowenthal, D. (1994) 'European and English landscapes as national symbols' in Hooson, D. (ed.) *Geography and National Identity*, Oxford: Blackwell, pp. 15–38.

Lutter, H. (2005) 'Raumordnungsberichte', in Akademie fur Raumordnung und Landesplanung *Handworterbuch der Raumordnung*, Hanover: ARL, pp. 872–877.

McCracken, R. (2009) 'Infrastructure Planning Commission: Challenge or opportunity', *Journal of Planning and Environment Law*, 13, supplement, pp. 7–23.

Macdonald, R. and Thomas, H. (eds) (1997) *Nationality and Planning in Scotland and Wales*, Cardiff: University of Wales Press.

McGowan, F. (2009) 'International regimes for energy: Finding the right level for policy', in Scrase, I. and MacKerron, G. (eds) *Energy for the Future*, Basingstoke: Palgrave, pp. 20–34.

MacKay, D. (2009) *Sustainable Energy: Without the Hot Air*, Cambridge: UIT.

Mackay, G. (1984) 'North sea oil: The British experience', in Cope, D., Hills, P. and James, P. (eds) *Energy Policy and Land-use Planning*, Oxford: Pergamon, pp. 69–99.

McNeill, D. (2004) *New Europe: Imagined Spaces*, London: Arnold.

Majoor, S. (2008) *Disconnected Innovations*, Delft: Eburon.

Malina, R. (2010) 'Competition in the German airport market: An empirical investigation', in Forsyth, P., Gillen, D., Mueller, J. and Niemeier, H-M. (eds) *Airport Competition: The European Experience*, Farnham: Ashgate, pp. 239–253.

Mander, S. and Randles, S. (2009) 'Aviation coalitions: Drivers of growth and implications for carbon dioxide emissions reduction', in Gossling, S. and Upham, P. (eds) *Climate Change and Aviation* London: Earthscan, pp. 273–290.

Marine Scotland (2010) *Draft Plan for Offshore Wind Energy in Scottish Territorial Waters*, Edinburgh: Marine Scotland.

Marsh, D., Smith, N. and Hothi, N. (2008) 'Globalization and the state', in Hay, C., Lister, M. and Marsh, D. (eds) *The State*, Basingstoke: Palgrave, pp. 172–189.

Marshall, T. (1994) 'Barcelona and the delta: Metropolitan infrastructure planning and socio-ecological projects', *Journal of Environmental Planning and Management*, 37, 4, 395–414.

Marshall, T. (1996) 'Catalan nationalism, the Catalan government and the environment', *Environmental Politics*, 5, 542–550.

Marshall, T. (2010a) 'History of the reforms in infrastructure planning 1990–2010, Working Paper, at http://planning.brookes.ac.uk/projects/resources/reformshistorymarchand-sept2010.pdf, accessed 29/2/2012.

Marshall, T. (2010b) 'Scotland working paper, at http://planning.brookes.ac.uk/projects/resources/Scotlandnov17final.pdf, accessed 29/2/2012.

Martin, R. (2008) 'National growth versus regional equality? A cautionary note on the new trade-off thinking in regional policy discourse', *Regional Science, Policy and Practice*, 1, 3–13.

Martinez Alier, J. (1987) *Ecological Economics: Energy, Environment and Society*, Oxford: Basil Blackwell.

Martinez Montes, G., Prados Martin, E. and Ordonez Garcia, J. (2005) 'The current situation of wind energy in Spain', *Renewable and Sustainable Energy Review*, 11, 467–481.

Mastop, H. (2001) 'Dutch national planning at the turning point: Rethinking institutional arrangements', in Alterman, R. ed., *National Level Planning in Democratic Countries*, Liverpool: Liverpool University Press, pp. 219–256.

Mastop, H. and Faludi, A. (1997) 'Evaluation of strategic plans: The performance principle', *Environment and Planning B*, 24, 815–832.

MEEDDAT (Ministere de l'Ecologie, du Developpement durable, des Transports et du Logement) (2010a) *Schema National des Infrastructures de Transport Soumis a Concertation*, Paris: MEEDDAT.

MEEDDAT (Ministere de l'Ecologie, du Developpement durable, des Transports et du Logement) (2010b) *Deuzieme Rapport Annuel au Parlement sur la Mise en Oeuvrre des Engagements du Grenelle Environnment*, November 2010, Paris: MEEDDAT,

MEEDDAT (Ministere de l'Ecologie, du Developpement durable, des Transports et du Logement) (2011a) *Schema National des Infrastructures de Transport*, January 2011, Avant-projet consolide, Paris: MEEDDAT.

MEEDDAT (Ministere de l'Ecologie, du Developpement durable, des Transports et du Logement) (2011b) *Installation de 3000 MW d'eoliennes en mer*, Dossier de Presse 26 January 2011, Paris: MEEDDAT.

Meek, R. (1962) *Economics of Physiocracy*, London: Allen and Unwin.

Merlin, P. (2007) *L'Amenagement du Territoire en france*, Paris: La Documentation Francaise.

Meunier, D. and Quinet, E. (2006) 'Motorway provision and management in France: Some lessons and perspectives', unpublished paper.

Michel, D. (2005) 'Ministerkonferenz fur Raumordnung', in Akademie fur Raumordnung und Landesplanung, *Handworterbuch der Raumordnung* Hanover: ARL, pp. 651–654.

Ministere de L'Ecologie et du Developpement Durable (2007) *Les 9es Programmes d'Intervention des Agences de l'Eau 2007–2012*, Paris: MEDD.

Ministere des Affaires Etrangeres (2006) *Spatial Planning and Sustainable Development Policy in France*, Paris: Direction Generale de la Cooperation Internationale et du Developpement, Ministere des Affaires Etrangeres.

Ministerio de Fomento (2005) *Plan Estrategico de Infraestructuras y Transporte* (PEIT), Madrid: Ministerio de Fomento (also available in English).

Ministerio de Obras Publicas, Transportes y Medio Ambiente (1994) *Plan Director de Infraestructuras 1993–2007*, Madrid : MOPTMA.

Ministry of Transport (1962) *Report of the Committee of Inquiry into the Major Ports of Great Britain*, (Rochdale report), London: HMSO.

Mintzberg, H. (2000) *The Rise and Fall of Strategic Planning*, London: Financial Times Prentice Hall.

Mitchell, C. (2008) *The Political Economy of Sustainable Energy*, Basingstoke: Palgrave.

MKRO (2006) 'Aus- und neubaubedarf des Höchstspannungsnetzes – raumplanerische Konsequenzen', Decision note at 33rd MKRO meeting, Berlin: Ministerkonferenz fur Raumordnung (MKRO).

Moore, V. (2010) *A Practical Approach to Planning Law*, Oxford: Oxford University Press.

Moragues-Faus, A. M. and Ortiz-Miranda, D. (2010) 'Local mobilization against windfarm developments in Spanish rural areas : New actors in the regulation arena', *Energy Policy*, 38, 4232–4240.

Moral, L. del (2000) 'Problems and trends in water management within the framework of autonomous organisation of the Spanish state', UGI congress Seoul 2000.

Moral, L. del (2006) 'Planificacion hidrologica y politica territorial en Espana', in Cuadrat Prats, J. M. ed, *El Agua en el Siglo XXI*, Zaragoza: Institucion Fernando el Catolico, seminar paper of 2003.

Moral, L. del (2008) 'Integracion de politicas sectoriales: Agua y territorio', Fundacion Nueva Cultura del Agua, Panel Cientifico-tecnico de seguimiento de la politica de aguas, Convenio Universidad de Sevilla – Ministerio de Medio Ambiente.

Moran, M. (2006) 'Economic institutions' in Rhodes, R., Binder, S. and Rockman, B. (eds) *Oxford Handbook of Political Institutions*, Oxford: Oxford University Press, pp. 144–162.

Morphet, J. (2011) *Effective Practice in Spatial Planning*, Abingdon: Routledge.

Moss, T. (2003) 'Solving problems of "fit" at the expense of problems of "interplay"? The spatial reorganisation of water management following the EU water framework directive', in Breit, H. et al (eds) *How Institutions Change*, Opladen: Leske and Budrich, pp. 85–121.

Moss, T. (2004) 'The governance of land use in river basins: Prospects for overcoming problems of institutional interplay with the EU Water Framework Directive', *Land Use Policy*, 21, 85–94.

Moss, T. (2011) 'Infrastrukturplanung fur die Raumentwicklung: Anspruche und Herausforderungen in Deutschland', in Tietz H-P and Huhner, T. (eds) *Zukunftsfahige Infrastruktur und Raumentwicklung*, Hanover: ARL, pp. 64–84.

Mouffe, C. (2000) *The Democratic Paradox*, London: Verso.

Muller-Rostin, C., Ehmer, H., Hannak, I., Ivanova, P., Niemeier, H. M. and Muller, J., (2010) 'Airport entry and exit: A European analysis', in Forsyth, P., Gillen, D., Muller, J. and Niemeier, H. M. (eds) *Airport Competition: The European Experience*, Farnham: Ashgate, pp. 27–45.

Nadai, A. (2007) '"Planning", "siting" and the local acceptance of wind power: Some lessons from the French case', *Energy Policy*, 35, 2715–2726.

NAO (National Audit Office) (2009) *DEFRA – Managing the Waste PFI Programme*, London: NAO.

Naredo, J. M. (2006) 'La encrucijada actual de la gestion del agua in Espana', in Cuadrat Prats, J. M. ed *El agua en el siglo XXI*, Zaragoza: Institucion Fernando el Catolico, seminar paper of 2003.

Naredo, J. M. (2008) 'Lo publico y lo privado, la planificacion y el mercado, en la encrucijada actual de la gestion del agua in Espana', Fundacion Nueva Cultura del Agua, Panel Cientifico-tecnico de seguimiento de la politica de aguas, Convenio Universidad de Sevilla – Ministerio de Medio Ambiente.

National Assembly for Wales (2011) *Inquiry into Planning in Wales, January 2011*, Cardiff: Sustainability Committee, National Assembly for Wales.

Needham, B. (2007) *Dutch Land Use Planning*, The Hague: SDU Uitgevers.

Nello, O. (2007a) 'Spain: Changing century, changing cycle? Large Spanish cities on the threshold of the twenty-first century', in van den Berg, L., Braun, E. and van der Meer, J. (eds) *National Policy Responses to Urban Challenges in Europe*, Aldershot: Ashgate, pp. 333–359.

Nello, O. (2007b) 'La nueva politica territorial de Cataluna (2003–2006)', in Farinos Dasi, J. and Romero Gonzalez, J. (eds) *Territorialidad y Buen Gobierno para el Desarollo Sostenible*, Valencia: Universitat de Valencia.

Nello, O. (2010) 'El planeamiento territorial en Cataluna', *Cuadernos Geograficos*, 47, 2, 131–167.

Netherlands Government (2009) *National Water Plan*, The Hague: Netherlands Government, December 2009 (English translation), http://english.verkeerenwaterstaat.nl/english/Images/NWP%20english_tcm249-274704.pdf, accessed 1/3/2012.

Neuman, M. (1996) 'The imaginary institution: Planning and politics in Madrid', *Planning Theory*, 15, 120–131.

Neuman, M. (1998) 'Does planning need the plan?', *Journal of the American Planning Association*, 64, 2, 208–220.

Newman, J. and Clarke, J. (2009) *Publics, Politics and Power*, London: Sage.

Newman, P. and Thornley, A. (1996) *Urban Planning in Europe*, London: Routledge.

Niedersachsisches Ministerium fur Umwelt und Klimaschutz (2010a), *Abfallwirtschaftsplan Niedersachsen, Teilplan Sonderabfall*, Hanover: Ministerium fur Umwelt und Klimaschutz.

Niedersachsisches Ministerium fur Umwelt und Klimaschutz (2010a), *Abfallwirtschaftsplan Niedersachsen, Teilplan Siedlungsabfalle und Nicht Gefahrliche Abfalle*, Hanover: Ministerium fur Umwelt und Klimaschutz.

Nogue-Font, J. (1991) *Els Nacionalismes i el Territori*, Barcelona: El Llamp.

Notteboom, T., Ducruet, C. and de Langen, P. (eds) (2009) *Ports in Proximity*, Farnham: Ashgate.

NRA (National Rivers Authority) (1992) *Water Resources Development Strategy, A Discussion Document,* London: NRA.

NRA (National Rivers Authority) (1994) *Water: Nature's Precious Resource,* London: NRA.

Nueva Cultura del Territorio (2006) 'Manifiesto por una nueva cultura del territorio', http://age.ieg.csic.es/docs_externos/06-05-manifiesto_cultura_territorio.pdf, accessed 29/2/2012.

Nuffield Foundation (1986) *Town and Country Planning*, London: Nuffield Foundation.

O'Connor, M. (ed) (1994) *Is Capitalism Sustainable?*, New York: Guilford Press.

ODPM (Office of the Deputy Prime Minister) (2002) *The Government's Response to the Transport, Local Government and Regional Affairs Committee's Report, The Planning Green Paper*, London: ODPM.

ODPM (Office of the Deputy Prime Minister) (2005) *Planning Policy Statement 10: Planning for Sustainable Waste Management,* London: ODPM.

ODPM (Office of the Deputy Prime Minister) (2006) *Planning Policy Statement 10: Planning for Sustainable Waste Management: Companion* London: ODPM.

OECD (2006) *Infrastructure to 2030: Telecom, Land Transport, Water and Electricity*, Paris: OECD.

OECD (2007) *Infrastructure to 2030: Mapping Policy for Electricity, Water and Transport*, Paris: OECD.

OECD (2009) *Going for Growth*, Paris: OECD.

Ohl, C. and Eichhorn, M. (2008) 'The mismatch between regional spatial planning for wind power development in Germany and national eligibility criteria for feed-in tariffs, a case study in West Saxony', *Land Use Policy*, 27, 243–254.

Ollivier-Trigalo, M. (2002*) Instituer la Mulimodalite avec les Schemas de Services de Transport*, (Les collections de l'Inrets 248), Paris: INRETS.

Ollivier-Trigalo, M. (ed) (2007) *Six Regions a l'Epreuve des Politiques de Transport*, (Les collections de l'Inrets 273), Paris: INRETS.

Ollivier-Trigalo, M. and Piechaczyk, X. (2001) *Evaluer, Debattre or Negocier l'Utilite Publique?*, (Les collections de l'Inrets 233), Paris: INRETS.

Ollman, B. (1993) *Dialectical Investigations*, London: Routledge.

O'Neill, P. (2010) 'Infrastructure financing and operation in the contemporary city', *Geographical Research*, 48, 3–12.

Openshaw, S. (1986) *Nuclear Power: Siting and Safety*, London: Routledge and Kegan Paul.

Pahl-Weber, E. (2010) 'Informelle Planung in der Stadt- und regionalplanung', in Henckel, D. et al, (2010) *Planen – Bauen – Umwelt. Ein Handbuch*, Wiesbaden: VS Verlag, pp. 227–232.

Pahl-Weber, E. and Henckel, D. (eds) (2008) *The Planning System and Planning Terms in Germany*, Hanover: ARL.

Pallis, A. and Tsiotsis, G.-S. (2008) 'Maritime interests and the EU port services directive', *European Transport/Trasporti Europei*, 38, 17–31.

Parker, D. (2008) *The Official History of Privatisation: The Formative Years 1970–1987*, Abingdon: Routledge.

Parker, D. and Penning-Rowsell, E. (1980) *Water Planning in Britain,* London: Allen and Unwin.

Parrado, S. (2008) 'The role of the Spanish central government in a multi-level state', paper given to SOG conference May 2008 Paris.

Payne, D. and Reid, C. (forthcoming) 'Longer term environmental challenges', in Swain, C., Baden, T. and Marshall, T. (eds) *English Regional Planning 2000–2010: Lessons for the Future*, Abingdon: Routledge.

Peel, D. and Lloyd, G. (2007) 'Civic formation and a new vocabulary for national planning', *International Planning Studies*, 12, 4, 391–411.

Perez Andres, A. (1998) *La Ordenacion del Territorio en el Estado de las Autonomias*, Madrid: Marcial Pons.

Peters, D. (2007) 'Decision-making for mega-urban transport infrastructure projects: A German case study', working paper prepared for the Omega project, based at University College London.

Pezon, C. (2009) 'Decentralization and delegation of water and sanitation services in France', in Castro, J. E. and Heller, L. (eds) *Water and Sanitation Services: Public Policy and Management*, London: Earthscan.

Pike, A., Rodriguez Pose, A. and Tomaney, J. (2006) *Local and Regional Development*, London: Routledge.

Pinder, D. (2008) 'Economic versus environmental sustainability for ports and shipping: Charting a new course?' in Docherty, I. and Shaw, J. (eds) *Traffic Jam*, Bristol: Policy Press, pp. 161–180.

Plowden, W. (1971) *The Motor Car and Politics 1896–1970,* London: Bodley Head.

Pontier, J.-M. (2003) *Les Schemas de Services Collectifs*, Paris: LGDJ.

Portswatch (2003) *Troubled Waters*, manifesto, December 2003.

Prat, N. (2008) 'El debate del agua', *El Periodico*, 11/12/2008, p. 6.

Priebs, A. (2011) 'Regionale Abfallwirtshaft in der Region Hannover', in Tietz. H.-P. and Huhner, T. (eds) *Zukunftsfahige Infrastruktur und Raumentwicklung*, Hanover: ARL, pp. 208–217.

Priemus, H. (2004) 'Spatial memorandum 2004: A turning point in the Netherlands' spatial development policy', *Tijdschrift voor Economische en Sociale Geographie*, 95, 5, 578–583.

Priemus, H., Flyvbjerg, B. and van Wee, B. (eds) (2008) *Decision-making on Mega-projects: Cost-benefit Analysis, Planning and Innovation*, Cheltenham: Edward Elgar.

Purdue, M. and Popham, J. (2002) 'The future of the major inquiry', *Journal of Planning and Environment Law*, 137–150.

Purves, G. (2006) 'Quality and connectivity: The continuing tradition of strategic spatial planning in Scotland', in Adams, N., Alden, J. and Harris, N. (eds) *Regional Development and Spatial Planning in an Enlarged European Union,* Aldershot: Ashgate.

Purves, G. (2008) 'National strategic planning', *Town and Country Planning Supplement: Planning Summer School 2008*, p. 5.

Ramboll/Mercados (2008) *TEN-E Energy Priority Corridors for Energy Transmission*, report for European Commission, November 2008.

Republique Francaise (2010) *National Sustainable Development Strategy 2010–2013*, English translation at www.developpement-durable.gouv.fr/IMG/pdf/NSDS4p.pdf accessed 1/3/2012.

Ribalaygua, C. et al (2002) 'Efectos territoriales de la alta velocidad ferroviaria: Estrategias para el planeamiento supramunicipal', *Ingenieria y Territorio*, 60, 74–83.

RICS (1992) *Shaping Britain for the 21st Century,* London: RICS.

Roberts, P. and Shaw, T. (1984) 'Planning for gas in the United Kingdom', in Cope, D., Hills, P. and James, P. (eds) *Energy Policy and Land-use Planning,* Oxford: Pergamon, pp. 101–122.

Robinson, P. (2009) 'Energy planning in 2009 – all systems go?', *Journal of Planning and Environment Law*, 13, supplement, pp. 53–77.

Rodriguez, F. (2010) 'El estado de la ordenacion del territorio en Espana', *Cuadernos Geograficos*, 47, 2, pp. 9–14.

Romero Gonzalez, J. (2002) "Nationalities and regions in Spain: The limits of the autonomic state', from webpages July 2009, net.lib.byu.edu

Romero Gonzalez, J. (2005) 'El gobierno del territorio en Espana: Balance de iniciativas de coordinacion y cooperacion territorial', *Boletin de la A.G.E*, 39, 59–86.

Romero Gonzalez, J. (2009) *Geopolitica y Gobierno del Territorio en Espana*, Valencia: Padilla Libros.

Roodbol-Mekkes, P. and van der Valk, A (2008) 'Disorder in the house: Spatial planning doctrine in the twenty first century', Paper presented to AESOP congress, Chicago, July 2008.

Rosewell, B. (2010) *Planning Curses: How to Deliver Long-term Investment in Infrastructure*, London: Planning Exchange.

Roskill, E. (1971) *Report of the Commission on the Third London Airport*, London: HMSO.

Rostow, W. (1960) *The Stages of Economic Growth*, Cambridge: Cambridge University Press.

Rothengatter, W. (2005) 'National systems of transport infrastructure planning: The case of Germany', in ECMT, *Round Table 128: National Systems of Transport Infrastructure Planning*, Paris: ECMT.

RREEF (2005) *Understanding Infrastructure*, RREEF (Real Estate and Infrastructure), London: Deutsche Bank.

RREEF (2008) *Infrastructure Goes Global*, RREEF (Real Estate and Infrastructure), London: Deutsche Bank.

RSPB (1997) *Port Development and Nature Conservation,* Sandy: RSPB.

RTE (2007) *Generation Adequacy Report on the Electricity Supply-demand Balance in France*, Paris: RTE.

RTPI (2006) *Uniting Britain*, London: RTPI.

Rubio Alferez, J. and Borrajo Sebastian, J. (2009) 'Un cambio de paradigma en la planificacion de infraesturas', *Rutas*, Jan-Feb 2009, 13–19.

Saalfeld, T. (2006) 'The costs and risks of democratic decision-making' in Sakwa, R. and Stevens, A. (eds) *Contemporary Europe*, Basingstoke: Palgrave.

Salet, W. and Gualini, E. (eds) (2007) *Framing Strategic Urban Projects*, London: Routledge.

Salet, W., Thornley, A. and Kreukels, A. (eds) (2003) *Metropolitan Governance and Spatial Planning*, London: Spon.

Salez, P. (2008) 'La France vue d'Europe', in Jean, Y. and Vanier, M. (eds) *La France, Amenager les Territoires*, Paris: Armand Colin.

Sauri, D., Olcina, J. and Rico, A. (2009) 'The state of urban water supply and sanitation in Spain: Issues, debates and conflicts', in Castro, J. E. and Heller, L. (eds) *Water and Sanitation Services*, London: Earthscan, pp. 207–217.

Saward, M. (2003) *Democracy*, Cambridge: Polity Press.

Scharpf, F. (2008) 'Community, diversity and autonomy: The challenges of reforming German federalism', *German Politics*, 17, 4, 509–521.

Schmidt, M. (2003) *Political Institutions in the Federal Republic of Germany*, Oxford: Oxford University Press.

Schmidt-Eichstaedt, G. (2001) 'National-level planning institutions and decisions in the federal republic of Germany', in Alterman, R. (ed.) *National-level Planning in Democracies*, Liverpool: Liverpool University Press, pp. 127–147.

Scholl, B. and Seidemann, D. (2010) 'Strategische Ausrichtung der Verkehrs- und Raumentwicklung am Beispiel der Nord-Sud-Transversale fur Europa von Rotterdam nach Genua', in Hesse, M. (ed.) *Neue Rahmenbedingungen, Herausforderungen und Strategien fur die grossraumige Verkehrsentwicklung*, Hanover: ARL, pp. 20–39.

Scottish Enterprise (2009) *National Renewables Infrastructure Plan*, Glasgow: Scottish Enterprise, with Highlands and Islands Enterprise.

Scottish Enterprise (2010) *Towards a Low Carbon Economy for Scotland: A Discussion Paper*, Glasgow: Scottish Enterprise, with Highlands and Islands Enterprise.

Scottish Executive (2004) *National Planning Framework for Scotland*, Edinburgh: Scottish Executive.

Scottish Executive (2006) *Scotland's National Transport Strategy*, Edinburgh: Scottish Executive.

Scottish Government (2008) *Infrastructure Investment Plan*, Edinburgh: Scottish Government.

Scottish Government (2009a) *National Planning Framework for Scotland 2*, Edinburgh: Scottish Government.

Scottish Government (2009b) *Renewables Energy Plan*, Glasgow: Renewable Energy Division, Energy Directorate.

Scrase, I. and MacKerron, G. (2009) 'Lock-in', in Scrase, I. and MacKerron, G. (eds) *Energy for the Future,* Macmillan: Palgrave, pp. 89–100.

Sealy, K. (1976) *Airport Strategy and Planning,* Oxford: OUP.

Sealy, K. (1992) 'International air transport', in Hoyle, B. and Knowles, R. (eds) *Modern Transport Geography,* London: Belhaven.

Seligmann, B. (2005) 'National systems of transport infrastructure planning: The case of France', in *National Systems of Transport Infrastructure Planning*, Paris: ECMT.

Senternovem (2008) *Energy Innovation Agenda*, Amsterdam: Senternovem.

Serrano, A. (2007) 'El uso del agua en la economia espanola', inaugural presentation, 28 February 2007, Fundacion Biodiversidad, ciclo de debate.

Serrano, A. (2009a) 'La influencia del territorio y su biodiversidad en las politicas de planificacion de la obra publica en Espana', unpublished paper, developed from presentation in March 2008 at Ingenieria para un Mundo Sostenible, at Escuela de Caminos de Galicia.

Serrano, A. (2009b) *Cambio Global: Espana 2020*, Programa Transporte Informe Base, May 2009, Madrid: Fundicot.

Simms, A. and Boyle, D. (2010) *Eminent Corporations,* London: Constable.

Sheail, J. (1986) 'Government and the perception of reservoir development in Britain: An historical perspective', *Planning Perspectives*, 1, 45–60.

Sinz, M. (2005) 'Raumordnung/Raumordnungspolitik', in Akademie fur Raumordnung und Landesplanung, *Handworterbuch der Raumordnung*, Hanover: ARL, pp. 863–872.

Sinz, M. (2006) 'Die neuen Leitbilder der Raumentwicklung – Anmerkungen zu einem politischen Diskurs', *Informationen zur Raumentwicklung*, 11/12, pp.III-XIV.

Smith, A. (2006) 'The government of the European Union and a changing France', in Culpepper, P., Hall, P. and Palier, B. (eds) (2006) *Changing France*, Basingstoke: Palgrave, pp. 179–197.

Smith, A. (2010) *Nationalism,* Cambridge: Polity.

Staats, J. (2006) 'Die neuen Leitbilder der Raumentwicklung – Moglichkeiten zur Umsetzung durch die Bundesraumordnung', *Informationen zur Raumentwiclung*, 111/12.

Starkie, D. (1982) *The Motorway Age,* Oxford: Pergamon.

Steenhuisen, B., Dicke, W. and de Bruijn, H. (unpublished) '*"Soft" public values in jeopardy',* TU Delft.

Streeck, W. (2009) *Re-Forming Capitalism*, Oxford: Oxford University Press.

Suarez de Vivero, J. and Rodriguez Mateos, J. (2002) 'Spain and the sea: The decline of an ideology, crisis in the maritime sector and the challenges of globalization', *Marine Policy*, 26, 143–153.

Subra, P. (2007) *Geopolitique de l'Amenagement du Territoire*, Paris: Armand Colin.

SURF (Centre for Sustainable Urban and Regional Futures) (2007a) *City-regions Shaping Transitions in Critical Infrastructures*, (Report for Northern Way Sustainable Communities Team), Manchester: SURF.

SURF (Centre for Sustainable Urban and Regional Futures) (2007b) *City-regions and Critical Infrastructure: Meeting Growth Targets Sustainably*, (Report for Northern Way Sustainable Communities Team), Manchester: SURF.

Sustainable Development Commission (2007) *Turning the Tide: Tidal Power in the UK*, London: SDC.

Sustainable Development Commission (2011) *National Infrastructure: Embedding Sustainable Development in Decision Making*, London: SDC.

Swyngedouw, E. (1997) 'Neither global nor local: "Glocalization" and the politics of scale', in Cox, K. (ed.) *Spaces of Globalization: Reassessing the Power of the Local*, New York: Guildford, pp. 137–166.

Swyngedouw, E. (2010) 'Trouble with nature: "Ecology as the new opium for the masses"', in Hillier, J. and Healey, P. (eds) *The Ashgate Companion to Planning Theory*, Farnham: Ashgate, pp. 299–318.

Szarka, J. (2007) *Wind Power in Europe: Politics, Business and Society*, Basingstoke: Palgrave.

TCPA (2006) *Connecting England*, London: TCPA.

Tewdwr-Jones, M. (2002) *The Planning Polity*, London: Routledge.

Thatcher, M. (2002) 'Analysing regulatory reform in Europe', *Journal of European Public Policy*, 9, 859–872.

Thatcher, M. (2007) 'Reforming national regulatory institutions: The EU and cross-national variety in European network industries', in Hancke, B., Rhodes, M. and Thatcher, M. (eds) *Beyond Varieties of Capitalism*, Oxford: Oxford University Press.

Thomas, S. (2009) *An Analysis of the Contemporary Developments and Corporate Policies in the European Energy Sector*, London: PSIRU.

Thompson, P. (2002) 'Major infrastructure projects – where to now?', *Journal of Planning and Environment Law*, Occasional Papers No 30, pp. 25–46.

Tietz, H. P. (2005) 'Ver- und entsorgung', in Akademie fur Raumordnung und Landesplanung, *Handworterbuch der Raumordnung*, Hanover: ARL, pp. 1239–1245.

Tietz, H. P. (2007) 'Raumplanerische Ansatze zur Beeinflussung und Steuerung kunftiger Standort- und trassenanspruche', in Gust, D. (ed) *Wandel der Stromversorgung und raumliche Politik*, Hanover: Akademie fur Raumforschung und Landesplanung, pp. 153–172.

Tietz, H. P. (2011) 'Funktionen und raumliche Strukturen kommunaler Ver- und Entsorgungsysteme', in Tietz, H. P. and Huhner, T. (eds) *Zukunftsfahige Infrastruktur und Raumentwicklung*, Hanover: ARL, pp.13–25.

Tietz, H. P. and Huhner, T. (eds) (2011) *Zukunftsfahige Infrastruktur und Raumentwicklung*, Hanover: ARL.

Tolley, R. and Turton, B. (1995) *Transport Systems, Policy and Planning*, Harlow: Longman.

Torrance, M. (2007a) 'The power of governance in financial relationships: Governing tensions in exotic infrastructure territory', Working Paper in Employment, Work and Finance, WPG 07–06, Geography Department, Oxford University.

Torrance, M. (2007b) *Forging glocal governance? Urban infrastructures as networked financial products*, Working Paper in Employment, Work and Finance, WPG 07–05, Geography Department, Oxford University.

Townsend, S. (2011) 'Town halls link up to fight rail route', *Planning*, 14 January 2011, pp. 12–13.

Transport Scotland (2008) *Strategic Transport Projects Review: Report 4: Summary Report,* Glasgow: Transport Scotland.

Turton, B. (1999) 'Transport', in Gardner, V. and Matthews, H. (eds) *The Changing Geography of the UK,* London: Routledge, pp. 108–128.

Urena, J. M. (2002) 'Escalas, territorios y enfoques de la ordenacion del territorio', *Ingenieria y Territorio*, 60, 4–9.

Urena, J. M. et al, (2006) 'Situaciones y retos territoriales de la Alta Velocidad Ferroviaria en Espana', *Ciudad y Territorio Estudios Territoriales*, 148, 397–424.

van der Vleuten, E. (2004) 'Infrastructures and societal change: A view from the Large Technical Systems field', *Technology Analysis and Strategic Management*, 16, 3, 395–414.

van der Vleuten, E. (2006) 'Understanding network societies', in Van der Vleuten, E. and Kaijser, A. (eds) *Networking Europe*, Sagamore Beach: Science History Publications, pp. 279–314.

van der Wouden, R., Dammers, E. and van Ravesteyn, N. (2006) 'Knowledge and policy in the Netherlands', *disP*, 165, 2, 34–42.

van Duinen, L. (2004) *Planning Imagery*, published by van Duinen, L. as a doctoral thesis.

Varlet, J. (2008) 'Les reseaux de transports rapides : Du descenclavement interregional aux dualismes intermodaux', in Jean, Y. and Vanier, M. (eds) *La France, Amenager les Territoires*, Paris: Armand Colin.

VenW (2008) *Ontwerp Beleidsnota Noordzee*, The Hague: Rijksoverheid, VenW.

Verbong, G. and van der Vleuten, E. (2004) 'Under construction: Material integration of the Netherlands 1800–2000', *History and Technology*, 20, 3, 205–226.

Vigar, G. (2009) 'Towards an integrated spatial planning?', *European Planning Studies*, 17, 11, 1571–1590.

VROM (2005) *National Spatial Strategy (Nota Ruimte: Ruimte voor ontwikkeling)*, The Hague: Ministries of VROM, LNV, VenW and EZ.

Wallace, H., Pollack, M. and Young, A. (eds) (2010) *Policy-Making in the European Union*, Oxford: Oxford University Press.

Wang, J., Olivier, D., Notteboom, T. and Slack, B. (eds) (2007) *Ports, Cities and Global Supply Chains*, Aldershot: Ashgate.

Ward, S. (1999) 'The international diffusion of planning: A review and a Canadian case study', *International Planning Studies*, 4, 1, 53–77.

WIDP (Waste Infrastructure Development Programme) (2006) 'An action plan for the Waste Infrastructure Development Programme', November 2006, WIDP, at http://archive.defra.gov.uk/environment/waste/residual/widp/documents/widp-actionplan.pdf, accessed 1/3/2012.

Welsh Assembly Government (2004) *People, Places, Futures: The Wales Spatial Plan,* Cardiff: WAG.

Welsh Assembly Government (2005) *Technical Advice Note 8: Planning for Renewable Energy*, Cardiff: WAG.

Welsh Assembly Government (2008) *People, Places, Futures: The Wales Spatial Plan Update 2008*, Cardiff: WAG.

Wenban-Smith, A. (2009) 'Complementary measures to facilitate regional economic benefits from high speed rail', Final report to Greengauge 21, by Urban and Regional Policy, June 2009.

Wendling, R. (2008) 'Facing up to a drier future: The Iberian experience', *ENDS Europe Report*, 24/04/2008, 18–19.

Whitfield, D. (2010) *Global Auction of Public Assets,* Nottingham: Spokesman.

Wilson, E. and Piper, J. (2010) *Spatial Planning and Climate Change*, Abingdon: Routledge.

Wolmar, C. (2004) *On the Wrong Line*, London: Aurum.

Wolsink, M. (2003) 'Reshaping the Dutch planning system: A learning process?', *Environment and Planning A,* 35, 705–723.

Wolsink, M. (2004) 'Policy beliefs in spatial decisions: Contrasting core beliefs concerning space-making for waste infrastructure', *Urban Studies*, 41, 13, 2669–2690.

Wray, I. (2010) 'Has England got a plan?', *Town and Country Planning*, January, 20–22.

WRR (1999) *Spatial Development Policy* (summary of the 53rd report), The Hague: WRR.

WRR (2008) *Infrastructure. Time to Invest*, Amsterdam: WRR, Amsterdam University Press.

Yergin, D. (1991) *The Prize*, New York: Simon and Schuster.

Zeller, T. (2007), *Driving Germany*, Oxford: Berghahn Books.

Zembri, P. (1997) 'Les fondements de la remise en cause du Schema Directeur des liaisons ferroviaires a grande vitesse: Des faiblesses avant tout structurelles', *Annales de Geographie*, 106, 593/594, 183–194.

Zembri, P. (2004) *La Planification des Transports au Niveau Regional*, Paris: Certu Dossier 155.

Zembri, P. (2005) 'El TGV, la red ferroviaria y el territorio en Francia', *Ingeneria y Territorio*, 70, 12–19.

Zonneveld, W. (2005) 'In search of conceptual modernization: The new Dutch "national spatial strategy"', *Journal of Housing and the Built Environment*, 425–443.

Zonneveld, W. (2006) 'Planning in retreat? The changing importance of Dutch national spatial planning', paper presented at the EGPA conference 6–9 September 2006, Universita Bocconi, Milan.

LIST OF INTERVIEWEES

NETHERLANDS
Government ministries
Vrom (Ministry of Housing, Planning and Environment):
- Arjen van der Burg, Spatial Planning.
- Andre Rodenburg, Spatial Planning.
- Loek Bergman, Waste Management.

VenW (Ministry of Transport and Water):
- Roger Demkes, Rijkswaterstaat.
- Maarten van der Vlist, Rijkswaterstaat.
- Robert van Winden, Rijkswaterstaat.
- Huub van der Kolk, Mobility.
- Caspar de Jonge, Mobility.
- Gerard Snel, Maritime Affairs.

EZ (Ministry of Economic Affairs):
- Otto Bitter, Regional Economic Policy.
- Joost van der Vleuten, Energy and Telecom.

Research/Advisory Bureaux
- Hugo Gordijn, Planbureau voor de Leefomgeving.
- Bram van der Klundert and Mirjan Bouwman, Vromraad.
- Gerbert Romijn, Centraal Planbureau.
- Johan Visser, Kennisinstituut voor Mobiliteitsbeleid.

Technical University Delft – Departments
- Aad Correlje, TPM.
- Willemijn Dicke, TPM.
- Andreas Faludi, OTB.
- Menno Huys, TPM.
- Hugo Priemus, OTB.
- Joost Schrijnen, Urbanism (and Province of Zeeland).
- Pieter Schrijnen, Civil Engineering and Geosciences.
- Marjolein Spaans, OTB.
- Wil Zonneveld, OTB.

Others
- Barrie Needham, ex Nijmegen University.
- Arnold van der Valk, Wageningen University.
- Rianne Zandee and Douwe Tiemersma , Natuur en Milieu.

FRANCE
Government ministries and agencies
- Nadia Boeglin, Commissariat general au developpement durable, MEEDDAT.
- Alain Glevarac, DG de l'amenagement, du logement et de la nature, MEEDDAT.
- Richard Lavergne, Commissariat general au developpement durable, MEEDDAT.

- Philippe Marzolf, vice-president, CNDP.
- Brice Masselot, DG de l'aviation civile, MEEDDAT.
- Pascal Mignerey, DIACT.
- Dominique Ritz, DG des infrastructures, des transports et de la mer, MEEDDAT.
- Jacques Sironneau, DG de l'amenagement, du logement et de la nature, MEEDDAT.
- Bruno Vergobbi, France Ports.
- Serge Wachter, Commissariat general au developpement durable, MEEDDAT.

Companies
- Francois Tainturier, RFF.
- Gro Waeraas de Saint Martin, RTE.

Academics
- Bernard Barraque, ENGREF.
- Antoine Fremont, INRETS (SPLOTT).
- Elizabeth Gouvernal, INRETS (SPLOTT).
- Charlotte Halpern, Universite de Lyon.
- Pierre Musso, Universite de Rennes II/Telecomm Paristech.
- Marianne Ollivier-Trigalo, INRETS (LVMT).
- Emile Quinet, ENPC/École Polytechnique Fédérale de Lausanne.
- Philippe Subra, Universite de Paris 8 (Institut francais de geopolitique).
- Genevieve Zembri-Mary, Universite de Cergy-Pointoise.

I would also like to offer special thanks to Patrick Le Gales at CEVIPOF Sciences Po, for advice and support from the beginning of my brief Paris immersion, and to several researchers at LATTS, including particularly Sylvy Jaglin, Olivier Coutard and Jonathan Rutherford, who kindly offered me a base for a short period at the beginning of my research, and gave me helpful advice on contacts. Others offering friendly support included Eric Charmes at IFU.

SPAIN

Government ministries

Ministerio de Fomento:
- Eduardo Pallardo Comas (transport infrastructure planning).
- Justo Borrajo Sebastian (road).
- Rafael Garcia Alcolea (rail).
- Javier Gese Aperte (Puertos del Estado, ports).

Ministerio de Industria, Turismo y Comercio:
- Eva Arenas Pinilla (energy planning).

Comunidad de Madrid
- Alberto Leboreiro Amaro (regional planning).
- Alberto Manzano (waste planning).

Universidad Politecnica de Madrid, Departamento de Urbanistica
- Ramon Lopez de Lucio.
- Julio Pozueta.
- Inez Sanchez de Madariaga.

Other academics

- Pedro Linares, Universidad Pontificia Comillas, Madrid (energy analysis).
- Antonio Serrano Rodriguez, Universidad Politecnica de Valencia, and Fundicot.

Catalonia, Generalitat, government ministries

Departament de Politica Territorial i Obres Publiques:

- Oriol Nello (territorial policy).
- Juli Esteban (regional planning).
- Manel Villalante (land transport).
- Jordi Follia and Josep Marti (roads).
- Josep Maria Carrera (Barcelona metropolitan plan at the Institut d'Estudis Territorials).

Departament de Medi Ambient i Habitatge:

- Gabriel Borràs (water planning at the Agencia Catalana de L'Aigua).
- Jordi Renom and Daniel Villaro (waste planning at the Agència de Residus de Catalunya).

Departament d'Economia i Finances:

- Agustí Maure (energy policy).

GERMANY

BMVBS (Federal Ministry of Transport, Building and Urban Development)

- Jan Dirks (ports).
- Hendrik Hassheider (BVWP).
- Marina Koester (airports).
- Roman Limbach (roads).
- Friederike Reineke (rail).
- Manfred Sinz (spatial planning).

BMWi (Federal Ministry of Economics and Technology)

- Till Spannagel (energy policy).
- Armin Steinbach (electricity grids).

BMU (Federal Ministry for the Environment, Nature Conservation and Nuclear Safety)

- Andreas Jaron (waste).
- Heide Jekel (water).

BBSR (Federal Institute for Research on Building, Urban Affairs and Spatial Development)

- Bernd Buthe.

Baden-Wurttemberg, Umweltministerium (Environment Ministry)

- Joachim Bley, water policy (by telephone).

Bremen (Free Hanseatic City of Bremen)

- Iven Kramer, ports (by telephone).

**Gemeinsame Landesplanungsabteilung Berlin–Brandenburg
(Joint spatial planning department of Berlin and Brandenburg)**

- Horst Sauer and Ulrike Assig.

Academics

- Melf-Hinrich Ehlers, Division of Resource Economics, Humboldt University Berlin.
- Klaus Kunzmann, ex Dortmund University.
- Tim Moss, Leibniz Institute for Regional Development and Structural Planning (by phone).

I would also like to thank for their various kinds of very valuable help, written and spoken, Elke Bruns (Berlin Technical University), Klaus Einig (BBSR), Tim Engartner (Duisburg-Essen University), Deike Peters (Berlin Technical University), Stefan Preuss (National Grid UK), and Andreas Thiel (Humboldt University).

SCOTLAND

- Amanda Chisholm and Lewis Hurley, Directorate for the Built Environment, Scottish Government.
- Iain Docherty, Glasgow University.
- Frances Duffy, Transport Scotland.
- Colin Imrie, Energy Directorate, Scottish Government.
- Paul McGhee, Finance Directorate, Scottish Government.
- Duncan McLaren, Friends of the Earth Scotland.
- Graeme Purves, Directorate for the Built Environment, Scottish Government.
- Aedan Smith, RSPB.

Also thanks to Roddy Macdonald, Directorate for the Built Environment, Scottish Government, for help early on and during my visit.

EU IN BRUSSELS

- Helmut Adelsberger, Transport Directorate.
- Kitti Nyitrai, Energy Directorate.
- Jean Peyrony, Regional Directorate.

INDEX